Faith and Narrative

FAITH AND NARRATIVE

Edited by

KEITH E. YANDELL

OXFORD

UNIVERSITY PRESS

2001

OXFORD
UNIVERSITY PRESS

Oxford   New York

Athens   Auckland   Bangkok   Bogotá   Buenos Aires   Cape Town
Chennai   Dar es Salaam   Delhi   Florence   Hong Kong   Istanbul   Karachi
Kolkata   Kuala Lumpur   Madrid   Melbourne   Mexico City   Mumbai   Nairobi
Paris   São Paulo   Shanghai   Singapore   Taipei   Tokyo   Toronto   Warsaw

and associated companies in
Berlin   Ibadan

Copyright © 2001 by Oxford University Press

Published by Oxford University Press, Inc.
198 Madison Avenue, New York, New York 10016

Oxford is a registered trademark of Oxford University Press.

Library of Congress Cataloging-in-Publication Data
Faith and narrative / edited by Keith E. Yandell.
p.   cm.
Includes bibliographical references and index.
ISBN 0-19-513145-2
1. Storytelling—Religious aspects.   2. Knowledge, Theory of (Religion)   I. Yandell,
Keith E., 1938–
BL628.7.F35   2001
121'.68—dc21   00-058478

1 3 5 7 9 8 6 4 2
Printed in the United States of America
on acid-free paper

Contents

PART III   The Promise of Narrative

PART IV   The Problems of Narrative

Contributors

James Billington, Librarian of Congress, Library of Congress

John B. Carman, Parker Professor of Divinity and Professor of Comparative Religion Emeritus, Harvard Divinity School

Gabriel Fackre, Abbot Professor of Christian Theology Emeritus, Andover-Newton Theological School

Robert E. Frykenberg, Professor of History and South Asian Studies Emeritus, University of Wisconsin-Madison

Paul Griffiths, Charles J. Schmitt Professor of Catholic Studies, University of Illinois-Chicago

David L. Jeffrey, Professor of English, Baylor University

Jon N. Moline, President and Professor of Philosophy, Texas Lutheran University

Lamin Sanneh, Professor of History, Missions, and World Christianity, Yale University

George Steiner, Professor of English and Comparative Literature, University of Geneva; Extraordinary Fellow of Churchill College, Cambridge University

Eleonore Stump, Paul Henle Professor of Philosophy, St. Louis University

Paul Vitz, Professor of Psychology, New York University

Nicholas Wolterstorff, Noah Porter Professor of Philosophical Theology, Yale Divinity School

Keith E. Yandell, Professor of Philosophy, University of Wisconsin-Madison

Faith and Narrative

Introduction

Everyone loves a story. From epic to limerick, novel to anecdote, literary narratives entertain and engage us. From individual autobiography and biography to accounts of familial ethnic generations, narratives define communities. Myths and histories loom large in religious traditions. No one doubts the affective potency and pedagogical power of narrative. But what is its role in knowledge? Does narrative discourse provide enjoyment and persuasion but fail us when we turn to it for reliable information? Do narratives yield knowledge available from no other source? Or does the truth of the matter lie in between these extremes?

In the essays that follow, these questions are addressed anew. The essays naturally group into four parts. In the first, *The Power of Narrative*, Professors Lamin Sanneh (Yale), David L. Jeffrey (Baylor), George Steiner (Geneva/Cambridge), and Eleonore Stump (St. Louis) focus on literary texts. In part 2, *The Place of Narrative*, Dr. James Billington (Library of Congress) and Professors Robert E. Frykenberg (Wisconsin) and John B. Carman (Harvard) deal with historical narratives of various sorts. In the third, *The Promise of Narrative*, Professors Paul Vitz (New York University), Jon N. Moline (Texas Lutheran University), Gabriel Fackre (Andover-Newton), and Nicholas Wolterstorff (Yale) consider the normative roles of narrative in psychology, ethics, and theology. The final grouping of writers, Professors Paul Griffiths (Illinois-Chicago) and Keith E. Yandell (Wisconsin), in *The Problems of Narrative*, grant the considerable virtues of narration but contend that narrative discourse is neither a source of religious or moral knowledge not otherwise available, nor a basis for principled assessment of competing theological or ethical claims.

The Power of Narrative

Lamin Sanneh approaches the question concerning the impact of European Christian missionaries on African culture by considering the enterprise of translating biblical and other non-African materials into African languages. Among the missionaries, some insisted that Africans should learn the language the missionaries spoke; therein lay the path of cultural and intellectual progress. Other missionaries insisted instead that the Bible be made available in the indigenous languages; such discourse was proper not only for the conduct of everyday affairs but also for the communication of the Christian message. Since typically the indigenous language had hitherto not possessed a script, and since the biblical message itself generated considerable indigenous respect, the effect was a reaffirmation of not only African languages but also their associated cultures. Furthermore, translation into an indigenous language spoken by the entire community militated against both cultural elitism and permanent missionary control. The result was a deepened awareness by Africans of the value of their own cultural heritage, now itself enriched by new content from which it received illumination and to which its fresh nuances and contexts provided further meanings and applications.

Sanneh's comparison of the translation of biblical and other material into the languages of various cultures provides a more general context from within which to see the translation enterprises that are his focus.

David L. Jeffrey argues against treatments of texts that, as Luther accused the pope of doing to the Bible, make them into wax noses to be twisted into whatever shape one wishes. Gnostic readings of a literary text treat it as a code, a bearer of an esoteric message available only to the duly initiated. Deconstructionist hermeneutics treat literary texts as tantamount to a box of paints, brushes, and canvases, material to be shaped by the "reader" as she likes. Realistic renderings of literary texts see them as relating possible events, creating worlds that might have existed and that bear significant resemblance to our own.

Asked to name documents that demand realistic treatment, one naturally thinks of works in the natural sciences. Perhaps, say, experimental reports and texts in chemistry, botany, and geology are safer examples than those in such more abstract and speculative fields as contemporary cosmology, but natural science (and its associated technologies) would seem to provide a plethora of examples of writings immune to gnostic or deconstructionist treatment. Nearer to literary texts are narrative histories, at least those produced by the majority of historians who continue to believe that *historical research* is not an oxymoron. But David L. Jeffrey does not find his favored counterexamples from natural science or history. His examples come from the literature of repentance.

Lamin Sanneh considers translations of texts with non-African origins (especially biblical texts) into African languages, a process that inherently focuses on and values indigenous persons and cultures and serves as a source of reinforcement for indigenous values. The translator serves his audience, not his peers. David L. Jeffrey discusses, as it were, texts that interpret readers. Regarding the literature of repentance, competent readers are changed by the texts that they read in ways determined by those texts, under whose authority and in conformity to whose content the reader comes to live.

While these reversals are not directly challenged by George Steiner's essay, the perspectives from which they are written are called into question. Both Jeffrey and Sanneh believe in a God before whom repentance is appropriate and about whom the Bible reliably speaks. Read in one natural way, at least, Steiner's essay—

self-described as denying any principled difference between sacred and secular texts, any reasoned distinction between revelation and its absence—favors a different perspective. He uses the death of Socrates and the death of Jesus as symbols for two literary and cultural traditions. Themes and artifacts, events and movements, are placed (some with clearer rationale than others) under these two rubrics.

Each event, in Steiner's conception, is a significant singularity, an event-and-symbol significant in that much of later history can be seen in its light and singular in its resistance to being reduced to a mere representative member of a class of events or symbols of some genus or kind of event. The suggestion is that, given either symbol, a certain salient if limited sense can be made of the tragedies of life and the vagaries of history. Much that is good, and much that is evil, can be understood in these terms. But hatred and death, the Holocaust and anti-Semitism, remain, neither prevented from occurring nor resolved in thought by the resources of either symbol. Hence, two contentions: there is no reason to regard either symbol as sacred rather than secular and no reason to grant either the status of revelation. *Transcendent revelation* is a neologism and evidence for transcendence is lacking. Curiously, this conclusion is based on considerations concerning genre and readers' phenomenology, whereas those who accept transcendent revelation typically appeal to content.

Steiner offers themes woven largely from examples and allusions. Insofar as he offers an argument, it proceeds by way of placing data in one setting that could easily have been located in various other settings. In at least one respect, Steiner's juxtaposition is strained. No tradition (unless Nietzsche and Steiner comprise such) looks to the death of Socrates as providing the key to life's meaning or the source of human redemption; for no one is history Socrates' story. For that matter, no one views the death of Jesus as the key to life's meaning. Only those who believe in a crucifixion followed by a resurrection assign cosmic significance to a grisly execution performed on a modest hill outside a holy city. Nor is it easy to see how one could, with even faint plausibility, construe the death of Socrates as the cornerstone of a metaphysic or a religion. This, of course, has been done regarding the death of Jesus.

One feature of the conduct of Steiner's reasoning calls for comment. It is the "strangeness" of Jesus and the strained-for "strangeness" of Socrates, on which their alleged mutual significant similarity is based. This suggested strangeness resides, at least in part, in comprehensibility in terms of categories not native to the neighborhoods of the symbols with which they are associated. This militates against reduction of these symbols to a lowest common denominator, though other powerful antireductionist strategies are available. But it has its prices. One who has waxed Romantic or Barthian about the strangeness of the object of his discourse has lost all right to complain that Thomistic arguments and empirical evidences are unavailable in support of claims concerning that object.

Eleonore Stump considers the Book of Job in the Hebrew Bible and Christian Old Testament in connection with the question as to how a good God can permit evil. She contends that second-person discourse—the discourse of address from one person to another—is central here. God, according to her reading of Job, neither refuses altogether to answer nor puts the question off for another time. The answer comes to Job in terms of God addressing Job, personal Creator to created person, in

a way that does answer his question. The answer does not come in terms of arguments that the existence of evil in general, or the particular sufferings of Job, are
logically consistent with, and do not provide evidence against, the claim that God
loves Job. It comes primarily in terms of Job having seen God—having had an experience or series of experiences in which he is, so to say, aware of God's feelings
about him, regard for him, and concern for his well-being. It is like the reassurance
felt when one reencounters someone who you thought had betrayed you but who
returns to reestablish contact, and even before any explanation is offered, you are
aware that betrayal was never an option. While it seems too dry a way to put
Stump's claim, roughly her view is that Job the book recounts the religious experience of Job the person, as his doubts and distresses are dissolved in the loving presence of God, the sort of resolution a mystic might be more likely to report, and for
that matter to seek, than a philosopher. Of course, God's second-person discourse to
Job is set in the context of narrative or narrative-like poetry concerning God described as in second-person relations with creation as a whole. (How this is to be
understood is of course another question. Even if God can be literally second-
person related to, say, gorillas and golden retrievers, ivy plants and rocks are another
matter.) In sum, Stump sees Job as a second-person approach to a solution to the
problem of evil—or, perhaps better, to that portion of the problem that is constituted by the believer feeling alone and betrayed.

The Place of Narrative

In a moving essay that defies summation, James Billington, an expert on Russian
history who was present in Moscow on the eve of the events that led to the fall of
the Russian Communist government, places the astounding political events of that
pivotal period in the context of the stories, the beliefs, the values, and the practices
of Russian Orthodox Christianity. His remarks illumine the manner in which a living religion, submerged but alive, underground but vibrant, provided stories that
saturated the life of a people and the lives of particular people. The power of its
eruption to the surface shocked the world.

John B. Carman begins by noting that it is often said that India lacks history,
both in the sense that serious historical works are absent from Indian culture and in
the even more demeaning sense that nothing much has happened in India. It is
true that one can read thousands of pages of Sanskrit text without coming upon a
reference to a person or event, and that the influential Advaita Vedanta religious
and philosophical perspective that all that really exists is Brahman-without-qualities
hardly places high value on what occurs in space and time. The words of the sacred
Vedas were viewed as eternal and the norm for knowledge was knowledge of the
Vedas. Nonetheless, Carman argues that one should not generalize about an entire
complex culture on the basis simply of certain of its texts and the influence of some
of its authorities. Advaita is only one variety of Vedanta, however influential were
the views of medieval Brahman pundits. Carman sees an indigenous Indian sense
of history of two sorts. One is a sense of one's temporal place in cosmic history in
which aeons of time are divided into four recurring cycles, the last of which (the

age of Kali) is bleak and evil. Typically, it is held that this is the current age. The other is the sense of one's own place in a religious community with its own history, a history typically centered around its founding and succeeding saints and its temples. Both hagiographies and temple histories abound in Hindu, Jain, and Sikh communities. The local Hindu narratives typically include the claim that God, or Brahman-with-qualities, has released the members of one's community from such bad features of the current age as inability to act rightly and unavailability of enlightenment and liberation from the cycle of rebirth.

While it is widely assumed both that it is to the writings ascribed to an author that we best turn to understand him and that hagiographies are inherently unreliable, Carman argues that the texts ascribed to the great *Vsistadvaita* saint and pundit Ramanuja leave us puzzled regarding his views and history, but the hagiographies or saint-stories written by his closest associates seem to provide more reliable historical information. He suggests a careful reexamination of hagiography as a source of historically reliable narration.

If Carman finds history in hagiographies and temple traditions, Robert E. Frykenberg finds it as well in family histories. Since through most of its history the Indian subcontinent has not been united under a single government, but has instead been divided among political bodies of highly diverse interests, structures, practices, economies, and powers, it has been possible for families to control large tracts for not merely decades but centuries. Their interest in recording the identity of their own members and their relationships with other power-holders, their deeds and accomplishments has been great. Such families have often, to a significant extent, controlled their own small part of the world, and if their records of historical events are presented from their own distinctive perspective, their histories do not differ in that respect from those produced by historians whose center of focus has been their own country. Indocentric history, on a microscopic or a macroscopic scale, is not less worthy than Eurocentric.

The familial histories are largely anecdotal. This, Frykenberg argues, does not prevent the family stories from being histories. History at its best, he contends, is comprised of duly sifted and extended anecdotes. If science is the long arm of common sense, history is the long arm of anecdote.

The Promise of Narrative

Paul Vitz highlights and contrasts the narrative contents of the psychologies of Freud and Jung. Freud claimed that psychoanalysis was a natural science. His theory of motivation views motivation as a matter of drives, quantities of psychic energy, that are repressed, bound, released, or converted from one form to another; the analogy is with force conceived in deterministic and mechanistic terms. But while Freud apparently viewed this as of one piece with his early training in neurology and physiology, his theory of motivation engages with no current work in the scientific study of the mind. His Nobel Prize was in literature, not science; his influence lies in literary and other narrative fields, not in the natural sciences. His theory of the Oedipus conflict made waves while his theory of motivation sank to the bottom. Freudian theory, Vitz argues, is best seen in literary terms. His theories are past-oriented and predict tragedy. There is no real resolution of the Oedipal conflict, no way the story of the young male will end happily.

Lacking a developmental psychology, Jung nonetheless emphasizes teleology, purpose, and self-realization. His theories are future-oriented and predict well-being for those who are able to come to terms with their archetypes. Jungian self-realization involves learning one's unconscious personal and collective archetypes (the masculine, the feminine, etc., typically personified), experiencing them in a symbolic environment of which the client, if all goes well, becomes the controlling author. The only Jungian tragedy is failure in self-fulfillment.

Vitz claims that the Freudian fall/winter, and the Jungian spring/summer, each deal only with part of the human drama. One majors in tragedy, one in comedy; life contains both. Both make fundamental assumptions concerning human nature (assumptions, one may note, not themselves narrative in nature). Vitz argues that it is appropriate to shift, as he has done, from a psychological interpretation of literature to a literary interpretation of psychology. The literary and narrative concepts are the more fundamental; they are of the higher explanatory order. Once this move is made, Vitz then proposes a narrative theological perspective, in which the insights of Freud and Jung can be retained and their limitations overcome.

Jon N. Moline develops and defends an ethic Aristotelian in structure and narrative in its foundations. He offers what, after Aristotle, he calls phenomena—a good ethic saves or accords with these. The phenomena are common sense judgments or opinions regarding specific cases—either a very concrete story is told in which a moral judgment must be made, or one reflects on what sort of person one would want for some role or task or relationship. Insofar as generalizations are possible, what is generalized is judgments about such relatively or precisely concrete matters. The phenomena are, or are closely connected to, narratives that invite moral reflection and conclusion, and that conclusion is itself partly constitutive of the phenomena. But also constitutive is the object of that judgment—the person or action about which a moral opinion is held—and the circumstances which frame that action or person.

Historically viewed, a Christian theology is evangelical if it is committed to scriptural authority in matters of faith and practice and teaches salvation by divine grace rather than human effort. "Narrative," in the sense relevant to Gabriel Fackre's notion of a narrative evangelical theology, means something like "plot and characters moving through conflict to resolution." Christian theology has always been narratively shaped: Creation, Fall, Redemption (the calling of Israel, the coming of Christ), Final Judgment. This structure is reflected in texts in systematic theology that standardly run: God, Humanity, Christ, Last Things, with a section on Soteriology falling within the section on Christ. In addition to accepting this narrative and theological framework, evangelical piety, as evidenced in its popular hymnology, emphasizes personal conversion; the believing individual sees her life as a converted person having its source and pattern in the life of Christ. The cosmic story (history seen as strung between Creation and Judgment) is mediated to one's personal story as a member of the Christian church through biblical stories—Old Testament stories about Israel and the nations and the prophets and the people, plus dominical stories concerning the life, parables, death, and resurrection of Jesus. Again historically, those who have embraced evangelical theology have been best at evangelism and personal piety. Emphasis on personal salvation gone awry tends to narcissism, but the biblical stories model and demand social justice and the emphasis on charity and grace encourages humility and service.

On the whole, then, Fackre sees evangelical theology and an emphasis on narration, as walking hand in hand, with one crucial proviso. Evangelical theology, however empathetic to and involved in narration, has always insisted that it matters that its central stories have external reference—that whether or not the nation of Israel or the person of Jesus have graced history by their actual presence matters deeply. In this respect, it contrasts sharply with those trends in narrative theology that see religious significance as limited to affective influence independent of the actual occurrence of such events as the death and resurrection of Christ.

Nicholas Wolterstorff reminds us that an effect of historical criticism of the Bible is this: whereas once readers of the Bible viewed themselves as living in a history defined by that text, now such readers view the Bible itself within the context of a larger history that exceeds its spatial and temporal boundaries and that it does not define. This reversal diminished de facto biblical authority, as did the idea that what were hitherto viewed as infallible statements could and even should now be checked against the data provided by historians and biblical critics. In an attempt to protect biblical authority, some theologians have endeavored to empty the biblical narratives of factual reference, with the intent of making the truth of what is said independent of whether what the text, on any realistic reading, said occurred did in fact occur. Along similar lines, revisionary interpretations were offered that, whatever their intent, trimmed the sails of biblical teaching to the winds of whatever ideology prevailed.

Wolterstorff's focus is on the question as to whether it is today viable and defensible still to "live in" the biblical text, and what doing this might mean. One thing it does not simply mean is understanding oneself as belonging within a history narrated by the Bible; Hebrew prophetic literature and Christian epistles are not narrative, but they traditionally have provided guidance, comfort, and imperatives.

One can, Wolterstorff suggests, "live in" a text by way of being a component of a world to which the text refers; one can do so by way of being part of a community that was early in its historical career defined by a text and continues to define itself by reference to that text—one's person and actions continue a narrative one neither began nor defines; one can do so by attempting to live in conformity to a pattern that is articulated textually.

Having discussed each of these senses of "living in" a text, Wolterstorff ends with a question: assuming that it is necessary to discriminatingly live within any text that provides us a dwelling, what are the proper parameters of such discrimination?

The Problems of Narrative

Our concluding essays, without denying the many merits of narrative, protest against narrativist imperialism; like good bread, narrative is wonderful but not everything. Paul Griffiths notes that narrative is composed of tensed sentences, sentences dated (at least relative to one another) by their relation to what is related in other sentences from the same narrative or by reference, explicit or implicit, to matters external to the narrative. In contrast, systematic discourse is composed of sentences not tensed to any times. Either sort of discourse may be embedded in the other. "Aristotle first reflected that the principle of noncontradiction is a law of both thought and things after breakfast on the day before he became Plato's student" embeds the intrinsically tenseless (or everlastingly tensed) "The principle of noncontradiction is a law of both thought and things" in a biographical report. Similarly, "An example of a statement that is not self-contradictory and the denial of which is not self-contradictory is: 'Aristotle first reflected that the principle of noncontradiction is a law of both thought and things after breakfast on the day before he became Plato's student'" embeds a biographical report in a tenseless illustration. Neither discourse is walled off from the other.

Both explicitly and implicitly, religious traditions, as a matter of necessity as well as history, include doctrines and creeds. Doctrines and creeds contain claims about what there is and about what is good to be and do; both metaphysics and ethics fall within their scope. Such claims are inherently systematic, not narrative, in nature.

Narratives are especially appropriate for relating the phenomenology of lived psychological experience, the fabric of physical and social life in particular places and times, and the meaning of historical events. Narrative is crucial in the process that yields the sort of cognitive and affective transformation typically called "conversion" and in making it possible for a person to deeply identify with a religious tradition, history, and lifestyle. All of this Griffiths regards as uncontroversial or at any rate plainly true.

Griffiths adds that seeing things narratively involves seeing-as as well as seeing-that. With the familiar duck-rabbit figure that can be seen as representing either a furry or a feathered creature in the background, the idea is that one who reads the Old Testament or Hebrew Bible and comes to believe that God was active in the history of Israel comes to see a certain history as providentially guided. She believes that it was; otherwise, she does not see it so. But seeing it so is not simply a matter of believing that it was providentially guided; it is to regard that history in cognitive and affective ways capturable only narratively. So far will Griffiths go with those who make high claims for narrative.

He will go a step further by way of supposing it true that there may be an irreducible particularity to knowledge of what it is right that one do and how it can be done that no appeal to moral principles and descriptive data will explain. (Here he agrees with a perspective that Moline embraces and Yandell challenges.) Having gone so far, Griffiths will go no further. When it comes to stating principles, elucidating a metaethic, or articulating and assessing ethical theories, systematic discourse is requisite and narrative must step aside. The same holds for the precision, systematization, universalization, and justification required in the lives of religious traditions—in theology, apologetics, catechetical instruction, and preaching (which of course typically contains both narrative and systematic components).

What, then, is Griffiths denying? While perhaps no one strictly claims that one can do absolutely everything in narrative discourse that one can do in systematic, many do claim narration is independent of and prior to systematic discourse, particularly in the central cases of religious stories and religious morality. To this Griffiths replies that the claims regarding God and human nature as they appear in the doctrines and creeds of monotheistic traditions are not adequately narratively expressible and that without the systematic seeing-that element of the seeing-as that narrative provides no seeing-as remains. Griffiths sees as ironic, and more important as self-refuting, the fact that in the very sentences in which narrativist imperialists express the views by which they endeavor to expunge all significant roles to systematic discourse, they themselves ineliminatively use systematic discourse which lacks a narrative base — something their own view denies.

Keith E. Yandell advocates nonnarrative approaches to ethics. He defends the claim that there is no possibility of an ethic not ultimately based on ahistorical moral principles, which in turn depend for their force on nonnarrative claims regarding human nature and ultimate reality. Narrative ethics (like narrative theology) is, by itself, relativistic. There is an infinity of possible, and a plethora of actual, narratives embraced by real people. Rational assessment of a narrative is not itself a narrational enterprise; no narrative can assess its own claim to truth, and if it makes no such claim then no ethic worth believing could be based on it. No narrative can contain within itself a rational assessment of its own claim to reliability as contested by analogous claims by other narratives. Limit ethics to narration and there is no such thing as a mistaken morality in any sense other than one that does not happen to jibe with some narrative tradition which is neither better nor worse than its multitudinous competitors.

There are purely physicalistic or materialist narratives in which ethics necessarily has no place. A purist narrativist — one who restricts his discourse regarding ethics to narration — can express dislike of such narratives but not argue against them. Even in offering a coherent narrative, he will be assuming laws of logic whose basis, he claims, is narrational; hence, the purist narrativist embraces conventionalism regarding logic. But conventionalism — even setting its enormous difficulties aside — is neither expressible nor assessable in narrative terms. In sum, Yandell argues that the ship of ethical narration sails on a sea of systematic discourse without which it could neither sail nor remain intact.

Conclusion

In ways but suggested by these remarks, the essays comprised in this volume address common questions and propound mutually relevant — sometimes complementary, sometimes competing — views of the scope, worth, and limitations of narrative discourse. That narration has an important role in history, theology, ethics, psychology, and (of course) literature is a point of agreement. Whether, for example, there is moral or theological knowledge accessible only through narrative is more controversial; both positive and negative answers to these questions are defended in the following pages. It is generally agreed by our authors that at least nonliterary narrative is referential in that it purports to describe nonlinguistic and typically nonartifactual entities—things, events, and the like. Some emphasize the necessity of leaving the narrative mode when one endeavors to verify such purported reference; others do not. My intent here has merely been to map out the cognitive geography covered by the essays that follow, highlighting some points of common interest, some matters of controversy, some salient common themes and perspectives, thus making clear some (but only some) of their rich interconnections. Another contributor would have drawn the map differently. The real interest, of course, lies in the intellectual terrain itself.

PART I

THE POWER OF NARRATIVE

LAMIN SANNEH

"They Stooped to Conquer": Cultural Vitality and the Narrative Impulse

Introduction

Two major cultural themes helped shape the modern missionary movement and they deserve close study. One is the idea of mother tongues being at the root of the cultural narrative, and the other is vernacular scriptural translations as the motor of mother tongue literacy in Africa and elsewhere. Two further issues are the nature of Christianity as a "translated" religion linguistically, and perhaps even theologically, and the continuity of that "translation" theme into the history of the modern missionary movement. The renewal of indigenous tradition and its narrative genius is thus connected to the translation work of mission. The essentially "translatable" character of Christianity, on the one hand, and, on the other, the story of Western expansion are the two folds between which I attempt to place the African material, both to show thematic continuity for translation and contextual specificity with African materials.

It is within that framework that we should examine the bond between "the noble character of common speech" that was such a distinctive trait of vernacular literary activity in general, as illustrated, for example, in John Bunyan's work, and the common stirrings of soil, blood, and breeding that have been the spark in movements of cultural revitalization, something that translating the Bible into mother tongues did much to inspire. Erasmus (d. 1536) expressed a sentiment that might stand as a flagship for Renaissance humanism.[1] He spoke of the social and cultural effects of making Christian Scriptures available to ordinary, as well as exotic, people in their own tongues. He had the vision not that farmers, fishermen, and weavers should abandon plow, shore, and shuttle and flock to the academy, but that translating the Scriptures would help achieve for the common and humble people the humanist ideal. Aware of the revolutionary social implications of his view, Erasmus defended himself by arguing that the religion of Christ is imbued with a populist, republican principle, for whereas, in his words, "the mysteries of kings, perhaps, are better concealed," those of Christ are meant to be "published as openly as possible."

Erasmus's contention about the Bible as common property is relevant to the story of nonliterate societies and cultures, such as those of Africa. By giving these societies the Scriptures in their own tongue, the translators of the Bible stimulated cultural and linguistic responses from the detailed, copious labor necessary to reduce these languages to writing and to furnish them with self-sustaining resources, including a dictionary and a grammar.

The African Crucible

An important consequence of adopting the mother tongue for the Bible was the awakening of communities and individuals toward a sense of opposition to colonial control. Two powerful currents, arising from a common source in Europe, swept through Africa by divergent channels. Colonial rule carried the current of foreign political tutelage, with the requirement that colonial administrations remedy the inadequacies of local leaders and institutions, while Christian missions, or at least those so involved, adopted local languages as the basis for religious work, as well as for the wider cultural revitalization by virtue of which specific religious responses could be shaped and guided. Thus, the linguistic procedure the missionaries adopted for establishing the spiritual kingdom allowed Africans to acquire mother tongue literacy with which they could explain to themselves the rapid changes affecting their societies.

Africans responded enthusiastically to Christianity, yet, as they pondered the omens, a subconscious alarm at the European assault on their societies dawned on them and reverberated across the continent. A sense of disillusionment spread as Africans realized from acquaintance with the vernacular Scriptures that the promises and hopes aroused with the first proclamation of the gospel were no longer being honored by the new generation of missionaries. Added to that was the growing realization of the strain and stress being put on traditional institutions and social structures. Instead of African societies being renewed and strengthened, they were weakened and demolished. Looking for security, Africans found insecurity. Instead of missionaries being their friends and protectors, they became their enemies and detractors.

In these circumstances of attraction to the Gospel, coupled with distrust of missionaries, Africans still embraced Christianity for two complementary reasons, a positive and a negative. On the positive side, Christianity became an ally amid the new changes that were being introduced into tribal societies. Christianity gave people a sense of assurance through the stories of suffering, violence, exile, and restoration, with the possibility of a similar happy ending for colonial Africa. On the negative side, Christianity inspired resistance to foreign domination, its message of redemption and freedom appropriated as a nationalist charter. Thus, the song, "Nkosike Leli Afrika," which became the South African national anthem, was a hymn of missionary inspiration. The missionary and the colonial movement was a disillusioning experience and contact with white people brought on calamity for the tribes. For the first time in the continent's history, the tribes were subjected to a single, uniform external fact of European control, and that control, when challenged by Africans, was defended as a Christian hegemony, as Ian Smith insisted in Southern Rhodesia, now Zimbabwe. Africans looked for a corresponding universal answer in mother tongue Christianity, with the storytelling character of mother tongue culture fusing with the human interest-driven, telos-laden, and perspective-changing accounts of Scripture. Actions, events, and experiences require a narrative for their understanding, and mother tongue Scripture enabled the old cultural forms and structures to serve the challenge and demands of the new historical experience of white control.

In his Marett lecture at the University of Oxford, the British sociologist John Peel described this narrative theme by construing it as a unique instrument of human agency, giving human beings the means to make sense of the temporal exigencies of their activities, of the arch of actions, memories, and experiences that spans their life.[2] Most important, narrative bestows the power of knowledge of an outcome, and so is different from the chronicle and its linear enumeration of events. The Bible was the paradigmatic narrative, with power to console and inspire, and with foresight to anticipate a conclusion and construct a meaning and a purpose. The victims of the events taking place in African society assimilated their experience into the wider frame of the biblical world. Thus could the Yoruba pastor Samuel Pearse, despairing of events in his hometown, Badagry, a slave port, speak of the house of God there deserted "as a cottage in a vineyard, as a lodge in a garden of cucumbers," citing Isaiah 1:8, and of his own unrequited labors thus: "Like the Galilean fishermen, we have toiled all night and caught nothing," citing Luke 5:5.2. Thus, too, could Samuel Ajayi Crowther (c. 1806–1891) speak of his rescue from slavery and his return to his native Yorubaland like the story of Joseph. The story of his eventual reunion with his mother, Afala, after nearly thirty years of separation, Crowther conflated with a biblical parallel. He baptized his mother as Hannah, so that he as Samuel was reunited with his now elderly mother by baptism. The biblical parallel, in 1 Samuel 1:2ff., with its striking African undertones, has the polygamous Elkanah, the Ephraimite, presiding unevenly over two wives, the barren but favored Hannah, and the much envied Peninnah blessed with children. Stigmatized by Peninnah, the tormented Hannah pleaded with God for a child to save her honor, saying she would devote the child to God's work. The son she later bore she named Samuel, and, as promised, gave him over to God's service. By analogy, thus did an old African woman, Afala, rendered "childless" by the cruelty of slavery, have her maternal prayer answered and regain her son, now a priest of God as Samuel, the most important African churchman of the nineteenth century.

Given the significance of narrative in the Bible, the publication of the Christian Scriptures in the language of a tribe was an event of major importance. Through mother tongue literacy Africans reassembled the torn pieces of their history and fit them into a coherent, meaningful account. Possessing the book written in their own language, Africans found meaning for the events that were changing their societies, events whose eventual outcome they divined from biblical inspiration. Thus, Jomo Kenyatta, the founding president of Kenya, spoke already in the 1930s of reading in the Ibuka ria Ngai, the Gikuyu Bible, the assurance that the spirit of God, Roho Motheru, would deliver his people from colonial oppression, as God did the ancient Israelites under slavery in Egypt. He would be the Moses of his people. Missionary agents and institutions created and guided the sentiment for the national cause, whatever their intentions. By introducing so wholeheartedly materials from local languages into Christianity, missionaries allowed Africans to rebound from defeat and domination. Hearing about how God helped the ancient tribes of Scripture through adversity and reversal, Africans claimed that as a parallel of their own story, and that gave them an agency role in the current of rapid social change convulsing their communities. Ultimately, mother tongue sentiments fused with the revolutionary message of the Bible concerning the favor of God toward all peoples and races and inveighed against the machinery of continued colonial rule and the doctrine of white racial supremacy.

Missionary translators themselves sometimes stumbled on the significance of mother tongue primacy even before Africans came to a similar realization. One missionary, Edwin Smith, argued that the experience gained from translating the Scriptures into African languages was decisive for the view that no insuperable barrier existed against adopting these languages as mediums of instruction in schools. These languages, he argued, were "rich, flexible, expressive, musical, capable of infinite development."[3] Therefore, he persisted, "to insist upon an African abandoning his own tongue and to speak and read and think in a language so different as English, is like demanding that the various Italian peoples should learn Chinese in order to overcome their linguistic problem."[4] In time, missionary confidence elicited a corresponding African confidence, and the two sides coalesced into a common conviction to break surface in organized efforts for cultural advancement. There was a historical coincidence between vernacular development and mother tongue aspirations which in turn supplied the motivation for the early forms of nationalist ferment. The political and social implications of Erasmus's observations found parallels in these responses.

Two general ideas growing out of the vernacular translation ferment and having considerable impact on Africans may be identified here. One was how ecumenical forms of the Christian religion embraced the local idiom rather than employing an imported professional language. African Christianity rejected such professionalization of language and its elitist tendencies. Instead, the language of worship, prayer, devotion, and preaching was the mother tongue, in a form that related it to the mundane, workaday world. Second, ordinary Africans, including women, appreciated that in principle they suffered no stigma of a ritual or cultural nature to prevent them from participating fully in the religious life, whatever foreign obstacles might be placed in their path. From the perspective of those receiving the message, the indigenous enterprise became necessary for religious and cultural fulfillment, so that communities and individuals that henceforth stood affirmed as without stigma before God felt empowered to demand equality of treatment before colonial rulers. Their religious insight, matured by mother tongue assurance, gained political significance.

Equipped with mother tongue resources, Africans embraced Christianity without taking in the corresponding Eurocentric chauvinism, for the tribes, too, had had their fill of chauvinistic pride. All of that left them open to fundamental stocktaking and repositioning, and so the weary cycle of accumulated antagonism, defeat, revenge, further enmity, strife, and estrangement created a longing for a new order. Christianity met this need, and so was adopted as the means by which Africa's fundamental spiritual realignment could be effected. The effects were felt not only on the plane of the people's worldview, where the old divination ideas of retribution and restitution for past breaches and the system of spirit possession and witchcraft eradication were replaced by the new ideas of ethical prophecy and divine reconciliation, but also reverberations were felt in the whole rhythm and fabric of daily life. It turned out that biblical Christianity had a profound resonance with the native outlook, and that the European practice of compartmentalizing religion was too radical an alteration of the message of the Bible. At any rate, Africans proceeded to relate Christianity to the whole system of life, missionary or colonial skepticism notwithstanding. In the old system, if the accumulation of centuries of experience and practice may be called a system, religion influenced the social structure from its foundation, beginning with the rearing of children.[5] Responding to missionary inquiries about where religion and other forms of indoctrination occurred in the syllabus, one old schoolteacher in Africa insisted thus:

> We teach it all day long. We teach it in arithmetic, by accuracy. We teach it in language, by learning to say what we mean — "Yea, yea, and nay, nay." We teach it in history, by humanity. We teach it in geography, by breadth of mind. We teach it in handicraft, by thoroughness. We teach it in astronomy, by reverence. We teach it in the playground, by fair play. We teach it by kindness to animals, by courtesy to servants, by good manners to one another, and by truthfulness in all things. We teach it by showing the children that we, their elders, are their friends and not their enemies.[6]

Many missionaries saw and welcomed the liberating effects of vernacular literacy. Others, however, saw and feared it. Accordingly, in much of French and Portuguese-speaking Africa, for example, vernacular scriptural translation was discouraged, in large part because the authorities suspected it of fomenting dangerous nationalism. The slow painful emergence of vernacular projects in culture, language, and literature, or the highly ambivalent attitudes that have long prevailed in these and other countries, show the importance of mother tongue consciousness to modern African culture. The point was underscored by one assessment which states that "hardly any writing is done in the vernaculars" in former French, Belgian, and Portuguese territories, in contrast to English-speaking Africa where "indirect rule and the concern of Protestant missionaries to make the Bible available to native populations have encouraged the new writers' attachment to their mother tongues."[7] Thus, in this matter, the negative aids the cause as much as the positive, for disallowing the vernacular because it stiffens the resolve for autonomy and self-reliance concedes its power.

The linguistic method of missions shifts the ground to the indigenous sources for cultural and artistic creativity and away from the themes of colonial control and domination. Colonial rule admittedly promoted the superiority of Western norms and relegated local languages to an inferior position. Neglect of these languages in African education, for example, conformed to the inferior rule prescribed for them. Adopting these languages for Bible translation came as a sharp and striking contrast and attracted the critical attention of Africans. Introduced to their own languages in church and school, Africans embraced them as a riposte to missionary domination and foreign rule. Rather than being exhausted, they felt invigorated sufficiently to turn from lamenting their fate to celebrating the promise of their freedom. As such, mother tongue literacy afforded new possibilities for dealing with the Western encounter by appealing to indigenous values and consecrating them in connection with the people's spiritual and social needs. Mother tongue literacy outlasted both the colonial and missionary phase of Africa's encounter with the West. It retained the advantage in local hands.

A sensitive cultural critic, Dr. Edward Blyden, eloquently observed long ago that Africa's future lay in systematic attention to Africa's aboriginal heritage. Dependence on foreign ideas and institutions would, he cautioned, reduce Africans to the status of those plants that have the local name, 'Life everlasting'—no botanical name exists. The leaves, severed from the stem, appear to survive apart from the whole plant, with no connection with root or branch. They can be pinned up against a wall or anywhere and yet appear to be green. But we know that the condition is not permanent. Africans assimilating into Western culture are like that plant, severed from the parent stock—the aborigines—who are the root, branch, and flower of Africa and of any lasting hope for local advancement.[8]

Historical Precedents and Comparative Perspective

By investing mother tongues with the Scriptures, missionary translators gave an elevated status to the affected cultures. A few historical examples show how such linguistic work led to wider cultural interest, and with those examples we can establish African affinities with biblical themes. Coptic Christianity is a good illustration. From about the middle of the third century, Coptic villages along the Nile began converting to Christianity. At first, Greek was the predominant language of religion and scholarship, having been in wide currency in neighboring Alexandria, the home of a famous catechetical school, but the language was viewed as foreign. As the new religion gained ground, it spawned the need to move beyond Greek, or the little of it that was employed, and in the late fourth century and the early fifth steps were taken to produce material in the vernacular, allowing Egypt to make its unique contribution to Christianity. As Kenneth Scott Latourette put it:

> In Egypt it was the successful effort to provide the masses of the population with a literature in the speech of everyday life which halted the exclusive use of the alien Greek for the written page and which stimulated the development of an alphabet which could be quickly and easily learned by the multitude in place of the ancient hieroglyphics which could be the property only of the few. Through this medium Coptic Christian literature came into being, largely the work of monks.[9]

A similar phenomenon occurred in Ethiopia where by the middle of the seventh century the great vernacular work in Amharic and Ge'ez within the Ethiopian Orthodox Church had been accomplished. With the foundation thus laid, a new intellectual movement developed when in the fourteenth century a member of the

Ethiopian clergy translated from an Arabic source a work we know as the Kebra Nagast, "the Book of the Glory of Kings." The Kebra Nagast secured Ethiopia's national identity by rehearsing the mythical story of the Queen of Sheba and King Solomon. Their union produced Menelik, the creator of Ethiopia's Solomonid dynasty. But the Kebra Nagast was not only a chronicle but also a stimulus of religious, linguistic, and cultural revival. Its impact was to give Ethiopia a powerful national and cultural sense of her heritage,[10] and was an effective barrier against wholesale Islamization.

Parallel developments took place in Europe itself. In the Carolingian empire, for instance, significant attention was devoted to the vernacular cause, with mission again providing the impetus. A modern scholarly evaluation of the Frankish church identified the vernacular work as a force in the rise of German national sensibility.

> The impetus to write the vernacular still came from the mission-field and to it the emperor [i.e., Charlemagne] had something to say. There can be no doubt that to him, as to all his contemporaries, the language of Christianity in the liturgical sense remained Latin, one of the three sacred languages. . . . But the Anglo-Saxons and the Goths had shown that the language of religious exposition could be vernacular; and this was to be encouraged. . . . Most significant . . . are the very large number of vernacular glosses, sermons, hymns, and confessions that survive. . . . This wide-ranging reach of the written vernacular for religious purposes throughout the Carolingian world is of first significance . . . That people should understand underlies a large part of all surviving vernacular translation of the period.[11]

Someone who strengthened this vernacular effort was Otfrid von Weissenburg, active between 863 and 871. He appealed to the people to remain faithful to the vernacular cause and to adopt measures to ensure its faithful transmission. The critical account of his work says he called on his learned contemporaries "who knew how to think and who can be encouraged through the vernacular to read more for themselves. Moreover, he combines learning with piety with great technical skill; something which no one had hitherto attempted in German on such a scale. Like the Heliand [*sic*] poet, Otfrid moved within the Germanic thought-world of warrior ethos, loyalty, and obedience, the lord-man relationship."[12]

Religious translation work sparked the great cultural impulse of northern European tribes, articulating afresh older cultural themes and examples in the midst of cultural change.[13] The translated manuscripts themselves are a unique historical source, as well as being literary specimens that leavened the surrounding culture. One of the most explicit and ambitious attempts during this early period to adopt the vernacular was the effort in Moravia, where in the ninth century two Byzantine missionaries went to work. These were the brothers Constantine-Cyril, who died young at forty-two (Feb. 869), and Methodius (d. Apr. 885). They were both committed champions of the vernacular. They invented the Slavonic alphabet, known after its creator as the Cyrillic alphabet, the standard usage in the Eastern Orthodox Church, including Russia. Of the wide-ranging effects on Slavonic society and culture of the vernacular translation inaugurated by Constantine-Cyril and developed by Methodius, a modern authority summed it up as follows:

His translation is in many ways an adaptation of the peculiar genius of the Slavic idiom elevated to a literary language and to the needs of the young Moravian church. . . . Constantine was well acquainted with the translations of the Gospels into other eastern languages. . . . He stressed his intention of translating the Gospels as accurately as possible, respecting, however, the difference in expression and in the meaning of certain words of both languages. In such cases he thought himself entitled to a more independent rendering of some of the passages in order to be able to explain the true meaning of the original.

In his translation Constantine followed the principles expounded in his treatise. Slavic philologists recognize the excellent qualities of his translation, which reveals a very deep knowledge of the Greek and Slavic languages and of their character. The translation is sometimes not verbal, as Constantine tried to make Greek expressions more understandable to the Slavic Christians . . . Constantine introduced his translations of the four Gospels in a special poetic composition . . . We read there a passionate appeal to the Slavs to cherish their books written in their own language . . . this was the first translation of the Gospels into a vernacular language to appear in the West.[14]

Modern commentators trace the idea of the unique character of Czech-Slavic culture and national identity to the vernacular translation work of the ninth century. The modern scholar Weingart, for example, affirms that "this Czech-Slavic type of culture was of paramount importance for the preservation, or at least, for the strengthening of the national character. If the Czechs did not succumb to germanization as quickly and to such an extent as the Wends [i.e., the Slavs of eastern Germany], this is indeed due to the growth of the Czech Old Church Slavonic letters."[15]

On the occasion of the 1,100th anniversary of the Moravian Mission, His Beatitude Dorotheos, Metropolitan of Prague and All Czechoslovakia, held the vernacular work of Constantine and Methodius as responsible for preserving the Slavic national idea. He commented:

The testament of Orthodox Moravia, left to us by St. Methodius, has been the keynote throughout the history of our nation; it has become the guide of the Slavic idea. . . . Methodius and Cyril helped to develop the culture of Great Moravia, especially the language . . . thus uniting [the] separate Slavic tribes into well-organized states. In so doing, they [awakened] in the nation a sense of national self-awareness.[16]

In the subsequent history of the Eastern Orthodox Church, this vernacular emphasis distinguished its own mission into other cultures. For example, St. Stephen of Perm (1340–1396) led a mission to the Zyrian tribes of the northern forest, creating a Zyrian alphabet and translating some religious works into the language. He encouraged vernacular literacy.[17] A long period of regression followed with imperial Russia intervening, but in the nineteenth century Orthodoxy's vernacular policy was revived with the production of a modern Russian translation of the Old Testament by the versatile Macarius Gloukharev (1792–1847), coupling that with a translation of Western works.[18] And then Nicholas Ilminski (1821–1891), a brilliant linguist who traveled to Cairo to study Arabic, carried the vernacular cause among the Russian Tartars whose language he treated not as a subspecimen of Arabic, as had been the wont, but as a language in its own right. The story is told of an elderly Tartar who was so struck by the genius of Ilminski's translation that he felt it affirmed the best in his culture. Thus, when he heard devotions in Ilminski's translation, he "fell on his knees . . . , and with tears in his eyes thanked God for having vouchsafed to him at least once in his life to pray as he should."[19] The devout Tartar had been stirred in the depths of blood, soul, and tongue. Ilminski illuminated what he called "the living tongue of the Tartars"[20] by giving the Tartars their own Bible, so that the popular, everyday language of the people was connected directly to "their deepest thought and religious consciousness."[21]

"It is in us, in our blood"

It is the same vernacular note that sounds like a drumroll in the rise and spread of the sense of social and cultural self-awareness, not in some refined if ephemeral Pan-African cultural project that is inclined to overlook linguistic and social particularity, but in the detailed, single-minded missionary cultivation of vernacular specificity, including the preservation of dialectical distinctions. A missionary linguist who left a permanent mark on the African vernacular scene was Johannes Christaller, a Basel missionary of German origin who arrived in Ghana in the 1840s and soon after embarked on an enormous translation project that took him deep into the intricacies of Akan life and culture. His work has been received by modern Ghanaians as a manifesto of cultural nationalism. After Christaller left Ghana in the mid-1870s to return to Basel, he continued with his vernacular work. Of the fruits of his labor was an impressive compilation in 1879 of some 3,600 Twi proverbs and idioms that provides an invaluable and unique insight into the Akan worldview. The British anthropologist, R. S. Rattray, produced an abridged and translated version of the proverbs for the Oxford series in African literature. Of the significance of proverbs for the African, Rattray elsewhere testifies as follows: "No one can become eloquent or well versed in the vernacular who has not a large stock of such sayings at his disposal. The best answer to any new-fangled suggestion or argument, however convincing and subtle, is to quote some proverb, however banal or inept, for such a retort is invested with all the force and sanctity of immemorial usage and is therefore—in the African's estimation—conclusive."[22] Similarly, in the preface to the collection Christaller acknowledged the great wealth of wisdom whose source, he felt, was no other than the Creator of the universe, a view that left the Akan and other Africans unbeholden to Western cultural scruples. He wrote:

> May this collection give a new stimulus to the diligent gathering of folk-lore and to the increasing cultivation of native literature. May those Africans who are enjoying the benefit of a Christian education, make the best of the privilege; but let them not despise the sparks of truth entrusted to and preserved by their own people, and let them not forget that by entering into their way of thinking and by acknowledging what is good and expounding [sic] what is wrong they will gain the more access to the hearts and minds of their less favoured countrymen.[23]

In 1881, Christaller published to critical acclaim his Twi dictionary, a monument of indigenous scholarship and an impetus to cultural revitalization. The Twi dictionary systematized and articulated a wealth of linguistic and cultural materials, and established bonds of relationship and mutual influence among neighboring languages and societies. Combined with the grammar of the Twi language that Christaller also wrote, the Twi dictionary gave the Akan an important instrument for cultural advantage in the context of the advancing machinery of colonial subjugation. Christaller also helped found a paper, the *Christian Messenger*, in Basel in 1883, devoted to the promotion of Akan culture and social life. From 1905 to 1917, when it was transferred to Ghana, it published articles in Twi, Ga, and English and covered local as well as international events, such as the news of the Russo-Japanese War of 1905, an event in which there was considerable local interest; Halley's Comet of 1910; and the sinking of the *Titanic* in 1912. If I may repeat what I said elsewhere, "The use of the vernacular to report on world news and instruct its readers in local affairs was a major contribution of the paper, for it suggests that its audience could keep abreast of happenings without literacy in the European languages."[24]

David Asante, a native of Akropong, Ghana, and trained between 1857 and 1862 at Basel, inherited Christaller's devotion to the vernacular cause. Commenting on Christaller's translation of the Psalms into Twi, Asante, evoking the sentiments of the elderly Tartar, testified:

> The Psalms are translated perfectly and brilliantly. Nobody can read this translation without deep feelings of awe. They resemble in many ways the songs of mourning [Kwadwom] in our Twi language; the Twi people will be glad to read them. May the Lord give His blessing to your labours. I want to congratulate you personally and in the name of Africa. May the Lord give you strength for more such work.[25]

Such pioneer linguistic work was important for reinforcing the indigenous narrative predilection, as Asante's work makes clear. He translated many works from the German and English into Akan, including John Bunyan's *Pilgrim's Progress*, that perennial of the genre. Arguably, his significance for Ghanaian letters and literature is considerable. "But such is the preoccupation of Ghanaian biographers with 'merchant princes' and nationalist firebrands that, outside a small circle of the Presbyterian Church and an entry in the Encyclopaedia Africana, not much is known of such pioneers as Asante. Yet in the translation of the Bible and in his other books he helped to introduce new concepts, new words and phrases into Ghanaian literature."[26]

Another local pioneer was Carl Christian Reindorf, who in 1889 wrote a history of his people, *The History of the Gold Coast and Asante*, a work that was first written in Ga, the vernacular of the Ghanaian littoral. The book made extensive use of oral traditions as a source comparable to documentary evidence, thus representing the kind of historical methodology that scholars thought they were pioneering in the 1960s. All of this immense vernacular work had a predictable effect on national sentiment. Reindorf said that was one of his aims, to give his compatriots a progressive sense of their place in history.

In part in response to that vernacular theme in Christaller and David Asante, a local quasi-political organization was founded, called the Reference Group, comprising educated Akan who pressed for the retention of the vernacular in church and social life. For it, too, religious activity increased political awareness to the extent that its members were, therefore, considered early pioneers of African nationalism. In the case of South Africa, a similar vernacular process can be discerned, and, given the historic controversy there, we should expect that the kind of criticism Erasmus leveled at elite monopoly of truth would assume a particularly explosive form. Vernacular sentiments became a potent force in this context.[27] The turning point came when missionaries adopted the African name for God as the God of Christianity, so that the Zulu word UnKulunkulu, for instance, was adopted for the God of the Christian Scriptures. Nothing in their previous training or religious preparation had prepared the missionaries for such a shift and its intellectual consequences. God is the great archetypal theme in African narrative life, since the first stories about the race and its lapsarian afflictions come out of that source, the paradigmatic story in the light of which other stories can be told and retold. In the vernacular field setting, it turns out, the missionaries were overtaken by Africans who had heard of God and the special forms by which knowledge of this God is cherished in the applied parts of the old narrative. Old men and old women handed down stories they in turn had received from their elders, stories about creation, fertility, kinship relations, and the other myriad ways in which the tribe was led, chastened, sheltered, and restored. No wonder many missionaries felt themselves preempted. The story of their arrival among the people, though a major historical event, was, in the light of the old narratives, something hinted at in the myths and legends that spoke of spirit and matter, of good and evil, and of the faithfulness and mystery of God. The old narratives are the people's hallowed memory, the canonical deposit as well as the shaping power of their collective experience.

The religious and theological aspects of vernacular translation belong to a later stage of our discussion. What I should stress here is that missionary transmitters, having stooped to conquer the native idiom, set off ripples in African society and commenced a transformation process in culture by drawing on mother tongues and giving them documentary backing. There was change involved in this, for while it might be possible in the pre-Christian period for Africans to think of God in highly refracted tribal and clan terms, terms that were inclined to be uncritical and inward looking, now a new scale of identity was introduced that included a critical, outward looking view of God as the God of all tribes and races, of God, in fact, as the clue to all history. That generalization, however, was arrived at through the transcribed medium of the mother tongue, a mother tongue, in the bargain, that retained the marks of the people's practice.

We should not be deterred by the scruples of anthropological purity or cultural superiority from seeing how, through mother tongue literacy, Africans entered an immensely important stage of human consciousness in which the printed word helped to renew and strengthen the oral culture. As a consequence, a wide-ranging renewal process was sparked in the religious, linguistic, cultural, social, political, and economic life of the people. Armed now with the vernacular Bible, Africans dealt in deliberate fashion with the problems induced by the irruption of the West into their societies, and did so in the reassuring symbols of the ancient narratives that told of God's faithful mindfulness for the race and the tribe. Anyone who has learnt first to think and write in the mother tongue has an advantage that subsequent exposure to another medium can only reinforce rather than displace, and if the mother tongue were to be a channel for the narrative themes of Scripture, as it often was, then it would impact the entire range of life and experience. Fidelity to the past could then coexist with accommodation to change. Religious thought and reflection, and whatever else is involved in conversion, would in that context occur within the search for new forms of identity and personal fulfillment.

What is illuminating in the indigenous cultural process is how the Christian Scriptures, cast into the vernacular medium, gave the native idiom and its aspirations a fresh horizon. It allowed Africans to configure their place in the new order and the possibilities within that for their own advancement and possibility. In the Mandinka language, for example, the verse "he had pity on him" (Lk. 10:33) can be translated as "Abala fata ye," which, with its hint of a woman's compassion, carries the literal sense of suffering in the flesh in solidarity with the weak and needy, a glimpse of the crucifixion. As a result, language was organized and integrated with the simplest and most eloquent rules, with the idioms of everyday speech and their common sense power engaged for moral and ethical instruction. Thus were men, women, and children appealed to without regard to economic or social status—and in some significant cases, in defiance of such status. It was the kind of intellectual revolution that in the West produced the idea of the primacy of conscience, and thus of the free individual as the linchpin of personal autonomy and social advancement. In Africa, by contrast, it produced a fresh narrative and a cultural identity set in the context of family, tribe, and nation.

Whatever their scruples or reservations, and whatever their motives or principles, missionaries found themselves drawn into documenting relevant instances of cultural observance, ritual, ceremony, and practice in order to ensure effectiveness in translation. The religious nature of the Bible resonated with natural ease with the religious character of traditional culture, and in that natural convergence Europe's 'civilising mission' in Africa was overwhelmed. Instead of the normative rationality of science wedded to universal progress, European missionaries found themselves cultivating for the first time remote, isolated African languages in their own right. Many missionaries consoled themselves with the forlorn thought that the admirable and complex systems of those languages were proof that the tribes had once attained a high degree of development from which they had inexplicably fallen but to which European agency might once again restore them. In that restoration process, however, missionaries first compiled the systematic linguistic tools needed to gather oral tradition, ethnographic details, and ritual observances, and to pursue wider and deeper theological, cultural, and historical connections. It led missionaries into uncharted waters. Many of them, for example, pursuing the logic of a primitive monotheism, plunged headlong into adopting the African name for God as the God of the Bible without fully knowing where that might lead. For example, the Zulu word for God, or what was imagined as the Zulu word for God, was embraced as the God of the Christian creed. On reflection, however, some missionaries began to demur, putting up a dogged resistance to such a hasty theological step. Remedial steps were taken, including imposing on African converts humiliating sanctions for using mother tongues and for practicing other native customs on missionary premises. The aim was to take back the advantage that the mother tongue Bible appeared to concede to the natives. It had never been the intention of missionaries that mother tongue literacy should undercut or replace the superior Western values contained in European languages and over which control could never be handed to the tribes. Yet once the vernacular Bible was produced, the beast of the tribe was beyond taming, one consequence being that even the seclusion of mission enclaves failed to secure final immunity against indigenous claims.[28]

The vernacular crucible forged a vigorous culture of indigenous renewal and focused attention on colonial subjugation as a contradiction of the gospel of freedom and equality before God. The rituals, prayers, and hymns of the new Christian communities were stacked with images and symbols favorable to the tribes, however veiled the allusions. The meticulous and painstaking task of learning African languages, of producing very careful scientific linguistic materials as an aid to translation, including the creation of alphabets, all this constituted an unprecedented advantge for the culture, and it redefined Africa's material and intellectual values by placing them meaningfully in the liberating setting of mother tongue pride. It is a matter of incalculable significance that on the historic front-line of cross-cultural encounter, Europeans should meet Africans not just as vanquished populations but as inalienable possessors of their own languages. It may not have averted eventual European mastery of the continent and its peoples, but at least it introduced greater complexity and irony into the encounter.

Thus, before the first complete Zulu Bible was produced in 1883 by the American Board of Commissioners for Foreign Missions, there had been a generation or so of preparatory work. In 1850, Hans Schreuder published a grammar of Zulu, followed in 1855 by the Anglican Bishop John Colenso's grammar of the same language. In 1859, Lewis Grout of the American Board produced in Natal his own grammar of Zulu. Grout also wrote an account of the Zulu called *Zulu-Land; or, Life among the Zulu-Kafirs of Natal and Zulu-Land, South Africa* (Philadelphia: Presbyterian Publication Committee, 1864). He offered an appreciation of the Zulu language as follows:

> Perhaps no language can lay a better claim than the Zulu to an exemption from two great faults—on the one hand, that superabundance of vowels and liquids which produces excessive softness; and, on the other, that superabundance of consonants which produces excessive harshness. That happy mean which it has observed in its intermixture of mute consonants with vocalic and liquid sounds makes it both pleasing to the ear and easy to speak. . . . And then the language is yet young as it were, uncultivated, waiting to be developed and fashioned for the largest and noblest ends. One root will often give you a large stem, with a good number of branches, and no small amount of fruit.[29]

Similar attention was paid to Zulu dictionaries. In 1855, Perrin's dictionary was published, and in 1861, Colenso's Zulu-English dictionary came out, and in 1880, Charles Roberts produced a similar work. Colenso was prominent in a landmark event in the history of the Zulu language when in 1859 he visited the Zulu King Mpande. He took with him two Zulu schoolboys, Magema and Ndiyane, and a schoolteacher, William. Following their visit they published a book containing accounts in Zulu of the meeting with the king. The three texts, written by Magema, Ndiyane, and William, were the earliest published contribution by a Zulu to the language.[30] Professor Nyembezi's general observation is worth reiterating here, to wit, that missionary translation was connected with indigenous cultural revitalization. He says it was not simply that "missionaries concerned themselves primarily with grammars, dictionaries and the translation of the Scriptures, [as that] some of them recorded folk-lore, proverbs and valuable historical material."[31] C. M. Doke, whose pioneering and definitive studies of Zulu[32] take in the missionary factor, in his review of the development of Bantu languages has also drawn attention to the indispensable role of Bible translation in establishing these languages. Beginning with early Portuguese missionary translations in the seventeenth century, through Moffat, Krapf, and Livingstone in the nineteenth century, and to Pilkington, W. H. Murray, and Alexander Hetherick in the twentieth, an unprecedented linguistic enterprise was carried through that transformed the face of modern Africa. Doke admits, "The story of this achievement of translation work, if written, would constitute a stirring romance. It will never be realized what privation, intensity of purpose, continued study, painstaking labour and pious devotion all this has meant, often in unhealthy climate, amid active opposition, with weak equipment or lack of support."[33]

John Colenso was representative of those Western missionaries who saw mother tongue development as a strategic way of opening the door into creative regions of the culture. For example, when he visited the Zulu king in 1859, Colenso had each of his three Zulu companions subsequently write an account of the event in Zulu, because, Colenso reasoned, it would encourage the men in question to "make a first attempt at keeping journals in their own language, which might be useful in showing how some of our proceedings looked from a native point of view,"[34] a native point of view that naturally left a stamp on whatever it touched. One of the results in this case was that Colenso found a deep natural piety in some of the Zulu material of the journals kept, with a strong rhythmic structure that lent itself to measured meter. Colenso commented: "The words run almost of themselves into rhythm and he [William Ngidi, one of the Zulu companions mentioned] has since thrown them into a metrical form, which is here added, in translation, as a specimen of a Zulu hymn, written by a native."[35]

> My brethren, let our weapons,
> Our warlike weapons all,
> Be beaten into ploughshares
> Wherewith to till the soil;
> Our shields, our shields of battle,
> For garments be they sewed,
> And peace both North and Southward
> Be shouted loud abroad.
>
> Northward, I say, and Southward,
> And far on every side,
> Through Him who ever liveth,
> The Father of our Lord,
> Who is our very Father;

And, as for evil all,
Through Him let all be peaceful,
I say, let all be good.

Our soldiers be they gathered,
For those who others harm;
For those, who seek to injure
The men who live in peace,
Gathered to make the highways
That go from land to land,
Till every tribe shall utter,
He is, indeed, our Lord!

He is the Lord, our Master!
He is the Lord our God!
He is the Lord Almighty,
Who liveth evermore!
Yes! dead is now all evil!
Goodness alone abides!
For Jesus Christ has conquered,
Who's risen from the dead.

Through Him we too, my brethren,
The world have overcome;
Have vanquished it entirely,
With all its evil things.
Yes! dead is now all evil!
Goodness alone abides!
For He, of Good the Father,
He liveth evermore.

The father died of evil,
And evil too, is dead;
Now ever lives all Goodness,
Now ever lives all Love;
And Northward and Southward,
And far on every side,
Peace lives, and lives forever,
The Peace of Christ our Lord![36]

The hymn reveals striking resonance with the old African narrative themes and employs all the well-known rules of reversal in Scripture of the weak made strong, the bellicose meek, the last and the lowly exalted. It takes in one hand all the great themes of faith and goodness and turns them over to the homecoming power of storytelling and praise-singing (izibongo) to confirm a revitalized potential for the African heritage. Critics of mission argue, however, that the hymn exhibits all the classic marks of African acquiescence to white supremacy, of Africans ingratiating themselves with their missionary benefactors. They contend that the hymn is proof, if proof be needed, of Christianity taming Africans, of missionaries placing natives under supervised guidance, with the Zulu hymnwright giving vent to sentiments that would please his new masters. It is the kind of invasive subversion of African culture that missionary translators had set out to achieve, we are told.[37] The difference between such gestures and the native reflex, such critics say, is tantamount to the difference between the private and amusing gambols of a lion-cub and the wild thunder of the tribal hunt that has tasted blood. African Christians, according to this reasoning, are held under cultural quarantine.

Yet this taming, if taming it be, this apparent socializing of the savage nerve, may be said to be the captivity of the beast in its native habitat, of Africans infusing from a stream to which the primordial paths of hunting and gathering had led them. The sound and tones of native speech, of which the English translation can convey an impression only as evocative rhythms, may now carry a new theme and burden, but they keep to the stamp and pace of ancient energy. The difference now is that the bush resounds with a strange familiarity, the dawn of the age when promises would be kept even after the oracles fell silent. The old ways led to new paths, and turning from them would not be a forsaking.

Christian Africans, let us recall, are naturally multilingual, with proficiency in several mediums. They are also naturally multicultural, in the sense of being steeped in their own customs and traditions, as well as being aware of their participation in the white man's world. They do not ignore the distinctions between their own and other people's culture—Africa's native pluralism gave them plenty of practice in cultural differentiation. So when Africans speak, or are assumed to speak, confidently in the language they learned from the West, so that the West hears the tones that reassure it of the effectiveness of its power, there are often in those tones echoes of the very confidence that threatened continued Western domination. Nowhere was this double effect more prominent and more persistent than in the translation projects of missions. Africans made their presence felt in this field, almost like uncaged beasts following the maternal scent. There is a much greater difference between traditional Africa and the secular West, say, than between Africa and the Bible, a difference that fused Christianity with the narrative deposit of collective security and promise.

Historical accounts are full of references to traditional Africa being deeply religious. Europeans were ambivalent about this fact. Religion, they felt, could be an obstacle in their plans for the takeover of African societies, and so it should be countered with imported values. On the other hand, religion might be strategic in offering a way of approach to the primitive mind where other methods were unavailing. In the end, the sources agree that religion could not be ignored, whether it was suppressed or encouraged. From the vantage point of natural advantage, religion aided the African cause, either directly from missionary encouragement or indirectly from foreign confrontation that stiffened the tribal resolve. Christianity stepped into the breach by offering Africans a revitalized version of their heritage in the translated Bible and in the grammars and dictionaries that accompanied it. So Africans possessed the translated Scriptures like the ancient Israelites the promised land. The old wisdom of the tribes was given written form, and that in turn sanctioned the ethics of resistance to wholesale overthrow of the heritage. The heritage could be saved; there was a new reason to live for; there was a new story worth telling; and there was an end worth looking forward to.

It was the peculiar advantage of the vernacular Bible that it held together the character of spoken language alongside its literate form, so that the speech habits of the people persisted through the written vernacular version. How one spoke and listened took precedent over how one read and studied. The much more marked transition into literacy as the scientific arbiter of a new system of values, as the passage from a rustic, provincial simplicity to an urbane metropolitan sensibility, was largely missing in preindustrial Africa. And this is still further from that crucial cultural stage of literacy preparing the way for textuality as the linear arbiter of values in a hierarchy of power, with epistolary elegance predominating over homiletic informality. We should recall that in medieval Europe literacy and administration were two sides of the same coin. Writing was a political act, the written record a legal rule. It is understandable that we should wish to extend into Africa this idea of literacy as objective rationality and argue that, perhaps, the vernacular Scriptures did set a cumulative precedent by broadcasting into the potent environment of oral culture the signals of the written code. Yet in so far as the long-range cultural effects are concerned, vernacular literacy seldom carried over into the differentiation of social stratification, let alone into the formation of independent urban elite groups. The vernacular Scriptures continued to resonate with popular consciousness and to preserve speech habits that drew their potency from a diverse indigenous exuberance. As one writer observed in a different connection, the African seems "to be so made as to worship a book. It comes as a new thing to him, but it is not strange to his mind that a material object can convey a message from the unseen world."[38]

In effect, Western scruples about religion, including the overzealous missionary preachiness that assumed unbelief as the point of departure and ontological proofs as part of the Western intellectual aid program, failed to carry with Africans. In response to the encounter with Bible translation, African speech forms persisted into scriptural usage, sometimes successfully, in any case self-consciously, and almost invariably in ways adapted to the continuity of the old narrative codes. The same rule that said that, given the demands of the extended family, the African should never pass muster as a person of independent means was also the rule that determined that the religious question should become one for community understanding and collective self-representation. In Africa we should make a distinction, however tentative, between the effects of European colonial rule, on the one hand, and, on the other, the modern missionary enterprise. Colonial rule assumed little by way of partnership with local leaders, and, too, assumed little or no role for native languages except in quarantine. By contrast, the modern missionary movement launched a full-scale investigation into local languages, and although not every person who acquired mother tongue literacy read or knew the Bible or joined the church, few who acquired such literacy did so without the grammars and dictionaries produced by the missions. Missionary motives or intentions had a limited effect in that regard.

Where Christianity took root, there was brought into being an indigenous self-reflection and understanding, a self-reflection that thrived on the remembered past and on the narrative that glued it together, rather than on disparate or dismembered parts of the culture. As psychology has taught us, it is the forgotten past, the dim, undeciphered images buried we forget where, that enslave us, not the images and symbols summoned by effort and choice. This is a truth that some missionaries appreciated, suggesting there was often a two-way process of transmission and respon-

sive adaptation.[39] Some Western missionaries were able to slip out of their own eth-
nocentric obsession to embrace indigenous confidence, a process that marked people like John Colenso. He was led to observe that Africans were also caught up in
the same narrative sweep of God's dealings with all humanity. He testified:

> I believe that, by thus meeting the heathen, half way, as it were, upon the ground
> of our common humanity, and with the recollection that humanity is now blessed
> and redeemed in Christ . . . we may [l]ook for far greater success in Missionary
> labours, and far more of stability in the converts that may be made, than by seeking
> to make all things new to them—to uproot altogether their old religion, scoffing at
> the things which they hold most sacred, deriding the fears, which alone have stood
> to them, for so many years long, as the representatives of the spiritual world.[40]

Suitably chastened by his African experience, John Colenso had his thinking
readjusted in Africa, and by virtue of that he came to exert a mutually transforming
influence upon the Africans of his time and place. This is so because of long-
standing contacts he had with native agents, one of whom was Magema Fuze, a
convert in the late nineteenth century who went on to write a valuable account in
the mother tongue of his Zulu people *Abantu Abamnyama* ("The Black People").
The book was finally published in 1922, and a critical modern translation in English
came out in 1979. Fuze's observations have been recognized for their unique ethnographic, linguistic, and historical importance, while he himself "stood at the
frontier of the clash of cultures, values and interests. In fact the teacher's [i.e.,
Colenso's] tolerance and sympathy towards local customs and attitudes laid an even
greater responsibility and difficulty upon the convert. That he did not violently resist, that he did not completely capitulate, that he thought about the problems and
came to his own conclusions, as these early chapters most clearly reflect, is a tribute
to the man and to the many Zulu people like him." The account continues:

> A major interest of the book is the way in which Fuze lives in several worlds at
> once. He came to Bishop Colenso's mission station, Ekukhanyeni (the place of en-
> lightenment), from a country background, the influence of which remained with
> him throughout his life. The care and accuracy with which he describes the details
> of Zulu rural life suggest not only that he was still in sympathy with it, but that he
> was still in constant touch with it, even at the mission. . . . It is clear that it was
> the wider world of the mission that fostered a wider sense of identity and nation-
> ality . . . on his travels through Natal and Zululand on mission business, [Fuze]
> gained a wider view than he could have gained from his original circumscribed
> background. It is also clear that the mission gave him a stronger sense of Zulu na-
> tionalism, for it was through the mission that he became acquainted with the Zulu
> royal family and with the issues borne by emissaries backwards and forwards across
> the Tugela River.[41]

Thus did Fuze weave together in his own life and work the several distinctive
strands of the old Africa and the new Christian religion, of the local and the national, of the Zulu ethnic impulse and the wider African connections Christianity
was bringing, of the force of cultural particularity and the historical unity of the
people of the world. The editor of his book felt constrained to the view that "the his-

torical and sociological value of Fuze's book lies largely in the way it 'straddles the several worlds he inhabits' and shows 'the linkages he forges between them.'"[42]

Fuze's residence at a mission station did not deprive him of his African sensibilities or undercut his political loyalty to his people. Instead his attention was turned not inward, to the routines and affairs of the mission station, but outward, to events and matters in the wider society. His book is strong evidence of his roots in his own society, with mission residence serving as a hidden platform for the enactment of a drama and story in which local interlocutors held center stage. Fuze could have spoken eloquently of how life at Ekukhanyeni, for example, was designed for the stripping of the natives, for the suppressing of their voice and rewarding them for their compliance. But if he had he would have been unable to take up with the zeal he did the native cause. With his attention shifted to missionaries, Africans would have emerged from his account as residual actors on their own continent. His own Christianity, the one mediated to him through his mother tongue, would under such circumstances have remained a function of distance: the farther away from the mission station the better the prospects.

Speculation aside, it says something of real value that Fuze's exposure to Christianity at the mission produced instead such careful and thoughtful interest in the constructive and imaginative resources of culture. He shows how his own primary sensibility was matured in a narrative wit that became part of his national heritage. In terms of power relations, we have, not the forcible uprooting of Africans and their barracooning in mission stations, but the vernacular transformation, where the native voice was given a natural outlet and the cause of mother tongue assurance deepened. Colenso's Ekukhanyeni gave an example of the process by which Africa domesticated Christianity, expressing through it indigenous themes and convictions even while Christianity itself was causing alterations in old habits and idioms. If missions had adopted a deliberate policy of advancing Africa's native aspirations, then they could not have chosen a more effective instrument than the mother tongue. That was the African advantage, and, against the Europeans, a crucial one at that.

Christianity and African culture were involved in a symbiosis, a symbiosis that involved considerable variation on the pattern of inferiority missionaries imposed on Africans. Missionaires employed mother tongues as a way of transposing Christianity into familiar local terms, and thereby tacitly adopted the indigenous cause as their own. The business of mission under those circumstances became the business of indigenous actors like Fuze. No one can read his book without a sense of someone in deep touch with his own roots, as confident about where he and his people came from as about where they were going. His infectious humor, his uncontrived candor, his faith in new possibilities, his natural flair for idioms rooted in a living, dynamic culture, his alertness to what animates and constrains his people, their ideals and fears, their strengths and weaknesses, all these leap from the page. In Fuze's hands the light of genuine affirmation falls naturally on the Africa he knew so well, an Africa reeling from the fateful impact of Europe.

Mother tongue development belonged with the changes Europeans introduced in Africa. Yet the effects of such mother tongue development have been far more beneficial to the cultures affected than those that attach to vernacular suppression and neglect. Even in the most ambiguous cases, such as when a linguistic federation was willed into existence in disregard of regional and dialectical differences, or when a heavy penalty was imposed on local custom to breach it with the requirement of the adoption of European languages and usage, the continued use of the vernacular Scriptures often generated important intellectual discussion about historical forms, about the issue of cultural origin and affinity, about the nature of language as an attribute of the human mind, and about the dynamic nature of the political encounter with the West. At any rate, let not a subtle, avuncular protectiveness push us to the point of depicting Africans as inherently incapable of coping with Western or other extraneous contact or meddling on the questionable grounds of Africans being an exception to the normal human traffic involved in historical exposure and struggle. We would be in danger of promoting such a view were we to disallow any possibility for complexity in indigenous categories and values or for Africans' ability to draw from mother tongue literacy lessons and insights for their own self-renewal vis-à-vis Europeans. Accordingly, mother tongue literacy enabled peaceful intertribal contact to occur and to alter political and social relationships in the precolonial period.

Thus, when the Yoruba clergyman, Rev. Samuel Johnson, wrote his magnificent *The History of the Yorubas* in 1897,[43] he devoted considerable space in his introductory remarks to a discussion of linguistic matters pertaining to Yoruba. Thus, he expounded his theme with the use of scientific, literary, historical, religious, social, political, geographical, and economic examples. He also describes the contributions of European scholars, missionaries, clergymen, and other interested writers by virtue of which the African heritage could be improved and strengthened. He remained true to his African heritage in spite of the European name he bore, aided in that cause by possessing the Scriptures in the mother tongue.

Johnson's career proves that contact with the West through Christian missions contributed often in unexpected ways in bringing about fresh adaptations and renewed vigor, with people like him and Fuze, for example, finding their vocation within the critical and dense milieu of Africa's encounter with Europe. Missionaries could not claim all the credit for the good that Africans derived from the introduction of the vernacular Scriptures. On the contrary, in many significant cases missionaries encouraged and rewarded in their converts an uncritical imitation of the West, with some hapless missionaries paying a personal price for flagrant cultural insensitivity. It is a theme Noël Coward has caricatured with merciless humor in the musical *Pacific*, some of the lines of his doggerel running thus:

> Poor Uncle Harry having become a missionary,
> found the native's words rather crude.
> He and Aunt Mary swiftly imposed an arbitrary ban
> upon them shopping in the nude.
> They all considered this silly and decided to rebel,
> They burnt his boots and several suits,
> which made a horrible smell.
> The subtle implication was that Uncle could go to hell.[44]

Any consideration of the full record of the missionary movement must include such examples of missionary caricature, and also, as Vilakazi eloquently put it, the numerous instances when missions distorted African social relations by altering relationships and networks of affiliation. In many places the church became "a new form of organization, usurping the functions previously performed by traditional institutions."[45] Church organization introduced new rules and patterns of administration, bureaucracy, formal procedures, communication, correspondence, and recordkeeping. It might be right to press the view from such a situation that Christianity allowed missionaries to mount a systematic assault on Africa's ancient dispensation and put in place a replacement civilization: schools, hospitals, clinics, chapels, and scientific methods of agriculture, health, communication, and commerce. Undoubtedly, such power would tempt even the most saintly of missionaries with impulses of superiority over Africans.

Images abound of children in Africa or Papua, New Guinea, or anywhere else, playing cricket, working diligently at their table manners, or comporting themselves to the measured jig of Scottish country dance, all their consecrated hours overshadowed by a bucolic missionary chapel on the hill and a long way from the village. How many African choirs had not tugged and otherwise labored gallantly at the strains of Gounod or Handel while the harmonic rhythms of a different music stayed throbbing in their veins? These or even worse travesties can be recounted ad nauseam.

However, missionary interference was often a passing phase, and where it persisted it was as often as not redirected into unsuspecting channels of adaptive local response. As a commission into the use of African languages in schools reported, "the mother tongue is the true vehicle of mother wit."[46] It is a fact that missions made possible the documenting of the creative impulses in the vernacular in a way that resonated with the older narrative tradition. That encouraged an intellectual process leading to the growth of an indigenous literary and national culture. It is hard even today to find mother tongue literary flowering anywhere in Africa untouched by the missionary movement.

There was an inconclusiveness as well as an element of ambiguity in the task of transcribing the mother tongue, especially when missionaries were doing so for the first time. It was difficult enough to attempt to cover all the ground of current usage, let alone trying to delve into deep and obscure pockets of memory to identify and retrieve half-forgotten treasures and their barely legible traces across ethnic lines. Furthermore, the translator would wish to establish a catalogue and inventory not just of the lexical properties of the language but the infinite and myriad occasions on which people used and produced language. The principles for organizing, explaining, interpreting, and utilizing hitherto unwritten languages were, to complicate matters, similarly innumerable. Yet something really unexpected and incalculable happened when a mother tongue was furnished with a new transcription and launched under its own steam. It moved not just to the formulas of imitation, subjugation, and conformity contrived for it, but to the free rhythms and resonances of its hidden life and logic. One impulse in it was charged with more significance than all the nonbiodegradable erudition that buoyed up imported classics in colonial Africa.

One other matter should not escape attention. In the field of Bible translation as such, there was a built-in principle of progressive improvement in the versions that were produced. If the job was done well enough, a newly translated version would impose a grip and solidify a position for itself, thus discouraging further translations from occurring too soon or occurring in any way that might challenge existing forms, as happened with the King James version. On one level this might not be bad in itself, since any new translation would have to compete against a tough, worthy predecessor. On the other hand, it could be predicted that forms and idioms that had been successfully pioneered in scriptural translation would, even without further Bible translation, take on a life of their own in fields besides the religious, fields as varied as literature, music, art, psychology, and customary law. With mother tongue literacy, the die is cast. Literacy is a catalyst of cultural change, ushering in transformations far beyond any obvious agenda or intention of the missionary. Under the circumstances, we would have no choice except to leave the door open to new possibilities and developments, precisely the space any dynamic cultural system requires in order to live and flourish. We cannot exclude this possibility for African culture once we concede the historical fact of the mother tongue projects of missions.

To turn to another example, Robert Moffat (1795–1883) was fairly representative of his age, too, and so something of his personal story may reveal clues into the cultural dynamics of missionary translation. No sooner had he arrived in South Africa early in 1817, than was Moffat confronted with the language barrier. Very little systematic work had been done in the indigenous languages, apart from Cardoso's catechism of 1624 and that of Pacconio and de Couto of 1643. To remedy the situation, Moffat decided to go and settle among the Africans, which he did in 1827. He acquired fluency in Setswana and was able to do preaching work in that language. From this time on, Moffat became the sponsor of translation work and publication in the language. When he had done a translation of the Gospel of Luke, for example, he rode four hundred miles to Cape Town with the manuscript in his pocket to try to find a printer, and when he found a printing press, its rather archaic state was aggravated by the unavailability of printers with adequate skill. It left Moffat with little choice except to learn the skill himself, which he proceeded to do. The printing press gave Moffat an effective tool for advancing the cause of Setswana vernacular literacy and confirmed him in the front ranks of linguistic development and study.

Moffat found that he could not successfully or unthinkingly assume Western theological terms for the vernacular and decided instead to follow the internal logic of Setswana in the rendering of religious concepts and ideas. "The Sechuana language," he confessed, "though exceedingly copious, is of course deficient in theological terms. . . . This at first occasioned considerable difficulty; but research has convinced me, that the language itself possesses an ample source of suitable words to convey with wonderful clearness, the language and meaning of the Scriptures."[47]

Apart from the theological issue, Moffat saw a similar problem in persisting with the Western ecclesiastic tradition for Africa. In particular, denominational sectarianism such as had marked modern European Christianity was, he felt, out of place in the faithful transmission of the message in the vernacular idiom, an idiom as yet untainted with credal uncharitableness. "I have studiously avoided," he testified, "giving the slightest tinge to any rendering in favour of any creed."[48] It is very difficult if, for example, in an African language the word for "church" means the same as community, as it most assuredly does in many African languages, to use it also to mean "stranger" or "excluded outsider." Whatever the case, Moffat's biographer wrote:

> In the famous library at the Bible House in London there is a memorial window figuring great translators: William Tyndale, Jerome, Cyril and Methodius, Martin Luther, John Eliot, William Carey, Robert Morrison, Henry Martyn, and—Robert Moffat, who takes his place naturally in the far-shining company, most of whom were greater scholars than he, but none of whom surpassed him in single-hearted devotion.[49]

Moffat claimed much less for himself, content merely to say, "I felt it to be an awful thing to translate the Book of God."[50]

The work of translating the Scriptures also involved being out of step with Western cultural suppositions and proceeding on the terms of indigenous societies and at their pace. Dr. Henry Callaway, a pioneer missionary translator in Zulu, spoke of his experience of having to defer to "native experts," even though he was impatient to press on with the job. In a letter he admitted: "I have a 'committee' of natives sitting on the translation! Each of the three natives has a translation by someone else in his hand, and I read ours, verse by verse. We do not get on very fast, but I am quite satisfied with what we have done. It corroborates me in the belief that hitherto nothing has been printed which at all approaches to what ours will be when completed."[51]

It is in the very nature of scriptural translation that sooner or later revisions should follow, and older forms and conceits, having exhausted their staying power, yield place to new. Such a process developed in African language translations, though often it was a slow process, either because the earlier versions, such as had happened with the Authorized (King James) Version for English, had succeeded too well to be easily dislodged, or because new experts were slow to arrive on the scene, or both. In any case, revision work helped to carry forward the impulse for cultural renovation by inscribing new words and concepts into the cultural memory and bringing them into fruitful convergence with past usage and custom. Although we can criticize what may sometimes appear to be the stifling effects of scriptural translation on new initiatives and the spirit of independence, especially where we find a slavish adherence to older versions, we must be balanced even here. We need to remember the contrasting case of neoclassical literature in the European Renaissance when writers before Shakespeare, Corneille, and Lope de Vega copied ancient forms mechanically without a true appreciation of the function of such works. Aristotle and Seneca were norms of imitation then, not a spur to free imagination. What we can say, therefore, is that when it came to be done, revised translation necessitated augmenting existing resources, raising and refining standards, and widening areas of contact and affinity, precisely the sort of intellectual activity by which a culture propagates itself and overcomes the hazard of foreign domination. Eventually, when Western contact became the single most important fact for modern Africans and assimilation unavoidable, it was mother tongue affirmation that acted as reassurance and smoothed out considerably the serrated edge of Western intrusion.

The question whose deafening echo has settled on the field like a thunderclap is the view that Christian missions opened the way for the suppression of African and other cultures, a view that leaves us with a victim notion of Africa and a residual understanding of its cultures. In fact, the missionary and the colonizer in Africa might be likened to Virgil's Juno and Jupiter on Olympus deciding the fate of Rome before a victorious Troy. The missionary, like Juno, acquiesced in the conquest of Africa, but the ground she, or, through her, the African convert yielded to the colonial Jupiter is actually reserved for native speech and dress. In Virgil's hands, the Trojan invasion is absorbed and naturalized into the subjugated Latin culture, so that the cultural weapon, what Virgil calls simply "the tongue of their fathers and their ancient ways," more than compensates for the march and thunder of Jupiter's foreign cohorts. Virgil's perspective of representing the cause of the vanquished carries this vernacular mark, and in the harsh, bitter conditions of foreign defeat the Latin tongue is invoked to allay ultimate disenchantment. In that sense his words ring with assurance for Africans, too:

> Never command the land's own Latin folk
> To change their old name, to become new Trojans,
> Known as Teucrians; never make them alter
> Dialect or dress. Let Latium be.
> Let there be Alban kings for generations
> And let Italian valor be the strength
> Of Rome in after times. Once and for all
> Troy fell, and with her name, let her lie fallen.[52]

Such a device Virgil employs to transcend the phantom of imperial subjugation by appealing meaningfully to provincial pride, much against the tendency of later classical learning to stress cosmopolitan standardization. Similarly, the fact of Western colonial suppression of Africans would undoubtedly have been far harsher, far more comprehensive, and far longer enduring without the cushioning effects of mother tongue literacy and the narrative flash they kindled in people's heart, whatever motives missionaries shared or did not share with colonialists.[53]

One indication that commitment to mother tongue literacy alerted missionaries to the political aspirations of the subject races was contained in a specific policy directive by Dr. Robert Mann, the colonial superintendent of education in South Africa. In 1864, he proposed making an appropriation from the colonial Reserve Fund in the form of an annual grant for schools with the prerequisite that all instruction be in English. Rufus Anderson, the secretary at the time of the American Board of Commissioners for Foreign Missions, opposed the plan on the grounds partly that government sponsorship of mission schools would bring them under government control and end their independence, suggesting that government and mission were not necessarily natural allies on the ground and partly that English would then supplant Zulu. Daniel Lindley, a missionary of the American Board of Commissioners for Foreign Missions,[54] took up these objections and expanded on them, in particular, on the language issue. He said while he understood that it was natural in an English colony for government to want to promote English and that whites and blacks needed to have a common language, and that, equally important, Africans needed to acquire fluency in English as the language of government and administration, he was opposed to dropping Zulu altogether. "The time is probably much nearer to us than it is to our friends in some New England States when black men with certain qualifications will be allowed the right of suffrage," he speculated innocently, but Christianity could not dispense with Zulu. He would settle for a compromise: the Gospel would be preached in Zulu; translating the Bible in Zulu would continue; other Zulu literature would continue to be produced; and English would be taught only to those who could already read and write Zulu. So he settled on the slogan: "Some English for some Zulus."[55] Even the English instruction that they would give, Lindley insisted, the mission agencies would refuse to accept payment for from government because, he said, such instruction would be done not for money or pandering to government "but for the good of the Zulus."[56] Missionary practice in such regard retained the advantage for the African.

So the question of Christian collaboration with colonialism looks very different when viewed from the angle of the vernacular paradigm, especially when we remember that in societies unhomogenized by technological impact, language and culture are inextricably intertwined,[57] so that the missionary effort in reducing these languages to writing and pioneering their development in other ways produced indigenous repercussions in numerous creative fields. It thus followed that "the same missionaries who promoted 'modernization' of African languages through codification in writing, standardization, and diffusion of printed texts also used language to defend traditional culture."[58]

David Livingstone, the famous Scottish missionary who dominated the world of missions in his day and beyond, reflected on the value of language as a bearer of Christianity, a reflection that alerted him to the distorting effects of Western contact. Scriptural translation, he thought, would activate the wider Christian process and help preserve the culture before (and after) it had come into contact with domineering Europeans, and it ought, therefore, to be encouraged. He contended:

> It is fortunate that the translation of the Bible has been effected before the language became adulterated with half-uttered foreign words, and while those who have heard the eloquence of the native assemblies are still living; for the young, who are brought up in our schools, know less of the language than the missionaries; and Europeans born in the country, while possessed of the idiom perfectly, if not otherwise educated, cannot be referred to for explanation of any uncommon word.[59]

Livingstone paid close attention to what might be implied by the adoption of the vernacular for scriptural translation. He called attention to Robert Moffat's translation of the Setswana Bible, saying Moffat had demonstrated the superiority of Setswana, so "that the Pentateuch is fully expressed . . . in fewer words than in the Greek Septuagint, and in a very considerably smaller number than in our own English version."[60] All this led Livingstone to appeal to the norm that had also constrained the framers of the American Constitution, namely, that "all men," Africans included, are endowed by their Creator with basic inalienable possessions, above all the gift of humanity which is not a matter of selective attainment. Livingstone insisted, "The existence, therefore, of the various instruments in use among the Africans . . . indicates the communication of instruction at some period from some Being superior to man himself. . . . The argument for an original revelation to man," he continues, "though quite independent of the Bible history, tends to confirm that history. It is of the same nature with this, that man could not have made himself, and therefore must have had a Divine Creator. Mankind could not, in the first instance, have civilized themselves, and therefore must have had a superhuman Instructor."[61]

It is the more reasonable conclusion to claim for the African genius the same divine status that we do for Europeans than to give credence to the theory that Africans subsisted in a state that would otherwise prove fatal to all the descendants of the race. Africans are not an exception to the human race, a thought that would be an unacceptable affront to the Creator. Thus, Livingstone felt that even though they stood outside the Greco-Roman civilization, Africans, too, participated in the general human process. "Language," he challenged, "seems to be an attribute of the human mind and thought, and the inflections, various as they are in the most barbarous tongues [thinking here, perhaps, of the clicks], as that of the Bushmen, are probably only proofs of the race being human, and endowed with the power of thinking; the fuller development of language taking place as the improvement of our other faculties goes on."[62]

The veteran missionary Edwin Smith, a translator of the New Testament in Zambia, stated the reasons, as he saw them, why scriptural translation seeks in authentic mother tongues the sources and forms of cultural originality, why the translation avoids artificial or foreign materials that restrict the range to current or contemporary fashion. He observed that

> men need two kinds of language, in fact; a language of the home, of emotion, of unexpressed associations; and a language of knowledge, exact argument, scientific truth, one in which words are world-current and steadfast in their meanings. Where the mother tongue does not answer both needs, the people must inevitably become bilingual; but however fluent they may succeed in being in the foreign speech, its words can never feel to them as their native words. To express the dear and intimate things which are the very breath and substance of life a man will fall back on the tongue he learnt not at school, but in the house—how, he remembers not. He may bargain in the other, or pass examinations in it, but he will pray in his home speech. If you wish to reach his heart you will address him in that language.[63]

Introducing a subject of pivotal interest and relevance to creative literary activity the world over, the reference to "home speech" as the pulse of the imaginative life identifies the heart of the cultural process. It was alluded to by Christaller in speaking about "the sparks of truth entrusted to our people," those flashes of matured brilliance and insight conveyed to us in the innumerable tiny vessels of custom, usage, sign and symbol, and the myriad other artful means that are our bequest. It was also pointed out by Professor Diedrich Westermann of Berlin, a former missionary to Africa, who wrote:

Language and the mental life are so closely connected that any educational work which does not take into consideration the inseparable unity between African language and African thinking is based on false principles and must lead to an alienation of the individual from his own self, his past, his traditions and his people. If the African is to keep and develop his own soul and is to become a separate personality, his education must not begin by inoculating him with a foreign civilization, but it must implant respect for the indigenous racial life, it must teach him to love his country and tribe as gifts given by God which are to be purified and brought to full growth by the new divine life. One of these gifts is the vernacular, it is the vessel in which the whole national life is contained and through which it finds expression.[64]

The great and costly work of William Tyndale (1490–1536) and Miles Coverdale (1488–1568) in giving us the English of the Scriptures, and thus helping to open a worldwide channel for the language, is a relevant reminder to us of the intellectual roots of a medium we have learned now to take for granted. In a work on the Igbo language, the achievement of Tyndale and Coverdale in creating the vernacular English Bible is quoted in support of pioneer language development.[65] The English Bible, in being simple and succinct, became the repository of those sparks and impulses that have animated the soul of a people. There are only about 6,000 words in the English Bible compared with Shakespeare's considerably greater number (some sources putting it as high as 32,000), so economical and direct was the language of the Bible.

This point of economy was remarked on by John Ruskin in his comments on Sir Philip Sidney (1554–1586). "Sir Philip Sidney," Ruskin wrote, "will only use any cowboy's or tinker's words, if only they help him to say precisely in English what David said in Hebrew; impressed the while himself so vividly by the majesty of the thought itself, that no tinker's language can lower it or vulgarize it in his mind."[66] William Wordsworth (1770–1850) recalls the words of Erasmus with the following poetic lines:

> But to outweigh all harm, the sacred Book,
> In dusty sequestration wrapt too long,
> Assumes the accents of our tongue;
> And he who guides the plow or wields the crook,
> With understanding spirit now may look
> Upon her records, listen to her song.

Walt Whitman (1819–1892), himself an architect of language, speaks in his *November Boughs* of the translated Bible as the seed and symbol of the creative life. He affirms: "I've said nothing yet of the Bible as a poetic entity, and of every portion of it. . . . How many ages and generations have brooded and wept and agonized over this book! . . . Translated in all languages, how it has united the diverse world! Not only does it bring us what is clasped within its covers. Of its thousands there is not a verse, not a word, but is thick-studded with human emotion." The special character of the Bible, according to Whitman, consists in its "incredible, all-inclusive non-worldliness and dew-scented illiteracy (the antipodes of our Nineteenth Century business absorption and morbid refinement)—no hair-splitting doubts, no sickly sulking and sniffling, no 'Hamlet,' no 'Adonais,' no 'Thanatopsis,' no 'In Memoriam.'"[67] It is the special power of the Bible, thus clothed in the mother tongue, to harmonize individuality and universality, to harmonize pithy anecdote with general norm, so that simple parable breaks into sublime truth.

So much of the Bible is packed with tribal matters, so much of it resonates with the strains of illiterate speech and with the earthy impulse of living humanity, that we forget that sophisticated elites recoil at its populist bias. Instead, it is upon the people who have walked in darkness and who dwell in the land of the shadow of death that the light has shone. The tribes who embraced Christianity had seen the fires extinguished at the altars of their fallen deities, and yet, nagged by a clamorous chauvinism, they persisted for a sign. The story, their story, deserved a happy outcome if only they would persist while the ground gave under them. There were enough hints in the promises to Abraham and Sarah, in the parting of the Red Sea, in the commendations of Elizabeth and Mary, and, supremely, in the narrative of Good Friday and Easter, to warrant faith in a coming new covenant and in a divine vindication. Such were the advantages that possessing the Bible in the mother tongue entailed for Africa's besieged tribes.

In Western culture, an identical process was at work, as several examples show. Thus, for instance, did Joseph Addison (1672–1719), the editor of the short-lived but influential periodical *The Spectator*, reflect on the legacy of the Bible in Western literature and letters:

> Homer has innumerable flights that Virgil was not able to reach, and in the Old Testament we find several passages more elevated and sublime than any in Homer. After perusing the Book of Psalms, let a judge of the beauties of poetry read a literal translation of Homer or Pindar, and he will find in these last two such an absurdity and confusion of style, with such a comparative poverty of imagination, as will make him sensible of the vast superiority of the Scripture style.

Speaking of "beauty," the literary critic Henry Bradley pointed out that the word "beautiful" did not exist in English literature until Tyndale used it.[68] Hilaire Belloc, the English literary figure and a stern judge of Tyndale, admitted nevertheless that Tyndale "had created the glories of English prose," and that Tyndale's "rhythms had begun to vibrate in the minds of a younger generation" as his "spirit still moved through" the majestic cadences of the language.[69] In his *Grammar of New Testament Greek*, Professor A. T. Robertson remarks on the creative force of the language of the Bible. He says, "The Christian spirit put a new flavor into this vernacular and lifted it to a new elevation and dignity of style that unify and glorify the language."[70]

It is not necessary to recount here the tragic fate of Tyndale in stooping to the English vernacular for Scripture, since the consequences of his achievement are undeniable. The great Sir Arthur Quiller-Couch in his Cambridge lectures pointed to what he considered the self-evident matter of our Bible being a translated book. Isaiah, he said, did not write the cadences of his prophecies as we know them; Christ did not speak the cadences of the Parables or of the Sermon on the Mount as we know them. "These have been supplied by the translators. By all means let us study them and learn to delight in them; but Christ did not suffer for . . . the cadences invented by Englishmen almost 1600 years later."[71] Quiller-Couch then took a panoramic view of the development of the language and assessed in that the role of the translated Bible, in particular, the Authorized Version. He says the English Bible has cadences homely and sublime, yet so harmonizes them that the voice is always one.

> Simple men—holy and humble men of heart like Izaak Walton and Bunyan—have their lips touched and speak to the homelier tongue. Proud men, scholars—Milton, Sir Thomas Browne—practice the rolling Latin sentence; but upon the rhythm of our Bible they, too, fall back. . . . The precise man Addison cannot excel one parable in brevity or in heavenly clarity; the two parts of Johnson's antithesis come to no more than this: "Our Lord has gone up to the sound of a trump; with the sound of a trump our Lord has gone up." The Bible controls its enemy Gibbon as surely as it haunts the music of a light sentence of Thackeray's. It is everything we see, hear, feel, because it is in us, in our blood.[72]

"It is in us, in our blood" is a sentiment passionately expressed by Thomas Carlyle when he wrote: "Of this one thing, however, be certain: wouldst thou plant for Eternity, then plant into the deep infinite faculties of man, his Fantasy and Heart! wouldst thou plant for Year and Day, then plant into his shallow superficial faculties, his self-love and arithmetical understanding, what will grow there."[73] That sentiment might stand as the motto of the vernacular cause. Speaking with reference to the early modern Catholic missions to India, the biographer of the Jesuit Robert de Nobili, a seventeenth-century Italian missionary, underlined his vernacular commitment, saying de Nobili "was aware that no amount of learning [which in de Nobili's case was considerable] could replace the deepest springs within the soul, fed by blood, tradition and climate, and crystallized in a mother tongue."[74]

Dante in his *Divine Comedy* called attention to a common fact, namely, that no aid is so resented as the bread of dependence, and no movement so painful as on the ladder of one's captor. He might have added that no language is so barren as that imposed by one's conqueror. But in matters concerning our ultimate destiny as moral beings, adopting the mother tongue, the mother tongue that in Africa could be characterized in the words of Whitman as "dew-scented illiteracy," guarantees a future for the heritage. Adolf Deissmann, in his Haskell Lectures at Oberlin College, appealed to an aspect of this "dew-scented illiteracy" when he spoke of the New Testament idiom as being "the underground stream of the people's language," not a shrine for "the mysteries of kings" and the upper classes.[75]

We might add to all these examples the testimony of Robert Louis Stevenson. He spoke of the cultural importance of missionary translations of the Bible and other literary materials for the Samoan people among whom he settled in the nineteenth century. He testified:

> Well, after this excursion into tongues that have never been alive—though I assure you we have one capital book in the language, a book of fables by an old missionary of the unpromising name of Pratt, which is simply the best and the most literary version of the fables known to me. I suppose I should except La Fontaine, but L.F. takes a long time; these are brief as the books of our childhood, and full of wit and literary colour; and O, Colvin, what a tongue it would be to write, if one only knew it. . . . Its curse in common use is an incredible left-handed wordiness; but

in the hands of a man like Pratt it is succinct as Latin, compact of long rolling poly-
syllables and little and often pithy particles, and for beauty of sound a dream.[76]

We may return to Erasmus's theme of the cultural and ideological implications
of Bible translation. While Erasmus saw Bible translation as empowering the public
associated with lowbrow culture, critics of Bible translation see it differently, convinced that Bible translation can have unsalutary effects on the simple and the
young. There is always the danger, these critics charge, of Bible translation inciting
wrongheaded fanatics and peddlers of sectarian doctrine. Perhaps these critics are
pointing to the fact that there can be no literal faithfulness to the text, because the
Bible comes to us already preloaded with prior assumptions and nuanced evoca-
tions of the human condition, in other words with biases of past cultures that defy
literalness. Biblicists are deaf to that and so take the Bible amiss. Therefore, the critics conclude, Bible translation is dangerous and should be discouraged, unless it
was safeguarded by sound doctrinal exposition.

Yet Erasmus's point is a valid one, namely, the religion of Jesus is already imbued with a bias toward ordinary and simple people, and there simply is no way
around making their voice stand out in Bible translation. It is, however, still the
case that translation should be pursued as a responsive, interpretive process that
takes due cognizance of the deeper culture of the Bible itself. That was the point
C. S. Lewis made in his observation that "all translations of scripture are tendentious: translation, by its very nature, is a continuous implicit commentary. It can become less tendentious only by becoming less of a translation."[77] What that means is
that when it is done well Bible translation can initiate a sustained intercultural
process, with or without religious underpinnings. After all, the languages of Christianity are the peoples' languages: there is no special language exclusive to the religion, so that believers and nonbelievers alike share a common language and culture. Erasmus was pointing to that fact when he insisted on Scripture being
available in the common idiom of the people.

Conclusions

In conclusion, we should draw an important distinction between missionary translations of the modern era and Enlightenment views. Enlightenment scholars defended translation on the grounds that all languages obeyed the same laws of reason, so that the diversity and variety of tongues and idioms merely concealed an
inner uniformity of structure, which translation, in their view, supported. For that
reason, Enlightenment writers felt a duty to write a universal grammar in order to
break free of contingency in pursuit of the universal efficacy of abstract generalizations. The Enlightenment view that cultural differences conceal and thus distort
the truth of one humanity is akin to the prevailing monism, and would, if followed
to the letter, make submission, imitation, and conformity the rule and ideal of narrative description.

In a significant departure from this point of view, scriptural translations
deemed cultural and linguistic distinctions as reason for recognizing vernacular

particularity, so that no one language or culture may promote itself as the universal exclusive norm of religion. Thus, in missionary translations even minute dialectical differences were noted, bringing variety and diversity into creative convergence with pluralism.[78] This had momentous consequences for African culture and literature, for that was how Africa's languages for the first time came to possess a literature of their own, namely, mother tongue Scripture, even though we deem the mother tongue unworthy of Shakespeare or Milton.[79]

There was, admittedly, a worldwide general ambition motivating missionary translations, namely, to secure converts for the church, often with Western cultural values as a precondition. However, it is interesting to reflect that critics of missions thought the idea of cultural relativism would effectively demolish the case or need for missions, yet cultural relativism as empirical practice was what distinguished missionary linguistic research and development. That empirical practice says that since all languages are equal in their capacity to receive and mediate the Gospel, then the act of making each receptor language sufficient for conveying the message, with the message already predisposed to the terms of the local idiom, is justified, and that fact no cultural or racial distinctions should alter or be allowed to alter. However, in contrast to the claims of cultural relativism, all languages in the religious view are equally inadequate vis-à-vis God's sovereign truth.

Accordingly, the variety and diversity of the plethora of languages employed in scriptural translation promoted, as nothing else has, cultural specificity and particularity, the notion the Enlightenment found such a stumbling block to its quest for an original purity and an objective unity. The mother tongue projects of missions helped indigenous revitalization, spawning projects more distinguished by their "common tellurian" bias than by uprooted assertions of Western cultural rhetoric. Thus, cultural relativism was scarcely consistent with itself when it opposed interference in African societies on the principle of the absolute autonomy of these societies, an idea that, because it assumes these societies to be in a state of original purity, actually hinders their growth and development. They can only revert to ethnocentrism.

However ambiguous the record, it can be said that a scripturally based mother tongue assurance became a salient part of the missionary record, and a pluralist Africa was thereby reinvigorated. Thus, neo-Enlightenment scruples on native innocence in fact became a native curse, opening the way for a hostile chauvinism that fed on ethnic isolation and fragmentation and fear of difference. Native innocence is native malice, and the cultural relativism that begot it was its deserving partner. Thus, it is no more responsible to present non-Western cultures as repositories of cultural purity than it is to promote the West as the universal arbiter of moral perfection. The evidence is that we are all implicated in the consequences of mother tongue development, as well as in ideas of cultural relativism. It is, therefore, a matter of great consequence that we do not set the laudable goals of inclusiveness, equality, tolerance, and diversity against the logic and consequences of mother tongue development. On the contrary, instead of a false choice between mother tongue equality and Western cultural arbitration, there is an interconnectedness between the two.[80]

Mother tongue equality was the operative method in Bible translation, with consequences that are plain for all to see. From that position, we come upon the springs of cultural particularity and renewal in indigenous societies, the very basis on which significant literary and artistic creation in Africa, for example, has gone forward and entered the dynamic stream of world history. The modern Christian missionary impulse staked the enterprise as much on the viability of local cultural forms as on the hoped-for numerical outcome, and by attending first to the essential preparatory linguistic and cultural work of the message and leaving issues of local response to an indefinite future, as Livingstone urged on his missionary colleagues, the conveyers of the message put in place an authentic mother tongue system that time and opportunity reinforced.

An enduring cultural awakening resulted from this system and allowed local populations to construct for themselves projects of cultural renewal and intellectual awakening that often went far beyond the narrow walls of membership in the church. It does not discredit the missionary enterprise to say that one of its fruits was the preservation of mother tongue identity, so that conventional views of Western missions as destructive of nonliterate cultures, however justified in certain cases, overlook perhaps the most critical frontier of the encounter, namely, the missionary pioneering of non-Western languages.

Consequently, we may make the following observation: the real worth and value of numerous African languages are no different in kind or degree from what is true for long-established literate societies: all languages are particular vehicles with which human beings construct meaning, transmit the heritage, and in other ways communicate. It is true that many languages are more widely used and articulated, have a longer documentary history, have a greater and more cultivated body of literature, and are more ably serviced with texts and resources than others, but all languages serve an identical need and purpose. The great effect of using mother tongues for translating the Bible was to move these languages toward their fullest inherent capacity and to equip their speakers to participate in the worldwide historical stream through the native idiom. It is not enough to look upon such linguistic and cultural innovation as the triumph of medium as message, as proof that traditional mystical thought that once dissolved God into an amorphous deity became demystified in the many forms and functions of culture and context, as if the modest loin cloth of custom became shredded by the cutting edge of literacy. Rather, we should see how religious doctrine acted to carry hitherto unwritten languages beyond the blind alley of tribal chauvinism, how religious doctrine drew their exclusivist poison and anointed their wholesome power and vitality. The coping stone of the narrative form was the personal testimony in which biographical and autobiographical subjects are illuminated with the authority of personal recognition. A moral shift was often involved with this sense of personal responsibility, the shift from religion as rules and the sanctions of taboo to religion as the domain of personal conscience. It was that moral shift that produced the sense of personal worth and dignity. It fueled transformation of what the Apostle calls "the inward man" (Rom. 2:29), a subject of limitless possibility, as St. Augustine has taught us. These linguistic pioneers, missionary as well as African, supplied the forces that shaped the narrative impulse, that became the seed from which would spring the full flowering of the sense of personal responsibility.

Thus, even if nonliterate languages could serve only a limited purpose, even if they could not escape the limitations of a primitive culture and could cope with Christianity's complex and subtle demands only with outside oversight, it was still significant that the languages were developed as carriers of the message of Christianity and, as such, became a formative frame for conveying the universal story of salvation, whatever the reservations. The Christian message was transmitted with the aid of the vernacular Bible, supported by rituals, hymns, and prayers in the same medium. Christianity strengthened the mother tongue foundations of African culture. It led in due time to the flowering, to the cultural renaissance, of the narrative seeds that were first sown with the ancient myths and sagas and with the perennial urge for community with the ancestors. We might amend the words of Charles Lamb (1775–1834) to the effect that if Shakespeare were to come into the room, even in African translation, we should, by choice, perhaps all rise out of respect, but if Scripture, in its mother tongue appeal, should speak to us of eternal assurance, it would stir us in the depths of blood, soul, and tongue, and we should, then, like the venerable Tartar, greet it devoutly on our knees.

Notes

An adapted and abridged version of this chapter was published in *Research in African Literatures*, Summer, 1992.

1. Desiderius Erasmus, *Christian Humanism and the Reformation: Selected Writings, with the "Life of Erasmus" by Beatus Rhenanus*, ed. John C. Olin (New York: Harper Torchbooks, 1965), 96–97.

2. J. D. Y. Peel, "For Who Hath Despised the Day of Small Things? Missionary Narratives and Historical Anthropology," *Comparative Studies in Society and History, an International Quarterly* 37, no. 3 (July 1995), 581–607.

3. Edwin W. Smith, *The Golden Stool: Some Aspects of the Conflict of Cultures in Modern Africa* (London: Holborn Publishing House, 1926), 302.

4. Smith, *Golden Stool*, 303.

5. R. S. Rattray, "The African Child in Proverb, Folk-Lore, and Fact," *Africa* 6, no. 4 (Oct. 1933), 456–471.

6. Cited in Smith, *Golden Stool*, 311.

7. Albert S. Gerard, *Four African Literatures: Xhosa, Sotho, Zulu, Amharic* (Berkeley & Los Angeles: University of California Press, 1971), 382. Edwin Smith also observed that the French, the Belgians, and the Portuguese adopt policies that suppress African languages "not on educational, but on political grounds." Smith calls it "an injustice." Smith, *Golden Stool*, 301–2.

8. E. W. Blyden, *The Three Needs of Liberia: A Lecture Delivered at Lower Buchanan, Grand Bassa County, Liberia, January 26, 1908* (London: C. M. Phillips, 1908), 2. Blyden was writing of the future of imported American institutions in Liberia with particular reference to the isolated nature of the Americo-Liberians from indigenous populations.

9. Kenneth Scott Latourette, *A History of Christianity*, 2 vols. (New York: Harper & Row, 1953; reprint, 1975), 1: 250–51.

10. Taddesse Tamrat, *Church and State in Ethiopia: 1270–1527*, (Oxford: Clarendon Press, 1972); also E. Ullendorf, *Ethiopia and the Bible* (London: Oxford University Press, 1988); Asa J. Davis, "The Orthodoxy of the Ethiopian Church," *Tarikh* 2, no. 1 (1967); Getatchew Haile, "A Christ for the Gentiles: the Case of the za-Krestos of Ethiopia," *Journal*

of Religion in Africa 15, no. 2 (1985). See also E. A. Wallis Budge, *The Queen of Sheba and Her Only Son Menyelek* (London: Oxford University Press, 1922).

11. John Michael Wallace-Hadrill, *The Frankish Church* (Oxford: Clarendon Press, 1983), 378ff.

12. Wallace-Hadrill, *The Frankish Church*, 386.

13. Matthew Arnold (1822–1888) is correct to credit what he calls the northern Barbarians with a leavening influence on Western cultural refinement, but Barbarians only after their fateful encounter with Christianity. Arnold, "Culture and Anarchy," *Selected Prose* (New York: Penguin Classics, 1987), chap. 3.

14. Francis Dvornik, *Byzantine Missions among the Slavs: SS. Constantine-Cyril and Methodius* (New Brunswick, N.J.: Rutgers University Press, 1970), 117ff.

15. Cited in Metropolitan Dorotheos, "The Influence of the Moravian Mission of the Orthodox Church in Czechoslovakia," *International Review of Missions* 74 (April 1985), 224.

16. Ibid., 225, 219. I have reorganized the passages in the interests of logical coherence, with resulting awkward pagination.

17. James J. Stamoolis, *Eastern Orthodox Mission Theology Today* (Maryknoll, N.Y.: Orbis Books, 1986), 26ff.

18. Stamoolis, *Eastern Orthodox Mission*, 30ff.

19. Ibid., 32.

20. Ibid., 33.

21. Ibid.

22. Rattray, "African Child," 458.

23. Cited in Dr. J. B. Danquah, *The Akan Doctrine of God* (London: Lutterworth Press, 1944), 186.

24. Lamin Sanneh, *Translating the Message: The Missionary Impact on Culture* (Maryknoll, N.Y.: Orbis Books, 1989; 9th printing, 1998), 180.

25. Cited in Hans W. Debrunner, *A History of Christianity in Ghana* (Accra, Ghana: Waterville Publishing House, 1967), 144.

26. Andrew W. Amegatcher, "Akropong: 150 Years Old," *West Africa* (July 14, 1986), 1472.

27. Patrick Harries describes how the new ethnic identity of the Tsonga of southern Africa was rooted in the linguistic work of the early Swiss Protestant missionaries. Patrick Harries, "Discovering Languages: the Historical Origins of Standard Tsonga in Southern Africa," in *Language and Social History: Studies in South African Sociolinguistics*, ed. Rajend Mesthrie (Cape Town and Johannesburg: David Philip, 1995), 154–175, 155.

28. I have examined this question of missionary enclavement in "The Yogi and the Commissar: Christian Missions and the African Response," *International Bulletin of Missionary Research* (Jan. 1991).

29. Rev. Lewis Grout, *Zulu-Land: Or Life Among the Zulu-Kafirs of Natal and Zulu-Land, South Africa* (Philadelphia: Presbyterian Publication Committee, 1864), 191–192.

30. C. L. Sibusiso Nyembezi, *A Review of Zulu Literature* (Pietermaritzburg: University of Natal Press, 1961), 3ff.

31. Nyembezi, *Review of Zulu Literature*, 3.

32. One of his first linguistic works is still considered a classic: Clement M. Doke, "The Phonetics of the Zulu Language," a special publication of *Bantu Studies* (Journal devoted to the Scientific Study of Bantu, Hottentot, and Bushmen) 2, (July, 1926).

33. C. M. Doke, "Scripture Translation into Bantu Languages," in *Contributions to the History of Bantu Linguistics*, ed. C. M. Doke and D. T. Cole, (Johannesburg: Witwatersrand University Press, 1961), 110.

34. John W. Colenso, *Bringing Forth Light: Five Tracts on Bishop Colenso's Zulu Mission* (Pietermaritzburg: University of Natal, and Durban: Killie Campbell Africana Library, 1982), 51.

35. Colenso, *Bringing Forth Light*, 194.

36. Colenso, *Bringing Forth Light*, 194–95.

37. Jean and John Comaroff, *Of Revelation and Revolution: Christianity, Colonialism and Consciousness in South Africa* (Chicago: University of Chicago Press, 1991), 213–30. This book is a sophisticated presentation of the classical theory of Christianity as a tool of colonial subjugation and of Africans as victims. As such, the book represents the European metropolitan viewpoint, the viewpoint of the transmitters over the recipients of the message.

38. Smith, *Golden Stool*, 226. Georg Simmel made much of the idea of literacy as a form of secrecy. *The Sociology of Georg Simmel*, ed. & tr. Kurt H. Wolff (New York: The Free Press, and London: Collier-Macmillan, 1950; reprint, 1964), 35–55. Patrick Harries writes that Tsonga Christians in southern Africa believed that "a sheet of writing paper could serve as a talisman or protective charm, a source of authority and wealth or, simply, as 'the medicine of knowledge.' The hymns printed in the buku appealed to the same constituency, as they carried a written message in oral form." Harries, "Discovering Languages," 164.

39. For example, Edwin Smith, a veteran missionary of southern Africa, wrote about this, saying, "The personality of the African is rooted in the past—the past of the African's own race. He cannot be treated as if he were a European who happened to be born black. He ought not to be regarded as if he were a building so badly constructed that it must be pulled down, its foundations torn up and a new structure erected on the site, on a totally new plan and with entirely new materials. Any such attitude is psychologically absurd." Smith, *Golden Stool*, 295.

40. Jeff Guy, *The Heretic: A Study of the Life of John William Colenso: 1814–1883* (Johannesburg: Ravan Press, and Pietermaritzburg: University of Natal Press, 1983), 45. This biography is considered by critics far superior to anything that has hitherto appeared on Colenso.

41. Magema M. Fuze, *The Black People: And Whence They Came* (Pietermaritzburg: University of Natal Press, 1922; reprint, Durban: Killie Campbell Africana Library, 1979), xi.

42. Fuze, *Black People*, xii.

43. The book was finally published in 1921; reprint (London: Routledge & Kegan Paul, 1969).

44. Cited in Julian Pettifer and Richard Bradley, *Missionaries* (London: BBC Books, 1990), 20.

45. Absalom Vilakazi, *Zulu Transformations: A Study of the Dynamics of Social Change* (Pietermaritzburg: University of Natal Press, 1962), 94; also 97ff.

46. Cited in Smith, *Golden Stool*, 303.

47. Cited in Doke, "Scripture Translation," 111.

48. Ibid.

49. Edwin W. Smith, *Robert Moffat, One of God's Gardeners* (London: Student Christian Movement, 1925), 245.

50. Doke, "Scripture Translation," 111.

51. Cited in Doke, "Scripture Translation," 115.

52. Virgil, *Aeneid*, Book 12, trans. Robert Fitzgerald (New York: Penguin Classics, 1990), 398. Compare this with Shakespeare's *Richard II* 1.2, where the Duke of Norfolk laments his banishment because it would sentence him "to speechless death" and rob "his tongue from breathing native breath."

53. The prototype colonialist is Cecil Rhodes who, in his "Confession of Faith" in 1877, spoke of 'English' colonialism as the messianic destiny of his race. He lamented the loss of

America, saying there might be time to avert a similar thing elsewhere, if necessary, even with secret designs to reclaim America! Rhodes was convinced of the English being "the finest race in the world and that the more of the world we inhabit the better it is for the human race." He continued: "Africa is still lying ready for us[.] [It] is our duty to take it. It is our duty to seize every opportunity of acquiring more territory[,] and we should keep this one idea steadily before our eyes[:] that more territory simply means more of the Anglo-Saxon race[,] more of the best[,] the most human, most honourable race the world possesses." Cited in John Flint, *Cecil Rhodes* (Boston: Little, Brown, 1974), 248, 250.

54. On Lindley and the American Board missionaries in South Africa, see Grout, *Zulu-Land*, 201–226.

55. Edwin W. Smith, *The Life and Times of Daniel Lindley* (1801–80) (London: The Epworth Press, 1949), 388.

56. Smith, *Lindley*, 389.

57. The Kenyan novelist, Ngugi wa Thiong'o, argues for the close link between language and culture, a link that European rulers in Africa tried to break. Accordingly, Ngugi calls for the retrieval and redeployment of mother tongues to remove the vestiges of colonial hegemony. Ngugi wa Thiong'o, *Decolonising the Mind* (Portsmouth: Heinemann, 1986), and *Moving the Center* (Portsmouth: Heinemann, 1993).

58. Johannes Fabian, *Language and Colonial Power: The Appropriation of Swahili in the Former Belgian Congo 1880–1938* (Cambridge: Cambridge University Press, 1986), 78. One guarded study of the subject is nevertheless prepared to present the view that missionary expertise in African languages grew naturally out of a commitment to African particularity, and in the process it led to the creation of "oral literature texts [that] often come closer to the ideals of contemporary scholars than do those of [European colonial] administrators." Ralph Austen, "Africans Speak: Colonialism Writes: The Transcription and Translation of Oral Literature Before World War II," Boston University Discussion Paper AH no. 8, 1990, 3.

59. David Livingstone, *Missionary Researches and Travels in South Africa* (London: John Murray, 1857), 114.

60. Livingstone, *Missionary Researches*, 114.

61. David and Charles Livingstone, *Narrative of an Expedition to the Zambesi and its Tributaries and of the Discovery of the Lakes Shirwa and Nyassa: 1858–1864* (New York: Harper & Brothers, 1866), 533–34.

62. Livingstone, *Missionary Researches*, 114.

63. Edwin Smith, *In the Mother Tongue* (London: British and Foreign Bible Society, 1930), 8. Oliver Wendell Holmes expressed a similar sentiment in pithy words thus: "Language is a solemn thing; it grows out of life, out of its agonies, its wants and its weariness. Every language is a temple in which the soul of those who speak it is enshrined." Oliver W. Holmes, *The Autocrat at the Breakfast Table* (Boston: Houghton Mifflin, 1906).

64. Diedrich Westermann, "The Place and Function of the Vernacular in African Education," *International Review of Mission* (Jan. 1925).

65. Rev. G. E. Igwe and M. M. Green, *Igbo Language Course: Book 3: Dialogue, Sayings, Translation* (Ibadan, Nigeria: Oxford University Press, 1970), 69. The authors cite the words of I. Williams as follows: "No book has had an equal influence on the English people. Apart from its religious considerations, it gave to all classes alike an idiom in which the deeper emotions of life could be recalled. It gives grace to the speech of the unlettered and it entered into the style of the most ambitious writers. Its phrasing coloured the work of poets, and its language has so embedded itself in our national tradition that if the Bible is forgotten, a precious possession will be lost." This quote is given in Igbo in a parallel translation (68–70).

66. Cited in *The Influence of the English Bible upon the English Language and upon English and American Literatures* (New York: American Bible Society, 1947 ed.), 7.

67. Walt Whitman, "The Bible as Poetry," in *November Boughs, Complete Poetry and Collected Prose* (New York: Library of America, 1982), 1140–1142.

68. Henry Bradley, *The Making of English* (New York & London: Macmillan, 1904), 220.

69. Hilaire Belloc, *Cranmer, Archbishop of Canterbury, 1533–1556* (Philadelphia: J.P. Lippincott, 1931), 193ff. Though his literary reputation is acknowledged, Belloc is less worthily regarded by historians.

70. A. T. Robertson, *Grammar of New Testament Greek* (New York: Hodder and Stoughton, 1915), 7.

71. Sir Arthur Quiller-Couch, *On The Art of Reading: Lectures Delivered in the University of Cambridge* (Cambridge: Cambridge University Press, 1920), 137.

72. Quiller-Couch, *On The Art of Reading*, 155–56.

73. Cited in Smith, *Lindley*, 387.

74. Vincent Cronin, *A Pearl to India: The Life of Robert de Nobili* (London: Rupert Hart Davis, 1959), 173.

75. Adolf Deissmann, *The New Testament in the Light of Modern Research: The Haskell Lectures, 1929* (New York: Doubleday, Doran & Co., 1929), 80. A study of the impact of Bible translation on medieval Europe has made the point that the Latin Bible drew heavily on colloquial usage. That in turn influenced speech patterns among Christian communities, reflecting the popular social roots of Christian converts. "The blending of classical stylistics and biblical themes greatly influenced the development of medieval Latin and the Romance languages." Brian Stock, *The Implications of Literacy: Written Language and Models of Interpretation in the Eleventh and Twelfth Centuries* (Princeton: Princeton University Press, 1983), 23.

76. Robert Louis Stevenson, *The Works of Robert Louis Stevenson: The Vailima Letters* (Edinburgh: Longmans, Green & Co., 1897), 46. For Stevenson's comments on Bible translation, see H. J. Moors, *With Stevenson in Samoa* (London, n.d.), 69.

77. C. S. Lewis, "Drab Age Prose–Religious Controversy and Translation," in *English Literature in the Sixteenth Century* (Oxford: Oxford University Press, 1954), 157–221, 206.

78. Holger Pedersen argues in this connection that modern linguistic science is a child of Christian missionary activity. Holger Pedersen, *The Discovery of Language: Linguistic Science in the Nineteenth Century*, tr. John Webster Spargo (Bloomington, Ind.: Indiana University Press, 1962).

79. Saul Bellow, the Nobel laureate, attacked African culture precisely for not having produced a Western literary prototype, evidence, he thinks, of intrinsic inferiority. "Who is the Tolstoy of the Zulus? The Proust of the Papuans? I'll gladly read them," he sneered.

80. In an article entitled, "The Diversity Myth: America's Leading Export," Benjamin Schwartz, a historian and foreign policy analyst, speaks of the "diversity myth" that frames America's perception of, and prescription for, the world. Although it is a distortion and an oversimplification, that myth constitutes "America's leading export." He says that the immigrant populations that flocked into the United States were subjected to a cultural stripping process that did not so much cleanse America of its ethnic minorities as cleanse those minorities of their ethnicity. The American melting pot, he points out, "celebrated not tolerance but conformity to a narrow conception of American nationality by depicting strangely attired foreigners stepping into a huge pot and emerging as immaculate, well-dressed, accent-free 'American-looking' Americans—that is, Anglo-Americans. Sinclair Lewis recognized the melting pot, in Main Street, as a means by which 'the sound American customs

absorbed without one trace of pollution another alien invasion.'" Benjamin Schwartz, "The Diversity Myth: America's Leading Export," *The Atlantic* (May 1995), 57–67, 62. For a recent discussion of how language origins might be located in a single universal tongue, see Robert Wright, "Quest for the Mother Tongue: Is the Search for an Ancestor of all Modern Languages Sober Science or Simple Romanticism?" *The Atlantic* (April 1991), 39–68.

2

DAVID L. JEFFREY

Gnosis, Narrative, and the Occasion of Repentance

Among scholars and critics of "primary narrative," it is widely recognized that the emergence to prominence of literary theory over "explication de texte" despite certain evident attractions, carries with it a disturbing proclivity to occlude the texts that were once, ostensibly, theory's justification. One may confirm this readily in such theorizing as one now associates with figures as widely various in their focus as Gadamer, Barthes, Derrida, Eagleton, and Lacan. But it is important also to recognize that this general displacement is not unprecedented; it holds much in common with usurpation of authority from the narratives that traditionally bear it in other eras. One thinks here not only of Marxism, as one might recently have first imagined, but also more anciently, of Neoplatonist systems of all kinds. Embarrassment with biblical narrative and flight from its "shameful simplicities" (the phrase is Augustine's) is highly visible in Philo Judaeus and Origen, for example, each of whose method of dealing with primary biblical narrative is antirealist, prophylactic, and cultivating of what we may call, in the informal sense, an elite gnosis.[1] And it may be, as some would argue, that the reflex of allegorism in late antiquity and the Middle Ages is but one pulse of a historical dialectic for which we might find analogues in any textual tradition.[2]

The Awkwardness of Realistic Narrative

Among literary critics, self-consciousness about gnostic impulses is not a recent phenomenon either. But in recent years, acknowledged or not, these impulses have come aggressively to the forefront of the discipline.[3] Few types of contemporary theorizing about literature and its interpretation, we are obliged to reflect, are innocent of the association. It has been persuasively argued by Hans Jonas, for example, that Heidegger's phenomenology is an elaborate analogue of second-century gnosticism.[4] Harold Bloom, the romanticist and literary theorist whose transgressive impulses have so often stimulated reflection, is a self-confessed gnostic. As such, he regards literary language as totally "overdetermined" and "magical," an approach he presents as similar to that of the Kabbalists.[5] Bloom thinks of deconstruction—described by him as "a thoroughgoing linguistic nihilism" which views language operating in "absolute randomness" and exhibiting a "dearth of meaning"—as polar to his own gnosticism. But deconstruction is itself arguably one of the most evidently gnostic varieties of poststructuralist theory. Like its second-century predecessor as much as the antinomian structuralism of Barthes on which it more nearly draws,[6] deconstruction *ad finem* strives to separate its form of knowledge from any reference to external nature, experience, or historical process.[7] The transcendent principle in both ancient gnosticism and modern deconstruction is an absence, not a presence; its mode of operation in either system is, though said to be constitutive, strictly speaking undemonstrable (or incomprehensible). Deconstruction, as its chief proponent Jacques Derrida proclaims, is also antitheological—yet it desires transcendence, to be "elsewhere": completely other than in the mundane and gritty world. Finally, like Valentinian gnosis, in which the fall of Sophia, the primordial wisdom-emanation, was explicitly conceived as the consequence of her mimetic folly, deconstruction especially is "dogmatically antimimetic,"[8] resisting absolutely those modes of linguistic representation that might once have been described as "realistic." The least we can conclude from these observations is that no contemporary theory can make unique claim to a "gnostic" poetic.

We should not be surprised that in such an intellectual climate—a rivalry of competing gnosticisms, so to speak—certain kinds of realistic narrative come to seem "awkward" and accordingly fall into comparative neglect. I want to elicit only one type—a persistent and centrally formative group of traditional stories that for convenience we may call narratives of repentance. This category would include not only biblical narrative but also classic works of both literary autobiography and representative fiction, such as may be conjured by a list which includes texts as diverse as Augustine's *Confessions*, Dostoevski's *Crime and Punishment*, and, though it is outside the scope of this study, Isaac Bashevis Singer's *The Penitent*. I want to suggest that the gradual eclipse of such narratives in theoretically motivated studies of Western literature raises serious questions about the capacity of the occluding discourse to give a balanced or "realistic" account of its ostensible subject, especially when a concern for ethics or virtue is part of that subject.[9]

Even the nonspecialist, of course, can guess what must be one of the leading sources of offense in such an increasingly "marginalized" text as the narrative of repentance: not so much an obtrusive credalism, actually, as its explicit insistence on being read as in some fundamental sense "realistic," psychologically, spiritually, or politically.[10] Moreover, and progenitively, repentance narratives are presented as second-order discourse—a reader's response to some other and primary book. These neglected "responsory" texts, whether narratives of social realism or spiritual odyssey, may remain of interest to Marxists, let us say, or to Sartrian cultural critics, or perhaps to sociologists of religion, but they will make relatively little sense in the repertoire of the poststructuralist theorist whose agenda is preoccupied with the reconstituting of criticism itself as first-order discourse.

To this latter enterprise, in fact, a good deal of the narrative that has been most culturally formative in Western tradition can be seen as irrelevant. More precisely, if allowed to remain present in cultural reflection, such narratives tend to be unsettling to the motives which led to their rejection or downgrading in the first place. Some such works may remain somewhere on the syllabus but cease to get much attention. Or if they do, the motivation may simply be to expose them as, from the point of view of contemporary theoretical discourse, "problematic."

This "canonical" awkwardness seems to be analogous to the reflex Kierkegaard identified as fashionable more than a century ago. In an extended critical review of the 1840s, Kierkegaard described the efforts of eighteenth- and nineteenth-century biblical criticism to "problematize" the text as an explicit strategy to make the Bible a text with little or no ethical application, a species of betrayal by interpretation—a classic *trahison des clercs*. In Kierkegaard's uncompromising characterization, interestingly, this is to be understood as the subterfuge of a phony revolution:

> A passionate and tumultuous age will overthrow everything, pull everything down; but a revolutionary age, that is at the same time reflective and passionless, transforms that expression of strength into a feat of dialectics: it leaves everything standing but cunningly empties it of significance. Instead of culminating in a rebellion it reduces the inward reality of all relationships to a reflective tension which leaves everything standing but leaves the whole of life ambiguous: so that everything continues to exist factually whilst by a dialectical deceit, *privatissime*, it supplies a *secret interpretation* that it does not exist.[11]

Kierkegaard was a biblical theist. Consequently, for him any realistic account of the problem of subjectivity in understanding must acknowledge *ab initio* the persistence of sin. "Sin" he defines as a rejection of Truth, of reality—especially of realism about one's own actual mode of being.[12] Its patent device—endless artifices for flight from this truth—means that no person "by himself and of himself can explain what sin is, precisely because he is in sin," and explanation, if there is to be one, must come via the instrumentation of an external Revelation, the mediation of a penetratingly knowing Other.[13] But each person knows the *effects* of sin as evasion of truth about the self: that is to say, as despair—manifest in the impulse to create unlikely fictions, implausible narratives, reinventing the world. Hence, for Kierkegaard, "the seriousness of sin is its reality in the individual, whether it be thou or I.[14]

Theoretical discourse, which Kierkegaard calls the "dialectic of speculation," is required by its own mode to "look away from the individual" and so becomes abstraction. It focuses, we might now agree, on language, another abstraction, more than on speech, the concrete manifestation. Which is to say, it tends to eschew "reality in the individual, whether it be thou or I."[15] The question which, with Kierkegaard, we might wish to ask in our parallel situation is, what mode of discourse can deal plausibly with this subjective personal reality, put it into relation with other reality, even that announced by Revelation, so as to treat personhood with the "seriousness" which is its due? Kierkegaard's answer is the "dialectic of sin," which he describes as "directly contrary to that of Speculation." And here is where the shadow of primary narrative slips in again by the back door. Where it is read accountably, that is, where some mode of relation to a penetratingly knowing Other is available, a narrative attempt at realism may become at least provisionally objectifiable as discourse, in part because it is accountable to that Other. This consciousness of the condition of accountability as the matrix of composition assures us, in Kierkegaard's view, that the resulting narrative will be capable of generating a "dialectic of sin." To put it another way, such a narrative will be all the more candidly human — that is to say, personal. Could this be why stories about repentance, whether first- or third-person narrative, include some of the most intensely "realistic" texts in our literary tradition? Yet these are typically texts of which some contemporary theories can speak only frivolously or not at all.

Biblical Repentance Narratives

The Bible, of course, features repentance narratives centrally. There are two foundational types. In the Hebrew Scriptures, these may be represented respectively in the stories of David and Josiah. There are few more memorable narratives than the prophet Nathan's confrontation with the adulterous and murderous David (2 Sam. 12), his unmasking parable prompting that terribly unwitting response, a self-condemnation which strips away from the poet-king his own self-justifying fictions and exposes him in — and to — the reality of his wrongdoing. As A. S. Herbert remarks, Old Testament parable, *mashal*, "had a clearly recognizable purpose: that of quickening an apprehension of the real as distinct from the wished for,"[16] and this particular narrative makes the point forever memorable. Forced into unwelcome self-understanding, the king is overwhelmed by his transgression, and the subsequent chronicle and corresponding poem (Ps. 51) are a dialectic of sin brought to repentance and atonement.

The second basic type of repentance narrative is that modeled in the chronicle of Josiah (2 Kings 22), concerning a discovery among the detritus of abuse, in a temple long bereft of its original purpose, of a book, a copy of an unknown scroll. As the king hears the Torah read aloud by one of the few members of his court still literate enough to read it, he rends his clothes and tears his hair in anguished and penitent remorse. There is nothing hypothetical or aesthetic in this response. Immediately, Josiah moves to enact a transformed identity: he sets about setting things right again, instituting the Law in every sphere of personal and national life.

The David story, earlier in the annals of the kings of Israel, might seem to be an instance of repentance affected by means of interpretation, as though the king finally understood the parable as an allegory and perforce as a summons to accountability. But in truth, this notion misconstrues the dialectic of sin precipitated by biblical narrative and made especially transparent in *mashal*. It is the parable that interprets the sinner, "dividing asunder the thoughts and intentions of the heart," as the New Testament writer to the Hebrews puts it (4:12). Which is as much as to say that, when read accountably, the text is not first and foremost an invitation to an act of criticism. Rather, the story breaks the reader's heart to hear it.

The Josiah narrative offers a parallel calling to accounts, in which discovery of the very existence of Revelation, the impact of Torah itself concerning sin, the integrity of God, and evidence of collective disobedience, breaks the heart of a king over the loss of national purpose incurred through ignorance and neglect of the Law. Though the focus of this narrative is political more than personal, the action in which it ensues is similarly a cognitive and moral revolution, a transforming of personal story in which old things pass away and all things become new. We may note: though the catalyst to David's personal repentance is a plausible fiction, while the catalyst to Josiah's communal repentance is overt revelation discourse, the character and effect of their understood readings are virtually the same.

New Testament writing echoes and amplifies each type of repentance narrative, that projected by parable, or *mashal*, and that summoned by prophetic word.[17] It may at first seem surprising that a celebrated literary study of New Testament parable, Frank Kermode's *The Genesis of Secrecy: On the Interpretation of Narrative* (1979), illuminating and challenging as it is in many respects, is strangely inarticulate on the subject of repentance narrative in general and parables concerning repentance in particular. But the lapse is explicable upon reflection. Kermode's central thesis depends upon his view that (cf. Mark 4: 10–11; Matt. 13:10ff.) Jesus spoke in parables as a means of excluding "outsiders" from the knowledge of a salvation that can be made evident to the understanding of "insiders" alone. On Kermode's reckoning, the parables thus become a kind of gnostic encoding, like the conventions of any schooled theory, an instrument for effecting the institutional control of interpretation. While this is conceivably one of the possibilities latent in the cryptic distinction Jesus gives the disciples (in Mark) between themselves and "those without," and has its place in the history of exegesis, it is hardly the only one and certainly not that which the Gospels themselves elsewhere underscore. As the longer version of the account in Matthew confirms, "those without," in the case of Jesus' parables, are typically those most evidently implicated in the institutional control of interpretation. In fact, their heavy investment in institutional (and hence elite) discourse is what Jesus tells them makes their typical acts of interpretation little more than exercises in self-justification. Given that they claim to be persons for whom Torah is the ultimate authority and "getting it right" their vocation and profession, this complete misplacement of focus renders their "reading" axiomatically meretricious. Or, to put it in typical biblical fashion, it reveals them as readers whose hearts have become hardened to what actually "the law and the prophets have been saying."

One parable from Luke, and a narrative of response following it, must here suffice to clarify a central distinction concerning interpretation repeatedly elaborated in biblical narratives—the split between unrepentant and repentant hearers of the Word, or to put it in still more biblical idiom, between the hard-hearted and broken-hearted reader. I refer to the parable Jesus tells, according to Luke, to "some who trusted in themselves that they were righteous and regarded others with contempt":

> Two men went up to the temple to pray, one a Pharisee and the other a tax collector. The Pharisee, standing by himself, was praying thus, "God, I thank you that I am not like other people, thieves, adulterers, or even like this tax collector. I fast twice a week; I give a tenth of all my income." But the tax collector, standing far off, would not even look up to heaven, but was beating his breast and saying, "God, be merciful to me, a sinner!" I tell you, this man went down to his home justified rather than the other; for all who exalt themselves will be humbled, but all who humble themselves will be exalted. (Luke 18:10–14)

The context of this parable in Luke is a series of parables, *mashalim*, told by Jesus to indicate the sort of "interpretation" that is to be expected in the Last Judgment. Here the Pharisee is as much an example of the hard-hearted reader as Pharaoh; the Law is unable to call him to repentance because he is after all Master of the Law, not one mastered by it.

The wretched tax collector, whose predatory crimes make him a universal object of contempt, is beyond any such imagination of mastery. He is to the occupying state which employs him a groveling toady, to his neighbors an oppressive traitor. A man without community, without acceptance, without self-respect, and perhaps even without love—all he can do in his miserable moment in the temple is cry out for mercy. He knows himself a sinner under judgment and pleads for remission, for pardon. The parable manifestly subverts institutional decorum: the one who "gets it right" is the one who seems heretofore to have gotten nothing right. On the plain interpretation of Jesus, it is the self-confessedly sinful man who is justified in his response to the Torah. Why? Because by candid participation in the dialectic of sin and repentance he has, like Josiah, "read" the Torah story in the way it most obviously cries out to be read. The condescending Pharisee's motive from the beginning is here unmasked as a decorum for self-justification, a confusion of institutional membership with personal right-mindedness so thoroughgoing that he can no longer conceive of a reason for repentance.

A primary function of Jesus' parables seems to be simply to distinguish or "judge" between these two types of readers. Who is broken-hearted? Who is capable of repentance? As a narrative of repentance, the purpose of such a parable is evidently to initiate the possibility of repentance in a reader who is not yet irremediably hard-hearted. The succeeding narrative tells of a rich young ruler who, though even in Jesus' eyes an earnest observer of the Law, could not repent of his self-serving, sell all his goods, "and distribute the money to the poor" (v. 24). As the man unwilling to part with his riches walks sorrowing away, he illustrates another order of broken heart—but not one open to repentance. Having heard Jesus' *mashal*, he edges toward response: surely, I have done what is required, he says, to have kept the Law since my youth. In speaking to Jesus, perhaps he seeks to be assured he has *kapparah*, acquittal from sin or atonement. But he is not willing to follow through with *taharah*, purification or catharsis, the crucial second step in what Rabbi Joseph Soloveitchik has called the restoration of "spiritual viability."[18] If we may follow Soloveitchik formally: for the narrative of repentance to become efficacious, it must pass beyond the remorse of *kapparah*, which seeks acquittal of sin, to a willed removal of the self from "the path of sin," *taharah*. In the terms of the present discussion, this final move is what might grant such a narrative its closure—a closure that in the case of the rich young ruler is lamentably not forthcoming.

In the account of the conversion of the tax collector Zacchaeus in the next chapter, who gives half of what he possesses to the poor and uses what is left to restore fourfold to any he has cheated (19: 1-10), repentance is, by contrast, brought to its purpose: *mashal* gives rise to *mishpat*, "right reading" emerges, in performance, participation, ethical action. In this way Zacchaeus acquires again his full ethical status as a Jew under the Law: "he too," Jesus says, is now "a son of Abraham" (19:9). To apply Soloveitchik's phrase, by his *taharah* he has truly entered into the

Covenant of the Lord."[19] Indeed, it is the typical claim of biblical narratives that no reading which is not performative (actualized, or in the strictest sense mimetic) can be right—or to use our abstracted word, prove responsibly "ethical" at all.

It is noteworthy in this respect that the parable is no less authoritative in its call to repentance than are the explicit imperatives of the Law. *Mashal*, in Hebrew as in other Semitic languages (Aramaic, Akkadian, Arabic), signified figurative discourse generally, not only the narrative units we call parables, but also tropes such as similes or metaphors, enigmatic sayings, and proverbs.[20] But in Hebrew alone among Semitic languages the word has another meaning. Its radical is the verb, spelled and pointed in identical fashion, which means "to rule: to have dominion," "to govern." *Mashal* is employed this way in Proverbs 16:32: "One who is slow to anger is better than the mighty, and he who rules his spirit than he who takes a city," and this is the sense invoked when God speaks to Cain about the consequences of obedience and disobedience in Genesis 4:7. In Psalm 78, the verb signifies the lesson to be learned from Israel's history about God's repeated judgment upon sin and calling to accounts. And it is also, in Psalm 89, a "*Mashal* of Ethan the Ezrahite" used in praise of God's absolute authority over his creation: "You rule the raging of the sea; when its waves rise, you still them" (v. 9). Though it may denominate figurative discourse, *mashal* is thus deeply imprinted with a sense of ultimate authority,[21] the weight of historical truth—even the resonance of divine creative fiat itself. Much of the most formative narrative in Western tradition is comprised of stories of the broken-hearted, and much of that wrought in repentance or to speak of repentance. Written after the fact, or in the constructs afforded by third-person voice, such narratives are often intentionally corrective of critical judgment; they constitute an ostensibly more convincing reading of life evidences. Formal confessional narrative is of the most obvious pertinence. Augustine's *Confessions*, for example, models the characteristic mimesis: a wishful but falsifying fiction is at last owned as being such, then corrected or replaced by a more realistic representation of the self, a new story.[22] Such a confessional narrative is written in self-conscious retrospect and thus forms part of the *taharah* or reconstitutive and cathartic performance consistent with the broken-hearted repentance (*kapparah*) which initiated it. It is usually assumed that confessional narrative may (and intentionally) precipitate repentance in another.[23] But so, of course, may a retelling of biblical narrative, or the writing of a fictional analogue, a *mashal*.

The most important flowerings of vernacular drama in the Middle Ages, whether biblical cycle plays or saints plays (such as the Digby *Mary Magdalen*), are offered (often explicitly) to their readers as occasions for repentance. As is recognized by disparaging and adulatory commentary alike, so are Dante's *Vita Nuova* and *Commedia*. Chaucer's florilegium of pilgrimage narratives, *The Canterbury Tales*, moves toward its closure in a call to repentance following examination of conscience in which the author himself necessarily participates (formally, in his "Retraction"). But the list could be extended almost indefinitely. Medieval writers such as St. Bernard of Clairvaux, St. Bonaventure, and the author of the widely popular *Meditations on the Life of Christ*, all insist that efficacious response to the biblical narrative of redemption cannot occur unless an "intellective" engagement is embedded in a prior "affective" engagement of the story. "Think, *in your heart*, how Christ was tortured to death on the Cross," Giovanni de Caulibus writes. "Look at him attentively, then, as He goes along bowed down by the cross and gasping aloud. Feel as much compassion for Him as you can, placed in such anguish and renewed derision." "Place yourself there," is the insistent and repeated invitation of the text: as elsewhere in medieval writing, "contemplation" and "meditation" are explicitly mimetic activities, identification with Christ in his atoning sacrifice. Or the contemplation may be mediated: "Think of how his Mother felt," and "have compassion for her whom you see thus afflicted." But this applies to the entire life of Christ in the world: commenting on Jesus visiting the disciples after the Resurrection "as if they were friends and not servants," the writer adds, "Reflect on this well, and admire and try to imitate it."[24] Otherwise, he says, you read the text in vain.

Imitatio Christi, as in the radical identification with Christ's Passion championed by Franciscan spirituality and symbolized hagiographically in the *stigmata* of St. Francis, is perhaps the most powerfully mimetic of readings, one which can take the text as far as literal emulation.[25] But *lebensnachfolge* (the term used by later theologians to describe precipitated, enacted reading as the script for a whole Christian life) considerably extends the narrative's mimetic reach. Specifically, it is by means of such a mimetic extension—that is to say, a reading in repentance or broken-hearted reading—that foundational narrative achieves in the reader its ethical authority.[26]

It is possible, of course, to write a history of Western narrative in which every example so far adduced is edited out of the record as impertinent to the question of "realism" as variously and more narrowly defined since Kant, the positivists, and Zola. One might then present a contrary or at least relativizing historical thesis—for example, that mimetic reading of biblical narrative began after all to disappear from serious intellectual consideration following the emergence of Martin Luther's independent Bible reader and especially after the post-Enlightenment antirealism of German Romanticism. But one could only hope to make the case for impertinence stick, I think, by omitting from such a thesis any serious critical consideration of the persistent textual treatment of the matter of repentance.

Frank Kermode's *Genesis of Secrecy* is written in the shadow of such a thesis incorporated as presupposition. The source he cites is "a subtle and interesting book" by Hans Frei, *The Eclipse of Biblical Narrative*, an invaluable resource for the history of late eighteenth-and-nineteenth century professional biblical interpretation.[27] Frei's contention is that any residual "narrative sense" in the reading of the Bible remained primary after the Enlightenment only in allegory, such as imitated in Bunyan's *Pilgrim's Progress*, or "directly, as in the Methodists' devout use of the Bible . . . in tracing and treading the path from sin to perfection."[28] Moreover, on the basis of this paradigm he projects the view that "evangelical piety" is in its own way a rejection of realistic biblical narrative: "though real in his own right, the atoning Redeemer is at the same time a figure or type of the Christian's journey," and so "what is real, and what therefore the Christian lives, is his own pilgrimage."[29] Perhaps if Puritan spiritual autobiographies and their American counterparts were the only expression of "evangelical piety," Frei's might be a tenable theses. His larger claims are compromised, however, by evident dependence upon too narrow a sample of Christian readers, even from within that portion of the tradition which might be imagined as most open to his charge.

Here, in a way that helps to explain how Kermode's derivative argument goes wrong, we can see how Frei's subtlety has proved misleading. For the actual textual record of homiletic and practical biblical exegesis among Christians from the time of the Great Revival of the eighteenth century to the Great Awakening of the nineteenth century is replete with almost innumerable examples of detailed narrative exposition that can only be regarded as reading the Bible "realistically." Notably, in these readings, repentance figures prominently as both subject and motive.

Again, examples abound, yet two or three must suffice. The poet William Cowper, converted through the intercession of his Methodist cousin Martin Madan, and pastored by John Newton, wrote thousands of lines of poetry that manifestly afford a "realistic" reading of biblical narrative. These poems bespeak as indubitable a sense of Scripture's imperative to performative response as do the published sermons of his distinguished parish priest.[30] Cowper's spiritual autobiography (1816), modeled transparently on the *Confessions* of Augustine, also clearly articulates the mimetic relation of biblical and subsequent Christian repentance narrative to his own narrative transformed. This is preeminently the case in the spiritual autobiography of Newton himself, titled *Authentic Narrative* (1764).[31] Though the primary influence in Newton's conversion is a transparent reading of biblical narrative, a mediating book which he says made him able to "view the Bible accountably" was Thomas à Kempis's spiritually mimetic reading, the *Imitation of Christ*. Each in his own fashion, Newton, the hard-headed former slave-trader, and Cowper, the psychologically unstable recluse, offers a classic paradigm of the brokenhearted reader.

But in post-Enlightenment literature, convincing *fictional* repentance narratives also occur; notable nineteenth-century examples include the chapter entitled "Janet's Repentance" in George Eliot's *Scenes from Clerical Life* and, more magisterially, Dostoevski's *Crime and Punishment*. These are, of course, written from the third-person point of view. In Eliot's case the writer's stance involves an ostensibly greater psychological distance from her protagonist, though not at significant loss to psychological realism in the chapter. Dostoevski as writer is more obviously implicated in his protagonist's crisis. But he is correspondingly more transparent about his vulnerability to the self-righteous rejection of mundane reality represented in that protagonist. The student Raskolnikov's monstrous and proleptic Nietzschean inability to read any other text than the agenda for his own will to power can only be broken down by a combination of realistically read biblical narrative (the resurrection of Lazarus) and Sonya the prostitute's vivid (and mimetic) narrative of personal repentance. The novel's very closure is correspondingly affected through the protagonist's own commencement toward repentance, his giving up his pretense to verbal fiat, the symbol and symptom of his will to power, which is to say, he gives up his dearest implausible fiction, the conviction that he can save himself by extraordinary command of thought and language, by "uttering a new word."[32]

I do not mean to suggest that only contemporary literary theory, or even hermeneutics since the Enlightenment, finds particularly awkward such narratives of repentance. The paradigm-driven theorist is not the only hard-hearted reader. What I do mean to say is that the marginalization of this tradition of repentance texts, as Kierkegaard's analysis long ago anticipated, is a phenomenon that deserves to be considered at several levels. In one form or another, a split something like that which I have called (in biblical fashion) a divide between the hard-hearted and the broken-hearted reader has troubled thoughtful contemporary commentators and writers alike for some time. George Steiner's seminal "Critic / Reader" essay helps to make evident why the stance of the formal critic entails as axiom a decorum of disengagement, sometimes making the "reader" in the "critic" less accessible. But as Steiner suggests, the polarity artificializes: though it explains, it does not describe an ideal state of affairs.[33]

Italo Calvino's novel *If on a Winter's Night a Traveler*, with its ideological and theory-minded Ludmilla resisting the author's story, unlike her more open-hearted sister who reads to engage, somehow, the man behind the pen, evokes a split between reader and writer to some degree compatible with that between reader and critic described by Steiner. And Walker Percy takes up allied issues, both in his books of essays[34] and in his Kierkegaardian novel *Second Coming*. There, the inscribed reader, an escaped psychiatric patient whose willed deliverance from unsustainable pretension lets her see "thou and I" more realistically, is, however embarrassingly, akin to Dostoevski's Sonya in being crucially proactive, precipitating the kind of dialectic that the narrative of repentance seeks. In all of these cases that dialectic requires a mimetic, realistic reading.

What is it that the greatest Teller of parables prayed? "I thank you Father, Lord of heaven and earth, because You have hidden these things from the wise and the intelligent, and have revealed them to infants . . ." (Matt. 11:25; cf. Luke 18:15–17). Is this not the very sticking point—the stumbling block of critical embarrassment with a certain type of literature, biblical and otherwise, parable or historical narrative—that it makes lack of critical distance the indispensable condition of "getting it right"? Jesus is not speaking here anymore than he is two chapters later (13:10–17) of privileging for understanding those with special knowledge or those who govern institutional interpretation. He is saying precisely the opposite.

Francois Mauriac's *Le noeud de viperes*[35] is among the most effective twentieth-century works employing psychological realism in a narrative of repentance. It purports to be the diary of a self-consumed, hateful, and hate-driven invalid, a miser, recording the strategies whereby he will effect revenge on his alienated wife and vulture-like family, who wait in an anteroom for him to die so they can swoop in on his money. In the process, he is also recollecting his life: his diary is his autobiography, a kind of *Confessions* of a materialist. In the act of recollection, however, something happens. Out of a morass of hate and fear, remembrances of brief encounters with love, however fleeting, have gradually emerged to consciousness—a beloved daughter who died young, an unself-centered nephew, a decent priest. As these recollections begin to weave their way into his narrative, we see that the original purpose of the narrative, and certainly his judgment on those around him, have begun to change. At the end, though the narrative is broken off in midsentence by his final heart attack, we realize that his process of repentance has brought him to New Life.

Appended to the diary and last testament of Louis are two letters. The first is from his grossly materialistic, hard-hearted son, who has immediately ransacked his father's papers. "Which of us," he writes to his sister, "is not maliciously treated in these pages?" The diary, he tells his sister, should be immediately destroyed by her after reading it, lest it fall into the wrong hands and prove an embarrassment to the family. Having long anticipated disinheritance or at least diminishment of his "due" and taken shameful steps to try to prevent it, he focuses on a small portion of the early part of his father's text and writes, "I thank God that he has granted that these lines of our father's should justify me" (192). The echo of Luke 18 is unmistakable.

The second letter is from the first reader's daughter, Louis's granddaughter. After abandonment by her husband, mental breakdown, and subsequent release from the psychiatric hospital, she has come to live with the old invalid. During this time a healing relationship is formed with a man who now seems to her to be an entirely new person. Her "reading" of him is accordingly shockingly contrary to that of the rest of the family: "Grandfather," she writes, "is the only religious man I have ever met." "We were wrong," she continues, "our principles remained separate from our lives. Our thoughts, our desires, our actions struck no roots in that faith to which we adhered with our lips . . . we were [the ones] devoted to material things" (198–99). She begs to be allowed to read the diary, which her parents who have authority over the estate have denied her, because even though she has yet to see it, she believes that it will bear "decisive witness" to her grandfather's transformation.

Here Mauriac has provided us a choice between two diametrically opposed "readings" of the same repentance narrative: we may side with either the hard-hearted or the broken-hearted reader. But as to which disposition is likely to be of most help in helping us to understand the apparent shift of motive, the spiritual transformation in the protagonist, we can be of little doubt. The first reader, we are unsurprised, reads each evidence of changing intention—of transformation—simply as a sign of "confusion" in his father's text.

Is there a kind of text that discriminates between readers, not because it is "closed up" by one sort of institutional encoding, or made to seem confused and unrealistic by another, but rather because against its transparent motives the intentions of the reader with hardened categories are implacable? It would seem so. And yet the recurrent value of such ethically powerful texts is that they are the ones which seem able to generate *new story*, to make old new, and so to move to bind up the broken-hearted and heal the crushed in spirit.

How might a hermeneutic be developed to deal more adequately with such texts? Well, perhaps, by taking better account of critical misprision, of the interpreter's strategies for avoiding embarrassment, and of the consequences of such evasion. In short, by engaging seriously in a critical "dialectic of sin," as well as the "dialectic of speculation." From this might even follow a fresh insight into contemporary debate over how to incorporate the category of the "ethical" more coherently in literary theory.

What really is required for a sensitive reading of repentance narrative? Clearly, I want to say, a way of reading that does not construe itself as a means to power, but

rather as a recognition of "legitimate dominion" in that other sense of *mashal*—
recognition of the authority of the primary text. This way of reading would express a
theory that does not so imperiously privilege method, mastery, or membership as
acknowledge and respect the intimacy of the encounter between the reader and
such a text. Let me put this point interrogatively: Should not our periodic examination of critical conscience affirm that we are maintaining an active category for texts
for which understanding comes about not because we interpret the text, but because, when read accountably, the text interprets us?

Notes

1. Another way of putting this, of course, would simply be to note that allegorists such as
Philo and Origen resist reading many parts of the biblical texts literally. Origen exclaims, for
example, "Who is so silly as to believe that God, after the manner of a farmer, planted a paradise eastward in Eden and set in it a visible and palpable 'tree of life' of such a sort that anyone who tasted its fruit with his bodily teeth would gain life; and again that one could par-
take of 'good and evil' by masticating the fruit taken from the tree of that name" (*De
principiis*, 4.3.1). The more significant effect of such reading is to be found, however, in the
typologizing of NT as well as OT narrative, in which the realistic surface of representative
narrative is taken to be frivolous. Here, as in Origen's elaborately rationalized allegory of the
six waterpots mentioned in the marriage of Cana story (John 2), the "logical and literal
meaning" is held to be simply inconsistent with the purpose of divine intellect (*De principiis*,
4.2.5–6; 9)—that is, it is assumed that God would not condescend to the authorization of
such trivialities. In biblical narrative, rather, the Spirit will "wrap up and conceal within
ordinary language under cover of some historical record or account of visible things . . .
secret mysteries" (4.2.8). The unambiguous bias against realism privileges "the more skillful
and inquiring readers, in order that these, by giving themselves to the toil of examining what
is written, may gain a sound conviction of the necessity of seeking in such instances a meaning worthy of God" (4.2.9). Origen's gnostic "saving of the appearances" is based upon a view
of God that is effectively almost nonincarnational, and in this respect compares with that of
Philo of Alexandria and some other Jewish writers of the tannaitic period.
2. One modern analogue must here suffice: in her essay "Narrative Emotions: Beckett's
Genealogy of Love," Martha Nussbaum suggests, for example, that an "unwriting" of narrative and a positing of an alternative account is required in a prophetic critique of society's
dominant self-understanding (*Ethics* 98.2 [1981]: 225–54). Though Beckett's "unwriting" is
still recognizably narrative, its antirealism and antinomian idiom invites—and still obtains—
inculcation into a liturgy of calculated mystification.
3. The pretension of much poststructuralist critical and theoretical writing to be first-
order discourse has, of course, occasioned concern among those who believe a central task of
critical writing is to rank, value, and preserve the contribution of primary narrative. Frank
Kermode, for example, argues in *Forms of Attention* (Chicago: University of Chicago Press,
1985) for the traditional place of interpretative criticism as subordinate, a second-order discourse. The success of interpretative argument as a means of conferring or endorsing value,
he contends, is, accordingly, not to be measured by the survival of the comment but by the
survival of its object.
4. Hans Jonas, *The Gnostic Religion*, 2nd ed. (Boston: Beacon Press, 1963), and "Delim-
itation of the Gnostic Phenomenon—Typological and Historical," in *The Origins of Gnosticism*, ed. V. Bianchi (Leiden: Brill, 1970).

5. See Bloom's "The Breaking of Form," in his edited collection, *Deconstruction and Criticism* (New York: Seabury, 1979).

6. D. L. Jeffrey, "*Caveat Lector,* Structuralism, Deconstruction and Ideology," *Christian Scholars Review* 17, no. 4 (1988): 436–48.

7. For an extensive critique see John Ellis, *Against Deconstruction* (Princeton: Princeton University Press, 1989); cf. Cedric Watts, "Bottom's Children: The Fallacies of Structuralist and Deconstructionist Literary Theory," in *Reconstructing Literature,* ed. L. Lerner (Oxford: Blackwell, 1983), 106–22.

8. These points are argued usefully by Michael H. Keefer, "Deconstruction and the Gnostics," *University of Toronto Quarterly* 55, no. 1 (1985): 74–93.

9. This tends to be a *lapsus* in Marxist theory as well. An example is the survey of Terry Eagleton in *Literary Theory: An Introduction* (Minneapolis: University of Minnesota, 1983).

10. "Realism" continues to be a bedeviled and unstable term in contemporary theoretical writing. Late nineteenth-century and early twentieth-century proponents of "literary naturalism" and "social realism" defined realism partly in terms of what it was *not*: a documentary, unexpurgated examination of life lived in disarray was "realism"; any comedic plot or romance with a happy ending was not. In biblical criticism, the movement away from "realistic narrative" in interpretation, especially after the nineteenth century, denotes the rejection of any sense of the task of the interpreter in which "realism" would mean something like "naively treating the text as though it described something which really happened" (cf n. 1). In certain types of contemporary theory, notably deconstruction, rejection of realism entails a conviction that meaning and reality have no evident connection, that any imagination of their stable correlation is purely chimerical.

11. Soren Kierkegaard, *The Present Age,* trans. Alexander Dru (New York: Harper, 1962), 42–43, emphasis mine.

12. Indicatively, he says in *The Concept of Irony,* trans. Lee Capel (New York: Harper & Row, 1966), "sin is inconsistency"(64).

13. Soren Kierkegaard, *Sickness Unto Death,* trans. Walter Lowrie (Garden City, N.Y.: Doubleday, 1954), 162–63, 232, 251. In this corollary sense, for Kierkegaard as for the medieval philosopher St. Anselm, a search for realism about one's own actual mode of being entails the search for Being, or God, a search that at once defines the searcher's perpetual corrigibility: "God is near enough, but no one can see God without purity, and sin is impurity, and therefore no one can take cognizance of God without becoming a sinner" *(Thoughts on Critical Situations,* trans. D. F. Swenson [Minneapolis: Augsburg, 1941], 25).

14. Kierkegaard, *Sickness Unto Death,* 239–40.

15. Kierkegaard's point here is not unrelated to the formulations of Buber or Levinas. For a usefully contextualized assessment of the contribution of Levinas in this regard see Susan Handelman, "Facing the Other: Levinas, Perelman, and Rosenzweig," *Religion and Literature* 22–23 (1990): 61–84. If there is a deconstructionist method which makes plausible address to ethics, then it seems to me to be rabbinic, and that the most articulate proponent is Levinas. For a thought-provoking reflection see Jill Robbins, *Prodigal Son/Elder Brother: Interpretation and Alterity in Augustine, Petrarch, Kafka, Levinas* (Chicago: University of Chicago Press, 1991).

16. A. S. Herbert, "The Parable (Masal) in the Old Testament," *Scottish Journal of Theology* 7 (1954): 180–96.

17. "Prophetic word" may include, of course, a parable understood (as in the case of the example of Nathan), whether or not it is acted upon in repentance, as it is not in the case of Micaiah's parable to Ahab (I Kings 22).

18. As recorded in Pinchas H. Peh, *Soleveitchik on Repentance: The Thought and Oral*

Discourses of Rabbi Joseph B. Soloveitchik (New York: Paulist Press, 1984), 49–52. (It should be remembered here that in Judaism during this period, one in a state of evident lapse from obedience to Torah lost his legal status and could not, for example, in that condition even serve as witness in a judicial hearing.)

19. His fourfold restitution is, of course, precisely what is required of him under the Law (cf. Exod. 22:1). Soloveitchik observes that this covenant restitution made possible by repentance is an effect of *hesed*, God's "covenant love." On this point Soloveitchik concludes: "Through repentance of purification man is reborn and he gains a new heart, a renewed spirit, another outlook on life and different horizons. One man enters the bath of ritual immersion and another emerges from the water. The sinful person emerges as a pure one. And, indeed, our sages have pointed out that changing one's name is especially beneficial for penitents" (59).

20. See Joachim Jeremias, *Parables of Jesus* (London: SPCK, 1963), 22ff.

21. Seen in this context of the Jewish narrative practice which features the *mashal*, the modern critical category of New Testament scholars, "Parables of the kingdom," can seem ripe with double-sense.

22. Saints' lives, the most popular vernacular genre in Christian Europe before the Reformation, stylize or typologize but do not alter the pattern; the occasion of repentance can be almost as easily prompted by reading a noncanonical repentance narrative as by a direct encounter with divine writ.

23. Augustine says he hopes for such a response from some readers.

24. The entire *Meditations of the Life of Christ*, which has been translated from a fourteenth-century ms. by Isa Ragusa and Rosalie B. Green (Princeton: Princeton University Press, 1961), is rife with such invitations. Cited here are passages from Meditations 77 and 85. For a general discussion of affective spirituality in the Franciscan tradition, see D. L. Jeffrey, *The Early English Lyric and Franciscan Spirituality* (Lincoln: University of Nebraska Press, 1975), chaps. 2–3.

25. See *Early English Lyric and Franciscan Spirituality*, 48–72. Less extreme examples abound in literature of the Franciscans: Jacopone da Todi's *Stabat mater*, with or without the heart-breaking setting by Pergolesi, may still be one of the most compellingly realistic "readings" of the crucifixion narratives. Its purpose is the prompting of a specific act of contrition.

26. Cf. Alasdair MacIntyre's *After Virtue: A Study in Moral Theory*, 2nd ed. (Notre Dame: University of Notre Dame Press, 1984), 214–17.

27. Hans W. Frei, *The Eclipse of Biblical Narrative: A Study in Eighteenth and Nineteenth Century Hermeneutics* (New Haven: Yale University Press, 1974).

28. Ibid., 149ff., esp. 152.

29. Ibid., 154.

30. Cowper's use of the Bible has yet to be studied as thoroughly as the subject deserves. An early and exploratory treatment may be found in Mary Seeley, The *Later Evangelical Fathers: John Thornton, John Newton, and William Cowper* (London: SPCK, 1914).

31. See G. A. Starr, *Defoe and Spiritual Autobiography* (Princeton: Princeton University Press, 1965), and Leopold Damrosch, *God's Plot and Man's Stories* (Chicago: University of Chicago Press, 1985).

32. The famous phrase is Nietzschean, but here, two decades earlier, is articulated by Raskolnikov in his article championing "those who Possess the gift or talent to say a *new word. . . .*" Fyodor Dostoevski, *Crime and Punishment*, trans. David Magarshak (London: Penguin, 1951; reprint, 1966), 277. That in his own mind this theory justifies murder is a central element in the novel's ambiguous problematic.

33. This essay, first published in *New Literary History* (1979), is conveniently available in *George Steiner—A Reader* (New York: Oxford University Press, 1984), 67–98.

34. *The Message in the Bottle: How Queer Man Is, How Queer Language Is, and What One Has to Do with the Other* (New York: Farrar, Straus and Giroux, 1975) and *Lost in the Cosmos: The Last Self-Help Book* (New York: Farrar, Straus & Giroux, 1983).

35. Francois Mauriac, *Le noeud de viperes* (Paris: Bernard Grasset, 1933); trans. Warre B. Wells, *Viper's Tangle* (New York: Image Books, 1957).

3

GEORGE STEINER

The Scandal of Revelation

Two deaths have, very largely, determined the fabric of Western sensibility. Two cases of capital punishment, of judicial murder, lie at the foundations of our religious, philosophic and political reflexes. One wonders: How different, how qualified in respect of tragic context, would Western history have been if it had at its source two acts of birth, if auroral celebration were its root instead of mourning and an eclipse of the sun? But it is two deaths that preside over our metaphysical and civic sense of self: that of Socrates and that of Jesus. We remain, to this day, children of those deaths.

The motives, be they compelling and fortuitous, of Socrates's execution are not, despite incessant scholarly inquiry, fully understood. Nor, one intuits, were they transparent to those who condemned and who mourned him. Our images of what came to pass in Athens in 400 or 399 B.C.—is it not striking that a degree of temporal uncertainty attaches to the two determinant dates in our history?—are primarily shaped by Plato's narrative. Indistinctly, we know of the conflicts between oligarchy and populism, between rhetorician or sophist and demagogue, which had enervated the *polis* and in which Socrates was, or was believed to be, culpably implicated. We know something of the weight which lay on what had been Pericles' city after its defeat by Sparta. Exhaustion and mutual recrimination poisoned the air. We need look no further than Aristophanes' *Clouds* to recall that Socrates had incensed his detractors, that he had goaded beyond patience certain "Pillars of society" (the Socratic inference in Ibsen's drama of the clash between truth and community is obvious). In its pitiless prescriptions, Book X of Plato's *Laws* reminds us of the archaic but constantly resurgent terrors that Attic public consciousness experienced in the face of impiety, of rationalistic provocations. Questionings as to the organization of the cosmos were one thing—they had already busied Anaximander and Heraclitus; questionings of the instrumentalities of convention and sanctioned discourse, which related the gods to the everyday stability of the state, were quite another.

But even if we observe these fatalities of political and personal circumstance

(Euripides also was to experience their menace), even if we register the deliberate "tactlessness" of Socrates' style of a density and plurality so great that it rebukes any confident analytic finding, the motives remain opaque. Nor must we overlook the dynamics of interaction of reflective mirroring and projection between earlier and later figurations. As we do not possess an exact chronology for either the Platonic and pseudo-Platonic dialogues on the one hand or for the four Gospels and their putative source on the other, we can only speculate. In what ways, say, does the "Socrates" of the *Gorgias* incorporate or alter the voice of the "Socrates," be he fictive or actually remembered, whom we meet in the *Protagoras*? What are the relations or distortions of identity affecting the presentation of Jesus not only within the Synoptic Gospels but also, drastically, in reference to St. John.

What is evident to any student of language and poetics is the pressure of literary unfolding in Plato's successive and self-modifying renditions ("inventions"?) of his Socrates. The Falstaff of *The Merry Wives of Windsor* is and is not the Falstaff of the two parts of *Henry IV*. But the informing genesis in this instance is almost simplistic when we compare it with the motions of verity and of fiction, of remembrance and of metamorphosis used by Plato to preserve, to communicate to and for himself and for us, the only individuality whose stamp on the memory of the rest can be set beside that of Jesus.

I know of only one iconic representation of the relevant paradoxes and intractabilities of interpretation, of the bounds which the material imposes on reason. It is a painting by an anonymous master in a late medieval Flemish style: on the rear wall of Mary's humble abode at the moment of Annunciation, we can make out a cross bearing the crucified Christ. Had Socrates paused to sniff or rub between his fingers the delicately divided leaves of a *Conium maculatum*, the hemlock plant, on one of his early walks?

Whether in religious or in secular history, whether in the "revealed" or the mundane canon (it is the aim of this chapter to ask whether any plausible distinction can be drawn between the two), "last words" of illustrious men form a distinctive genre. I say "men" because, disturbingly, we have hardly any examples of the last words of women. Are women more prone to silence in their death hour? Have their final utterances gone unrecorded? The masculine mode is, by contrast, rich. It extends from the heroic sublime to bathos, from stoical brevity to flowery bravado. We have sound reasons to suppose that such finalities are, perhaps more often than not, prepared before the midnight time, that they have, notably among high personages in the baroque and neoclassical periods, even been rehearsed. There is evidence that some of the most celebrated or notorious of valedictions are the result of misunderstanding by witnesses or of sheer hagiographic invention. Nonetheless, a crucial realization is in play. The "language animal" that is man (this designation lies at the heart of both Hebraic and Greek anthropologies) exercises his defining humanity one last time. Death is a cessation of speech. It is the end-stop that punctuates the script of articulate being. (How is this script finalized in the existence of the mute? What are the "last words" of the speechless?) At death, grammar and the anarchy of silence confront each other, closing the circle which began when the cry of the newborn infant laid claim to human significance. And it would seem indeed that it is language that substantiates our conclusive perception of self: we know of no composer whose "last words" took the form of musical notes, of no graphic artist who addressed his or her own death with a drawing.

"Crito, we owe a cock to Asclepios. Pay my debt, and do not forget it." That "we" remains as enigmatic as the nous, never reiterated or explained, in the opening sentence of Flaubert's *Madame Bovary*. Is Socrates identifying with collective mankind so as to remind us that death is the most total of generalizations, that it can be construed as the eradication of the first-person singular? In death we do become "we." If this is the intent of the syntax, modesty proved shortsighted. Socrates has, in the history and practice of Western logic, come to stand for "man." Innumerable are the syllogisms and the translations of natural 'Socrates' to represent man. From the medieval schools to Descartes and modern primers, countless schoolchildren and tyros in logic have recited the basic syllogism: "Socrates is a man. / All men are mortal. / Socrates is mortal." Being so flat and familiar, the sequence has lost its aura of enormity. Not until Leon Shestov, the twentieth-century Russian thinker against death, against our servile acquiescence in logical necessity, will anyone protest and point to the vital scandal of Socrates' existential presence in this formalization of doom. It is, so Shestov, terrible enough to apply this primary syllogism to a dog; it is an ontological outrage to mouth it, unthinking, about Socrates.

What we know is this: the Socrates who turns to Crito, who already feels in his groin the nearing death-chill of hemlock, chooses, in his last words, both a plural pronoun, "we owe," and a personal possessive, "my debt." He literally voices the threshold, the passing from ego to anonymity. He cannot know (would he have cared?) that anonymity will afford him no lodging, that logic and logical argument would make "Socrates" one of the two least nameless of men.

Given the music of discourse in the *Phaedo* and the poetic strengths of Plato, given the mastery over every technique of rhetoric and eloquence displayed by Socrates throughout his life trial—what Xenophon, with a point of reproof, perhaps, called his *megalogeria*—these last words surprise. Even Wittgenstein's plainness—"Tell them I have led a happy life"—is more charged with the unexpected, with the luminous authority of the occasion. Some have gone from us pronouncing malediction over their foes. Some have blessed them. Some have labored to encapsulate in a single phrase or lapidary tag the essence of their character and destiny (Talleyrand's quip about God's *metier* being forgiveness; Goethe's alleged call for "more light"). Had the master-builder of Western speech, knowing that these would be his final words, knowing, one has reason to believe, that they would be fervently recorded and passed on to others, nothing grander, nothing dialectically more stimulating to say?

Commentary and explication have been various. Scholars tell us that Asclepios was a newly imported deity in the Athenian pantheon. It is held that he originated from the north, possibly from Macedonia, that uncouth yet politically and militarily potent region whose shadow lay heavier and heavier on worn Greece. The cock is also a late arrival in mainland Hellas (no reference antedates c.550 B.C.). He seems to have come from Persia, as did Manichaeism and those dualistic forerunners that also attach to the Median-Persian world. Dualism, the polarization of light and dark, which is the foundation of Manichaean and Gnostic systems, relates forcefully to the cock. It is difficult to summarize even in shorthand a voluminous chapter in the study of comparative religion, mythology, ritual, and symbolism. The cock is Chaucer's Chantecleer. He is herald of dawn. If he fails to crow, legend has it, the sun will not rise. His argent flourish both announces and hails the daily miracle of light. His sexual prowess—in English, "cock" designates the male organ—enacts the life-giving potencies of the sun, the burst into heat which procreates life. In Gallic consciousness, the cock's strutting pride is that of the nation in flashing arms, in glory, when in turn, *gloire* is kindred to sunlight. Throughout Western practice and iconography, cock's feathers adorn the headdress of the warrior and the virile lover. On our weathervanes, the rooster tells of wind and weather, directing our notice skyward. Spurred, he engages in ferocious combat and exhibitions of male mastery.

In antithesis, however, the very same creature relates to darkness and the kingdoms of death. He is, in Petronius's *Satyricon*, the *bucinator*, the trumpeter of death. In Near-Eastern beliefs, in certain strands of classical and celtic mythology, the cock, most especially when he is himself black, is implicated in funeral rites and in the bestiary of the underworld. His blood figures explicitly in rituals of burial and the sacrificial propitiation of the departed. Gods and demons of the nether world have commerce with the bird. There are fables and ghostly tales in which the crowing of the cock does not attend on sunrise and new birth but on the imminence of death in the house. Unsurprisingly, it is Shakespeare who spins these ancient, contradictory threads.

> It faded on the crowing of the Cocke.
> Some sayes, that ever 'gainst that Season comes
> Wherein our Saviours Birth is celebrated,
> The Bird of Dawning singeth all night long:
> And then (they say) no Spirit can walke abroad,
> The nights are wholesome, then no Planets strike
> No Faiery talkes, nor Witch hath power to Charme
> So hallow'd and so gracious is the time.

A bird of dawn which sings all night in the season of Christ's nativity; but whose call summons back to Purgatory the wretched spirits such as Hamlet's father. A fowl of joyous coming which is simultaneously and literally the summoner out of and back to the sulphurous dark of death. The cock occupies Socrates' last thoughts and words. It crows news of the grace that comes of Jesus' birth. It is a frequent herald of death. We stand on puzzling ground.

Armed with revelation and the death-cry of the risen Christ, Church Fathers, Lactantius and Tertullian most prominently, derided Socrates' finale. What sounder proof than his trivial dictum of the fact that even the wisest, the most ethically in sport of pagan sages was, at the supreme hour, nothing more than a superstitious idolater? We knew already of Socrates' resort to his daimon—a word which in early Christian ears rang with sinister connotations. We have ample witness to his regard for the oracle at Delphi, symbol of that entire edifice of false or devilish prophecy laid waste by Christian revelation. Now that cock for Asclepios. Should this have been the parting reflection and bidding of a true teacher, of a seeker of moral and spiritual truth? Socrates' closing move, moreover, entails animal sacrifice. It is one of the just vaunts of Christian doctrine, of Jesus of Nazareth's exemplification of encompassing love, to have rejected the offering of animals, of any living creature, on the altars of God. In so doing, the new ecclesia had indeed surpassed the ethics and practice of both paganism and Judaism. It had, by virtue of this simple but "revolutionary" abstinence, proclaimed a truly novel perception of the sacredness and unison of all created life. What philosophic-moral trust can we invest in a man (Socrates) who, at the instant of death, seeks to honor or assuage some minor deity by blood-sacrifice? No, as so often, declared the Church Fathers, the triune God had convicted even the loftiest of a philosophy of puerile emptiness and had done so out of its own mouth.

A second line of interpretation is more generous. It was, we are informed, customary to offer to Asclepios a gift of thanks in prequital of healing, of recovery from illness. Socrates (this will be the Stoic reading and that of Montaigne) aims to teach us that death is a blessed recovery from the illness that is carnal existence. Specifically, according to Xenophon, Socrates had told Hermogenes that death freely chosen was far preferable to the ineluctable afflictions, infirmities, and decrepitude of old age. What wise man would choose to fall into risible decay of mind and body when he could die more or less painlessly and in possession of his faculties? Therefore, let us give thanks to the god of healing when he allows us to exit lightly. May the cock which we bring him in offering embody our indebtedness for deliverance into a true and lasting dawn. May it mark our reasoned acquiescence in the logic and benediction of our passing. Thus, the crowing of the cock sends our soul on its twofold journey through the black gates and into Elysian noon. This duality will impress itself on Nietzsche when he qualifies Socrates' last words as being both *lächerlich* & *furchtbar*—risible and terrible.

The ironies in the *Phaedo* are labyrinthine. The play of argument and of symbol is as manifold as any in Plato. One of the key motifs is that of Socrates' self-adjudication of innocence and public merit. It is Socrates (so Socrates) who is the veritably pious man. It is he who best honors the divinities of Athens. The charge of impiety applies to his accusers. It is their officious observance and adherence to unexamined gestures that makes religion vacant. Now, at the precise instant of his innocent death, Socrates elects to demonstrate his caring piety. He bids Crito sacrifice to a new cult, to a divinity which may have entered the religion of the city only recently. The cock for Asclepios signals Socrates' scrupulous alertness to appropriate ritual even where, particularly where, its context is new and as yet, perhaps, overlooked. "Do not forget." The ironies may lie gentle and deep. They are akin to those in Pascal's wager on transcendence: even the freest, wisest of mortal spirits adds a touch of potential insurance to his pilgrimage into death. Who knows? Asclepios may ease the transition. But the implications reach beyond irony. At other levels, the *Phaedo* invites us to discriminate courteously but stringently between the numerous, polymorphic deities whom we encounter in myths and inherited rites on the one hand, and the one supreme principle, the "unknown God" whose altar St. Paul will find, precisely in Athens, on the other. Of this first principle we know, *stricto sensu*, nothing. In significant part, however, its eternal, changeless truth and universality are revealed to us by the realm of Ideas, themselves analogously eternal and changeless. We are, at this point, distant from the early

Socratic "Socrates" and close to the transcendental Platonism that will become that of Plotinus, of Proclus, and of Augustinian Christianity. Without formal emphasis yet unmistakably, the *Phaedo* would have us distinguish the mythopoetic, civic polytheism as we find it in Homer and daily Athenian usage from the Demiurge and ascendant hierarchy of abstraction delineated in the *Timaeus*. Careful remembrance and public gestures (the sacrifice of a cock) are due to the former; metaphysical meditation and the soul's act of faith are owed to the latter.

Asclepios provides a pertinent figure in whose cult this distinction and the passage from one order of religious sentiment to a higher order is enacted. His inclusion in the Athenian panoply seems to have related to the spread of Orphic beliefs and rituals. Asclepios belongs to the "death and rebirth" constellation which is associated with Demeter and Dionysus and with the mimetic initiations into the afterlife practiced by their adepts. Thus, Socrates' final bidding could be said to educate us to the steps which must be taken if we are to progress from the naive religious imaginings and sacrificial obligations of a Crito (who is no philosopher) to the domain of eternal Forms and of their better, such as they are about to be revealed to Socrates. As so very often, a Socratic injunction is Janus-like, oriented toward two directions and two different capacities of reception. This, essentially, is the interpretation put forward by St. John Damascene. The song of the dying cock will accompany the voyage of the philosophic soul from a more or less material Hades to the pure absolute light of the *Logos*. "We" courteously includes both Crito and Socrates in a shared motion; the "I" tells of insights and expectations open to the enlightened.

As the law prescribes, Socrates dies at sundown. He invokes, with his dying breath, the bird whose cry proclaims sunrise. There could be no neater example of dialectic. In the *Symposium*, the cock rouses Aristodemus from drunken slumber, allowing him to report to Apollodorus the events and discourse of the night's banquet. We remember that this banquet closes with Socrates' proof—which Agathon and Aristophanes are too besotted to recall or reconstrue—that the writer of tragedy is also and equally the writer of comedy. This (lost) equation bridges the two polarities of eros, at once carnal and spiritual, immanent and transcendent, as they are celebrated in the *Symposium*. It relates also to the desolation and joy of mortal farewell and immortal felicity as expounded in the *Phaedo*. The cock of Socrates' adieu is veritably the summoner to darkness and the herald of everlasting dawn.

Let the cock guide us toward the question of whether the revealed admits of a rational hermeneutic. It is his annunciation of morning which rings out in the Christian liturgy: *Gallo canente spes redit*. In countless verbal, iconographic, and musical presentations of the theme of resurrection, the rooster, with his plumage of flame and sun, images the negation of death. We saw that in fable and in slang, this negation is associated with sexual drive, with the libidinous power of the "cock" to engender new life. Where the world is a barnyard—a current conceit in medieval, renaissance, and popular cultures—whose eggs symbolize the ancient riddle of the coming into being of the cosmos, the cock is God the Father.

But the episode that links the cock to the death of Jesus is of a humbler and sadder sort. In Mark 14:30, Jesus says to Peter: "Verily I say unto thee, that this day, even in this night, before the cock crow twice, thou shalt deny me thrice." That "twice" is lacking in Matthew. Luke (22:34) varies further: "The cock shall not crow this day that thou shalt thrice deny that thou knowest me." The Fourth Gospel closely echoes Matthew. The motif is unambiguous: the crowing of a cock, in the courtyard of the house of the High Priest, either singular or repeated, will accompany and declare a second betrayal of the Son of Man. In some respects, this betrayal cuts deeper than that of Judas. Simon Peter will be tested less by Satan (though all men are) than by natural frailty, by the solicitations of our fallen humanity. Peter, foremost of the disciples and the "rock" on whom the risen Saviour will found his church, fails his master in the hour of peril. The psychological drama of Peter's denial springs from the fact that it is committed voluntarily yet against his true intent. The enduring shock of Peter's inability to withstand the "temptation" (*peirasmos*) of fear vibrates in entry 317 of Pascal's "cinematic" *Arege de la vie de Jesus-Christ: Et neanmoins Pierre*. The uncannily compressed *neanmoins* stands both for the abjection of Peter's cowardice and for the remorse and heroic martyrdom to come. Though wholly familiar, the ensuing scene retains its sombre tension. Western literature adverts to it on numerous occasions (think of Donne or of Baudelaire). It inspires Western painters (Caravaggio, La Tour). Musical settings of the Passion mime the crow of the cock. Following on the Evangelists, Flemish painters, who so often depicted the narration, set a coal-brasier or hearthfire in the courtyard or interior of the house of Annas, the High Priest, or Caiphas his son-in-law (our testimonies differ). April evenings can be chilly in Jerusalem. All too meaningfully, Simon Peter has followed at a distance and not entered the house. Yet if Mark is to be credited, of all the disciples, Peter alone had not fled in the tumult of Jesus' arrest. Luke's chronicle is the most circumstantial. By the light of the fire, a servant girl denounces Peter to the other domestics and bystanders: "This man also was with him." Peter's emphatic negation (*arneisthai*) exactly fulfils the Lord's prediction: "Woman, I do not know him." The La Rochelle and Geneva Bible of 1616, rendering this same reply in St. John, gives it the lapidary concision of high drama: "*Je n'en fuis point.*" By inserting a separation in time between the successive denials, Luke conducts the action toward a more realistic hour for cockcrow. Peter has denied any knowledge of Jesus; he denies being among his companions and being one of those Galileans so specially implicated in Jesus' ministry and ascent to Jerusalem. Matthew has him "cursing" and "swearing." Human accents sharpen with fear: would this alone not have unmasked the Galilean fisherman? "And immediately, while he yet spake, the cock crew."

At that instant, the cock is indeed a bird of night, of ghastly omen. On a level as yet opaque, he affirms the complete validity and potential of grace in Jesus' oracular prediction. It is Luke, so much the "writer," who transcribes or imagines the crowning movement of sorrow and salvation: "The Lord turned and looked at Peter." It is this turning, this look at the exact instant of the cock's call, which poets and painters have labored to recapture, which cantatas and oratorios seek to translate. As in the case of the wordless kiss that Christ bestows on Dostoevski's Grand Inquisitor, the meanings are translucent, but of a clarity resistant to paraphrase or explication. Only in the motion and eyes of total love can there be the dark light of total sadness. Only in the sentence passed, as in a "first last judgement," by betrayed love, can there be, though as yet wholly imperceptible to Peter himself, the assurance of subsequent redemption and forgiveness. In Mark alone, the cock crows twice. May one take this to mean that the first call signifies the defeat and damning of Peter, where the second, already directed to the rising day, portends his later witness and glory?

Is there any other point or pericope at which the ambivalent, genuinely gnostic figure of the cock has bearing on Jesus? Hints of epilepsy, of the "holy sickness" and the visionary illuminations which may come of seizures, cling stubbornly to the mythographic traditions surrounding the riddling *persona* of the Nazarene. As late as the nineteenth century, cocks were sacrificed in the Scottish Highlands to ensure or to give thanks for recovery from epileptic fits. Bird and Saviour, sacred illness and clairvoyance, come together in "The Man Who Died," D. H. Lawrence's last and strangest story. In this tale, the horror and sanctity of resurrection in the torn flesh are "debated" (enacted) between Jesus and the solar cock. In unsettling play are the intimate bonds between healing and sexual potency on the one hand, and between death and disincarnate resurrection (*Verklarung*) on the other. No less than Plato and Luke, Lawrence dramatizes the divided nature, the duality of the "bird of dawning" whose song can be that of the sepulchral night.

Comparisons, parallels, studies in mirroring and asymmetry as between Jesus and Socrates, with special reference to their deaths are, since the neo-Platonism of the Renaissance at least, a commonplace in the West. When, in Jacques-Louis David's celebrated painting of Socrates' last moments, the sage is depicted with his index-finger pointing toward Elysium, this iconic posture explicitly "cites" the gesture of Christ in such renditions of the Last Judgment as Michelangelo's. When, in his bizarre paper of 1916, Walter Benjamin denounces Socrates' abuses of eros, the inferred corrective is that of Grünewald's image of Christ and of the Immaculate Conception. Strangely, there is, until now, no comprehensive treatment of this central *topos*; very likely, no bibliography, no iconological catalogue of thematic contrasts and analogues, could hope to be exhaustive.

Parallels drawn have been open or covert, theological and philosophic, ethical and psychological, historical and literary. In skeptical-libertine writings of the late seventeenth and eighteenth centuries, the death of Socrates and the Crucifixion are contrasted in what is frequently an "Aesopian" or clandestine code. Outwardly, Socrates' conduct in his final days and at the hemlock hour is characterized as being the supreme embodiment of a secular, pagan rationality and *dignitas*. The comeliness of his parting marks, as it were, the upper limit of pre-Christian humanism. But the kenosis of the god-man Christ and his agony on the Cross are taken to signify a "quantum jump" into revealed truth and the proffer of universal salvation. It is just the hideousness of Jesus' suffering, the abjection and ugliness which he endures in the flesh, in their stark contrast with the elegant nobility of Socrates' passing, that articulate the new message to man.

This is the explicit tenor of the comparison as it was taught and moralized upon in schools, in manuals of behavior and of rhetoric during the late Renaissance, baroque, and neoclassical generations. It is the official reading still provided by the more cautious of *philosophes* in the Enlightenment. But in key cases, the subtext is otherwise. To subversive spirits such as Pierre Bayle, to thinkers of beauty such as Winckelmann, it is the death of Socrates, not of the Galilean, that is exemplary. Socrates bears undying witness to the capacity of the human spirit to face and accept mortality, not in any animist or dogmatic reliance on celestial compensation, but by virtue of its love of moral and intellectual truth. Even in utmost torment—thus the implicit argument—Jesus is persuaded of his translation to heaven and of his return in cosmic majesty. Socrates has no such assurance. His intuitions of some kind of survivance for the enlightened soul, his prevision of Elysian fields, are either gently ironic means of teaching or, at best, metaphors of speculative reason. It may well be that in Socrates' inward mind, as in that of the wise Fool in Lear, dwells the perception that we are only "for the dark." What concerns Socrates, and most directly the "Socrates" who precedes with his death the Platonic modulation into transcendentalism, is the rational, virtuous conduct of our earthly lives and the humane quality of our acceptance of death. What he aims at in the *Crito*, as Montaigne understood so admiringly, is that discipline of decency, that tact of heart which should humanize even a cruel death.

In nineteenth-century philosophy and philosophy of religion, the Jesus-Socrates motif becomes almost obsessional. It is, famously, the pivot of Hegel's lifelong reflections on the philosophy of history and of religion. No other moments are as dramatically demonstrations of the *Bildungsroman*, of the evolutionary dynamics of human consciousness, as are those of the deaths of Socrates and of Christ. The execution of Socrates argues the creative dialectic of conflict between individuality and the state (as does the execution of Antigone in whom Hegel envisages an instinctual counterpart to Socrates). The phenomenology of Jesus' person and passion, their transgression of the Judaism of Abraham and of Moses, determine new categories of consciousness and of conscience, categories fundamental to the birth of modernity and to the self-realization of Geist. It is not only materialist interpreters and critics of Hegel who have pondered the concordance between the triple motion of Hegelian dialectical logic and the paradigm of the Trinity.

Any index to the topic of Socrates and Jesus, in similitude and contrast (even antithesis) in the works of Kierkegaard, would discern its references and discursive passages in almost every title. It is fair to say that Kierkegaard's structural axis—that of the steps from the aesthetic to the ethical and from the ethical to the religious—is traced in the constant evocation of Socrates and the man from Nazareth. Already in Kierkegaard's inspired dissertation on Socratic irony and on the pedagogic and heuristic modes of Socratic teaching, the contrasting theme of Jesus' homiletic and allegoric means is latent. Thereafter, and voluminously, Soren Kierkegaard will meditate on the contrarieties between Socrates' maieutic rationality and the existential "absurdity" and unreason of Jesus' life and preaching. The "guilt" of Socrates (a paradoxical issue already pursued in a number of fascinating and legalistic, though little known, eighteenth-century tracts, notably in France and Italy), is seen by Kierkegaard in ironic counterpoint to the innocence of Jesus. It was precisely because Kierkegaard intuited so acutely in himself the claims of the Socratic—he was a virtuoso questioner and dialectician, a gadfly and exasperation to his fellow-citizens in Copenhagen—that the "decision for Christ" was so taxing and had to be so uncompromisingly dramatized. And even as Hegel senses in Antigone some degree of fusion between absolute ethics and Socratic provocation on the one hand, and the sacrificial self-annulment of Jesus on the other, so Kierkegaard discovered in Job both the Socratic challenger and the acceptor of unmerited suffering and of submission to the mystery of divine love. The Either/Or emblematic of Kierkegaard, and the untenable mediation between them, is persistently that of Socrates and of Christ, of hemlock and Golgotha.

The dialogue continues in Feuerbach's reflections on death (his masterpiece) and critiques of religion. But it is, obviously, in Nietzsche that the duality and congruence of Jesus and of Socrates attain their most intense pitch. During the concluding ecstasies of vision and argument in Turin, it is Socrates/Christ who become(s) Nietzsche's obsession. Now the polemic against Socratic rationalism, against Socrates' physical ugliness, against the analytic sterility of his teachings and their corrosion of the primal genius of Greek tragedy with which the young Nietzsche had initiated his philosophic philology and cultural criticism, blend with the indictment of Jesus in the *Antichrist* and *Ecce Homo*. The Athenian pedant and the Galilean slave-moralist overlap in a kind of wild mental dance during Nietzsche's twilight. "*Ich bin dem Heiland Asklepios einen Hahn schuldig.*" By itself, this translation from the *Crito* speaks volumes. The word *Heiland* does not, of course, have any but punning relevance to Asclepios. The real presence in Nietzsche's version is that of Christ the Savior.

In mordant shorthand, the later Nietzsche interleaves what he takes to be the Socratic crimes against Dionysian vitality with the "slave-pathos," with the canting idealism and humbling of man's natural ego in "Judaic" Christianity. As libertines and ironists had done before him, Nietzsche mocks the Judaeo-Christian "obscenity" of a crucified God. Both Socrates, the simian-faced idealist, and the sufferer from Nazareth "do dirt on life" (the unnerving phrase is D. H. Lawrence's and encapsulates a faithful understanding of Nietzsche). The polemic is complex throughout, in that it amalgamates the Platonic Socrates with a Jesus seen in the light of Judaic utopian rationalism. Obliquely conjoined, the two figures and the laming weight of their deaths on the Western psyche provoke Nietzsche's critique from the early papers on Socrates and Greek tragedy to the debate on Strauss's *Life of Jesus*. Their adverse presence shadows the *Genealogy of Morals* and inspires, in ecstatic contrariety, the gospel and dialectic of *Zarathustra*. Socrates and the man Jesus preside, like malevolent idols, at the crazed epilogue. "When one reads the New Testament, one must wear gloves," says Nietzsche. The same gloves, one is given to understand, must be worn when reading the *Crito*. In it Nietzsche's unerring ear will have heard that same doctrine of nonviolence, of absolute forgiveness which so exasperated him in the Nazarean. (I will come back to this point.) The cock of *Zarathustra* sings neither death, nor betrayal, nor purgatorial superstitions. He clarions high noon and that promise of Eternal Return that is Nietzsche's (jealous) repartee to Christ's offer of resurrection.

And today? Never have the trial and death of Socrates been more insistently unfinished business. The dilemmas—*Das Problem des Sokrates* as Nietzsche calls it—have never been more acute. They comport the coexistence of the state and of intellectual freedom, of diverse forms of popular democracy and of intellectual excellence, of the conventions of coherence indispensable to a social order, and the anarchic, almost necessarily cynical, autarchy of the free spirit. Not only are these conflicts unresolved, but they are also, today, of peculiar discomfort (*Unbehagen*).

They are, in the proper, most vivid sense, dialectical: each proposition enforces culpability and self-questioning on the other. The Western *polis*, be it city-state or nation, is branded with the ineradicable guilt of having slain the archetypal thinker, the human being who, par excellence, lived the life of the mind. (We recall the dread charge, taken up by Luke and Paul from the Old Testament, that Jerusalem will always slay its prophets.) In turn, however, there is a real sense in which Socrates gives the city no choice, in which he forces on our "commonality," whether of character or of intellect, the enduring transgression enacted in his capital punishment. This, in the shadow of the Dreyfus affair, is the argument implicit in Georges Sorel's sophistic, incisive *Proces de Socrate* (Lenin had read Sorel). Socrates, moreover, by his very refusal of ordinariness and illusion, puts in question the possibility of the democratic compromise with human mediocrity. Hence, the revisionist counter to Socrates in I. F. Stone's recent version of the trial. Cities in the West could be defined as the "collective reality principles" that are compelled to try and condemn their Socrates. Observe how he insists.

By propounding his commitment to the body politic, by refusing privacy and solitude—he is wholly of the marketplace—Socrates forces the issue. A man or woman infected by the leprosy of pure thought, by the virus of questioning, can remain a hermit. He or she need not leave the desert or the bare room (Wittgenstein) for the *politeia* of Cleon or of Herod. Some of Socrates' true successors—Pascal, Spinoza, Kierkegaard, Nietzsche himself—will argue out of aloneness. They will shun politics. Not Socrates, who thrusts his presence on the daily life of the community, who demands that his life and ideas be examined and justified in the *agora*. The ambiguity of Plato's response to this Socratic strategy pervades the dialogues. Much in Plato cannot pardon Athens. Together with the Gospels, the *Apology*, *Phaedo*, and *Crito* remain the crucial passion-plays and indictments of human vileness in our Western world. They would renew each day our intimations of irreparable betrayal and loss. The idealized lineaments of Plato's *Republic* can be clearly seen as designed to prevent a social-political structure in which a Socrates can (has to be) convicted and done away with. Yet this is not Plato's final or complete perspective. The fierce interdict on religious-philosophic skepticism, on radical speculation, detailed in the draconian Tenth Book of the *Laws*, suggests a deep-seated apprehension. The despotism of virtue in the later Plato could not have housed Socrates. (Can, asks Dostoevski, any established church house the Galilean troublemaker?)

Our perplexities remain Plato's but have behind them a history crueller, more bewildered, than any that classical Greek political theory could have foreseen. We have accused and killed "Socrates" perennially. Each hounding, be it that of Galileo or Rousseau, each doing to death, be it that of Giordano Bruno or of Condorcet, is a footnote to the typological disaster in Athens. Every time a community attempts, by censorship, ostracism, or killing to silence the moral-intellectual outsider within its walls, to gag or efface his intolerable queries, it lives a Socratic hour. But concomitantly, the thinker, the scientist, the artist, the ironist, or satirist who presses *in extremis* his deconstructive doubts, who sets his addiction to what he takes to be the truth above the inherited beliefs and compromises essential to the continuance of the city, repeats the Socratic provocation. Consciously or not, whether on a secular level (that of a Karl Kraus) or on a religious-philosophic level (that of a Simone Weil), the "No-sayer" to injustice, to human greed and stupidity is not only risking but also soliciting a Socratic destiny. Is it fortuitous that the *agents provocateurs* of the spirit and the intellect, certainly in modern Western history, should so often have been Jews, as was Jesus before them? It is in the marginalization or destruction of so many Jewish questioners, from the rabbis of medieval Spain to Spinoza and to Freud, that the Western state has repeated the reflexes of self-defense and of alarmed vengeance at work in the dooming of Socrates. The killing of Socrates and Jew-hatred advertise the organic fears and loathing which tyranny and the mob feel toward the heresies of intelligence. The *Einsatzgruppen* of the German armies in the East culled and massacred first all those who could read.

Plato's profound ambivalence in respect of despotism, which almost proved fatal to him during his ill-fated involvements in Sicilian politics, has borne complex fruit. Far from acting as critics and opponents of totalitarianism, a clutch of eminent moralists and philosophers have been theoreticians and apologists for autocracy. They have found egalitarian politics and social justice either irrelevant to or more or less incompatible with ideals of absolute intellectual inquiry (has this finding ever been refuted?). Hegel's advocacy of the Prussian system was only tempered sentimentally by roseate memories of youth and revolution. In our times, the conjunction of philosophical-ethical mastery with political support for totalitarian regimes has taken on a sharp profile. We have only begun to come to uncertain terms with the Stalinism of Lukacs, with Sartre's repeated apologias for the Gulag, and the barbarism of the Maoist cultural revolution, or, most saliently, with the politics of Martin Heidegger. For the liberal faith these and lesser cases constitute what Goya would call a "nightmare of reason".

The paradox may not be one. The private existence of the mandarin, of the academic philosopher—Wittgenstein detested this rubric as cordially as Socrates would have—the immersion of the *maitre a penser* or pedagogue in abstraction, in the exigent dust of textuality, can generate a fascination with violence, with the scenarios of history at their most savage. Hegel's Napoleon-obsession is matched by that which Lenin and Stalin exercised on a Lukacs or a Kojeve. Bertrand Russell's pacifism is oddly kin to violence: shortly after the end of the Second World War, he called for a preventive nuclear strike against the Soviet Union. Heidegger's appetite for political might, for a Platonic mission of governance over the spiritual and social destiny of the state, was scarcely veiled. Once again, a Plato was more than ready to direct a Dionysius.

The "strangeness" of Socrates, like that of Jesus, remains intractable to any confident reconstruction. But the Socrates before Plato seems to have been nonacademic to the grain. His seminar rooms were the open street, the shaded banks of a stream, a dinner-party. It is the high academicism in Plato, the institutionalization of metaphysical instruction, the partly sophistic partly scientific redefinition of the philosopher and dialectician as an academic specialist after the time of Socrates, which allow the opportunistic, self-dramatizing commerce between intellect and power. So far as we can make out, Socrates' stance was at once that of the ordinary citizen and of a subverter of majority opinions. He was an exemplary foot-soldier—

itself an activity emblematic of democracy—and served with stoic good humor under stress of battle and retreat. At the same time, his awareness of the natural aristocracy of beauty and mental endowment was exceptionally acute and unconcealed. What appears to have had no hold on him whatever was the hypnosis of violence. Plato's uneasy jibe that Diogenes the Cynic was "Socrates gone mad" contains a piercing insight. Both Socrates and Diogenes are immune to the seductions of worldly power. An Alexander or a Stalin leave them unawed. The treasons of the clerics committed by a Fichte in his season of chauvinism and anti-Semitism, the errors of a Sartre or a Heidegger, are not of Socratic provenance. They originate, as it were, out of Alcibiades or, more precisely, out of the Plato whom Alcibiades spellbound (and whom Karl Popper was to excoriate).

As Gregory Vlastos has shown once again, in his deeply felt if controversial portrayal, Socrates' position in the *Phaedo* is crystal clear. A man or woman aspiring to virtue cannot willingly commit an injustice. To do evil to any other human being is to act without or against virtue. This axiom absolutely excludes retaliation, whatever the provocation. Socrates will do nothing that could harm or do offense to his unjust enemies. Thus, he will not avail himself of the chance to escape from prison and death. This would be to break the law and perform a flagrant injustice. Plato fully sets out Socrates' argument (if Vlastos is right, he does so uncomfortably). The position adopted by Socrates is indeed "scandalous" (in the sense of a "radiant enormity" such as we find it only in the use of this Greek word in 1 Corinthians 1). It contradicts not only natural instinct, but also the entirety of the heroic, masculine traditions in the ancient Mediterranean world. It is as alien to semitic criteria of retribution as it is to the fine discriminations drawn between condign and excessive retaliation and punishment in Aristotle's *Nichomachean Ethics*. The postulate of nonviolence, of nonretaliation in the face of evil and injury, the rejection of the law of the *talion* are (Vlastos again) not only at the innermost center of Socrates' being and teaching, but they are also his enduring challenge to mankind. Kant's moral imperatives come after Socrates and seem more complexly qualified. In the West, the doctrine of the *Phaedo* has one sole counterpart: it is Jesus' offering of "the other cheek" and the loving pardon he extends to his tormentors and executioners. Little wonder, then, that Proclus and the Neo-Platonists of the Florentine Renaissance regarded such texts as the *Apology* and the *Phaedo* as truly divine, that they cited them in exactly the same spirit in which St. Augustine or Anselm cite Scripture. In both instances, let us remember, the presence is that of a text.

No intellectual or historical mapping can fully locate the Cross in the landscape of concept and of sensibility in contemporary terms. For participants in an overwhelmingly secular, technologically-oriented society, this location is a "black hole" left by mythologies and unreason out of the past. For the majority, one suspects, of practicing Christians—and what does "practicing" entail in this context?—the Crucifixion remains an unexamined inheritance, a symbolic marker of familiar but vestigial recognitions. This marker is revered and invoked in conventional idiom and gestures. Its concrete status, the enormity of suffering and injustice it incarnates, would appear to have faded from felt immediacy. How many educated men or women now hear Pascal's cry that humanity must not sleep because Christ hangs on his Cross till the end of the world? A "rationalized" Christianity hovers between an untenable literalism and symbolic insubstantiality, in the indistinct spaces of fitful imagining that we call myth.

There *are* those—they need not be Christians or even religious believers—for whom the matter of Golgotha is the irreducible crux (let the pun be allowed) at the heart of our moral and political condition. There are those who feel that there can be no responsible, indeed and paradoxically, no rational endeavor to grasp the collapse of European values in this century and the regimen of the inhuman which obtains since 1914, without reference to Christ's agony. Without a stringent rethinking of that sense of total abandonment, of total defeat, voiced by the Son of Man on Gethsemane. There are among us those who are convinced that to perceive mankind as it actually is after Auschwitz and a century of licensed bestiality is to perceive Golgotha and the relation between the two realities.

Theologians, philosophic theologians, moralists, certain poets, and, no doubt, silent men and women who try to lead their lives in the acknowledged shadow of the unspeakable (cf. Ernst Wiechert's haunting novel *Missa sine nomine*) have engaged this relationship. They have pointed to the long and murderous history of Jew-hatred within Christendom. They have listened, with a new frankness and embarrassment, to the calls for the elimination of the Jews as these resound in the Church Fathers, in Luther. The widespread indifference of the churches, both Catholic and Protestant, to the coming and fulfillment of the Holocaust has been documented and debated. An entire school of post-Barthian theology, most notably in Germany, has argued that Christianity is now gravely ill, that its historical record on anti-Semitism and its lamentable weakness during the midnight of Western man have put in radical doubt the Christian message of love and salvation. Searching and sombre perceptions have emerged from these considerations. I am not persuaded that they reach deep enough.

There are taboos, politically and psychologically defensible, which surround any clear analysis of the fatalities of coexistence between Jew and Christian. Historically, we know next to nothing of the circumstances underlying the refusal of Christ's messianic claims by his Jewish contemporaries. The Psalms, deutero-Isaiah, manifold figurations in the Torah and the Prophets, had "foretold" the coming and the passion of the Suffering Servant out of the house of David. Rejecting the Galilean, the Jews of his time rejected something urgent in their own messianic expectations. Only if we could clarify the psychic sources of this rejection and the scars it left, could we put into focus the central truth that there is at the very roots of Christianity, a strong pulse of Jewish self-hatred (witness Mark and, principally, Paul of Tarsus). In the black light of the Shoah, one is very nearly tempted to define Christianity as the fruit of that self-hatred. The parallel with Marx's anti-Semitism is not fortuitous: Christianity and Marxism are the two major heresies out of messianic Judaism.

It may be that there are between Golgotha and Auschwitz symmetries unbearable to reasoned understanding. By refusing God's kenosis, His self-bestowal in the person of Jesus, Judaism judged spurious and contrary to reason the divinization of a man. At Auschwitz, the butchers reduced both their victims and themselves to a subhuman level. They "bestialized" humanity in the flesh of those who had denied the literal divinity of that same flesh in Jesus the Jew. Metaphors can kill. It would be idle to speculate on the future of Western ethics and metaphysics after these new Dark Ages. A certain economic rebound (always fragile), the explosive spread of crypto-religious and fundamentalist movements across the globe, are no proof of a renascence of spirit. The current collapse of Marxism, if it is that, is a profoundly ambiguous phenomenon. It is in Marxism that post-Christian Western messianic hopes were invested, that manifest expression was given to a hunger for justice on earth. Both the Sermon on the Mount and the Communist Manifesto proclaim their origin in Mosaic teachings and in Amos. The downfall of the Marxist ideal may bring with it the final enfeeblement of Christianity. Wrestlers succumb to mutual exhaustion. What is clear is that the venture of authentic humaneness in social, political man (*die Menschlichkeit im Menschen*) led to derision and defeat on the Cross and in the ash of the death camps. Neither the trope of Resurrection—so uncertain in Mark, so absent from Pascal's monition—nor the two-edged miracle of the rebirth of Israel can wipe out the terror at the heart of our history. Nor can pluralistic liberalism and legislated tolerance efface the killing of Socrates.

Where they are honest, where they do not deal with formalities or self-flattering exercises in academic analysis, attempts to face the insoluble end in images. It is pictures and stories that make endurable our losses. It is the telling of tales in the arts, in parables, where our two main threads draw together. In Caravaggio's *Denial of St. Peter*, which may have been that haunted master's last work, the head of the apostle is closely modeled on traditional busts of Socrates. In Baghdad, during the Gulf War, the cocks crowed in shrill song the night through. But the brilliant light over the city was not that of the sun. It is to this pass that we have been brought by two sets of texts out of antiquity.

To the one set, that of Scripture, there has attached, over almost two millennia, the designation of the "revealed." The corpus has been held to have originated more or less immediately in the word of God. Hermeneutically, this makes of Holy Writ what physics calls a "singularity." In respect of the biblical canon, normal laws of understanding and critical reception—criteria of logical causality, of empirical falsifiability, of historical or rational credibility—do not apply or apply only at the surface. The notion of normative conditions is itself suspended precisely in so far as it entails repeatability in other and comparable cases. Where the word of God and its revelation to man are concerned, no such investigative checks exist. The object offered to understanding is sui generis.

The Platonic set has, we have seen, also been acclaimed as divine. But such a claim has been put forward as a "hyper"-analogy. The author of the *Crito* or the *Phaedo* is not, in sobriety, considered a god. Where the concept of 'inspiration' is invoked, of philosophic and stylistic powers beyond the ordinary, this invocation, as in the references made to the Muses by poets, is a figure of discourse and explanatory fiction. The hermeneutic, the art of understanding brought to bear on a Platonic dialogue is, though perhaps in exalted measure, of the kind brought to bear on any semantic artifact produced by natural means and mortal hands. The cock destined for Asclepios is not "miraculous" in his crowing as is that chosen by Christ to attend on Simon Peter's denial. When the guests go "into the night" during the *Symposium*, this simple phrase may be identical with that which marks Judas's exit during the Last Supper narrative in St. John, but the status of transcendentally underwritten verity that tradition has assigned to the one does not apply to the other. Can responsible reading, today, make any sense of the difference, of the "surplus value" (I borrow and distort the Marxist term) said to be yielded by the words and sentences in Scripture beyond any to be harvested from the parallel or even identical components of language in a Platonic dialogue?

In both cases, which is simply to say for the sum of "sacred" and of secular texts in our civilization, the same instrumentalities of access are, certainly since Spinoza and the nineteenth-century "Higher Critics," in play. They are those of epigraphy, lexicography, comparative grammar, rhetorical and structural analysis, philological and historical verification. In both instances, the hermeneutic act is one of rational linguistics in the fullest sense of the term. Text-criticism, again in a comprehensive sense, is the sole approach available to the educated, to the rational recipient. Where, then, lies the difference? At present, any ascription of singularity in regard to "revealed speech and speech-acts"—for example, the narration and narratology of "miracles"—is, in the ordinary sense, scandalous. It is, literally, an "en-normity" outside reason. Today the proposition that certain ancient writings, formally (lexically, syntactically, structurally) homologous with any other body of texts, with any other communicative sequence, are to be set apart because they possess an authority, an immediacy of generation wholly singular to themselves, is, on any intelligible ground of which I am aware, unsustainable. It is an empowering fable, a myth of myths.

What could make such a claim verifiable? It might be argued that the pressure of the moral and "credential" imperatives in Scripture is of so unique a kind as to entail a realization in personal action, a transformation in the listener's or reader's existence. But such is the effect of much serious philosophy, literature, and art. As the archaic torso of Apollo in Rilke's sonnet proclaims, all great art bids us "change our lives." It has been propounded that the "word of God" exhibits an axiomatic, predictive force such as demarcates a mathematical or mathematical-physical system of laws from natural language. Plainly, this is not so. The long history of the preaching and interpretation of the Old and the New Testament has been that of an incessant deferral from the eschatological, of a postponement, via allegory and metaphor, of any material fulfillment. Might archaeology unearth, at some future date, evidence to demonstrate the process of supernatural origination in "revealed" texts, a process substantively other than that implied by allusion to the Muses, to poetic trance (as in Plato's *Phaedrus*), or to individual poetic genius? A moment's thought suggests that the mere notion of any such discovery of new "evidence" is an absurdity.

This absurdity is immune to the dogmatic alarms and linguistic obscurantism or innocence of all literalist and fundamentalist positions. It may well be that these positions are, numerically, again in the ascendant. It seems likely that human reason, undermined by political barbarism and intractable social dilemmas, will again seek refuge in intolerant fears. The closed minds, the hatreds of atavistic orthodoxies are on the march. But these cannot restore to intelligibility the dogmas of textual revelation. Subtler moves are possible. Vico, when adverting to Homer, Heidegger, when explicating the pre-Socratics, suggest that we do find in such texts vestiges of a phase in the condition of language and of exceptional sensibilities, in which signifier and signified, word and world, semantic marker and *Logos*, were concordant as they have not been since. This semiotic of the prelapsarian derives, fairly obviously, from the conceit of Adamic speech in Eden, of a lost Arcadia of linguistic equivalence with truth, as it haunts Western theories of meaning from Plato's *Cratylus* to Walter Benjamin. There was a time, so goes the argument, when the discourse of certain men and women was immediate and transparent to unambiguous sense, to truths and perceptions whose source was that of a fused social collectivity (Vico), of the Being of being (Heidegger), or of the proximate presence of God. Biblical texts would retain, or retain in considerable part, this Ur-permeability. An irreducible, although often enigmatic, core of significant "otherness," of transcendent reinsurance, inhabits the lexicon and grammar of the Torah and Gospels. In Judaism, the corollary is that of the cessation of direct linguistic exchanges with God after Elijah. In Islam, it is the hypothesis of a theology and philosophy born of a time of prophecy and of a theology and philosophy constructed thereafter. One recalls Meister Eckhardt's tremendous trope in his commentary *In Exodum* according to which Adamic speech, the "Hebrew of God," is itself "sent into exile" after the refusal of God to explain Himself to Moses out of the Burning Bush.

Intuitively, these paradigms of a semantic "break," of a rupture between a primal, authentically "divinized" mode of language and a subsequent, secular tenor, are attractive. They would account not only for biblical revelation, but also, by analogy, for the visionary splendors and lastingness of philosophic and poetic utterance in the "classics" (a splendor which many have felt to be tenaciously unrecapturable). In fact, there is no shred of evidence for them. On the biological timescale, the evolution of speech in our species represents no more than the blink of an eye. No trace subsists of any fall from linguistic grace, of any closure of discourse or of hearing to ontological originality and the revealed. We are exactly the same "language-animal" named by Greek anthropology. The Torah passage, the saying by Anaximander, the Homeric verse, does not evidence any mode of textuality prior to that of our own resources and hermeneutically nearer to dawn. Thus, if there is "revelation," it must lie in the eye and ear of the beholder. It is in the postulate and a priori of faith that he or she brings to the reception of the canonic. The 'revealed' is the fruit of the investment of credence, of mimetic resolve (rite, liturgy) made by the individual within the larger community of the faithful. It can, intelligibly, be nothing more. It is perfectly comparable with the investment, often determinant of life and death, made, say, by the communist in certain Marxist-Leninist source texts or by the Freudian in the sybilline books of the begetter. Strictly considered, the "holy" script is revealed to itself by its reader and exegete within the house of shared beliefs. Modern epistemology provides some access to this situation. The "language games" of the sacred may well be more widely sovereign, more poignant and unsettling, than any others played (i.e., spoken and written) by men. But they remain language-games whose only rules and validation must be internal. They cannot be demonstrated "from outside"; they have no self-evident proof. I take this to be the import, profound and far-reaching, of Wittgenstein's note in the *Philosophical Investigations* (I, 373): "Theology as grammar." Any reading of the cock of St. Peter as inserted in an ontologically different context from that of the sacrifice to Asclepios, is, in Kierkegaardian terminology, a leap into the light.

This leap may entail fundamentalist hermeneutic. It need not do so. Personally, I find scriptural literalism or any peremptory attribution to God of "speech acts," such as we know and use them, to be unacceptable, be they rabbinic, Muslim, or Evangelical (the Roman Catholic handling of biblical texts has long been of a wary sophistication). Such attribution only offends human reason and historical evidence—so much in the Old Testament burns with tribal folly. Literalism evades the paramount obligation of the individual.

Notes   For Ruth and Myles Burneat.

4

ELEONORE STUMP

Second-Person Accounts and the Problem of Evil

First-Person and Third-Person Accounts

It has become customary in philosophy to distinguish between what is often called a third-person point of view and a first-person point of view. The difference is hard to define precisely but easy to illustrate; it is perhaps most notable in philosophy of mind.[1] When, from my first-person point of view, I observe the mind I know best, my own, I am aware of beliefs, doubts, questions, desires, inclinations, willings, and things of this sort. But if a neurologist were to examine me, what he would perceive from his third-person point of view is something very different. He would observe synapses, neurochemicals and their receptors, neurons, clumps of nuclei and bands of fibers, topological maps, and things of this sort. He would not see beliefs and desires. None of the things he finds from his third-person point of view are observable to me from my first-person point of view when I introspect; and what I find from my first-person point of view, beliefs and desires and the rest, is not apparent to the neurologist from his third-person point of view.

Is there any alternative, however, to accepting either the first-person or the third-person point of view if there is a split between the two? In a recent lecture, Avishai Margalit suggested that we should try bridging this gap by means of what Margalit called "a second-person account." I am not sure what Margalit himself had in mind; but I want to consider his suggestion carefully because, whether or not it is a panacea for this problem in all areas of philosophy, I think there is something to be said for Margalit's suggestion with regard to certain issues in philosophy of religion.

Second-Person Experience

To make use of Margalit's suggestion, we first have to understand it. What is a second-person account, and how is it to be distinguished from its first-person and third-person analogues? Put very roughly, a first-person account is a report of something from the point of view of *my* experience, a first-person experience. So it seems that a second-person account must be some kind of report of an experience suitably characterized as second-person, as from a second-person point of view.

It is clear that a second-person experience is different from a first-person experience. In a first-person experience, I am directly and immediately consciously aware of a person as a person, but that person is only myself. A second-person experience is also different from the sort of experience a neurologist has of his subject. It is possible for the neurologist to function as a neurologist when he has only a brain of some dead person in front of him. Or, even if his subject is living and conscious as well, the neurologist can practice neurology just by interacting with some part of that subject, recording electrical potentials from the skull, for example. A neurologist can therefore do his work without being conscious of his subject as a person. There are, of course, cases where it seems as if the neurologist is conscious of his subject as a person. For example, there are cases where it is crucial for the neurologist to talk to his subject in order for him to carry out his neurological work, as when the neurologist is trying to determine whether stimulation of a particular area of the brain affects language function. In such cases, I am inclined to say that the neurologist uses a second-person experience of his patient in order to get information relevant to the third-person neurological account he is trying to construct. So a second-person experience is different in character from a first-person or a third-person experience because it is necessary for a second-person experience, as it isn't for a first- or third-person experience, that you interact consciously and directly with another person who is conscious and present to you as a person, in one way or another.

Second-Person Accounts

But what is an account of such a second-person experience? Why think it differs from either a first-person or third-person account? If everything knowable in a second-person experience could be expressed in expository descriptions[2] of oneself or of the others with whom one interacts, then no doubt a second-person experience could be captured by first-person and third-person accounts, and there would be no room for anything that could be considered a second-person account. In fact, however, there are some things we know in second-person experiences which are difficult or impossible to put in expository form at all.[3]

What could that possibly be?, a skeptical objector may ask. But, of course, if I give an answer to the skeptic's question, I will have an incoherent position: in answering the question, I will be presenting in expository prose what I said could not be presented that way. So is there another way of responding to the skeptical objector and showing that we learn something in a second-person experience that we can't express expositorily?

One way to answer the skeptic is by doing a thought experiment. Imagine someone, say, Mary, who from birth has been isolated by a mad scientist from contact with any other persons but who has had access to any and all information about the world, as long as that information is only in the form of third-person accounts.[4] So, for example, Mary has available to her the best science texts for any of the sciences, from physics to sociology. She knows that there are other people in the world, and (*mirabile dictu*) she knows all that science can teach her about them. But she has never had any personal interactions of an unmediated and direct sort with another person. She has read descriptions of human faces, for example, but she has never been face-to-face with another conscious person. She has read books that describe the process of human communication, including the role of melody in speech and body language; but she has never had a conversation of any sort with anyone, and she has never participated in any way, even as a bystander, in anyone else's real or imagined conversation. In short, Mary has been kept from anything that could count as a second-person experience. And then suppose that Mary is finally rescued from her imprisonment and united for the first time with her mother who loves her deeply.

When Mary is first united with her mother, it seems indisputable that Mary will know things she did not know before, even if she knew everything about her mother that could be made available to her in expository prose, including her mother's psychological states.[5] To begin with, although Mary knows her mother loves her before she meets her, when she is united with her mother, Mary will learn what it is like to be loved. And this will be new for her, even if in her isolated state she had as complete a scientific description as possible of what a human being feels like when she senses that she is loved by someone else. Furthermore, it is clear that this is only the beginning. She will also know what it is like to be touched by someone else, to be surprised by someone else, to ascertain someone else's mood, to detect affect in the melody of someone else's voice, to match thought for thought in conversation, and so on. These will be things she learns, even if before she had access to excellent books on human psychology and communication. In her first direct and immediate experience with another human being, Mary's mind is opened to all that we learn and experience in face-to-face contact, the complex give-and-take of interpersonal interactions. Mary will be surprised by the nature of a second-person experience, no matter how good her science textbooks have been or how rich her isolated introspective experience may have been. The surprise makes two things clear: first, that she is learning something she didn't know before the personal interaction, and, second, that it isn't possible to teach her by means of the expository prose (of the sort in the science books she has) what she comes to learn through personal interaction.

This thought experiment thus shows that there are things we come to know from our encounters with other people and that these things are difficult or impossible to describe from a third-person or a first-person point of view, because they are difficult or impossible to formulate in expository terms at all.[6]

So far I have argued that second-person experiences can't be reduced to first-person or third-person experiences without remainder; but I began this part of the discussion by asking what a second-person account might be, and my conclusion here might seem equivalent to the claim that a second-person account is impossible. If what we learn in second-person experiences is difficult or impossible to express in expository prose, how can any account of it be given at all?

In one sense, this point is right. There is no way to give an adequate expository account of a second-person experience. But it doesn't follow that no account of it is possible at all. While we cannot express the distinctive knowledge we gain in such an experience expositorily, we can do something to re-present the experience itself in such a way that we can share it with others who were not part of it.[7] This is generally what we do when we tell a story.[8] A story takes a real or imagined second-person experience and makes it available to a wider audience to share.[9] It does so by making it possible, to one degree or another, for a reader or listener to simulate what it would have been like for her if she had been a bystander in the second-person experience represented in the story.[10] That is, a story gives its reader some of what she would have had if she had had unmediated personal interaction with the characters in the story while they were conscious and interacting with each other, without actually making her part of the story itself, without her having to imagine or simulate the characters' having personal interaction with her. The re-presenting of a second-person experience in a story thus constitutes a second-person account. It is a report of a second-person experience that doesn't lose (at least doesn't lose entirely) the distinctively second-person character of the experience.

Some forms of literature that don't count as stories in any medium can also sometimes qualify as a second-person account. So, for example, some poems serve the same function as stories in portraying for us the interactions of persons;[11] and even some poems which have very few features of stories may still be successful in re-creating for us an image of one person's relations to others. So, for example, as I will discuss shortly, the poems which are God's speeches to Job present for the reader a picture of God's relations to his creatures, and the picture is vivid and lively enough to make it at least arguable that the poems are second-person accounts, too. But the clearest examples of second-person accounts are stories (in one medium or another) involving more than one person.

Whether second-person accounts are useful in bridging the gap between first-person and third-person accounts, as Margalit thinks they will be, depends in my view on the nature of the particular gap. I have no confidence that second-person accounts will be a universal remedy,[12] but I do think that they have a special place in some areas of philosophy, including philosophy of religion. The major monotheisms take God to be a person, with a mind and a will, and it matters to many issues in philosophy of religion, perhaps especially to the problem of evil, that God is taken to be a person who has personal relations with created persons. Insofar as these personal relations make a difference to such issues as the problem of evil, narratives about God and his relations to human beings have a role to play in our philosophical and theological thinking about such issues. And, of course, it is noteworthy that the sacred texts of all three major monotheisms include not only divine laws and commands, but also narratives about God and human persons.

I think that narratives representing second-person experiences that involve God's interactions with human persons are helpful in thinking about the problem of evil. Believers typically have available to them two main routes of accessing from a second-person point of view God's interactions with people. One comes from their own religious experience, which is taken by believers to be some sort of second-person experience of God. The other is the second-person accounts of God and human persons in biblical narratives. Insofar as personal interactions make a difference to such issues as the problem of evil, stories about God and his relations to human beings of the sort found in biblical narratives have a role to play in philosophical and theological thinking about such issues.

The classic biblical text having to do with the problem of evil is, of course, the Book of Job; and with this much explanation of the role of stories in philosophy of religion, I want now to turn to the Book of Job.

The Anchor Bible Interpretation of the Book of Job

The Book of Job has a complicated form. The heart of the book is a set of dialogues, but they are framed by a story about what God does both to Job and in interactions with others that crucially affect Job and cause him great suffering. The dialogues themselves consist in a heated debate about Job's suffering and God's role in it, so that the dialogues are a commentary on the story that frames them. But part of the dialogues is itself a conversation between God and Job, and so this part of the dialogues furthers the framing story because it consists in interaction between God and Job. In addition, in his part of this conversation, God re-presents for Job God's personal relations with his creatures. The divine speeches to Job consist in vivid descriptions of God's interactions with the nonhuman parts of his creation.

Consequently, there is an intricate set of nested second-person accounts in the Book of Job. The description of God's personal relations with the nonhuman parts of his creation is contained within an account of God's conversation with Job, which is part of the dialogues commenting on God's relations with Job, which are themselves the subject of the text framing the dialogues. All of this taken together constitutes the story of God and Job.

And yet the Book of Job is commonly treated as if it were little more than a philosophy treatise on the problem of evil. The details and intricacies of the narrative and its second-person context are neglected as unimportant or dismissed as uninteresting additions to the philosophically important debate in the dialogues. Furthermore, the debate in the dialogues is treated as an unsatisfactory philosophical discussion because it is taken to break off without a decisive conclusion regarding the problem of evil. The one thing Job wants, as he says over and over, is for God to explain to him why he suffers; and, on the common reading of Job, that is the one thing Job never gets from God.

The Anchor Bible commentary on Job is a good example of this sort of interpretation of Job, and I can show what I want to say about the Book of Job more easily by taking the Anchor Bible as my foil.[13] Contrary to the common interpretation, I think that Job does get what he wants in this story, namely, an explanation of why he suffers. Consequently, I also think that the Book of Job is helpful for thinking about *solutions* to the problem of evil, but only if it is read with careful attention to its character as a second-person account.

The Anchor Bible, on the other hand, supposes that the story of Job gives us no help with the problem of evil. The Anchor Bible commentator says:

It has been generally assumed that the purpose of the book [of Job] is to give an answer to the issue with which it deals, the problem of divine justice or theodicy. This question is raised inevitably by any and every instance of seemingly unmerited or purposeless suffering, and especially the suffering of a righteous man. Job's case . . . poses the problem in the most striking possible way. A man of exemplary rectitude and piety is suddenly overwhelmed with disasters and loathsome disease. How can such a situation be reconciled with divine justice and benevolent providence? It must be admitted first and last that the Book of Job fails to give a clear and definitive answer to this question.[14]

The Anchor Bible quite rightly sees Job's reaction to his suffering as passionately defiant. The commentator says, "Job bluntly calls into question divine justice and providence";[15] his "bitter complaints and charges of injustice against God shock his pious friends who doggedly defend divine justice."[16] Job, on the other hand, "vehemently denies that he has sinned, at least not seriously enough to merit such misery as has been inflicted on him. Justice, he argues, often appears abortive in the world and for this God must be held responsible. Hence, Job infers that God has no concern for justice or for human feelings. ". . . [Job] wishes to argue his case with God, but he cannot find God nor force him to grant a fair hearing."[17]

On the Anchor Bible reading of the story Job recognizes God's power,[18] but in a series of vehement protests against God he calls in question God's goodness. Here, at any rate, I think the Anchor Bible has it right. Job's own passionate insistence on moral goodness in the governance of the world underlies his violent protests against God and his demands that God be called to account. Job's friends are shocked at what they take to be his blasphemy. They repeatedly point out to Job the contrast between Job's limitedness, on the one hand, and God's power and knowledge, on the other.[19] "God's greatness is beyond man's comprehension . . ." the comforters say, and so, in their view, Job ought to appeal to God for mercy and forgiveness in order to be restored to God's favor.[20] But Job rejects the comforters' attitude with scorn. Job readily grants that God has power. What is at issue for Job is God's goodness. According to the Anchor Bible commentator, "[Job] charges God with vicious and unprovoked assaults. . . . He cries out for vindication. . . . God has afflicted him unjustly."[21] I agree entirely with the Anchor Bible on *this* score: Job will not submit to a God who is not good, no matter how powerful he is.

Because Job makes such a powerful indictment of God, the Anchor Bible maintains that God's answer to Job, which comes in God's speeches near the end of the book, is "something of a surprise and . . . a disappointment. The issue, as Job had posed it, is completely ignored. No explanation or excuse is offered for Job's suffering. . . . Job had already expressed his awe and wonder at God's power. . . . He had questioned not divine omnipotence but [divine] justice and mercy. The complete evasion of the issue as Job had posed it must be the poet's oblique way of admitting that there is no satisfactory answer available to man."[22] The Anchor Bible commentator says, "The fundamental question [about suffering], If not for sin, why then?, is completely ignored. It is quite understandable that readers . . . are left with a feeling of chagrin at the seemingly magnificent irrelevance of much of the content of the divine speeches."[23] What Job called into question with so much passion and rebellion was God's goodness. But, on the interpretation of the Anchor Bible, the only attribute of God's on display in God's speeches to Job is God's power.[24]

So the picture the Anchor Bible paints is this. Job, an innocent man, suffers horribly at God's hands. In his suffering, Job acknowledges God's great power, but he complains bitterly about God's apparent lack of goodness. When God finally appears on the scene to answer Job's charge, however, all God talks to Job about is God's power. So, as the Anchor Bible reads the story, God simply fails to address Job's charge—and if that is right, then this part of the story certainly is both surprising and disappointing, as the Anchor Bible commentator says.

A Puzzle for the Anchor Bible Interpretation

But I myself think that there is something even more surprising and puzzling about the story as the Anchor Bible interprets it, and it is something the Anchor Bible commentator fails to comment on at all. What does Job do in the face of the disappointing high-handed description of God's power that he gets in God's speeches to him? On the view of the Anchor Bible, Job "answers with humble acknowledgment of God's omnipotence and his own ignorance";[25] in the face of God's majestic declaration of his divine power, "Job repents and recants."[26] So on the Anchor Bible interpretation, Job not only takes back what he has been saying, but he also submits to God with a good deal of humility.

But isn't this a surprising response to find on Job's part? It seems to me so surprising as to call in question the fundamental conclusions of the Anchor Bible interpretation. Is it really credible that after all Job's passionate focus on goodness, after all his defiance of the power of God, he simply collapses into a heap of humility when the almighty ruler of the universe comes to talk to him and Job has impressed on him how really powerful God is? Are we to suppose that Job was a pompous windbag, willing to complain about the boss of the universe behind his back but utterly unable to stand up to him to his face? I don't see how anyone could read Job in this way. On this score, the Anchor Bible interpretation of the text seems to me thoroughly implausible.

Furthermore, the Anchor Bible interpretation can't account for the intensity with which Job repudiates his earlier accusations against God. After God's first speech, Job says (4:32), "Behold, I am vile";[27] and after God's second speech, Job says, "I recant and repent in dust and ashes" (42:6). If the divine speeches have as their only function reiterating the power of God, which Job has already acknowledged when he was alienated from God and insisting on an explanation of his suffering, why do God's speeches have this effect on Job? Why do they produce so powerful a repentance of his earlier attitude toward God? He could, after all, submit to God with suitable deference without going so far.

The Anchor Bible interpretation thus gives us a serious incongruity in the character of Job. In the speeches to his friends, he is heedless of everything except goodness, and he is willing to confront even the power of God to get it. But in his response to God's speeches, on the Anchor Bible interpretation, Job just cringes in front of power. Now we can, of course, always chalk up an incongruity of this sort to the artistic incompetence of the author or editor of the narrative, though in this case it would be a fairly serious and dramatic incompetence. Even if the author or editor of the book wanted Job to be submissive to God at the end of the book, there are ways to write the story more plausibly than simply to have the rebel turn at once into a lackey in the face of God's assertion of his power. Furthermore, impugning the competence of an author ought to be an interpretative strategy of last resort, to be employed when other attempts at explanation have failed. In this case, it is also a particularly lame strategy, because of the magnificent artistry that is readily recognizable in the rest of the book.

An Alternative Interpretation of the Divine Speeches

I am inclined to think that the problem in the Anchor Bible interpretation arises because the Anchor Bible commentator is oblivious to the fact that the divine speeches both are set in the context of second-person relations, in the story they are part of, and themselves constitute a second-person account, in their content.

Take, first of all, the content of the speeches. The Anchor Bible summarizes the divine speeches this way:

> Who is Job to speak out of ignorance? [God says, addressing Job.] What does [Job] know of the founding of the earth, the subjugation of the violent sea, the dawn of day, the depths of the infernal regions, the expanse of the earth, the abodes of light and darkness, the treasure houses of the snow and ice, the ordering of the constellations and the rains . . . ? Can Job provide food for the lion and the raven? Does he know the birth season of the wild goats, the habits of the wild ass? . . . Yahweh speaks to Job out of the storm and challenges him to show that he has divine powers.[28]

There is no question that the Anchor Bible commentator is right in thinking that these speeches of God describe God's power; God's power and knowledge are undoubtedly a central theme in the divine speeches. But the commentator seems to me to miss an equally important feature of the speeches that is crucial for an adequate interpretation of Job's response to them.

Consider, for example, the beginning of God's first speech, which the Anchor Bible characterizes as describing the power of God in the founding of the earth. That description is correct as far as it goes, but it is seriously incomplete. Here is what God says to Job:

> Where were you when I founded the earth? Tell me, if you know so much. Who drafted its dimensions? Surely you know? Who stretched the line over it? On what are its sockets sunk, who laid its cornerstone, while the morning stars sang together, and all the sons of God rejoiced?[29] (38:4–7)

As the Anchor Bible correctly maintains, these lines represent God as having the immense power to create the earth. But they also show God's role in a community that participates in God's creating by watching what he does and rejoicing in it. Furthermore, this community is not passive. It responds to what it sees God doing, and the response is communal, too: the morning stars sing together. When God creates the earth, then, he does not create alone. He shares his creating with a community of his creatures who rejoice together at his creating and sing, and clearly part of the point of the sharing is precisely to bring this joy to this community. Finally, it is important not to miss the parental imagery. The group that rejoices is the group of God's sons. From the beginning of creation, then, and from the start of the divine speeches God is portrayed as a parent. So what we see here in this part of the first divine speech is not just the metaphysical attributes of power and knowledge necessary for God's creation of the earth. We also see God as a person, in personal and parental relationships with his creatures, sharing what he has created with them and making them glad by doing so.

The Anchor Bible characterizes the next part of this divine speech as a description of God's subjugation of the sea. Now what God says in the part of the speech about the sea is this:

> Who shut the sea within doors, when it came gushing from the womb, when I made the cloud its garment, dark mist its swaddling bands, when I put bounds upon it, set up bars and doors, saying, "Thus far come, but no more. Here your wild waves halt?" (38:8–11)

It is important not to be oblivious to the second-person account in these lines. In the first place, the imagery here depicts maternal interactions between God and the sea. The sea is created by coming forth from a womb, and God deals with the sea as a mother deals with her child: he wraps it in swaddling bands; he clothes it with a garment. The description of the creation of the sea is thus couched in the sort of language we would ordinarily use to tell the story of a mother and her new baby.

Furthermore, the relations between God and the sea are described as personal relations.[30] The Anchor Bible characterizes these lines as a description of God's subjugating the sea; but it is noteworthy that God controls the sea by *talking* to it. In fact, it's hard to see these lines as a description of a *subjugation*. God does not simply bend the sea to his will. He doesn't just wield his great power to decree what the nature and attributes of a sea must be. Almighty God could do so with an act of will alone, without making any utterances. Or if he wanted to determine what the sea did by an utterance, he could make an impersonal statement, addressed to no one in particular, of this sort: "I decree that the sea will extend from here to there, but it will not extend any further." Instead, what we get in the speech is a description of a personal interaction between God and the sea. God addresses the sea directly, and he addresses it as if the sea were a rambunctious and exuberant child of his, but nonetheless a child who can hear him, understand him, and respond to him. God brings the sea into conformity to his will by talking to the sea itself and explaining to it what it can and cannot do.

The remainder of God's speech describing the inanimate parts of his creation continues in the same way. In this part of his speech, God portrays inanimate created things as if they were children of his with whom he has a personal relationship and for whom he has a parental concern. Furthermore, he not only describes himself as talking to inanimate creatures, as he does in the section on the sea, but he also describes these inanimate creatures as responding by talking to him. "Did you ever command a morning?" he asks Job (38:12), and a little later he says, "Where is the way to light's dwelling, darkness, where [is] its abode, that you may guide it to its bourne, [and] show it the way to go home? . . . Who cleft a channel for the downpour, [or] a path for the thundershower, to bring rain on no-man's land, [on] the wilderness with no man in it, to sate the desolate desert, [and] make the thirsty land sprout verdure?" (38:19–20, 25–27); "Can you send lightning scurrying, to say to you, 'Here we are'?" (38:35).

Darkness and light have dwelling places, and God guides them there; even darkness and light get to their proper place in the world because God shows them the way home. God talks to the morning; and when he sends the lightning where it should go, the lightning talks to him.

These parts of the divine speeches constitute a second-person account. They are not a story, but they are storylike. They convey in the vivid sort of way a story would a picture, an impression, of God's entering into personal relations with all parts of his creation and of his dealing with his creatures in maternal ways. That impression is only strengthened in the next part of the speeches which constitutes a second-person account of God's dealings with animals.

Here what God tells Job shows not only God's power over the animals and his knowledge of their nature and ways, as the Anchor Bible holds, but also his great care for them. He hunts the prey for the lions, makes a home for the wild donkeys, and gives the hawks the wisdom necessary for flight. Even in the case of the ostrich, who is portrayed as an inept and foolish mother, deprived of wisdom by God, there is a loving note in the description; and the implication is that if the ostrich's eggs and children survive, it is because God does the mother's job for the ostrich mother. She forgets, God says to Job, that the eggs she leaves in the sand are easily crushed and are vulnerable to animals that pass by. There is a maternal note in the complaint that the ostrich *forgets* who but God told her, or told her and reminded her, of what she is forgetting, and who but God preserves the eggs that the mother ostrich so forgetfully leaves vulnerable (39:14–15).

Furthermore, the animals are portrayed as responding to God's care by relating to him personally. For example, the raven's young don't just cry when they are hungry; they cry to God (38:41). Not only young and helpless animals but also powerful, fully grown animals are described as having an intimate personal relation to God. "Will the buffalo deign to serve you?" God asks Job. "Will he stay beside your crib? Can you hold him in the furrow with rope? Will he harrow the valley after you? Can you rely on his great strength, can you leave your labor to him? Can you trust him to return and gather the grain of your threshing floor" (39: 9–11)? The implication of these questions is that even if a human being such as Job couldn't have the close and trusting relationship with this fierce animal implied by the mention of all these activities characteristic of domesticated animals, God can and does.

The second of God's speeches to Job has to do with two great animals, behemoth and leviathan. Some of the second speech is devoted to describing the strength of these beasts and the even more impressive power God has over them, including the power to capture or even to kill them. But there are also passages such as this: "Will [leviathan] make long pleas to you, cajole you with tender words? Will he make a covenant with you, will you take him as [an] eternal slave? [Will you] [p]lay with him as with a bird, leash him for your girls" (41:3–5)? For Job, the obvious answer to all these questions is "no." For God, on the other hand, the answer is clearly different. God has a close relationship with these great beasts, who not only talk to him with tender words but also cajole him, plead with him, play with him, and make covenants with him.

It is a mistake, then, to characterize God's speeches as demonstrating nothing but God's power over creation. The speeches certainly do show God's power; but, equally importantly, they show God having personal interactions with all his creatures. He relates to everything he has made on a face-to-face basis, as it were; and in these personal interactions, God deals maternally with his creatures, from the sea and rain to the raven and the donkey and even the monstrous behemoth and leviathan. He brings them out of the womb, swaddles, feeds, and guides them, and even plays with them. Most important, he talks to them; and somehow, in some sense or other, they talk to him in return. These speeches thus show God as more than powerful; they show him as personally and intimately involved with his creation; they portray him as having a mother's care toward all his creatures, even the inanimate ones.

Explanations for Suffering

The divine speeches don't make claims about God's relations to creation. If they did, they would be a third-person account laying out some general theological claims. Instead, they constitute a second-person account that lets us participate, to some limited extent, in the perception of God's relation to inanimate things, plants, and animals. The speeches begin with a reference to the morning stars singing together and the sons of God rejoicing as they watch God's dealings with his creation. To some minimal degree, the speeches invite us to see what they saw. The implication is that if we see it, we also will be inclined to rejoice. What Job wanted was an explanation of God's relations with him, and he does get it, but in the form of a second-person account. He had demanded goodness. What he gets is what caused the sons of God not just to find God good but to rejoice in him and in his relations to his creatures.

But what exactly is this? For the reasons I gave above, I don't think that this question can be answered, or at least not answered without remainder. The question is a request that what is presented as a second-person account be translated into a third-person account, and I argued above that this could not be done without losing what is most important about the second-person account. Nonetheless, I want to say one thing which in my view is suggested by the second-person account of the relations between creator and creatures in the divine speeches.

The divine speeches suggest that God's relationship to all his creatures is personal, intimate, and parental or even maternal. Now a good mother will sometimes allow the children she loves to suffer—but only in case the suffering benefits the child who experiences the suffering, and benefits him in some way that couldn't have been equally well achieved without the suffering. A good mother, for example, wouldn't cause suffering to an innocent child for the sole purpose of getting the dean of her college to learn a lesson. In the divine speeches, God is portrayed as giving the animals what they need because they need it—food for the baby birds who cry to him, prey for the young lions, help in mothering for the foolish ostrich. Nothing in the speeches suggests that God considers whether the hunger of the baby birds might be a good thing for the cats in their neighborhood. God doesn't think about whether their need and weakness might not be turned to good account for some other part of his creation, so that letting them stay hungry is justified by the good it produces elsewhere in the world. He just considers what will be good for them, and so he feeds them when they cry. And so there is not a claim but a suggestion, a picture, a portrayal that leads us to think God operates on the principle I attributed to good mothers. This claim is not equivalent to the justly ridiculed Leibnizian principle that this is the best of all possible worlds in which everything that happens happens for the best. Rather, this is a point about one necessary condition for good mothering, namely, that, other things being equal, the benefit which justifies a mother in allowing some suffering to an innocent child of hers has to go to the child. If she let her child suffer for someone else's sake or for some abstract general good, to that extent she wouldn't count as a good mother.

Nothing in God's speeches to Job specifically describes God's relations with human beings, of course, but there is certainly a ready inference—both for Job and for readers of the book—from the way God deals with the rest of his creation to the way in which he deals with human persons. If God deals maternally with even the inanimate parts of his creation, if he seeks to produce good even for infant ravens, then a fortiori in his dealings with human beings God will operate in the same way, allowing their suffering only in case he can turn it to some good available to them. If an innocent person suffers, then, it will be because a good God, a loving God involved face-to-face with his creatures, produces out of the suffering a good meant for that person that in the circumstances couldn't have been produced, or produced as well, without the suffering. The inference to this explanation about suffering is available to Job, as I said, but if I am right about second-person accounts, Job doesn't need to draw it, since in the second-person account of the divine speeches he has something epistemically stronger than this inference.

In addition, however, Job has another source of information about God's reasons for allowing him to suffer, and it is even more powerful than the second-person account in the divine speeches. It is the experience of God that he has while God is talking to him. The Anchor Bible, which doesn't see or doesn't accord much weight to the personal interactions described in God's speeches, also doesn't recognize the importance of the context in which the divine speeches are set. While God has been talking to Job, what is the relation between Job and God supposed to be? We don't have to speculate because Job explains it in his last lines to God. "I had heard of you by the hearing of the ear," Job says to God, "but now my own eye has seen you" (42:5). While God has been talking, Job has been seeing God. The communication between God and Job is thus face-to-face communication; in the course of the divine speeches, God has been somehow directly present to Job. The second-person account of the divine speeches to Job is thus set in the context of a second-person experience of God for Job.

When Job complained bitterly about the goodness of God, his charge wasn't just a metaphysical complaint raised for philosophical reasons. It was a personal complaint. Job's history before the start of his suffering is a history of trust in God and obedience to him, as Job makes clear in his speeches to the comforters. His protest against God in the dialogues thus at least includes a charge of betrayal of trust. But for this charge, a face-to-face encounter can make all the difference. To answer a mistaken charge of betrayal, a person who loves you can try to explain, or he can just face you and let you see *him*. If Job can see the face of God who loves his creatures as a mother loves her children, then he will see, or feel in some other way, that he is encompassed by that love also. So in the sight of God which Job has in his second-person experience of God in the course of the divine speeches to him, Job has another powerful response on God's part to Job's demand for an explanation. The sight of the face of a God whose mothering love is directed even toward rain and ravens is also an explanation of Job's suffering.

It is, of course, an explanation that is short on what we might think of as engineering or medical details. A child with aggressive leukemia who is suffering the pains of a bone marrow transplant may want to know from his mother why she doesn't help him and stop his suffering when she so clearly could, just by taking him out of the hospital. She could respond to that demand for an explanation with the details about the benefits of the transplant, a third-person, quasi-engineering medical account about the reconstruction of healthy bone marrow. She might share that medical account with her son in this way: "Well, see, you have a cancer which affects the blood, and the major blood products are produced by stem cells in the bone marrow. So what we are doing is removing some of your stem cells; the lab hunts through those till it finds some that aren't diseased, and it clones them, for eventual reinfusion. Then we inject you with a series of cytotoxic drugs which destroy the diseased stem cells in your bone marrow. Those drugs work because they target fast-growing cells. The cancer cells in your bone marrow are fast-growing; but so are your hair cells, the cells in the mucus membranes which line your mouth, your esophagus, and your gut. The cytotoxic drugs kill those, too. That's why you have sores in your mouth; that's why you're throwing up, and why you're constipated." And so on and on.

It might be that this is the right explanation for her son. But then again it might not be. There are circumstances in which third-person explanations of this sort are utterly inefficacious to comfort. That's why, for example, even after all the explanation needed to take away from you the impression you had that your friend had betrayed your trust, even when you do see for yourself that there was nothing hurtful there, the breach may not be healed for you until you make eye contact, clasp hands, get a hug, or in some other way make personal contact with your friend. The child undergoing a painful medical procedure may be more hurt by what he takes to be her abandonment of him, her apparent indifference to his pain and need, than by anything that is happening to his bones and mucus membranes. In that case, the best response to his need for an explanation—perhaps the only efficacious response—is to show him, with some second-person experience of her, that she loves him, that she would only let him suffer in order to bring about some serious good for him which she couldn't get for him in any easier way.

The explanation that Job gets is of this second-person kind. What exactly the suffering effects in him, the medical or engineering details, aren't part of the explanation the divine speeches provide. But that they provide an explanation, and just the right kind of explanation for Job, is shown by Job's response. I began by asking how we could explain Job's subsiding into humility and acquiescence after all his defiance of God and his insistence on justice, if God's speeches to Job contain nothing but an assertion of God's power. What a closer look at the speeches makes clear is that this question rests on a false view of the content of the divine speeches and an obliviousness to their context. If we see the speeches in the way I have argued for, a second-person account set in the context of a second-person experience, showing Job the love of God, then we can understand better why Job reacts to them as he does.

Suppose you had been sure that the person who should love you the best had betrayed you, had abused your trust and used your vulnerability to him to cause you pain. Suppose that you've given vent to your anger and sense of betrayal in vehement speeches to his friends or to anyone who will listen; suppose you've made these views known to him, too. And then two things happen. First, you are forcefully reminded, with a vivid second-person account, of the deeply loving character of your supposed betrayer and all the good he has done in the past. And, second, you see that powerful goodness and love directed toward you in his face. How would you feel? You might very well feel stricken, abashed, ashamed, and repentant—just the sort of emotions we find in Job. Job says, "Now my own eye has seen you," and he follows that line with this one: "So I recant and repent in dust and ashes" (42:6). Job wanted bare justice, but his face-to-face experience with God goes past justice to love.

Conclusion

Job does, then, have an explanation of his suffering; but it isn't of the sort that philosophers have been interested in when they considered theodicies, because it isn't a third-person account. A second-person experience can constitute a good explanation of a mistaken charge of betrayal for the person who has that experience, but it will be hard for him to use that experience to convince a third party, for just the reasons I gave when I was explaining why second-person accounts differ from third-person accounts. How Job knows what he comes to know in the story—that his suffering is at the hands of a good and loving God—is hard to explain to someone who wasn't part of the same second-person experience. The best that can be done, as I argued above, is to turn that experience into a second-person account, of the sort we have in the story of God's conversation with Job. But stories aren't arguments; they can't compel a certain view of things as arguments can. Furthermore, they are much more likely to be persuasive to those who have had some experience of their own of the sort being described in the story. It is for that reason that people reveal themselves when they explain what novels they find moving.

Furthermore, what Job knows, that God loves him and didn't betray his trust, may not be what someone looking for a third-person account wants. It may be enough for the sick child, who has a shared history of loving relations with his mother, to know that she allows him to suffer only because she loves him. But an outsider who doesn't know the mother, who has no relation to her, may well want to know exactly what the connection between the suffering and the child's well-being is, before he is willing to grant that the mother is justified in allowing the child to suffer.

For both these reasons, the problem of evil presents itself differently to those within and those outside a religious community. Believers come to the problem of evil with what they take to be some sort of history of relations with the God they believe in. They can and they should draw on that history in reflections on suffering, in their own lives or in the lives of others. Furthermore, the second-person accounts of God, the stories about God in Scripture, will be read differently by believers, who have their own religious experiences to draw on as they read them, from the way in which they are read by nonbelievers, just as the second-person account in the divine speeches will strike Job differently from the way in which they strike an outsider.

Consequently, believers will not and need not think about the problem of evil in the same way nonbelievers do, and a believer's resolution of the problem may be successful, even if it isn't persuasive to nonbelievers. This is, in my view, one of the lessons of the Book of Job, which we learn when we are sensitive to the nested second-person accounts that make up much of the book. And it helps to explain why contemporary academic accounts of the book take the form we find in the Anchor Bible commentary, which sees the book as raising a charge of injustice against God that is never answered, while a committed believer such as Thomas Aquinas reads the same texts as constituting a good explanation of the way in which a loving Providence operates to govern the world.

Notes

1. In this chapter, I distinguish not only among first-person, second-person, and third-person points of view, but also among the corresponding experiences and accounts. I have no neat and precise definitions for any of these, but, put roughly, what I have in mind is this. A first-person experience is an experience I have with some degree or other of conscious awareness and which I could have by myself. A first-person point of view is my reflection on or observation of my (real or imagined) first-person experience considered as a first-person experience (as distinct, for example, from considering that experience as a neurologist or some other third person might consider it). And a first-person account is my account to someone else of my reflection on or observation of my (real or imagined) first-person experience qua first-person experience. So, my wanting a cup of coffee when I am in a normal cognitive and conative condition is a first-person experience; I want the coffee, and the desire is a conscious desire in me. My conscious, introspective reflection on or observation of that conscious desire is a first-person point of view. I can have a conscious state without a conscious reflection on it or observation of it, as I do when I drive to work, conscious of the state of the road but focused intently on the news on the radio, so that I don't attend to the conscious visual states that guide my driving. And my explaining my desire considered as a first-person experience to someone else is a first-person account. Something roughly similar

distinguishes experience, point of view, and account for the second- and third-person analogues.

2. For purposes of this chapter, I take "expository prose" to mean prose that does not constitute a story and that does not fall into some other genre of literature (such as certain sorts of poetry) that is storylike in its artistry.

3. I am not claiming that what makes second-person experiences different from first-person experiences is that only in second-person experiences is there something which can't be expressed in expository prose. In my view, part of what goes into at least some first-person experiences also can't be expressed expositorily, namely, what a conscious experience is like. My point here is rather that whatever is distinctive about a second-person experience is among the things that are not expressible expositorily.

4. I am here adapting an example from the literature in philosophy of mind which has been used to argue that qualia, the mental states one is in when one is conscious, can't be reduced to brain states. The example was originally introduced by Frank Jackson ("Epiphenomenal Qualia," *Philosophical Quarterly* 32 [1982], 127–136), who constructed a thought-experiment involving a neuroscientist Mary who knows everything there is to know about the brain but who has had no perceptual experience of color; although she knows the neurobiology of color perception, she will learn something new when she first perceives color, Jackson argued. However we adjudicate the dispute in the philosophy of mind about qualia, Jackson's thought-experiment seems to me also to show something he didn't construct it to show, namely, that certain first-person experiences are not expressible in expository prose. That is why Jackson's Mary doesn't know qualia, even though she has available to her a large scientific library. It isn't just that *neuroscience* books can't capture qualia, no expository books could. In my thought-experiment Mary comes to learn not the qualia associated with color perception but a particular sort of qualia or analogue to qualia that accompanies second-person experience.

5. Nicholas Wolterstorff has suggested to me in correspondence that if Mary had had the requisite sort of experience of personal interaction before her period of isolation, then it would have been possible to communicate to her in the expository prose of a third-person account what personal interaction with her mother would be like. On this view, the difficulty in communicating to Mary by a third-person account the nature of a second-person experience with her mother is just a function of Mary's innocence of second-person experiences. But I am inclined to think this diagnosis of Mary's difficulty is not correct. In ordinary circumstances involving persons socialized in the usual way, it remains true that when we meet a person for the first time, we learn something important we didn't know before, even if before the meeting we were given an excellent and detailed third-person account of that person.

6. In correspondence, Al Plantinga has suggested to me that I am here in fact explaining in expository prose what it is that Mary learns, namely, what it is like to be loved by her mother, and so on. But that some sort of description of what Mary learns is possible doesn't mean that we can explain it adequately with an expository account. Consider, for example, that while it is possible to describe the experience of seeing red to a person who has been blind from birth by saying that when a sighted person sees a red object, she knows what it is like to see red, this description isn't an adequate explanation in expository prose of what the sighted person knows in knowing what it is like to see red.

7. In this respect, a second-person experience differs from a first-person experience of the sort we have in perception. There is no way for me to convey to someone who has never seen colors what I know when I know what it is like to see red.

8. I am not here implying that the only function, or even the main function, of narra-

tives (in one medium or another) is to convey real or imagined second-person experiences. My claim is just that much less is lost of a second-person experience in a narrative account than in a third-person account, ceteris paribus.

9. Someone might suppose that any information that could be captured and conveyed by a story could also be conveyed by an expository account. I have no good argument against this claim, for the very reasons I have been urging, namely, that we can't give an expository description of what *else* is contained in a story; but I think the claim is false. Consider, for example, an excellent and current biography of Samuel Johnson, such as Robert DeMaria's *The Life of Samuel Johnson: A Critical Biography* (Oxford: Blackwell, 1993), and compare it to the pastiche of stories in Boswell's *Life of Johnson*, and you see the point. There is a great deal to be learned about Johnson from DeMaria's *The Life of Samuel Johnson*, but Boswell's stories give you the man as the biography can't.

10. On the role of simulation in audience reaction to fiction, see, for example, Kenneth Walton, "Spelunking, Simulation, and Slime: On Being Moved by Fiction," in *Emotion and the Arts*, ed. Mette Jhorte and Sue Laver (New York: Oxford University Press, 1997). On simulation theory in general, see, for example, Martin Davies and Tony Stone, *Mental Simulation* (Oxford: Blackwell, 1995).

11. And, of course, some poems, such as Homer's *Iliad* and *Odyssey* or Milton's *Paradise Lost*, are or at least include stories in an artistically complicated form.

Martha Nussbaum argues for the importance of narrative in philosophy in general but without giving much explanation of what narratives contribute that can't be provided by philosophy alone without narratives. See, for example, *The Fragility of Goodness. Luck and Ethics in Greek Tragedy and Philosophy* (Cambridge: Cambridge University Press, 1986, reprinted 1992), 45–47.

13. Marvin Pope, *Job*, The Anchor Bible (New York: Doubleday, 1965).

14. Ibid., lxxiii.

15. Ibid., xv.

16. Ibid., xxiii.

17. Ibid., lxxv.

18. Cf., e.g., lxxx.

19. Ibid., xvii-xxii.

20. Ibid., xviii.

21. Ibid., xix.

22. Ibid., lxxx.

23. Ibid., lxxxi.

24. Ibid., 291, note 3b; cf. also 318, note 9b.

25. Ibid., xxii.

26. Ibid., lxxx.

27. The Anchor Bible translates this line as "Lo, I am small"; the root meaning of the Hebrew word is to be contemptible or to be disgraced, so "vile" seems better than "small."

28. Ibid., xxii.

29. I have used the Anchor Bible translation throughout, except where noted, for the sake of fairness, since I am disputing its interpretation of the text. In this case, I have departed from the Anchor Bible translation at two points. The Anchor Bible commentator translates as "gods" a Hebrew phrase which it acknowledges to mean literally "sons of God." Since the Anchor Bible translation thus obscures just what I think is interesting about this phrase, I have translated it more literally. I have also translated as "rejoiced," what the Anchor Bible translator renders "exulted," but just because "exult" can carry an array of connotations, such as gloating, for example, that don't seem warranted by the Hebrew. Finally, the Anchor Bible

translator prints the text as if it were English poetry, in short broken lines beginning with words which are capitalized; but since there is no warrant in the Hebrew text for any such arrangement, I have simply omitted it.

30. These interactions don't count as personal, strictly speaking, on the interpretation of "personal interaction" that I gave above, because they are interactions between God and creatures that are not themselves persons. But insofar as these nonhuman creatures are portrayed in personal terms in the divine speeches, God's relations with them are also portrayed as personal interactions.

PART II

THE PLACE OF NARRATIVE

5

JAMES BILLINGTON

Social Transformation as Return of Story Tradition

There are, I take it, two premises underlying this discussion. One is that story rather than theory is the better way to understand reality as far as human beings are concerned; and the second is that the Judeo-Christian tradition is best understood as story rather than as theory. The astonishing developments in Russia in August 1991, which I was privileged to witness, illustrate, I believe, both of these propositions in a rich, interconnected way that I will try to describe.

The decisive historical event that ended Communism, the Soviet Union, and the Cold War was the unsuccessful putsch of August 19 and 20, 1991, and the sudden, successful resistance to it. If ever there was a victory of a story over a theory, it is the remarkable story of that remarkably minuscule resistance prevailing over the greatest intrusion of a theoretical construct into human life in modern times, the totalitarian Communist state. The inability of the Western socioscientific establishment to understand what happened then is illustrated by our continuing effort to describe it as a "revolution"[1]—even though all the key characteristics of a modern revolution were entirely absent from the events. Modern revolutions have been violent, highly political, secular, and led by intellectual elites with clear ideological blueprints. These events were strikingly nonviolent, largely uninspired by any political program, tinged with religious idealism, and the product of a spontaneous movement from below without any future blueprint at all. It is my contention that these events can be best understood as a legendary story with distinct Judeo-Christian dimensions.

Pasternak has suggested in *Doctor Zhivago* that the Russian revolution unfolded as a kind of ritual reenactment of Holy Week. George Steiner suggests at the end of his *Real Presences* that we "may all be living today in the Saturday between a good Friday and a perhaps better Sunday." Can it be that the most transforming political reality in our time follows more the pattern suggested by the novelist and the critic than the predictions of those whom society today subsidizes to divine events: historians, policy analysts, economic forecasters? Is it merely accidental, to begin with, that the sudden and altogether unexpected overthrow of Communism in Russia, perhaps the most stunning political event of the second half of the twentieth century, unfolded between two great feast days of the Christian East—precisely those that are least observed in and understood by the Christian West, the Feast of the Transfiguration and of the Assumption?

The doctrine of the Transfiguration was a major source of the deepening East-West separation in the troubled fourteenth century. The belief that there was a universal significance to Christ's appearance in a transfigured state before his disciples on Mount Tabor, even before his passion and final days, gave hope to the individual in his search for sanctity amid the social and imperial collapse of the Byzantine Empire. In the iconography of the Christian East, which developed at a time when verbal theology was prevailing in the West, Christ in his transfigured state is represented in pure white: a many-layered, rich white used only to represent the direct imposition of transcendence into human affairs. The icon suggested Christ's capacity to transfigure normal human limitations, to inspire directly holiness for the individual; the so-called *hesychast* movement specially inspired by this doctrine was responsible for the resurgence of monasticism in the late Byzantine world, which in turn became the main force of colonization for the rising Muscovite Empire on the northern Byzantine frontier.

The Russian putsch began on the Feast of the Transfiguration. The first Russian tanks rolled into Red Square precisely at the time the Patriarch of Moscow was, for the first time since the revolution, opening the doors (used for coronation addresses) at the Cathedral of the Assumption within the Kremlin after the liturgy to address a crowd about the possibilities of transfiguration. In the resistance that rapidly developed to this last great power play by the Leninist political machine, the color of white played a visually galvanizing role in the resistance. Moscow had always been the "white-stoned city" in ancient legends. Now it was the color of the site of the government of the Russian Republic, the White House, of Yeltsin's white hair, and of the shirt-sleeved crowd seen via a breakthrough of sun from the almost continuous rain during the period of doubt—all of this lent a magical and heroic aura to the resistance.

In the Orthodox iconography of the Transfiguration, the disciples fall away from the very brightness of the whiteness. They are dazzled by the intrusion of the "holy other" into ordinary life, the appearance of a new authority and model in the midst of their hitherto limited and mortal strivings. The resistance at the White House acquired something of that mythic heroic quality that emits from the sudden birth or intrusion of superhuman authority into ordinary human life. Yevtushenko, in his interview at the time, said he was suddenly living "as in a fairy tale" and used the image of falling in love to describe why he was attracted to and stood by Yeltsin at that first moment of resistance.

The resistance on the first day of the putsch, August 19, was very disjointed and involved relatively small groups of people around the White House. What was remarkable was the explosion of mythic and symbolic elements. First and foremost were the icons of St. Georges, in which the same pure white appears on the horse (an echo of the pre-Christian sun god). In the most famous of these icons, both the horse and the shield of St. Georges reflect the sun worship that preceded Christianity and added authority in the dark north to the bearer of victory over the dragons of evil. In addition to the icons of St. Georges, there was the tricolor lapel that became a tricolor flag.

Most fascinating of all was the way in which the major forms of the resistance were shaped not by anybody's theoretical program but by television images of earlier resistances to similar types of centralized Communist authority projecting sheer military power onto its own people. The image of Yeltsin stopping the tank was an amplified variation of the young man in Tiananmen Square stopping the tank, which became a kind of global icon of people resisting tyranny. The forming of a barricaded ring around the Parliament building was an almost exact echo of what had happened earlier in the year in Lithuania, defending against a committee on national salvation that tried to overthrow it. The continuing plans Gorbachev was making to restore order and authority in Russia were downgraded from a committee on "national salvation" to one on an "extraordinary situation." Moscow television under Gorbachev banned all depiction of the Lithuanian events. Yet, Russian television under Yeltsin had smuggled images of the Lithuanian conflict in belatedly, and pictures of it were in everyone's mind as a kind of iconic model of how people should behave once the committee on the extraordinary situation claimed power in Moscow. Without anyone's clear order, Moscow adopted the model that had previously been market-tested in Lithuania.

Three key elements in the resistance appeared on the first day. There was the appearance of a *hero*, a new *location for legitimacy,* and the *dispatch of messengers* to the people. All three of these are traditional themes of epic narrative, rather than programmatic prescriptions in anyone's military handbook. The image of the hero was galvanized popularly, not by anything Yeltsin said, but by the way he appeared and comported himself. In icon painting, the face and the hands are generally the only parts to appear in flesh color and to remain uncovered when metal casings are placed over them. The face and hands of Yeltsin—the confident smile and the hands uplifted in a confident fist atop the tank—were engraved in everyone's imagination. This picture was played back on CNN, transposed in xeroxed sketches, and talked about after work on that first day of the resistance. The image was made all the more powerful by means of the contrast with the televised press conference of the Committee on the Extraordinary Situation, whose nominal leader Yanev appeared with trembling hands reflecting his alcoholic condition and an uncertain shifting gaze that immediately made him seem (as one of my Russian friends put it at the time, watching this conference on television) "like one of the defendants at Nuremberg."

The new locus of legitimacy was of course, the White House, the home of Russia's first popularly elected president and its parliament. This suddenly became liberated space within a magic circle, giving spatial as well as historical reality to legend. Beginning at 3 P.M. on that first day, the decision was made to send messengers out to talk both with the surrounding troops that might attack and with the people of Moscow.

It is important to remember that the core resistance movement was totally insignificant and unreal by any normal standards. There were no more than 150 people with arms inside the White House, probably not many more than 10,000 outside on the first day. Only the hardcore opposition to Communist rule, based on deep moral commitment, had immediately rallied to the White House. It was now located all in one place and, from a technical point of view, could be easily destroyed. As one Communist official said to me at the time, "We have brought the infection to a head, all we need to do now is lance the boil." There was, moreover, the largest number of potential lancers probably ever assembled in one place in order to impose domestic tranquility inside a modern state. The largest army of all time in the largest empire of all time had concentrated its elite forces to a far greater degree than any of us realized at the time around Moscow, operating on a plan that had been very carefully worked up by the ministry of defense, interior forces, and the KGB, beginning the very day after Gorbachev had taken off for his summer vacation in the Crimea. Backed by the most powerful and long-lived political machine of the twentieth century, the Leninist Communist Party with its inner nomenklatura structure, the armed forces of the Soviet Union had drawn an iron ring around Moscow, and had at their disposal, unbeknown to the occupants of the White House, twenty-four subterranean entrance points (of which the defenders discovered only four, even after they were tipped off early in the game about such attack plans). There was every reason to believe that, having miscalculated that a mere show of force would suffice, a real attack on the second day would be rapid and successful. The junta believed an attack would take no more than twenty minutes, whether by airborne troops from above, subterranean troops from below, infiltrating troops from without, or rapidly striking with rockets, flame-throwers, or gas from a distance.

How then did the resistance prevail? How would a cynical, long-submissive people come alive? The answers may be as astonishing as the outcome. Mortal men may have come alive for a brief moment of time because a woman went to sleep in heaven for all time. The Feast of the Assumption in the Eastern rite is, in a way, a more mysterious miracle than that of the Resurrection. And yet, it has always represented the ultimate security policy for the Christian East. The Virgin has been the protector of Constantinople. When that "second Rome" fell and the great icon of the Vladimir Mother of God was borne through Kiev and Vladimir to Moscow, it enabled Moscow, the "third Rome," to resist a series of invasions from the East and occupations from the West. The Mother of God was seen in classic Russian Orthodoxy as the protectress of the white-stoned city of Moscow as well. Just after midnight on the second night (shortly after three young men were accidentally killed in a melee with tanks at some distance from the White House—the first and only bloodshed of the crisis), the Patriarch of Moscow broadcasted from the White House a prayer to the Virgin for the Feast of the Assumption, invoking Her protection on Moscow and anathematizing fraternal bloodshed. At almost exactly the same time, Father Gleb Yakunin (often a bitter opponent of the Patriarch) was talking on a megaphone to the excitable crowd gathered on the outer ring street at some distance from the White House, imploring the crowd in Christian terms not to retaliate with violence against the semiaccidental killing of the three young men.

How important those actions were in the overall drama of that night is open to dispute, but it is almost certain that there was never more praying done in Moscow since the revolution than on that night. Because the prayers were often from newly printed prayers focused on the Assumption, that Feast played a central role in the religious symbolism from which people from an almost entirely atheist formation were suddenly drawing during that dark, rainy, second night when a violent end was widely expected.

The transformation from Communism to new beginnings was, in a way, consecrated by two other liturgies in that same Cathedral of the Assumption, in the Kremlin: the first on August 26 commemorating the three young men who died and, at the same time, opening up the parliamentary session, and a second liturgy for the Feast of the Assumption itself on August 28.

Three groups were central to the messengers that were first sent out on the first day. These groups began to galvanize a more formidable resistance on the second day which in effect put enough human blood on the line that those who really did plan to attack the second day were deterred from doing so. The first group were the young priests (about a dozen) who conducted almost nonstop counseling, baptisms, improvised communion service, and hymn-sings. Particularly remarkable was the young delegate to the Moscow City Council and founder of the Russian Bible Society, Alexander Borisov, who distributed 2,000 New Testaments to the young men in the tanks with only one person refusing to accept one and who then returned to distribute the other remaining 2,000 to the resistance around the White House. Such activities led to a blurring of the distinction between the two groups. The movements of priests and others with icons of St. Georges, bibles, and halting prayers suggested that there was something common and unifying that both attackers and defenders might rally to.

The second group were the Afghan veterans, whose inner network just below the top surface of the Soviet command structure undercut the efforts of the top people to get their subordinates to mount an attack. Central to all this was the figure of Alexander Rutskoi, Yeltsin's vice president and a particular hero of the Afghan war. Little known is the fact that Rutskoi had two visions of the Virgin Mary before these events.

The first vision came in Afghanistan when he was about to commit suicide with a hand grenade rather than allow himself to be captured as an airman who had been shot down. A sudden vision of the Virgin convinced him not to take his own life, and a second vision had come to him just four days before the attempted putsch. He was in Novgorod with the Patriarch at the time when the oldest church in the Russian Republic, Santa Sophia in Novgorod, was being officially returned by the state to the church. When the sun came out on its newly illuminated golden dome, which of course symbolically represented the sun in the dark north, Rutskoi had a second vision of the Virgin, which seems to have given his leadership of the resistance added passion.[2]

The Patriarch too had been emboldened by this shared experience with Rutskoi, as well as by the experience of the Sunday before the putsch when he had presided over the reburial of the remains of the one great patriarch who had resisted Soviet authority unconditionally, Thikon, and whose remains were reburied in the monastery of Our Lady of the Don. Once again, the image of the protective Lady of the Don, who had turned back the Mongol horde, was seen as active in turning back the atheistic horde that had overtaken Russia.

Most important of all the three groups—even more than the priests and the

Afghans—was, however, the women. Women challenged the young men directly in the tanks and took the issue away from being a kind of virility contest between rival groups of men. It was particularly the old women who set up the canteens within the White House, prepared hospitals for the wounded, brought food to the young men on the barricades, engaged the rather frightened young men in the tanks in dialogue, and refused to leave on the night of the twentieth when the somewhat male chauvinist Afghan veterans insisted they vacate because fighting was near. They, it seems, were the surrogates of the lady in heaven, whose final rest contained the mystery of ultimate security.

What was striking during this time was the rediscovery of moral responsibility. Those at the White House were defending not only their newly won freedom but also their suddenly rediscovered responsibility, which is, of course, freedom's Siamese twin wherever it endures. Everyone had functioned for so long in a system where the secret was to avoid decisions. The great phrase was that "it does not depend on me," which is, of course, the rationalization of every bureaucracy that has reached its ultimate level in the totalitarian state. Suddenly, everyone was making decisions: whether or not to speak up within the family, within his or her organization, among friends; whether or not to go to the White House; how much to participate in the resistance; and so forth. In addition to the rediscovery of moral responsibility, a kind of purification of language occurred in the remarkable oratory that came from Radio White House. Even the most prosaic and didactic of figures, like Elena Bonner, ascended into poetry with a kind of simplified incantational beauty, saying "We are higher, we are cleaner." Yevtushenko wrote one of the shortest and best poems he has done in recent memory for the occasion, ending with those great lines, "the Russian parliament like a wounded marble swath of freedom, defended by our people, swings into immortality." After decades of language pollution by the acronymic horror of Soviet rhetoric, Russians had been treated to a kind of bathos of unending self-pity and self-righteousness in the self-indulgent oratory of their new parliament. Suddenly, everything was condensed and focused. The language itself was simplified, cleansed in the way that Pasternak had anticipated by talking about the young girl who returns at the end of *Doctor Zhivago* voicing Pasternak's hope for the future "from somewhere in Siberia where the language is still pure." This, of course, was the group that was central to the Yeltsin resistance: the Siberians, the sons and daughters of the gulag, who had come back to reclaim the heritage that Stalin had tried to kill off in one of the greatest acts of genocide by a political leader against its own people.

When Gorbachev returned—after the coup had been defeated, the troops withdrawn, and the junta dissolved—he provided a classic case of someone schooled in theory, unable to understand the moral meaning of a story. He began immediately talking about "stages of *perestroikala*" and giving an ideological gloss on what had happened—unable to understand that there had been a transformation, even a transfiguration, of his people. I remember standing in Dzerzhinsky Square the day after he returned, where the great statue of the founder of the secret police was being swept off its pedestal by four cranes that hovered over it like a hungry family of brontosauri slowly moving in on its dinner. Gorbachev's press conference was being broadcast, but when he answered the first question of "Why did you appoint all these people in the first place?" with a series of ideological evasions, everyone simply shouted, "Turn it off." Gorbachev lost his largest audience and his last serious listeners in a country with which he had totally lost spiritual contact.

The spiritual drama reached a climax on Saturday, less than a week after the putsch had started, with the funeral procession for the three young men who had been killed. This event echoed yet another Judeo-Christian theme: the redemptive value of innocent suffering. The young men were unconsciously likened to those first Russian saints, St. Boris and St. Gleb, the youthful sons of Prince Vladimir, who also accepted death in order to overcome the divisions of their people. The high point came when Boris Yeltsin emerged from the White House, went directly to the parents of the three young men, and said, "Forgive me, your President, that I was unable to defend and save your sons." "Forgive me," of course, is what Russians say to each other before they take communion and what that other Boris—Boris Godunov—said to the Russian people in his last words in the greatest of all Russian operas about that other "time of troubles."

Of course, the ending of this story is not yet known. Russia is still going through an inner moral catharsis but has so far avoided the vindictiveness of vengeance or scapegoating. They have accepted to an astonishing degree an act of corporate national repentance by opening their archives for an exhibit at the Library of Congress during the Yeltsin-Bush summit in June 1992. They are seeking new answers inside and above themselves in a transcendent ideal, rather than looking for scapegoats outside and below themselves in a common enemy. But the possibility remains that the other, more familiar kind of catharsis—a semifascist-type nationalism—may be the fallback position for the vast nineteen-million-person Communist Party that has been dispossessed. The Communists are, in a way, beneficiaries of the mildness and tolerance of the new democratic regime. The possibilities of a xenophobic catharsis remains with the so-called red/brown movement: former Communists who have become extreme nationalists. A hint of their violence is contained in the murder of the leading preacher of his generation, Father Alexander Men, an extraordinary and unique human bridge between the two long-alienated intellectual and religious communities of Russia and between Christians and Jews.

Let me say in conclusion what I think may be the meaning of all this—speaking probably presumptuously and certainly speculatively. The Russian Empire contained vital centers of all three of the great prophetic monotheisms—Judaism, Christianity, and Islam—on the eve of the first of the twentieth century's three world wars. I believe that now, as the last of three world wars has ended, the prophetic meaning of all this has something to do with all three of those monotheisms. The gathering around the barricades overcame classic divisions in Russian history between workers and intellectuals, Slavophile and Westernizing tendencies, Christians and Jews. One of the three boys killed was Jewish, and in the open-air funeral procession through Moscow, chants of the reformed Jewish Kaddish mixed with the "Eternal Memory" of Russian Orthodox cantillation. The two forms of cantillation blended together, and the three young men were buried together in an Orthodox graveyard. There was a sense of reconciliation that was evident not in passive speeches about brotherhood but in dynamic mutual rediscovery on the barricades.

Of course, no one supposes that Christian-Jewish tensions or Slavophile-Westernizer antagonisms can be overcome by one moment of shared exhilaration. Many Jews have emigrated and many who remained behind feel threatened. The question of whether the still-substantial surviving Jewish community does or does not play a fully accepted and integrated role in building the new Russia will be a key determinant of whether or not pluralism will take root in Russia.

Russian Orthodoxy is split today between two versions: one a reactionary reenforcement for the red/brown movement, supported by some of the old hierarchy closely connected with the Communist government and now popularly referred to as the *Mitropolitburo*. The other involves the refortifying of Orthodox theology with a passion for authentic social justice and concrete acts of charity and reconciliation. This protodemocratic trend among the younger clergy seeks to reassimilate into a heavily Hellenized Orthodoxy the Judaic emphasis on social justice that was represented by people like Alexander Men. His concept of Jewish-Christian interdependence and reconciliation was almost certainly the major cause of his murder. The outcome of Russia's current troubled transition depends on whether they fall back on a historic church structure heavily compromised with nationalism and the state or on the new prophetic Christianity exemplified on the barricades by the younger priests.

In the long run, however, the key split in the former Russian Empire will probably not be between different versions of Christianity but between Christianity and Islam, a dialogue that has hardly yet begun there any more than here. Here, too, Russia may find creative possibilities. The youngest member of the Russian parliament is a charismatic twenty-two-year-old Islamic modernist from Dagestan. If the Yeltsin government can establish a Muslim-Christian dialogue within Russia and with the newly independent Islamic states of the former Soviet Union, democratic pluralism will be advanced—and new possibilities created for Christian-Muslim understanding generally.

The mundane meaning of the changes in Russia can, I think, be understood through the concepts of a great suppressed humanistic critic of the Soviet period, Mikhail Bakhtin. He saw the medieval carnival as the vehicle for temporary liberation from restrictive authority and hierarchy in his famous book on Rabelais. What happened around the White House was, in many ways, a carnival of liberation which, however, proved not to be simply an interlude, a mere temporary escapevalve from the reigning hierarchies and restrictions on speech. Whether the festive two days on the barricades were only an interlude in Russia's enduring commitment to absolution or a real prelude to democracy is, of course, the key question for the Russian future.

Another of Bakhtin's concepts is his sense of the broader significance of the movement from the epic to the novel, which he analogizes as the movement from monologue to dialogue. During the decisive two days of meetings of the Russian Parliament as recorded and duplicated on Xerox machines, a new Russian identity appeared. The Xerox machine by exit 8 of the parliament was almost like a high altar, issuing forth sacred relics that were carried by the evangelists as they moved out from the White House to the factories and to the troops. Russians were challenged to move from a Soviet-style monologue to a new kind of dialogue by the proclamations from the White House. After August, the emergence of that new dia-logic form of government we call the separation of powers began to develop halt-ingly through the chaos.

Can Russia simultaneously move inward to recover its conservative religious tradition and outward to internalize a Western liberal democratic tradition? It is doubtful for reasons too long for me to go into here that they will be able to succeed in both rediscovering their religious roots and honoring all their democratic branches unless America, the other superpower scorpion in the bottle, and the hid-den model for much of their strivings, is not more deeply and actively involved than we are at the moment. Russia has been transformed, but that transformation could still tragically lead to new negative nationalism.

Much of the democratic movement comes from Siberia and in some dark Siberian versions of Russian folklore, the savage bear was originally just an ordinary man. But when he was denied the bread and salt of simple human hospitality by his neighbor, he retreated in humiliation into the forest and returned unexpectedly in a transformed state to take his revenge.

Notes

1. Documentation for this account—and some of this account itself—is contained in James Billington, *Russia Transformed: Breakthrough to Hope* (New York: The Free Press, 1991).
2. Rutskoi subsequently broke with Yeltsin and the reform movement during the con-troversy over the Referendum of April 1993 and adopted a reactionary position, openly dis-playing a map of the traditional Soviet Union in his office.

6

ROBERT E. FRYKENBERG

Anecdote as the Essence of Historical Understanding

Ideally, history itself should be rewritten entirely in terms of anecdote, for these alone assert their authenticity above the prejudice and conformism of the professional historian.

Richard N. Coe[1]

No element in history, I would argue, is more basic than narrative. Indeed, it is *the* basic and essential element. History *is* "*story.*" And, as such, "*anecdote*" is its very essence: its life, its blood, and its breath. The very word "story," in its now somewhat more obsolete and obscure meaning, is directly descended from the original Greek word "*istoria*" and the subsequent Latin word "*historia.*" Exactly how, when, or why, the word "story" became partially separated from its ancient ancestral root is a "story" in itself.[2] Yet, the fact remains that the term has never ceased to convey some of the original meaning found in its parental root; and "history" has never ceased to be and to mean "story." The original noun form "story," meaning "history," almost any standard dictionary informs us, is the more original, even if it is now more obscure and obsolete. In simple terms, a story is "a narrative, true or presumed to be true, of important events and celebrated persons";[3] "a narrative of events in their sequence." The word, moreover, pertains to that particular kind of "action" that is found in the very "relating" or "telling" or "writing" or "describing of things historically"—that action which adorns the present with "scenes from the past."[4]

But, in the expanded and fuller sense of the concept, as it is defined today, story as history is a particular kind of description: it covers or follows a sequence of actions, events, experiences, incidents, or episodes that have actually happened in the "life" or "lives" of one or more persons.[5] It contains a sequence of events that have actually occurred in *human* situation(s) or predicaments that are *typical.*[6] It also (usually) contains, and is enlivened by, a sequential chain of "little stories" or "*anecdotes.*" Both forms add deeper insights and arouse heightened awareness, consciousness, and interest. Story and anecdotes as history, moreover, are kinds of narrative descriptions of events in which *contingencies* (unexpected changes, reactions to change, or turns) affect situations in such a way as to lead those events to some sort of eventual climax or conclusion. By their very nature, both true anec-dote and true story bring to light hidden aspects of situations and of personalities within such situations. Either anecdote or story (and/or both together) can show how changes and consequences bring further changes or cumulative conse-quences, and how these in turn can lead to sudden, *unexpected turns* of events, con-tingencies, and/or predicaments. Chain reactions of events, actions, thoughts, and predicaments, even institutions, can, like living individuals or communities of peo-ple, acquire a kind of "life of their own." So it is that the responses to predica-ments—however "good" or "bad," however "successful" or "unsuccessful"—gradu-ally bring each anecdote, each sequence of anecdotes, and each larger story to some ultimate climax.[7]

Various elements and facets within any anecdote or any story serve to make it into a special vehicle for the appropriation of historical understanding. The sense in which history is "historical" or "true"—what makes a true anecdote or a true story *true*—is of extra special concern. As a form of creative art that calls forth or draws on every device of human imagination and reason, each true anecdote or true story is an attempt to imitate *true* life: the sense of human experience "as it happens" or "as it once happened" must be convincingly strong. Each tale, each story as history, and each anecdote within a larger story as history, draws on all avail-able resources and powers of the teller—all of the accumulated experience, imagi-nation, insight, memory, and sagacity, along with any or all other materials which come in hand, are brought together in order to "reconstruct life." Life as it is now or once was lived in some definite place and time in the past is described, examined, and followed step by step. Sequences of actions and events are recounted. One or more lines of action, possibly complex, interconnected, and tangled, are traced, taking the listener or reader (or researcher) from some beginning point (in space and time) through various contingencies, gradually building tension with each sud-den, unexpected, or surprising turn until, at last, the listener or reader is brought to some final, conclusive ending point. Narrative, if fully appreciated and compre-hended in all of its manifold or subtle implications, becomes *the* quintessentially ideal vehicle for acquainting people with—and for the acquisition and transmission of—"true" understandings of the past.

In its classic mold, any story—be it anecdote, saga, tale, or whatever—attempts to capture and to hold the imaginations of those recipients who are its listeners or readers. It does so by relating life in the present to things that have already hap-pened at some time (and place) in the past, whether recent or distant. However true a story may be, it makes its appeal to the past in terms understandable to contempo-rary human experience. Harking back to ageless conventions and formulas, an ar-chetypical story commences its primary functions of conveying understanding by simultaneously capturing and holding attention, by entertaining and exciting emo-tions, and by informing and instructing its recipient listeners or readers. It can do this with some stereotypical phrase comparable to those words recited to children: "Once upon a time . . ."[8] By employing a familiar cliché, set phrase, or ritual in-vocation, history as story moves from the familiar to the unfamiliar and "awakens," "brings back," or "calls out of the past" echoes of something that now no longer exists and restores awareness of things that once were and are no more.

Implicit within this essence of history are appeals to elemental emotions: feelings which lie deep within each and every human being. Mingled among such deep and innate feelings are the especially profound and primordial sensations: anxiety, curiosity, ecstasy, or morbidity. Curiosity about the unknown, about darkness and death, is universal and holds a special fascination within (most if not all of) us. Perhaps some insatiable craving to come to terms with what lies both within and beyond mortality, some refusal to accept the finality of death (or defeat, or loss) drives us: some hope that there is something within us that is "deathless," something that lives on (in us, or of us), something we strive to appropriate and better understand. What moves us to exquisite delight, to experiences of ecstasy,[9] or what arouses direst dread of impending tragedy: such things can, to borrow from Johnson's timeless phrase, so wonderfully "concentrate our minds." However captured or described, it is this striving "to know," this wish "to resurrect" what is gone, that compels attention and awakens imagination. History as story appeals to something that is beyond death, something deathless.

Often forgotten in our day is the fact that the way in which we understand history—the way all purposive human action and thought is understood—is basically and profoundly different from the way in which we understand natural phenomena. To understand "what happened" is to understand, at least in some measure, "how it happened" and even "why it happened." To understand in this way is to understand particular actions and events and thoughts within particular, if not peculiar, situations and circumstances and contexts. The "dominant empiricist epistemology" of our age does not appreciate this way of understanding. The concept of "story" or "narrative," as *the* foundation for historical knowledge and as a special or unique form of human understanding, is distinct (or sui generis) in its own right. W. B. Gaillie (1968), pursuing this argument, declared that "as in the sciences there is always a theory, so in history there is always a story."[10] As he saw it, just as a phenomenon selected for study is a starting point for "discovering" more comprehensive explanations and systematic general theories in any proper science, so an event (action, incident, or episode) is a starting point for historical study.[11] This is so, in his view, precisely because a particular event is thought to be so memorable or noteworthy—so "story-worthy." Such an event is compelling. We want to know more. We want to learn about a particular success or a tragedy (gain/victory or loss/defeat, etc.) so that we can know the more intimate circumstance, total context, and fuller detail. We want this either "for its own sake" (to satisfy curiosity, either cursory or deep) or for its comparability to concerns that are "our very own." Any action or being or event worth a story, in a broad and comprehensive sense, is an "adventure" for our minds and consciousnesses or emotions. This means that the event in question contains elements that are accidental, contingent, surprising, unforeseen, and/or unpredictable. It is this element in history-as-story that makes it worth following. History-as-story is always something *worth* following: worth following stage by stage and following until its details bring us to some sort of ultimate climax or ending-point. This is so because, ultimately, it is through the story itself, and through its telling, that the essentials of historical understanding are produced and transmitted. The story carries itself by the very compelling character of its essentials. The ingredients that make up such a story are, at the same time, the conditions that are necessary in order to make such a story into genuine history. It is these ingredients of story that concern us here.

What distinguishes "anecdote," as a special form of story, and what makes it so important is its peculiar and unique potential for conveying the very essence of truths and understandings about human experience. An "anecdote" is not just a "small story." It is a special kind of "small story," one which somehow "documents" an event. It possesses a capacity to convey the very sense of truth (or understanding) about particular "happenings" in the past: it illuminates human events and human experiences. Coming out of the mists of earliest consciousness and remnants of memory, linking it to origins of folklore and oral tradition, in times (and places) when facticity, historicity, and mythic verity were not yet separated into distinct categories or concepts, anecdote continues to retain a very powerful kind of authenticity and potentiality.

The classic Greek *anekdota*—literally "[thing]-not-given-out," "not-published," or yet "unpublished"[12]—is the "small hard truth."[13] It is a "brief account" or "short narrative" of a "memorable event," a "remarkable experience," or "striking incident" imbued with memorable significance and truth. Detailing some event or experience "as it happened" and graphically telling "how it was," drawing on some "hitherto unknown" or "unpublished" sources, often related out of someone's memory,[14] the really good anecdote, in its classic mold, requires formal structure. It must have a beginning, a middle, and an ending; and its facts must not contradict deeper substructures of historically verifiable truths. Used to give emphasis or make some point within a larger context (or longer work); employed for highlighting interest or for throwing new light upon life; or presented simply for its own sake, anecdote is betimes amusing, curious, gossipy, pungent, revealing and/or risqué; sometimes crude, grotesque, or vicious; and even, at times, inspiring or sublime. Yet, it has always retained some of its nature as an insightful recital of "small hard truths." This is so even as it makes a point, illuminates, or illustrates "how it really was," and drives home a particular idea. Artfully "done," a good anecdote is not just delivered; it is "performed." By means of explicit detail, implicit omission, captivating dialogue (mimicry, etc.), plays on words, spirited appeals (either droll, humorous, or pathetic, etc.), and climactic endings, all sorts of captivating devices are used to give listeners a "deeper glimpse of life," as it really was in a particular situation. Imaginative memory harnessed to narrative, in the form of anecdote, throws graphic light on a "larger picture"; and, by such means, a heavier subject can be "humanized."[15] Whatever its form, whether autobiographical, biographical, or nonbiographical, anecdote serves as an ideal vehicle for conveying factual details about an actual event.[16]

It is rather surprising to discover how little attention has been given to the inner nature and structure of the anecdote as such. While my searchings may yet uncover something more valuable, the best analysis of anecdote so far is found in an article by Richard N. Coe. In an enquiry into the origins of Stendhal's narrative technique, he has explored the inner structure of the anecdote, both in its classic and nonclassic forms. The classic anecdote, as he sees it in Stendhal, possesses at least five, if not six, distinguishing features.

First and foremost, an anecdote is effective or genuine only if, and to the degree that, it conveys something true. In other words: "No *truth, no anecdote!!*" Without truth, a "little story" or "funny story" or "joke" is merely and simply and nothing but that. Without story, on the other hand, a pithy insight or observation is no more than a maxim or an assertion with "truth-bearing" potentialities. A maxim is in no way similar, whether couched as aphorism, paradigm, proverb, theory, or "wise" truism (e.g., "Absolute power corrupts absolutely!"). A maxim states some general principle that serves as a guide or rule. An anecdote narrates facts and circumstances, giving details in sequence. An anecdote, even if and when it points to some conclusion or some general observation, will not do so explicitly. The anecdotist who knows his stuff studiously refrains from drawing any general conclusion. He leaves this entirely up to his audience. It is his audience (or readers) that draws inferences and connects the particular to the general. One form, whether anecdote or maxim, is the other form inside-out (or back-to-front): one gives a general conclusion or theory without supplying evidence; and the other does just the reverse, narrating details and providing evidence without drawing conclusions. The empirical and the theoretical, by nature, work in opposite ways.

Second, anecdote is what Stendhal called "*petit fait vrai*"—that is, it carries, within itself, a truth of such significance, exceptionality, and veracity that it is, for that very reason, memorable. The contrast between the "hard little truth" of anecdote and the softness (even "falseness" or "shallowness") of sweeping generalization highlights this feature in anecdote. Here there is a basic conflict: between the banality of composing averages of matters mundane and the insightfulness of startling exceptions that make-the-rule. Attempts to gain historical understanding, when devoid of anecdotal elements, all too quickly cease to assert truths that transcend the conforming restraints of general or theoretical explanation. Generalization, or theoretical explanation in history, is likely, by itself, more often than not, to degenerate into or to be driven by ossifying doctrines (which are often themselves merely agendas or covers for ideology).

Third, anecdote is extremely and profoundly personal, if not private. As a mode of expression, it calls for consummate skill and developed techniques. Accent, gesture, voice, and personality play crucial roles. The same anecdote, told by different persons, can convey different understandings. Anecdotal truth, embodied in dramatized intimacy and enhanced by theatrical technique, is narrated in proximity, bringing anecdotist and audience into closer relationship.

Fourth, as with any form of theater, anecdote creates illusion. The very impression of spontaneity and simplicity, even naïveté, that anecdote conveys is, in fact, anything but that. Anecdote, at its best, is nothing if not artful. Its cunning devices are ingeniously contrived, neatly balanced, carefully crafted, and shrewdly wrought. Its rhythm, timing, and tone are subtlety personified. Slyly lulling senses into comfortable conformity and a familiar mundanity, the anecdotist suddenly transforms soporific and deliberately murky shapelessness into something sharply edged. As the performance approaches its finale, tension builds, and then, with startling speed and flashing wit, a thunderous revelation breaks upon the listener.

Nothing, one must repeat and stress, can be less spontaneous than a really good anecdote.

Fifth, at its very epicenter, the good anecdote captures and captivates the human spirit. Any artistic masterpiece has this quality of touching the heart. Plumbing the very depths of despair and reaching for the heights of ecstasy, it plucks at the strings and strums the chords of every emotion. It breathes and echoes with sobs and hysterics, releasing gusts of humor or pathos that reverberate from those all who hear and listen. Alternatively, soft and tender, biting and bitter, grotesque and risqué, piquant or satirical and sublime, this kind of tale is driven home with force and verve. The anecdote is not worth the name that fails to "breathe" some wind and wit and "*hwyl.*"[17]

Sixth, and finally, anecdote conveys and possesses historical authenticity *as* anecdote only if, when, and to the degree that it demonstrates detachment. Between teller and thing told, between anecdotist and anecdote, distance is required. Objectivity separates the creator from the thing created. Self-effacing genius is not confused with what it has made. The performing self is not the story. No amount of personal brilliance or wit can be permitted to inflate the narrator. Narrator, as actor, can play, and be excused, any part but that of hero—witness, victim, simpleton, or butt—anything so long as the anecdotist is out of the spotlight. Let teller take the slightest merit or glory to himself and both he himself and his anecdote look ridiculous. Worse still, he and his "story" then commit the inexcusable crime of boredom.[18]

It is in this very last feature that the structure of the classic anecdote confronts us with a strange paradox. The very action that produces something supremely synthetic, sophisticated, and artificial also establishes the facticity and veracity of a genuine historical event. Historical events which, by themselves, obviously occur within an otherwise shapeless context and a seemingly unstructured environment require structured narration to document and establish authenticity. In other words, *a* truth is established at the expense of *the* truth. What is it that lies behind this apparent contradiction, raising questions and insinuating suspicions?

It is the very facts that make a genuine anecdote so good that establish its power. Details so improbable are able, by their very improbability, to make themselves convincing. No mere imagination, the audience feels, could invent facts so amazing. And hence, they must be true. The very exceptionality of the details and facts becomes the bond and seal of authenticity. In comparison, claims that are vague or general, propositions seemingly platitudinous or hypocritical, if not clearly a cliché or stereotype, become suspect. Worse yet, they need only an exception to be proved false or untrue. Many an axiom or maxim, as explanation or generalization, especially when inflated or sweeping, looks banal and sounds like so much "cant" in the presence of "hard little facts." Indeed, just as for historiography, factual authenticity and historicity "reside in" and "rest on" *documents*, resulting in calls for ever more rigorous "documentation," so for the anecdote, details told serve "to document" the facticity of the particular episode that it describes. This has been so since the time of the ancients, long before Herodotus and Thucydides employed them with such skill. It is this quality of intrinsic detachment, objectivity, and documentation within anecdotal description that poses a problem for the historian: namely, the dilemma of preserving the inherent "truth-bearing" authority of the anecdote while, at the same time, controlling or at least somehow downplaying (muting or disguising) the contrived character of its narrative. Anecdotal artificiality and sophistication, in short, are at odds with authenticity and detached documentation.

No clear or entirely satisfying answer or solution to this dilemma seems to have been found. How, in other words, does artificiality in narrative authenticate life in experiences and events? How are apparently unstructured and shapeless contexts of real events made understandable? The answers to such questions seem to lie in different kinds of artifices, ruses, and stratagems. One can, for example, downplay or disguise the artificiality of a given anecdote—by, for example, producing the evidence of events and experiences contained within an anecdote without actually producing the anecdote itself, thereby leaving others to draw their own conclusions about the historicity of what is related. Resort to this kind of device, and others too many to examine at length here, led to the production, in turn, of "nonclassical" forms of anecdote. Some anecdotes, as a consequence, have been deliberately "personalized" and "unstructured" (or "deconstructed": that is, left without their usual beginning, middle, and ending or without "punch line," finale, or hint of a "point"); "syncopated" (in which formal links in a sentence are cut and left entirely to the imagination, so as to provide a "neighbor's-eye-view"); or "extended" (or made into "*nouvelles*," wherein dialogue has replaced narrative and smaller anecdotes have been incorporated). Literary devices for fusing together many forms of anecdotes—classic, personal, extended, and so on—within longer short-stories have made possible the retention of the classic qualities of the true anecdote and, at the same time, have also satisfied a reluctance to draw conclusions, erect formal structures, or spell out truths.

Extended anecdotes that contain other anecdotes and that have been lengthened into increasingly longer episodes have eventually, in turn, been extended into full histories (or novels). These have then become, with each addition, more and more complex. During this process of extension, distinction between history and novel, between "faction" and "fiction," can be made clear or can remain murky. Much depends on degrees of detachment or personal involvement, in each kind and size of anecdote. Personal responses to historical events that cannot be expressed directly, or in simplistic terms, merely by inclusion in an anecdote or a maxim, can be shifted into the realms of fiction and allegory. The shifting of anecdotes from historical works into novels and short-stories, whereby a fictitious narrative presents a picture of "real life," especially focusing on crises in the lives or life-histories of men and women, has in no way altered the essential historical character of the genuine and true anecdote.

Nevertheless, due to its many uses, in its generic form, the anecdote remains ubiquitous. Its purposes in human affairs, in all places and times, have been manifold: whether historical, literary, pedagogical, political, rhetorical, theatrical, or whatever. Sometimes as "filler" or as added "sauce" or "spice" in public discourse, it has been "manufactured" synthetically, mass-produced, and marketed. Once made saleable as a synthetic product, it has been mixed with aphorisms and jokes for use in banquets or speaker circuits. Some anecdotes have become so famous and popular, traveling so far and wide, that their shadows have become by-words and metaphors. Removed from the original context of historical circumstance, carcasses or ghosts of powerful anecdotes become enshrined in such timeless shells, in fables and parables, as much as in metaphorical allusions, phrases, or proverbs. Whatever their far journeys, whether in factual or in fictional forms, short accounts of "hard little truths" about single, isolated events, experiences, or incidents taking place at crucial turning-points within larger courses of events have become the very essence of most genuine historical understandings. Within larger frameworks of narrative, where history-as-story, even when accompanied and surrounded by interpretive analysis, is still the most ideal and the most preferred vehicle for conveying the very essence of particular historical understandings, the place of anecdote remains unchallenged. No amount of secondary analysis, interpretive theorizing, or building of models and paradigms by professional scholars, among whom academic historians have been conspicuous during the past two decades, has yet been able to eradicate or undermine the paramount supremacy enjoyed by anecdotes.

Examples of anecdotes, of course, abound, both in history and in literature. On every hand, and in every clime and time, anecdotes lie thick upon the ground of cultural discourse. So ubiquitous and so universal has been their presence in human affairs and human history, so vast their numbers that they are, like the seed of Abraham, "as many as the stars of the sky and the sands of the seashore beyond counting."[19] Whether genuine or falsified, whether good or bad, comic or tragic, somber or jovial, effective or ineffective, famous or obscure, alive or dead: anecdotes come in every shape, size, and form. Anecdotes, in one form or another, still give meaning to many of the most classic of metaphors and myths. They even ornament some of the most tired platitudes, trite stereotypes, and banal clichés. Often, one phrase or even one, two, or three words within a particular cultural tradition encapsulates, encodes, or symbolizes a famous or popular anecdote. Virtually "everyone" within the Judeo-Christian world, if not within the Islamic world also, knows and even understands (down to finest details) what certain biblical allusions and metaphors mean. In Hebrew Scripture, such terms as "Curse of Cain" ("Am I my Brother's Keeper?"), "Babel," "Potiphar's Wife," "Passover," "Jericho," "Goliath," "Rivers of Babylon," "Fiery Chariot," "Fiery Furnace," "Handwriting on the Wall" conjure up whole anecdotes in an instant. Likewise, in the Christian Gospels (including Luke 2: The Acts of the Apostles), words like "Bethlehem" or "Manger," "Wise Men, or Magi," "Cana Wedding," "Prodigal Son," "Great Temptation," "Driving out the Money-Changers," "Last Supper," "Thirty Pieces of Silver," "Golgotha," "Damascus Road," and hosts more do the same thing. All classical cultures, whether from Greece, India, China, or elsewhere, are thick with threads and networks of anecdotal material.

However much one may value any particular or exemplary anecdote, the role played by anecdotes within the larger framework of historical narrative—"history-as-story"—is all pervasive. The pivotal and persuasive importance many a "little true tale" gives is just that essential flash of insight, that "revealing essence" within the framework of a larger story. In that very "moment-of-truth" light is thrown on some whole larger episode. Thereafter, the mythic and the historic are repeatedly subject to exegetical and hermeneutical examination and revision. At the same time, anecdote-as-history, by its very nature, also depends on the framework of the larger historical narrative for its veracity. Its energy comes from those critical turning points, those times of crisis, when "all history" (meaning all events in a crucial period) seems to "stand still" or "hang in the balance." No one, for example, can quote Wellington's memorable comment, that "Waterloo" was "a near run thing," without somehow appreciating how desperate was that fathomless panoply of awesome emotions, dreadful deeds, and suspense-filled moments—even the sense of "miraculous deliverance" from destruction—which lies behind it. Any action of private memory, making a nonpublic assessment public, can transform a previously obscure "hard little fact" into something at once contemplative, critical, cautionary, and timeless: so that all who read may remember, reflect, and take to heart the larger narrative of what happened. In cryptic, marvelously terse words (of wonderful economy and efficiency), a common understanding of "what really happened" is engendered and commitment to understanding occurs.

While many anecdotal traditions might be examined more closely here, undoubtedly some of the most famous and striking concentrations of anecdotes anywhere to be found are those collections and sequences contained within the historical parts of Hebrew and Christian Scriptures. Virtually every event recorded therein is, indeed, a carefully selected collection and a highly structured distillation of anecdotes, each a "document" put in place to carry forward the essentials of a larger (or master) narrative. Taken from oral traditions about happenings, "small hard truths" carefully remembered, handed down from generation to generation for some time before ultimately being recorded in writing, they represent facts, tightly packed, concentrated, and reduced to barest essentials. The very concentration, density, or economy of words, and precision of meanings in fact contained in these strings of anecdotes is truly astonishing. So also are the essences of historical truth, as well as mythic and theological verity, which they transmitted down through many passing millennia. Moreover, having survived ravages of time and turbulence, both natural and political, the credibility of these texts have withstood nearly three centuries of critical assault from scholars. Their rejection as a reliable record of events, starting in the time of Spinoza, gained momentum and speed during the Enlightenment.

The texts were subjected to severe scrutiny, driven by critical doubts that sometimes verged on fanaticism. Their composition, dating, content, and form were questioned; and they were pounced on and pronounced to be more didactic than historical, more the vehicles for myths rather than for hard facts. The events and personalities they described, from Abraham down to Jesus and his Apostles, were seen as artful "constructions" or carefully composed or even deceitful "fabrications." Not until the death and destruction of worldwide war and the horrors of the holocaust exposed depths of human depravity and wickedness as never before did the tide begin to turn. Then, respect for the dependability of these texts as reliable records slowly returned, restored by archeological findings and recovery of ancient texts that established the truth of dates, events, and persons described in the Torah. Those denying historicity have been put on the defensive, as detail after detail has been corroborated. Indeed, with exact datings now being made, it is possible to conclude that, in terms of reliability, historical anecdotes found in the narrative books of Samuel, Kings, and Chronicles are on a par with the finest works written by such Greeks as Herodotus and Thucydides. Better history was not produced by any other peoples in ancient times.

The anecdotes and stories contained in the historical records of the Jews, over a period of nearly four thousand years, contain historical understandings in many shapes and sizes. On the level of human relationships alone, much of what we learn is often filled with horror and tragedy. Exactly how horrible and how tragic cannot be appreciated without taking the whole history into account. All sorts of conclusions can be drawn from this history. Yet, nothing is more marked than the capacity for evil and folly, corruption and wickedness, by which mankind has brought pain and sorrow and suffering onto itself. It is difficult not to see now that the only restraints upon propensities for wrongdoing among the Jews seem to have come out of the central importance of religious faith in their history. This religious faith made it possible for countless generations, despite many personal, social, or political failures and despite countless oppressions, misfortunes, and sufferings, to establish foundations on which they were able to build lives of remarkable achievement, satisfaction, and security. Certainly, if the records have possessed any veracity at all, they still tell us—anecdote by anecdote—how, but for their faith, this small and seemingly insignificant people could never have survived and how many, especially those who lost their faith, were hounded and hunted down until they vanished from the earth.

The story of Christians, beginning with anecdotes of Jesus found in the Gospels and continuing with anecdotes found in the Acts of the Apostles, especially as recorded by Paul and his companions during their missionary journeys, is much the same. Mostly written down and then later "canonized," perhaps at about the same time or not long after the highly dense and tightly packed phrases found in the epistles, and built upon presumptions of understandings that assumed and presupposed knowledge of the historical events written in the Hebrew Scriptures, they are so filled with allusions to events related in previous anecdotes that comprehension of the New Testament is not possible apart from the "Old." Whether or not the epistles, filled with their profound doctrinal elements and their sophisticated theology, were written first, one of the Gospels may actually have been among the *last* elements of biblical literature to find an established place within the canon of Sacred Writ. With their entry, the records were closed and sacred memory-in-history became complete. That simple stories, in strings of anecdotes, might have come *after* the most complex treatises is a matter for no small wonder.

Some samples of anecdotes, taken from Scripture and taken from historical accounts, both in early modern and recent times, together with a sample of an anecdote that could be taken as a self-authenticating document with reference to a personal (family) history, will serve to put some substantive meat on the bones and some blood in the veins of what, to this point, may have seemed, at least to some readers, like a cold and sterile analysis. To write about anecdotes in any meaningful way, without actually demonstrating examples of their inner power, is to indulge in an empty, somewhat fatuous exercise. What follows, therefore, starts in Scripture and ends in personal experience. This chapter concludes by giving a few prime examples.

Two Anecdotes from the Gospel of John

The Samaritan Woman

"A report now reached the Pharisees: 'Jesus is winning and baptizing more disciples than John.' In fact, it was only the disciples who were baptizing and not Jesus himself. When Jesus learned this, he left Judaea and set out once more for Galilee. He had to pass through Samaria, and on his way he came to a Samaritan town called Sychar, near the plot of ground which Jacob gave to his son Joseph and the spring called Jacob's Well. It was about noon, and Jesus, tired after his journey, sat down by the well.

The disciples had gone away to the town to buy food. Meanwhile, a Samaritan woman came to draw water. Jesus said to her, 'Give me a drink.' The Samaritan woman said, 'What! You, a Jew, ask a drink of me, a Samaritan woman?' (Jews and Samaritans, it should be noted, did not use vessels in common.)

Jesus answered her, 'If only you knew what God gives, and who it is that is asking you for a drink, you would have asked him and he would have given you living water.'

'Sir,' the woman said, 'you have no bucket and this well is deep. How can you give me "living water"? Are you a greater man than Jacob our ancestor, who gave us the well, and drank from it himself, he and his sons, and his cattle too?'

Jesus said, 'Everyone who drinks this water will be thirsty again, but whoever drinks the water that I shall give him will never suffer thirst any more. The water that I shall give him will be an inner spring, always welling up for eternal life.'

'Sir,' said the woman, 'give me that water, and then I shall not be thirsty, nor have to come all this way to draw.'

Jesus replied, 'Go home, call your husband and come back.'

She answered, 'I have no husband.'

'You are right,' said Jesus, 'in saying that you have no husband, for, although you have had five husbands, the man with whom you are now living is not your husband. You told me the truth there.'

'Sir,' she replied, 'I can see that you are a prophet. Our fathers worshipped on this mountain, but you Jews say that the temple where God should be worshipped is in Jerusalem.'

'Believe me,' said Jesus, 'the time is coming when you will worship the Father neither on this mountain, nor in Jerusalem. You Samaritans worship without knowing what you worship, while we worship what we know. It is from the Jews that salvation comes. But the time approaches, indeed it is already here, when those who are real worshippers will worship the Father in spirit and in truth. Such are the worshippers whom the Father wants. God is spirit, and those who worship him must worship in spirit and in truth.'

The woman answered, 'I know that Messiah' (that is Christ) 'is coming. When he comes he will tell us everything.'

Jesus said, 'I am he, I who am speaking to you now.'

At that moment his disciples returned, and were astonished to find him talking with a woman. But none of them said, 'What do you want?' or 'Why are you talking with her?'

The woman put down her water jar and went away to the town, where she said to the people, 'Come and see a man who has told me everything I ever did. Could this be the Messiah?' They came out of the town and made their way towards him.

Meanwhile, the disciples were urging him, 'Rabbi, have something to eat.'

But he said, 'I have food to eat of which you know nothing.'

At this the disciples said to one another, 'Can someone have brought him food?'

But Jesus said, 'It is meat and drink for me to do the will of him who sent me until I have finished his work.'

'Do not say, "Four months more and then comes the harvest." But look, I tell you, look around on the fields. They are already white, ripe for harvest. The reaper is drawing his pay and gathering a crop for eternal life, so that the sower and reaper may rejoice together. That is how the saying comes to be true: "One sows, and another reaps." I sent you to reap a crop for which you have not toiled. Others toiled and you have come in for the harvest of their toil.'

Many Samaritans of that town came to believe in him because of the woman's testimony: 'He told me everything I ever did.' So when these Samaritans had come to him, they pressed him to stay with them; and he stayed there two days. Many more became believers because of what they heard from his own lips. They told the woman, 'It is no longer because of what you said that we believe, for we have heard him ourselves; and we know that this is in truth the Saviour of the world.'" (John 4:1-42, *New English Bible* [Oxford: 1971 ed.])

Lazarus, Mary, and Martha

"There was a man named Lazarus who had fallen ill. His home was at Bethany, the village of Mary and her sister Martha. (This Mary, whose brother Lazarus had fallen ill, was the woman who anointed the Lord with ointment and wiped his feet with her hair.)

The sisters sent a message to him: 'Sir you should know that your friend lies ill.'

When Jesus heard this he said, 'This illness will not end in death; it has come for the glory of God, to bring glory to the Son of God.' And therefore, though he loved Martha and her sister and Lazarus, after hearing of his illness Jesus waited for two days in the place where he was. After this, he said to disciples, 'Let us go back to Judaea.'

'Rabbi,' his disciples said, 'it is not long since the Jews there were wanting to stone you. Are you going there again?'

Jesus replied, 'Are there not twelve hours of daylight? Anyone can walk in daytime without stumbling, because he sees the light of this world. But if he walks after nightfall he stumbles, because the light fails him.'

After this, he added, 'Our friend Lazarus has fallen asleep, but I shall go and wake him.' The disciples said, 'Master, if he has fallen asleep he will recover.' Jesus, however, had been speaking of his death, but they thought he meant natural sleep.

Then Jesus spoke out plainly: 'Lazarus is dead. I am glad not to have been there; it will be for your good and for the good of your faith. But let us go to him.'

Thomas, called 'The Twin,' said to his fellow-disciples, 'Let us also go, that we may die with him.'

On his arrival, Jesus found that Lazarus had already been four days in the tomb. Bethany was just under two miles from Jerusalem, and many of the people had come from the city to Martha and Mary to condole with them on their brother's death. As soon as she heard that Jesus was on his way, Martha went to meet him, while Mary stayed at home.

Martha said to Jesus, 'If you had been here, sir, my brother would not have died. Even now I know that whatever you ask of God, God will grant you.'

Jesus said, 'Your brother will rise again.'

'I know that he will rise again', said Martha, 'at the resurrection on the last day.'

Jesus said, 'I am the resurrection and I am life. If any man has faith in me, even though he die, he shall come to life; and no one who is alive and has faith shall ever die. Do you believe this?'

'Lord, I do,' she answered. 'I now believe that you are the Messiah, the Son of God who was to come into the world.'

With these words she went to call her sister Mary, and taking her aside, she said, 'The Master is here; he is asking for you.'

When Mary heard this she rose up quickly and went to him. Jesus had not yet reached the village, but was still at the place where Martha had met him. The Jews who were in the house condoling with Mary, when they saw her start up and leave the house, went after her, for they supposed that she was going to the tomb to weep there.

So Mary came to the place where Jesus was. As soon as she caught sight of him, she fell at his feet and said, 'O sir, if you had only been here, my brother would not have died.'

When Jesus saw her weeping and the Jews her companions weeping, he sighed heavily and was deeply moved.

'Where have you laid him?' he asked.

They replied, 'Come and see, sir.'

Jesus wept.

The Jews said, 'How dearly he must have loved him!'

But some of them said, 'Could not this man who opened the blind man's eyes, have done something to keep Lazarus from dying?'

Jesus again sighed deeply. Then he went over to the tomb. It was a cave, with a stone placed against it. Jesus said, 'Take away the stone.'

Martha, the dead man's sister, said to him, 'Sir, by now there will be a stench. He has been there four days.'

Jesus said, 'Did I not tell you that if you have faith you will see the glory of God?'

So they removed the stone.

Then Jesus looked upwards and said, 'Father, I thank thee! Thou has heard me. I knew already that thou always hearest me, but I spoke for the sake of the people standing round, that they might believe that thou didst send me.'

Then he raised his voice in a great cry: 'Lazarus, come forth.'

The dead man came out, his hands and feet swathed in linen, his face wrapped in a cloth.

Jesus said, 'Loose him! Let him go.'

Now many of the Jews who had come to visit Mary and had seen what Jesus did, put their faith in him. But some of them went off to the Pharisees and reported what he had done." (John 11:1–46, *New English Bible* [Oxford: 1971 ed.])

Anecdote of a Famous Regicide

Charles I's Execution

"On the day of his execution, he dressed with special care, telling his servant Herbert, in combing his hair: 'Prithee, though it be not too long to stand upon my shoulders, take the same pains with it as you were wont to do: I am to be a bridegroom today and must be trimmed.' He added: 'Let me have a shirt on more than ordinary, by reason the season is so sharp as probably may make me shake, which some observers may imagine proceeds from fear. I fear not death. It is not terrible to me. I bless my God I am prepared.' He was kept waiting four hours, between ten and two, before being taken to the scaffold. There, he 'looked very earnestly upon the block and asked if it could be no higher'; but this was refused. After his last speech and his profession of faith, he handed his 'George' [garter] to Bishop Juxon to give to the Prince of Wales, with the word: 'Remember!' To Colonel Hacker, in charge of the guard, he said 'Take care that they do not put me in pain.' Then, to Juxon: 'I go from a corruptible to an incorruptible crown, where no disturbance can be, no disturbance at all.' Then, looking again at the block: 'Is it fast?' 'It is fast, Sir.' To the headsman, Young Gregory Brandon, disguised with false hair and a beard. 'Strike when I put my arms out this way' (stretching them). Then 'immediately stooping down, he laid his head on the block.' But his hair came loose, and Brandon put it back again; the King, thinking he was going to strike, said 'Stay for the sign.' Brandon: 'Yes I will, an it please Your Majesty.' Then the King gave the sign. Philip Henry, a seventeen-year-old Christ Church student, testified: 'At the instant when the blow was given there was such a dismal groan among the thousands of people that were within sight of it (as it were with one consent) as he had *never heard before*; and desired he might never hear the like again, nor see such a cause of it.' Then, 'immediately after the stroke was struck . . . according to order, one troop [began] marching from Charing Cross towards King Street, purposely to disperse and scatter the people.' Nevertheless, many crowded round the scaffold to 'dip their handkerchiefs' in the King's blood and were 'admitted for moneys.' The soldiers sold pieces of the blood-stained scaffold boarding, from a shilling to half a crown each, 'according to the quality of the persons that sought them.' Payment was also charged to see Charles in his coffin at St James's Palace, 'by which means the soldiers got store of moneys, insomuch as one was heard to say, "I would we could have two or three such majesties to behead, if we could but make such use of them."'" S. R. Gardiner, *History of the Commonwealth and Protectorate* (London, 1903)[20]

Anecdote from a Famous Charge of Impeachment

Warren Hastings's Trial

In 1788, Edmund Burke and other leading Whigs succeeded in bringing an impeachment charge against Warren Hastings, who had been governor-general of India. The trial opened before the House of Lords on 13 February 1788 and lasted until 1795, when Hastings was acquitted. Fanny Burney, one of the Queen's ladies, was present the first day.

"The business did not begin till near 12 o'clock. The opening of the whole then took place, by the entrance of the *Managers of the Prosecution*; all the company were already long in their boxes or galleries. I shuddered and drew involuntarily back when, as the doors were flung open, I saw Mr Burke, as Head of the Committee, make his solemn entry. He held a scroll in his hand and walked alone, his brow knit with corroding care and deep labouring thought—a brow how different to that which had proved so alluring to my warmest admiration when first I met him! so highly as he had been my favourite, so captivating as I had found his manners and conversation in our first acquaintance, and so much as I owed to his zeal and kindness to me and my affairs in its progress! How did I grieve to behold him now the cruel Prosecutor (such to me he appeared) of an injured and innocent man! Mr Fox followed next, Mr Sheridan, Mr Windham, Messrs Anstruther, Grey, Adam, Michaelangelo Taylor, Pelham, Colonel North, etc. . . . When the Committee Box was filled, the House of Commons at large took their seats on the green benches . . . Then began the procession, the Clerks entering first, then the lawyers according to their rank, and the peers, bishops and officers, all in their coronation robes; concluding with the Princes of the Blood—Prince William, son to the Duke of Gloucester coming first, then the Dukes of Cumberland, Gloucester and York, then the Prince of Wales; and the whole ending by the Chancellor, with his train borne.

Then they all took their seats. A Serjeant-at-Arms arose and commanded silence in the court on pain of imprisonment. Then some other officer, in a loud voice, called out as well as I can recollect words to this purpose: 'Warren Hastings, Esquire, come forth! Answer to the charges brought against you; save your bail or forfeit your recognizance!' Indeed I trembled at these words, and hardly could keep my place when I found Mr Hastings was being brought to the bar. He came forth from some place immediately under the Great Chamberlain's box and was preceded by Sir Francis Molyneux, Gentleman—Usher of the Black Rod; and at each side of him walked his bails, Messrs Sullivan and Sumner. The moment he came in sight, which was not for full ten minutes after his awful summons, he made a low bow to the Chancellor and court facing him. I saw not his face, as he was directly under me. He moved on slowly and, I think, supported between his two bails, to the opening of his own box; there, lower still, he bowed again; and then advancing to the bar he leant his hands upon it and dropped on his knees; but a voice in the same moment proclaiming he had leave to rise, he stood up almost instantaneously, and a third time profoundly bowed to the court.

What an awful moment this for such a man! A man fallen from such height of power to a situation so humiliating, from the almost unlimited command of so large a part of the Eastern World to be cast at the feet of his enemies, of the great tribunal of his country, and of the nation at large, assembled thus in a body to try and to judge him! Could even his prosecutors at that moment look on and not shudder at least, if they did not blush?

The cryer, I think it was, made in a loud and hollow voice, a public proclamation: 'That Warren Hastings, Esquire, late Governor General of Bengal, was now on his trial for high crimes and misdemeanours, with which he was charged by the Commons of Great Britain; and that all persons whatsoever who had sought to allege against him were now to stand forth.' A general silence followed and the Chancellor, Lord Thurlow, now made his speech . . . 'Warren Hastings, you are now brought into this court to answer the charges brought against you by the Knights, Esquires, Burgesses and Commons of Great Britain—Charges now standing only as allegations, by them to be legally proved, or by you to be disproved. Bring forth your answers and your defence, with that seriousness, respect and truth due to accusers so respectable. Time has been allowed you for preparation, proportioned to the intricacies in which the transactions are involved, and to the remote distances whence your documents may have been searched and required. You will still be allowed bail, for the better forwarding your defence and whatever you can require will still be yours, of time, witnesses and all things else you may hold necessary. This is not granted you as any indulgence: it is entirely your due: it is the privilege which every British subject has a right to claim and which is due to every one who is brought before this high Tribunal.'

This speech, uttered in a calm, equal, solemn manner, and in a voice mellow and penetrating, with eyes keen and black, yet softened into some degree of tenderness while fastened full upon the prisoner—this speech, its occasion, its portent and its object, had an effect upon every hearer of producing the most respectful attention and, out of the Committee Box at least, the strongest emotions in the cause of Mr Hastings. Again, Mr Hastings made the lowest reverence to the court and leaning over the bar answered, with much agitation, through evident efforts to suppress it: 'My Lords—impressed—deeply impressed—I come before your Lordships, equally confident in my own integrity, and in the justice of the court before which I am to clear it'. . . .

A general silence again ensued, and then one of the lawyers opened the cause. He began by reading from an immense roll of parchment the general charges against Mr Hastings, but he read in so monotonous a chant that nothing could I hear or understand, than now and then the name of Warren Hastings. During this reading, to which I vainly lent all my attention, Mr Hastings, finding it I presume equally impossible to hear a word, began to cast his eyes around the House, and having taken a survey of all in front and at the sides, he turned about and looked up; pale looked his face—pale, ill and altered. I was much affected by the sight of that dreadful harass which was written on his countenance. Had I looked at him without restraint, it could not have been without tears. I felt shocked too, shocked and ashamed to be seen by him in that place. I had wished to be present from an earnest interest in the business, joined to firm confidence in his powers of defence; but his eyes were not those I wished to meet in Westminster Hall. . . .

I hope Mr Hastings did not see us; but in a few minutes more, while this reading was still continued, I perceived Sir Joshua Reynolds in the midst of the Committee. He, at the same moment, saw me also and not only bowed but smiled and nodded with his usual good humour and intimacy, making at the same time a sign to his ear, by which I understood he had no trumpet. [She was joined in her box by one of the prosecutors, William Windham MP.] After the first compliments he looked around him and exclaimed: 'What an assembly is this! How striking a *spectacle*! I had not seen half its splendour down there. You have it here to great advantage; you lose some of the Lords but you gain all the Ladies. You have a very good place here.'

'Yes; and I may safely say I make a very impartial use of it: for since here I have sat, I have never discovered to which side I have been listening.'

He laughed, but told me they were then running through the charges.

'And is it essential', cried I, 'that they should so run them through that nobody can understand them? Is that a form of law?'

He agreed to the absurdity; and then, looking still at the spectacle, which indeed is the most splendid I ever saw, arrested his eyes upon the Chancellor. 'He looks very well from hence,' cried he, 'and how well he acquits himself on these solemn occasions! With what dignity, what loftiness, what high propriety he comports himself!' Looking still on, he next noticed the two Archbishops. 'And see,' cried he, 'the Archbishop of York, Markham—see how he affects to read the articles of impeachment, as if he was still open to either side! My good Lord Archbishop, your Grace might, with perfect safety, spare your eyes, for your mind has been made up upon this subject before ever it was investigated. He holds Hastings to be the greatest man in the world for Hastings promoted his son in the East Indies!' . . .

In the midst of the opening of a trial such as this, so important to the country as well as to the individual who is tried, what will you say to a man—a Member of the House of Commons—who kept exclaiming almost perpetually, just at my side: 'What a bore! When will it be over? Must one come any more? I had a great mind not to come at all. What's that?—Lady Hawkesbury and the Copes?—Yes. A pretty girl, Kitty. Well, when will they have done? I wish they'd call the question. I should vote it a bore at once!'" *The Diary of Fanny Burney*, 13 February 1788[21]

A Wellington Anecdote

The Iron Duke

Many anecdotes are recorded concerning Arthur Wellesley, the Duke of Wellington. Among the most famous is his remark that the Battle of Waterloo had been "a near run thing!" Another is as follows:

"Lady Salisbury asked which was the greatest military genius, Marlborough or Napoleon? 'Why, I don't know—it is very difficult to tell. I can hardly conceive anything greater than Napoleon at the head of an army—especially a French army. Then he had one prodigious advantage—he had no responsibility—he could do whatever he pleased; and no man ever lost more armies than he did. Now with me the loss of every man told. I could not risk so much; I knew that if I ever lost five hundred men without the clearest necessity, I should be brought upon my knees to the bar of the House of Commons.'" Earl of Stanhope, *Notes of conversations with Wellington, 1831–1851* (London: 1888)[22]

Two Classic Churchillian Anecdotes

Churchill's Bath

"Churchill contrived to meet nearly all the great wartime leaders while bathing himself, Stalin being the only notable exception; the CIGS, Sir Alan Brooke (later Lord Alanbrooke), described the procedure: *26 March 1943*. The PM sent for me. By the time I . . . reached him in the Annexe he was in his bath. However, he received me as soon as he came out, looking like a Roman centurion with nothing on except a large bath-towel draped round him. He shook me warmly by the hand in this get-up and told me to sit down while he dressed. A most interesting procedure. First he stepped into a white silk vest, then white silk drawers. Then a white shirt which refused to join comfortably round his neck and so was left open with a bow-tie to keep it together. Then the hair (what there was of it) took much attention, a handkerchief was sprayed with scent and then rubbed on his head. The few hairs were then brushed and finally sprayed direct. Finally, trousers, waistcoat and coat, and meanwhile he rippled on the whole time about Monty's baffle and our proposed visit to North Africa."[23] Bryant, *The Turn of the Tide* (London: 1957)[24]

Churchill's Twilight

"The last years were sad, but not as sad as some make out. He knew very well that his place in history was secure. The few friends he had were gone. The only person he ever loved, his wife, didn't like the Riviera, and liked Lord Beaverbrook still less; so he often went there alone. Once he rang up a friend of mine, who had a villa in Monte Carlo, and said that he would like to come to lunch. My friend was rather apprehensive, and invited Mrs (Daisy) Fellowes, the Singer sewing-machine heiress, who had known him for many years, to help him out. Soon after lunch began, he closed his eyes and appeared to pass out. Mrs Fellowes then said to her host: 'What a pity that so great a man should end his life in the company of Onassis and Wendy Reves.' Suddenly, to their horror, one eye opened and Churchill said: 'Daisy, Wendy Reves is something that you will never be. She is young, she is beautiful and she is kind.' Then the eye closed again." Lord Boothby, *Recollections of a Rebel*[25]

Anecdote as a Self-Authenticating "Document"

'Get Rid of Him! He's a Thief!'

"His name was Kanniyapa. He stood beneath a huge slowly moving fan hanging from the eighteen-foot ceiling in the grand dining room of 'Red Craig.' This stately 'garden house' in Nungambakkam, Madras, had been built two centuries earlier, by a sepoy general of the Honourable East India Company. It now belonged to the State Bank of India and served as the residence for its Chief Accountant, Stephen Chase. Stephen, a Madras native from an old Anglo-Indian family, had already helped us to find and rent a nice house; and now, in September 1965, he was helping us to staff it with servants. We needed a cook.

Kanniyapa's 'chits'—letters of reference—were glowing. One declared that his Swedish meatballs were 'out of this world.' Another extolled his delicious lemon pies. Our mouths watered: these were among our favourite dishes. With minds nearly made up, we were ready to make our decision. The salary request seemed reasonable—only one hundred rupees a month.

Our host turned to Kanniyapa and, looking at him over closely, remarked, 'I can see that you are a thief!' Visibly shaken, Kanniyapa's face darkened. We were shocked! How could anyone say such things to a complete stranger? To someone never before seen? Unpleasantness of this sort was not something to which we were accustomed. Something was wrong. In the face of this apparent insult, we kept silent. Kanniyapa, he eyes flashing with indignation, abruptly withdrew and left the house.

Turning to Stephen, we asked, 'How could you make such an accusation? You have never seen this fellow before!' Smiling, he replied, 'Did you not notice? Not one of those chits says that Kanniyapa is honest!! That omission alone is significant! But worse still, the fellow is insolent and surly. Did you not notice that he came into this room wearing shoes? Old tennis shoes at that? In India, no servant, certainly no person seeking employment as a family servant, will wear shoes within the house. These should have been left at the door.'

The matter did not end there. New and inexperienced, acutely conscious of the slight Kanniyapa had suffered, we brought him to our house for further consideration. Our mouths were still watering at the thought of the succulent dishes which he could put before us. Perhaps, as Americans, unaccustomed to unpleasant, seemingly unprovoked confrontations, we were too naive. Whatever the case, a few days after interviewing other candidates whose chits could not compare with those of Kanniyapa, we hired him.

The meatballs *were* delicious, and the lemon pies *were* beyond compare. Guests at are our table in Nungambakkam remarked upon the excellence of our cuisine. But one problem soon became apparent. However full we kept our refrigerator and larder, food disappeared, inexplicably and mysteriously. Moreover, butter and cheese and milk seemed to vanish at an ever more alarming speed. More food was disappearing than could possibly have been eaten by ourselves and our house guests. How could any one family, we asked, consume so much food? It was enough to run a small restaurant. But, without evidence, it was difficult to resolve this problem. We did not wish to be unjust—to presume guilt. Moreover, we did not wish to be without a cook, especially one whose dishes were so delicious.

One day, when the Swedish meatballs were especially tasty, I asked, casually and appreciatively, where in the world Kanniyapa had learned such a wonderful dish.

'Kodaikanal!' he replied. 'Amrikan missionary lady teaching me.'

'Is that so?' I pressed, 'Where in Kodaikanal?'

'Very steep hill. Baptisht Hill. Kodaikanal, my native place.'

'When was this?'

'Long, long ago! Maybe pforty-one, or pforty-two.'

'Where did this lady live on Baptist Hill?'

'Verrry top house.'

'What was its name?'

'House name "Eureta," I think.'

'What was missionary lady's name?'

'Lady name 'Prikinberg.'

Amazed, I suddenly realized that up to this point Kanniyapa never learned my name, or that of my family. Being literate *only* in Tamil, he had not been able to make out the roman letters spelling F-R-Y-K-E-N-B-E-R-G on the gatepost of our house at 2/A College Lane, Nungambakkam. Nor, as far as I knew, had he yet ever heard any-one pronounce the name 'Frykenberg' since taking employment with us. In short, there had been no way for him to know that Kodaikanal was the place where, from 1937 to 1942, I had gone to school—at the now famous American Kodai International School. Moreover, it had been during 1941 and 1942, precisely in those years, that my mother had come to spend months in Kodai—out of a mother's wish to give more loving attention to her children. The house in which we had lived during those years had been at the top of Baptist Hill. Its name had been 'Eureta'!!

'Kanniyapa,' I exclaimed, 'Do you not know my name? My *inti peru* (Telugu for 'home name') is 'Prikinberg!' That person, that American missionary lady who taught you how to make Swedish meatballs and lemon pie, was my mother!'

A look of shock and wonder crossed Kanniyapa's face. His amazement was truly as great as my own. I told him that I was going to write my mother about this marvelous coincidence. This I immediately did. In those days an airletter took over a fortnight to reach America. Two weeks later, Kanniyapa suddenly came to us at breakfast waving a telegram. His mother was seriously ill and he was urgently needed in Kodaikanal. He was very sorry, but it would be necessary for him to go immediately to Kodai to attend her. He asked for a leave of absence, promised to re-turn as soon as possible, and introduced us to his 'brother,' Muttu. Muttu, he as-sured us, was an excellent cook—almost as good as Kanniyapa himself.

Kanniyapa disappeared. We never saw him again. Muttu was a fine, if sloppy, cook—he tended to throw food about with reckless abandon, so that flies and other insects constantly endangered our health.

Two weeks later, a letter arrived from my mother. Her words were memorable indeed: 'Yes,' she wrote, 'I well remember Kanniyapa! He is a fine cook. But get rid of him! He is a thief!'" R. E. Frykenberg, A Personal Experience (Madras, Late October 1965)

Notes

Much of the argument and content of this essay has appeared in my book entitled *History and Belief: The Foundations of Historical Understanding* (Grand Rapids: Eerdmans, 1996), chap. 4, 96–122.

1. Richard N. Coe, "The Anecdote and the Novel: A Brief Enquiry into the Origins of Stendahl's Narrative Technique," *Australian Journal of French Studies* 20, no. 1 (Jan.–April 1985), 7.

2. The fascinating etymology of this word covers over six columns (more than three pages) in the OED: *The Compact Edition of the Oxford English Dictionary*, vol. 2 (1971), 1041–1043.

3. *OED*, vol. 2, 1041 (cols. 1 and 2).

4. E. M. Kirkpatrick, ed., *Chambers 20th Century Dictionary* (Edinburgh: 1983), 1276.

5. The difference between "real" and "imaginary," between "factual" and "fictional" history, lies not in their quality as narrative, but in the measure to which what they relate corresponds to actual events that can be supported by evidence ("documentation" and/or "verification").

6. Stories of nonhuman or inanimate objects, such as of an animal, forest, river, house, or even of a discovery (e.g., a test-tube experiment), are often "anthropomorphized" in the process of their telling.

7. W. B. Gaillie, *Philosophy and the Historical Understanding* (New York: Shocken Books, 1968; 2nd ed., 1969), chap. 2: "What Is Story," 22ff.

8. That this convention became more standard for "false" or fictional stories, and especially for fairy tales, does not thereby nullify their appeal, however unserious, to some past reality which was no longer real and to a "make believe" that things related were once real.

9. The name C. S. Lewis gave this feeling became the theme and title for his book *Surprised by Joy: The Shape of My Early Life* (London: Geoffrey Bles, 1955).

10. Gaillie, *Philosophy and the Historical Understanding*, Preface to 2nd ed.

11. Ibid. Or, in Gaillie's words: "Just as an investigation becomes scientific only as result of critical dissatisfaction with received theories and the consequent desire to find an agreed method for testing and selecting among these, so an investigation becomes historical only when critical minds are impelled to devise texts for the vague and often inconsistent claims to truth which most traditional stories contain."

12. Any standard reference, such as A. M. MacDonald, ed., *Chambers Twentieth Century Dictionary*, (Edinburgh: 1972), 46, so informs us that it comes from the Greek roots: *an-*, privative [consisting of the absence or removal of something: absence or negation] and *ekdotos-*, published, from *ek-*, "out," and *didonai-*, "to give," so as to make the word "*anecdota*."

13. It is what Stendhal described as the "*petit fait vrai*" of narrative—the "little actual happening," "little factual verity," "little hard truth," or "little true fact." Coe, "The Anecdote and the Novel," 7.

14. An "insider's" perspective or "private" knowledge, something which often, if not usually, puts a "different spin" on previously held understandings.

15. For variant comments, definitions, and expositions, see Kirk Polking, ed., *Writing from A to Z* (Cincinnati: Writer's Digest Books, 1990), 18–19; Raymond Berry, ed., *Literary Terms* (San Francisco: Chandler Publishing Company, 1966); A. F. Scott, ed., *Current Literary Terms* (New York: St. Martin's Press, 1965), 14; Northrup Frye, ed., *The Harper Handbook to Literature* (New York: Harper and Row, 1985).

16. At the same time, when used as a means of highlighting that event, it is often accompanied by parenthetical commentary or observations.

17. The old, yet still common Welch expression, with ancestry in old Anglo-Saxon (*segl*) and Latin (*vailum*) from which we get our word "sail," has many meanings and over-lapping connotations. At its center, like wind catching the sail, is a sense of infectious, even overpowering conviviality, ecstatic, fervent, hilarity and mirth, if not zest, alternately damp-ened by desolation and lamentation: all this and more in the course of a progress or journey from one place to another and one time to another. A *Dictionary of the Welch Language*, vol. G–L (Cardiff: University of Wales Press, 1968–87), 137–138.

18. Here, interestingly, a gender distinction arises: namely, a suggestion that anecdote seems to be a peculiarly masculine prerogative, a genre in which "no woman has truly left her mark." The feminine equivalent, as Coe (p. 6) sees it, is the Diary or the Letter. This an-ecdotal form, even when filled with anecdotal material, offers less room for the dynamics of drama. "By contrast, no male since Saint Paul has achieved immortality exclusively through his correspondence."

19. Epistle to the Hebrews (in the New Testament of the Holy Bible) 11:12.

20. Paul Johnson, ed., *The Oxford Book of Political Anecdotes* (Oxford: Oxford Univer-sity Press, 1986), 36–37 [Item 50].

21. Ibid., 80–84 [Item 107].

22. As found in *The Oxford Book of Political Anecdotes*, 111 [Item No. 138].

23. Classic anecdotes from the mouth of Abraham Lincoln are just as noteworthy and as numerous.

24. *The Oxford Book of Political Anecdotes*, 221.

25. Ibid., 222.

7

JOHN B. CARMAN

Hagiography and Hindu Historical Consciousness

In his book *An Area of Darkness*, the West Indian V. S. Naipaul gives vivid expression to his disappointment with India, the land of his ancestors:

> It is well that Indians are unable to look at their country directly, for the distress they would see would drive them mad. And it is well that they have no sense of history, for how then would they be able to continue to squat among their ruins, and which Indian would be able to read the history of his country for the last thousand years without anger and pain?[1]

Naipaul seems to be harking back to a Western view more commonly and boldly stated in the nineteenth century—that India has no history. Even in a book published in 1900, the professor of Sanskrit at Oxford, A. A. Macdonell, could say, "Early India wrote no history because it never made any."[2] This charge picks up both sides of the usual Western concept of history: both the events that have happened and the recounting of these events in some connected way that brings out their meaning. To say that ancient Indians did not compose histories is a serious charge, suggesting a marked peculiarity of their civilization, but to say that early India made no history is to say that this was a human community among whom nothing significant happened. This is the most dismissive form of Western scholarly judgment, and it was made by a professor who knew perfectly well that there was a Sanskrit equivalent for "history." Like the German word *Geschichte* or the Dutch word *geschiedenis*, the Sanskrit term *itihasa* stresses the objective side of history: it is "what happened." Naipaul's reaction to Indian history has a different emotional base. Indeed, the words I quoted come just after a statement that twenty years after British withdrawal from India, "India has almost faded out of British consciousness: the Raj was an expression of the English involvement with themselves rather than with the country they ruled."[3] He certainly thinks that something had happened in India and was continuing to happen, but he believes Indians have shielded themselves from contemplating the ruin of the past and the misery of the present in what he calls "fantasy and fatalism."

This chapter is about a particular form of narrative, history, which is a story about what the storyteller considers real events. Usually, the audience in some fashion participates in these events or their aftermath, but sometimes the storyteller talks or sings about what is long ago or far away. It is the art of the storyteller to make that distant story present, to persuade you that "you are there" or, at least, that the storyteller was there and personally witnessed what is beyond the experience of the listeners. The special difficulty in talking about Indian history is that we have often been told that India is a peculiar civilization without a history. I shall therefore need to convince you that Indians do indeed have both a history and a sense of history. More specifically, Hindu stories about their saints cannot be excluded from what we should consider history. Not only are the stories real for them, but they also already impinge on our colonial history.

Let us begin with the grain of truth in the Western scholarly assessment, which is well brought out in a recent article by Sheldon Pollock, now professor of Sanskrit at the University of Chicago. He first distances himself from Macdonell's position. We are no longer sure what history means, he states, and even using old categories there is a "massive amount of material" for the historian, including medieval dynastic accounts, "family lineages," and what he calls "historically coded iconography." Even so, Pollock continues, "there is a stunning absence of apparent historicality in orthodox Sanskrit discourse itself: tens of thousands of pages of Sanskrit text without a single useful, meaningful historical reference."[4] Pollock then proceeds to show how this negation of historical interest was itself a development in the interpretation of Vedic texts that led to the demise of a "historical" (*aitihasika*) interpretation and the triumph of a notion of timeless words in the Vedas. This had the further consequence that other disciplines, seeking to demonstrate their authority by virtue of their connection with the Vedas, also had to conform to this model of knowledge "and so to suppress or deny the evidence of their own historical existences, suppression that took place even in the case of *itihasa*, 'history' itself."[5] Pollock sees the apogee of this development in the late Vedanta. Appaya Dikshita went so far as to say that the Vedic word cancels phenomenal reality.[6] Pollock does not point out that this conclusion also reflects an interpretation confined to only one school of Vedanta, that all phenomenal existence is, viewed from the ultimate standpoint, illusory. Nor does he discuss to what extent other parts of Indian culture, which was also expressed through the many spoken languages, accepted the model of knowledge based on the eternal Veda. Certainly medieval Hindu consciousness was strongly influenced by the Vedic teaching of the Brahmin elite, but does that mean that medieval Hindus had, as Naipaul says, "no sense of history"?

It is my contention in this paper that many Hindus have what I would call a double "historical consciousness," even though neither "sense of history" is the same as that of Western historians since the Enlightenment. The first sense of history is cosmic and generally pessimistic: the awareness of the great cycles of cosmic time and their own participation in the worst of the four ages: the age under the demon Kali when human beings are scarcely able any longer to act rightly and to work toward their liberation from this cosmic line. The second sense of history is more paradoxical and more optimistic: the confidence that within their own community of devotees, their God has released them from the imprisonment of this evil age and instituted, or at least set the stage for, the return of the righteous age. We get a clearer picture of this possibility if we first look briefly at a neglected sphere of Indian scholarship that was outside of Brahmin control: the tradition of the Jains. The small but influential Jain minority has a continuous history going back twenty-five hundred years or longer, even earlier than the beginning of the Buddhist community.

In a recent paper for a symposium at the University of Virginia, my colleague John Cort contends that Jains have an acute awareness of themselves "as being historically constituted."[7] Their own sense of history has shaped their self-identity. Yet, he continues, "there has not been a reflexive, self-conscious science of history in the Jain tradition." What Dr. Cort has sorted out within an extensive body of Jain texts are "two different but closely related senses of history. The first is their location within cosmic history, as they interpret it, "their current location on the ever revolving wheel of time" coming after the twenty-four Victorious Souls (Jinas or *Tirthankaras*) of this span of cosmic time. They also locate themselves, however, within their own particular branch of the tradition, and indeed the sub-branch established in a particular geographical area. This second self-location is accomplished by relating themselves to the "history of important foundational individuals, most often monks but also frequently laymen (and only rarely nuns or laywomen)." The universal history includes virtually identical lifestories for all twenty-four Jinas and emphasizes a model of right action to counteract the previous bad action characteristic of this period of world history. The localized historian recognizes the repeated decline in standards of mendicant practice but highlights the reform affected by the founding monk or layman of that particular Jain community. There is also another kind of localized history, that of a particular temple. In his *Guidebook to Various Pilgrimage Shrines*, completed in 1333 C.E., Jinaprabhasuri to some extent combined the universal and localized histories.

Unlike the universal history, however, Jinaprabhasuri's concern is not with karma and its effects, it is with the ways in which the shrines through their close association with the beneficent events in the lives of the Jinas make accessible to his contemporaries special places of charged, salvific potency.[8] Despite the atemporal model and the lack of historical references of knowledge in thousands of pages of Sanskrit texts, it is quite evident that within the Hindu tradition there are also thousands of pages, or more to the point, tens of thousands of recited stories, of *both* the kinds of history that Cort has so usefully distinguished among the Jains. One aspect of this distinction is highlighted by the anthropologist David Pocock, who happens to be writing of Hindus in the same part of India (Gujarat) where Cort has conducted research among the Jains.

Pocock begins with the "commonplace that traditional Indian society sets little value upon history" but goes on to ask "what happens in that society to the experience of duration . . . of the particular?"[9] While the theory of the four declining world ages (yugas) seems to point to the annihilation of duration, we need to remember the awareness of all those who discuss this subject that they are living in the Kaliyuga, that is, in an age of degeneration. "The horror of duration and the human experience that things fall short of the ideal are made tolerable by being made understandable."[10] Pocock sees a parallel to the theory of the yugas and the theory of successive births. "I was struck by the indifference of the greater part of the peasantry in Gujarat to this belief which they still formally accepted." Their confidence in salvation at the end of this life through their devotion, especially in the nineteenth-century incarnation of Lord Vishnu in Swami Narayan, transcends their acceptance of standard Hindu belief in future reincarnations. Returning now to the theory of the cycles of time, Pocock sees a parallel to the two views of the possibility of the soul's salvation. While there is an inexorable "progression of the cycle from freshness to decay . . . we find the element of intervention even here: a growing belief from the Middle Ages onward that Vishnu plays with the cycles of time. His avatars come increasingly to be considered as interventions. . . . He is believed to break through the progressive decay, arrest its course, and even revive it. . . . just as bhakti is opposed to, cuts through, the inevitable succession of rebirths, so Vishnu cuts through the inevitable succession of the yugas."[11]

The two types of Jain history insight seem to be somewhat more harmoniously related than the two comparable Hindu types, since Jains believe in the possibility of progress toward eventual liberation through the moderation and partial asceticism of lay people and the radical asceticism of monks and nuns. However, official Jain doctrine does not admit the possibility that any human beings will win liberation at the present time. This first type of Jain history is thus very similar to Hindu pessimistic attitudes concerning the possibilities of moral and religious action in the Kaliyuga. Similarly, in practice, many localized Jain histories appear to believe that the most spiritually advanced monks and nuns may attain liberation at the end of the present life, just as many Hindus, at least those devoted to Lord Vishnu, believe in the possibility of liberation at the end of this lifetime as a result of the Lord's grace.

There is nothing new about recognizing either of these types of histories, or senses of history, except to admit that they are "histories." Western scholars have generally not treated either genre as historical. The cosmic history of the cycles and supercycles (yugas and mahayugas) are considered fantastic mythology, while the biographies of saints and sages are called hagiographies. It is to the genre of hagiography or sacred biography that we now turn.

When we use any English word to designate something in another culture called by some name in another language, we are involved in translation, which is often a more complicated comparison of similarities and differences than first appears. Both the Christian and the Greek intellectual traditions give us some confidence to engage in such translation. We tend to assume that there are universals in human cultural expression that can be quite adequately designated by one or more words in our own language. When we sense considerable difference between the meaning of our word (and the concept behind it) and what we have found in another language or cultural complex, we may have to choose between (1) considering the other language or culture more or less deficient in this respect, (2) seeking a more universal term than the name familiar to us, or (3) admitting that the "something" we are trying to name is not universal in human creativity or in human experience of reality. The more important is the subject under discussion, the harder it is to accept the third option. To pursue the second option, on the other hand, may require finding a more neutral term that does not pose the translation problem so sharply. We do this often in the modern history of religion: "Holiness" is more general than "divinity": "Transcendence" can substitute for "God," and instead of choosing between "history" and "hagiography," we can speak of "narrative." Some of these substitutions may prove more satisfactory than others. In the particular case to which I now turn, I want to argue that Hindu hagiography does correspond to both the subjective and objective sides of an older and more religious Western concept of history.

In September 1969, I was privileged to take part in a scholarly meeting of the Punjabi University in Patiala to celebrate the five hundredth anniversary of the birth of the first leader of the Sikhs, Guru Nanak. One scholar was conspicuous by his absence: Dr. W. H. McLeod of New Zealand. In his book *Guru Nanak and the Sikh Religion*, McLeod had given a brilliant analysis of Nanak's hymns in the Sikh Scripture, the *Adi Granth*. This part of the book delighted Sikh readers, but many of them were greatly disturbed by the other part of the book, in which he did what so few Western scholars have attempted: a careful examination of the hagiographies of the person whose writings they are studying, in this case, the *Janamsakhis*, the special Sikh term for the stories about Guru Nanak. On the basis of generally accepted criteria of Western historiography, McLeod could turn up what he considered the reliable historical evidence in less than a page. He concluded that "in the janamsakhis what we find is the Guru Nanak of legend and faith, the image of the Guru seen through the eye of popular piety seventy-five or a hundred years after his death."[12]

In my paper for that Patiala conference, I discussed the problem for the Sikh sense of history posed by McLeod's study or possible future studies using a modern Western historiography. I tried to state the problem quite directly: "Presenting the historical founder of the Sikh community to a world that is increasingly historically minded leads to both a reinforcement and a challenge to Sikh history. The traditional Sikh sense of the importance of the formative past is reinforced by the modern sense of the importance of historical events, but the . . . way in which Sikhs have traditionally told and retold their history from generation to generation is challenged by the historiography of the modern secular historian, not only in the West, but increasingly in India as well. In this seminar . . . the Sikhs have invited the world into their festive *pandal*, but having accepted the invitation and . . . come in, the world may stay to criticize as well as to pay its respects."[13]

The orthodox Sikh objection to McLeod's "historical" approach, I went on to suggest, "is all the more emphatic because of the traditional Sikh sense of history, in which the lives and teachings of the Gurus form an important part of the Sikh faith."[14] My contention in that paper is one of which I am now still more convinced: something of this same sense is present in other Indian religious movements whenever the founding teacher is considered by his followers to have opened a new channel of divine grace that redeems their lives.[15]

The rest of my paper then proceeded to compare the Sikh sense of historical importance of the First Guru and the lives of Gurus with the community of Ramanuja, in which there has been a highly developed historical sense and a corresponding interest in the lives of saints and teachers. With the benefit of twenty-three years of hindsight, I can now amend that sense of history to what I am here calling a double historical consciousness. I am reasonably sure of this formulation of the Srivaishnava community's sense of history. I suspect that a similar double consciousness exists in other Hindu devotional communities.

There are several verses in one section of Nammalvar's Tamil poem-cycle called the Tiruvaymoli (composed about 800 C.E.) that refer to the present evil age (Kaliyuga) and to the defeat of the demon Kali, who presides over the age. Let me first quote them in Vasudha Narayanan's translation.

> Rejoice! Rejoice! Rejoice! The persisting curse of life is gone, the agony of hell is destroyed, death has no place here. The force of Kali is destroyed. Look for yourself! The followers of the sea-colored Lord swell over this earth, singing with melody, dancing and whirling [with joy].

> We see them. The whirling age of Kali ends; the divine ones also enter [the earth]. The golden age dawns and floods of great joy sweep [over the land]. The followers of him who is dark as a cloud, my Lord, the sea-colored one, Fill this earth, singing with melody. They are all over this land.

> Pulling out like weeds all other religions of this earth, becoming the followers of the Lord who reclines on the deep sea, they fall on the ground, sit, rise, and sing many, many songs.

> They walk, fly, bend, acting out the drama.

> Those beloved of the discus-wielding Lord uproot disease, hatred, poverty, and suffering, which kill and conquer this earth.

> Singing melodiously, they jump, dance, and fly all over this earth.

> O servants [of the Lord]! worship, and live. Fix your minds [on Him].

> All over the worlds, the naked one (Siva), Brahma, Indra, and the hordes of immortal beings, worship the sacred form of Kannan everywhere.

> O servants [of the Lord]! If you worship him, there will be no more age of Kali.

> These glorious ten verses of the thousand [which speak of] the radiant Lord, the entrancing Lord, who shows grace to his servants, such that there is no more age of Kali composed by Catakopan Karimaran, of the beautiful Kurukur surrounded by paddy fields, will destroy the strains in our thoughts.[16]

On the face of it, these verses seem to describe a present reality, but it is not surprising that they were also interpreted as a prediction of the future, since according to one of the two Hindu senses of history, we are deeply mired in the Kaliyuga and shall continue to be for many years. The tenth verse does put the defeat of Kali in a conditional form: If you servants of the Lord worship him, there will be no more Kaliyuga. The first written commentary on these verses begins by treating the verses as the poet-saint's joyful benediction on those who had just become devotees of Vishnu. In paraphrasing the third verse of the set the commentator is emphatic: "The age of Kali is stopped for all time and only the golden age (Krta Yuga) exists." The commentary on the tenth verse simply repeats the conditional statement of the verse. The description in the final verse ("the entrancing Lord, who shows grace to his servants, such that there is no more age of Kali") is paraphrased as "the Lord, who has the nature of graciously changing Kali Yuga to Krta Yuga." This emphasizes the eternal nature of the Lord's grace and leaves the question open as to when the Lord will restore the age of complete dharma.

One interpretation of these verses by the later Srivaishnava community was to treat them as a prediction that would be fulfilled by Ramanuja (1017–1137 C.E.). Different versions of this community recognition are given in the different biographies, a recognition that is also included in three verses of an Ode of a hundred verses that claim to be composed by Amudanar, an immediate disciple. There are brief allusions in two verses ("uttering Ramanuja's name will remove Kali" in verse 43 and "Ramanuja took steps to remove the darkness of Kali," in verse 59); verse 49 contains a more elaborate statement: "When Ramanuja appeared in the world, the righteous path became straight, the false 'six religions' disintegrated, and cruel Kali died."

Exaggeration in an avowed statement of praise is well known in Indian parlance. This was especially the case when court poets praised the king. In her study of religious biographies, Phyllis Granoff has rightly pointed out how the figures of king and sage tend to coalesce.[17] It is therefore possible to give a quite minimal interpretation to this extraordinary recognition given to Ramanuja, which virtually recognizes him as Kalki (though that name is not mentioned): the avatara of the future who will end the reign of Kali and usher in the age of complete dharma, which is understood both as right social order and as enthusiastic devotion to Lord Vishnu. This royal note, however, may also be a clue to another interpretation of the theory of the four ages.

The leading French scholar of the dharma texts, Robert Lingat, has noted that one of the key formulations of this theory occurs in the Laws of Manu. There we find the celebrated metaphor of the bull of dharma who loses one foot in each successive age of decline, so that in the fourth age the bull must try to stand on only one leg. After this comes a verse in which the essential type of religious action for each age is indicated: austerity (*tapas*) for the Krta age, knowledge (*jnana*) for the Treta age, sacrifice (*yajna*) for the Dvapara age, and only the gift (*dana*) for the Kali age.[18] Lingat goes on to give one temporal and two nontemporal interpretations of this theory of four ages by later commentators on the dharma texts. The temporal interpretation is that "if the saving powers of dharma rules decrease through the ages, this should be ascribed less to the passage of time than to the declining ability of man to recall and to apply correctly the prescriptions of the Shastras."[19]

The first nontemporal interpretation is particularly appropriate for ascetics: The dharma, through its atemporal nature, is immune to the changes of the ages. The norms it propounds are valid for all time. The succession of the ages is but a delusion. The Sage can escape this Kali age by striving to conform his life to the prescripts of the Eternal Law. It cannot be said that he reverts to the past, he merely reinstates order.[20]

This reinstatement of order, however, has a different meaning for the ascetic, who has withdrawn from society, than for the king, who is obligated to protect and restore the order of society. "Upholding dharma constitutes above all the mission of the King. Indeed it behooves him to restore the Dharma bull. . . . The King, through his statecraft, founds the rule of dharma." As stated in the *Mahabharata*

(*Santiparvan*, 69, 103), he is the author of time, *Kalasya karanam*, not of the chronological time which is but an abstraction, but of the time which ripens the actions of men. Manu himself, expounding on the royal mission, declares that the king identifies himself in his conduct with the ages of the world: "Asleep he is the *kali* age, awake the *dvapara* age, about to act the *treta* age, and in action the *Krta* age" (IX, 301–02), thus indicating that, according to the way he fulfills his duty of protecting the dharma, the king institutes the Golden Age or the Iron Age. Here we are far off from the commonly given purely temporal interpretation of our verse 85.[21]

When "royal" praise is heaped on a teacher who bore the title "King of ascetics" (*Yatiraja*), perhaps it is not surprising that he should be credited with the fulfillment of the great saint's prophesy: turning the age in thralldom to Kali into the best of the four ages, the high throw of the dice (krta), or in classic Western terms, changing the age of iron into the age of gold. Whether this language is that of royal mandate from the legal tradition or the hyperbole of a poet-saint, it is but one of the ways in which Ramanuja is interpreted as a special person with a decisive role in the Srivaishnava community. His own ritual act of surrender to the Lord is not only the model for all later generations but also an assurance of his disciples' salvation; they will be accepted because of their connection to him, as well as their connection through him to the great saint Nammalvar, the gracious Goddess Sri, and the Lord Vishnu-Narayana himself. The *Prapannamrta* discussed by Phyllis Granoff is a much later hagiography that has become known throughout India because it was written in Sanskrit. It treats Ramanuja as an incarnation of the cosmic serpent Sesha on whom the Lord reclines on the milk ocean, the prototype of all servants of the Lord. It should be noted, however, that Ramanuja is not an avatara of Lord Vishnu. He is not even considered a soul liberated while still in this life (*jivanmutka*), and while his icon is given reverence with the other icons of the saints, the icon itself almost always shows Ramanuja as an humble devotee, hands folded together in the gesture of worship.

The special role of Ramanuja in the community is the feature of each hagiography that is most obviously "mythical" or suprahistorical. Even if we could be absolutely sure that his immediate disciples considered him the destroyer of the Kali age, we would still have no historical evidence that he did in fact destroy it. That "fact," so crucial for his disciples, is beyond any human discernment. Moreover, it contradicts what we think is the usual Hindu understanding of history. What we do know is that for many hundreds of years Ramanuja's disciples have considered his work, not only his writing and public debates, but also his great expansion of the community and reform of temple-worship, to have firmly established the community of God's servants who, sharing in the Divine grace showered on Ramanuja, are also assured of their own salvation. The entire community, including its monks, is still involved in the material world and in the moral compromises of society in an age of greatly reduced dharma. Nevertheless, those who acknowledge that they stand under God's constant protection (*rakshana*) and occasionally enjoy moments of intimate Divine communion already anticipate in their daily worship on earth their promised role as members of the heavenly chorus. In some sense for these devotees the power of Kali has been broken and they live their daily lives in the age of *dharma*. We might, with another risky translation, call this double sense of history a "realized eschatology," but it may be as paradoxical and as fleeting as the early Christian sense of living in two worlds. We might even describe this sense as the combination of two views of time: both the time of decay, in which human capacity seems less and less, *and* the time of opportunity, the right time (*samaya*), in which Divine grace abounds more and more.

So far our entire discussion has been about the subjective side of the Hindu sense of history, and certainly much more could be said about the theological and ritual concerns that shape all the narratives concerning Ramanuja and so many other Hindu saints and sages. From the standpoint of those standing within any one of the Hindu communities concerned, the faith in some decisive Divine intervention is crucial, and the special Divine powers of the central figures in their history are part of the objective history. Indeed, what is beyond our human gaze is precisely what constitutes this as history, as a chain of meaningful events stretching from God's saving action in the past to the daily life of the present members of the devotional community. For our purpose here, however, I should like to look at the objective side of Hindu history in a more restricted "secular" sense. I suggest that at least in the case of Ramanuja's hagiography, we ought, as modern historians, to treat this as biography and as history.

In 1980, W. H. McLeod published a sequel to his earlier book on Guru Nanak. This second study was entitled *Early Sikh Tradition: A Study of the Janam-sakhis.* He begins by stating that those stories about Guru Nanak "are certainly not biographies . . . but . . . hagiographic accounts of his life." "Even when stripped of all their wonder-stories," he maintains, the *janam-sakhis* "do not offer an account of the actual events of the Guru's life," but rather "provide an interpretation of that life . . . springing from the piety and commitment of later generations."[22]

Central to McLeod's argument is his concept of myth, which he describes as a "construct of human imagination, developing out of an actual situation and seeking to give meaning to that situation." It is such a myth that underlies the *janam-sakhis*, a myth that can be served by both legend and history. This myth is that Nanak was "the divinely commissioned giver of salvation. To all who would seek salvation the way lies open. The means of salvation consists in loyalty to the person of Babu Nanak and acceptance of his teachings."[23]

Myth, as what McLeod understands in the "myth of Nanak" or the "myth of Jesus," is not so different from what I just referred to as the suprahistorical fact that makes a communal history possible. With respect to such a "myth" or "fact," I agree with McLeod that the issue can be affirmed only by an "act of faith."[24] However, the term "myth" has an unhappy ambiguity stemming from over two thousand years of being unfavorably distinguished from the word (logos). All modern efforts to redeem the term for positive scholarly use have not removed the suspicion that a myth designates what someone else mistakenly thinks is a true story, and even if we insist that there is a social or metaphysical truth embedded in the story, it is a truth that those who "love to tell the story" often find hard to recognize. The term myth, moreover, suggests that the significance of the hagiography lies elsewhere than in objective or external history, that the eye of faith perceives a different object than the eye of rational scrutiny.

It is somewhat ironic that the term "hagiography," now so negative in its connotation for historians, once designated an important genre of Christian literature concerned with genuine human beings who succeeded in making God's presence palpable in a suffering world, whether through their own unmerited suffering or their power to relieve the suffering of others. Saintly people or their bodily remains could sometimes be the channels for remarkable hearings or other miraculous effects, and they would sometimes be the medium for supernatural communications. The canonization process in the Roman Catholic Church requires the attestation of miracles as evidence of genuine sainthood. In the modern assessment of hagiography, on the contrary, a miracle story is evidence for the spuriousness of an account, of its creation by religious fantasy or its determination by prescientific and therefore false views of natural process. Even if this miracle story is considered a legend that serves a functioning myth, it is moved in our modern historical sifting of evidence from objective to subjective history.

If we treat all hagiography, as Phyllis Granoff has done, as a particular kind of narrative, we can indeed notice both distinctive and common features of different narratives, but we are likely to see these differences only as varieties of religious imagination in the storytellers. Thus, the relatively small role of miracles in Buddhist and Jain hagiography may seem only to be evidence of the greater sobriety or rationality of the Buddhist and Jain worldviews. The Buddhists' own view, which Granoff reports, is that the monks in question had powers that would enable them to perform miracles but chose not to use them. "Holy men in the Buddhist tradition ought not to display their power before the lay public."[25] Ignoring the objective history in these miracles deprives us of greater understanding of the actual functioning of an important monastic virtue: self-restraint. In principle, McLeod's approach is different, since he tries to see how both legend and history are utilized in the service of the underlying myth. In practice, however, because of modern historical skepticism concerning the historicity of events reported in the stories, he places most of the material in the category of legend. Such material can be extremely valuable in our understanding the stories' "witness" (which is the literal meaning of *sakhi*) to Sikh faith in Guru Nanak, but the legendary material does not help us to understand Nanak as a historical figure in the wider social dimensions of what happened in the fifteenth and sixteenth centuries in the Punjab. We can learn much from Phyllis Granoff's comparative study of Indian religious hagiography, and we must admire the rigor of Hew McLeod's examination of Sikh hagiography. Certainly, both approaches are to be preferred to Western treatments of Indian religious leaders that simply ignore the traditional biographies or excuse their lack of attention to them on the grounds that they are interested in the thought rather than the person. Certainly, there are formidable difficulties in dealing with a variety of languages and a multiplicity of genres. The historian of religion, however, should be interested in the concrete expression of religion in general social history. Thought needs to be related, not only to the history of a particular person, but also to the history of that person's immediate community and wider society. To what extent it is able to construct a plausible historical narrative will vary from case to case. McLeod decided in his first book that the Sikh hagiographies were less helpful in a historical portrait of Guru Nanak than the collection of hymns attributed to him, which

McLeod considers indisputably genuine. The longer I ponder the puzzle of Ramanuja's biography, however, the more convinced I become that here the opposite is the case. The historical person Ramanuja seems to me more evident in his hagiographies than in his own writings.

Within the usual history of Hindu thought, Ramanuja is known as the first philosopher of Vedanta to challenge the interpretation of Sankara with a theistic interpretation of the relation of ultimate reality to the finite universe that is evidently affected by his devotion to Narayana (or Vishnu), whom he identifies as the Supreme Lord of the Universe and the ultimate principle of the Upanishads, Brahman. Modern followers of Sankara have often considered his teachings as well as still later theistic versions of the Vedanta as popular adaptations of the Vedantic teaching in higher spiritual insight and philosophical rigor. Although living in South India at a time when Sanskrit was known only by learned Brahmins and used only for scholarly discourse among themselves, Ramanuja writes only in Sanskrit and confines his references to a relatively few Sanskrit texts, those considered authoritative by the Vedantins. Unlike the tradition of Sankara, in which the earliest extant hagiography dates from seven or eight hundred years after his death, the earliest hagiography of Ramanuja dates from somewhere between his own lifetime (since some biographies claim to be by contemporary disciples) and two hundred years later. Some are in Tamil, some in Sanskrit, but all assume that Ramanuja knew and commented on the Tamil hymns of the earlier poet-saints of Vishnu called the Alvars, especially the long poem-cycle of Nammalvar from which we have quoted above. The later commentaries on these hymns, like the hagiographies, include Ramanuja's interpretation of particular verses. The earliest commentary, which the hagiographies say Ramanuja commissioned his cousin and disciple Pillan to undertake, is written in a peculiar Tamil, peculiar because it is filled with Sanskrit phrases that Ramanuja uses hundreds of times in his Sanskrit writings. Despite its later split, the Srivaishnava community agrees in interpreting Ramanuja as the authoritative teacher of the "Dual Vedanta": the same truth expressed in quite different ways in the Sanskrit Vedas, of which the Upanishads are the final part, and in the Tamil poems of the Alvars. When modern scholars outside the community compare Ramanuja's interpretation in Sanskrit of Sanskrit Scripture with the theology of the hagiographies, the Tamil commentaries, and indeed all of Ramanuja's disciples, marked differences are evident, not so much in the metaphysics as in the understanding of the path to salvation, specifically whether that path requires disciplined meditation on certain passages of the Upanishads leading to an unremitting devotion to the Lord, or rather a humble surrender to the Lord without regard to one's learning, social status, or spiritual attainment. The path open only to learned Brahmins, which generally meant Brahmin men, was called *bhakti-yoga*, the "discipline of devotion." The alternative was called *saranagati*, "taking refuge" or *prapatti*, meaning "humble approval" or "surrender."

The modern Western approach to Indian thought has generally considered a person's own writings to be the core of hard historical evidence. There are a few inscriptions that establish that Ramanuja did live at approximately the time the hagiogaphies state and did enjoy the favor of the king of a kingdom outside his Tamil homeland, a kingdom to which the tradition says he fled to escape religious persecution at home. Otherwise, there are the numerous hagiographies, as well as various writings in both poetry and prose, both Tamil and Sanskrit, that become more and more numerous, especially after the first two hundred years.

Those who restrict themselves in their historical portrait of Ramanuja to his Sanskrit writings face the further problem of assessing the differences between his more philosophical writings and a few much shorter devotional pieces with a doctrine of surrender that seems absent in his major works. If these devotional works are rejected as later compositions, the base of hard historical evidence is further restricted. The result is a supposed historical figure who was a Vedic Brahman quite isolated from the Tamil culture in which he seemed to have lived and quite distinct in his theology and practice from the religious community that claimed the authority of his leadership. I decided thirty years ago that it was not possible for me then to disprove this picture of Ramanuja, but one would have to accept far more improbabilities than one would in accepting the Srivaishnava claim that Ramanuja was their most important teacher and religious leader. It seemed to me then that studying the works attributed to Ramanuja's closest disciples would be one way to determine the connections between the historical Ramanuja and the figure presented in the more developed hagiographies, two or three hundred years later.[26] Some of us have since made a start on such a study. It seems to me quite probable that Ramanuja was a person who accepted the Tamil as well as the Sanskrit traditions of the worshipers of Vishnu among whom he lived in South India. He may not have been as aware of the difficulties in reconciling them as were later generations of his followers.[27]

What then are we to make of the many fascinating stories in the hagiographies? It seems to me that even to determine the characteristic features of the narrative, an examination is required as careful as that which McLeod undertook of the *janamsakhis*. That, to my knowledge, has not yet been done. Certainly, to consider questions of historical probability, we need to do as much as possible to determine the date and location of each version of what is called "the succession of teachers" (guruparampata). Even then there are likely to be varying opinions on whether certain events actually happened or whether certain prominent character traits in the hagiogaphies are historically accurate.

In contrast to the hagiographies of the rival Vedantic teachers Sankara and Madhva, Phyllis Granoff points out, the *Prapannamrta* "does not consistently present Ramanuja as a towering intellectual." Although it does report that he learned the Vedas when he was only eight days old, "in general the picture of the mature Ramanuja provided by the biography is of the pious devotee who achieves direct communication with his God, and not of the militant philosopher whose dialectical acumen is such that he marches from victory to victory in debate with other schools of philosophy." Indeed, this work "is unique in its singular lack of interest in the philosophical debate." Even when debates occur, it is through supernatural means that Ramanuja triumphs. Once this is by turning into "his divine self Sesa" who "hidden behind a curtain . . . fires off a thousand rejoinders to each of the arguments advanced by the Buddhists."[28] On another occasion he is unable to defeat a follower of Sankara named Yajnamurti. After Ramanuja prays for help the Lord appears to him in a dream and reminds him to use the arguments against

Sankara's position advanced by his great predecessor Yamuna. When Ramanuja wakes up he is filled with confidence, and he marches into the debating hall so proudly that Yajnamurti concedes in advance and becomes his disciple. Granoff quotes Ramanuja's response to this surprising development verbatim.

"There is no doubt that Yajnamurti is greater than I am, both by reason of his cleverness and his knowledge; he surpasses me in his inherent charisma, his fame and his glory. Such a one has became my disciple now only because of the Grace of the Lord of Lords."[29] Granoff concludes by summarizing the distinctive position taken by this text: "its lack of emphasis on Ramanuja's intellectual achievements in general . . . and its openly hostile attitude towards the intellectual approach to religion, with its strong support of surrender and devotion to God as the only means to release."[30] There is no doubt that this story and many other stories in the hagiography are told in such a way as to bring out the author's understanding of essential Srivaishnava doctrine. It would have been much easier to determine this specific author's contribution if the story in this hagiography had been compared with earlier versions. Certainly, when compared with the many philosophical works in this tradition, these stories show but little interest in the details of philosophical arguments. A picture is presented of Ramanuja as an authoritative interpreter of the scholarly tradition but also as the leader of a religious community that was attempting to overcome strongly felt differences between different castes, and even between one group of Brahmins and another. When prominent scholars are converted, they are given a new name and a new task. The works attributed to Yajnamurti after his conversion are more accessible doctrinal treatises—in Tamil. Each of Ramanuja's closest disciples has a distinctive role, and at least one, his secretary Kurattalvan, is also described as cleverer and on one occasion wiser than his master. This is indeed a story about the growth of a community of fallible mortals with a fallible leader, but a community trusting in the grace of God. It is more than a story, however. It is a connection back from the present to the early years of this religious community, a link back to a historical person Ramanuja, a leader who had to learn humility and then exemplify it, not by scorning intellectual gifts but by using them, his own and those of others, with a constant awareness of the pervasive grace and protection of God. With a vivid intimation of God's coming triumph, he and his followers could recite Nammalvar's disclosure:

> The persisting curse of life is gone, the agony of hell is destroyed, death has no place here.

> The force of Kali is destroyed.

Notes

1. V. S. Naipaul, *An Area of Darkness* (New York: Vintage Books, 1981), 212.
2. A. A. Macdonell, *History of Sanscrit Literature* (1900; reprint, New York: Haskell, 1996), 10–11.
3. Naipaul, *An Area of Darkness*, 212.

4. Sheldon Pollock, "From Discourse of Ritual to Discourse of Power in Sanskrit Culture," *Journal of Ritual Studies* 4, no. 2 (Summer 1990), 329.

5. Ibid., 332.

6. Ibid., 333.

7. John E. Cort, "Where Paradigms Meet: Jain History and the History of the Jains" (paper presented at the Second South Asia Symposium, University of Virginia, April 11, 1992).

8. Ibid., 22–23.

9. David F. Pocock, "Anthropology of Time-Reckoning," *Contributions to Indian Sociology*, no. 7 (1964), 26.

10. Ibid., 26–27.

11. Ibid., 28–29.

12. W. H. McLeod, *Guru Nanak and the Sikh Religion* (Oxford: Clarendon Press, 1968), 147.

13. J. B. Carman, "History and Historiography in the Study of Religious Movements: One Significance of Guru Nanak's Anniversary Celebration," in *Perspectives on Guru Nanak: Seminar Papers* (Patial: Guru Gobind Singh Department of Religious Studies, Punjabi University, 1975), 375.

14. Ibid.

15. Ibid.

16. Verses 5.2.1, 5.2.3, 5.2.4, 5.2.6, 5.2.10, 5.2.11, in John Carman and Vasudha Narayanan, *The Tamil Veda: Pillan's Interpretation of the Tiruvaymoli* (Chicago: University of Chicago Press, 1989), 210–215.

17. From her study of medieval Sanskrit biographies, Professor Phyllis Granoff of McMaster University has concluded that "both sage and king are regarded as *avataras*, incarnations of God, come to rescue mankind by ridding the earth of evil doers and heretics . . . and by giving their support to the pious and the good. . . . Both king and sage must wage war. . . . The war that kings fight is always violent; the war of the sages most often involves words, magical spells, miracles, and more subtle forms of persuasion." Phyllis Granoff, "Holy Warriors: A Preliminary Study of Some Biographies of Saints and Kings in the Classical Indian Tradition," *Journal of Indian Philosophy* 12 (1984), 291. Granoff summarizes the common feature of the saints' biographies as follows: "The saint described from childhood is different from others, he learns quickly, and begins to show a lack of interest in mundane and routine affairs. His progress is marked by miracles as he seeks his proper teacher and eventually his mission becomes clear to him and to the reader of his life, usually in a moment of divine revelation, where the saint encounters the chosen deity who speeds him on his course and instructs him in his quest."

18. Robert Lingat, "Time and the Dharma" (on Manu I, 85–86), *Contributions to Indian Sociology*, no. 6 (1962), 9.

19. Ibid., 10.

20. Ibid., 14.

21. Ibid., 14–15.

22. W. H. McLeod, *Early Sikh Tradition: A Study of the Janam-sakhis* (Oxford: Clarendon Press, 1980), 8.

23. Ibid., 10.

24. Ibid.

25. Phyllis Granoff, "The Miracle of a Hagiography without Miracles," *Journal of Indian Philosophy* 14 (1986), 39.

26. John Braisted Carman, "Ramanuja's Relations to His Successors: The Problem of

the Gadyas," in *The Theology of Ramanuja: An Essay in Interreligious Understanding* (New Haven and London: Yale University Press, 1974), chap. 17, 212–37.

27. Carman and Narayanan, *The Tamil Veda*, especially chap. 11, "The Commentator as Disciple: Pillan's Relation to Ramanuja," 145–58.

28. Phyllis Granoff, "Scholars and Wonder-Workers: Some Remarks on the Role of the Supernatural in Philosophical Contests in Vedantic Hagiographies," *Journal of the American Oriental Society* 105, no. 3 (1985), 462–63.

29. Ibid., 464.

30. Ibid.

PART III

THE PROMISE OF NARRATIVE

8

PAUL VITZ

Narrative and Theological Aspects of Freudian and Jungian Psychology

In this chapter I will look at narrative aspects of both Freudian and Jungian theory and practice. I will then note important liabilities, narrative and otherwise, of these two psychological approaches. Finally and briefly, concepts of a Christian narrative character will be applied to these two psychologies.

Sigmund Freud and Narrative: Oedipus

With the exception of Freud's notion of the unconscious, his best-known concept is probably the Oedipus complex. This idea is obviously a narrative one since it derives from Greek mythology—and in particular, from Sophocles' drama Oedipus Rex, one of a cycle of three plays on Oedipus.

Briefly, Freud's version goes as follows. The story is played out primarily in the psychological life of the male child, its first expression occurring around ages three to five. The drama takes place primarily in the unconscious of the child and will remain there throughout the boy's life, unless brought to consciousness through psychoanalysis or some accidentally equivalent activity. Aspects of the complex are normally reactivated in the boy's life around puberty. In addition, this internal unconscious drama can be activated at any time by certain external conditions related to the original childhood configuration. For example, strong father figures, the death of a father, and excessively doting mother figures can all tap into the power of this unconscious *ménage à trois*. The now familiar story begins with the three-year-old boy, filled with desire for his mother, of an immature undifferentiated generally erotic kind. Coexisting with this desire is his love, and especially his fear, of his father, whom he sees as the enemy, the rival, from whom he must take his mother. To do this he assumes he must challenge and kill his father, and thus at this stage dreams and fantasies, unconscious but foundational, of patricide are taking place along with the fantasies of obtaining the mother. The impossibility of the boy's achieving his unconscious desire is in time accepted, and the complex is "resolved" by his identifying with the aggressor—his father. This identification solidifies the boy's sexual identity and his love of his father, and brings into existence the super-ego, with its moralistic rejection of his still-unconscious aggressive and erotic desires. The fact that the complex is normally "resolved" should not blind us to the Freudian claim that it persists in its original form in the unconscious. This buried complex, with its murderous hatred and erotic desire centered on the parents, remains as the central aspect of male psychology throughout life, and, according to Freud, it remains the source of all neuroses. Patients with severe oedipal problems can benefit from psychoanalysis, by which serious neurotic dysfunction can be alleviated. However, as Freud himself said, the best that psychoanalysis can do "is to return the patient to the normal level of human misery." In other words, from the repressed oedipal hate and sexual desire, there can be significant but far from complete relief for the most severe sufferers. But for all us men, according to Freud, there is no ultimate answer or resolution. What this means is that a powerful psychological drama, involving the most intense of human feelings (sex and aggression) and the most important people in our lives (our parents and ourselves), remains at least unconsciously at the heart of Freudian "human nature." My point is not to accept Freud's claims that such oedipal motivation is universal. Unlike most psychoanalysts, I certainly do not accept that, nor, I should add, do the great majority of nonpsychoanalytic psychologists today. However, it certainly seems to have been true of Freud's own personal psychology, and most therapists are occasionally aware of the appropriateness of the oedipal framework for some clients. And, of course, Freud's theories, especially this one, have had a profound impact on Western culture.

What we must note is the way in which the Oedipus complex exposes the fundamentally narrative character of Freud's theories. Freud himself, at least at a conscious level, commonly claimed that his theories of the mind were part of natural science and not part of literature and the humanities. His metapsychological theory was derived from nineteenth-century deterministic and positivistic models of science. Trained as a physician and as a graduate student in neurology and physiology, Freud portrayed his move into psychoanalysis as an extension of natural science, especially biology, to a new area. This general claim led him to postulate his well-known "drive theory" of motivation. This theory assumed that there was a kind of psychic "energy" that was bubbling about, so to speak, in the mind. This energy was captured by certain psychic structures and led to conflicts between opposing structures such as the superego, the ego, and the id. Psychic energy was repressed, cathected, bound up, or converted from one form to another. This level of Freud's thinking has fallen into considerable disuse, especially in the past few decades. In fact, Freud's energy-based psychology is now recognized as an application of outdated nineteenth-century scientific concepts. In any case, Freud's work has shown no evidence of being a "primitive" or young scientific theory. Scientific study of the mind, especially contemporary neuroscience, has no links to Freudian concepts, and the impact of Freud on the natural science of the mind has been virtually nil.

In contrast, Freud's significance for literary studies—and other narrative disciplines—has been immense, and increasingly, Freudian scholars are understanding this narrative significance (e.g., Ricoeur, 1970; Schafer, 1980; Spence, 1982, 1987;

Steele, 1982; Vitz, 1988). As a result of this understanding, it is retrospectively highly appropriate that Freud received the Goethe Prize for Literature—but never the Nobel Prize for Science. In fundamental respects, his rewriting of the Oedipus story is analogous to Goethe's rewriting of the Faust myth: it is a great modern writer's homage to a great earlier writer's work.

Let us take a more detailed look at the narrative significance of the Oedipus complex. The most important point to make here is the obvious one: Freud's Oedipus story, for all of its differences from that of Sophocles, remains a tragedy. Of course, the resolution of the complex is not a tragedy, but the unconscious complex remains one. Indeed, it is a triple tragedy. First, because in the psychic story the boy does kill his father—over and over—and seize his mother. Second, although typically the male is never aware of this internal drama, his ignorance is no release from being made perpetually unhappy and unfulfilled. Finally, and perhaps most important, this is a drama that cannot end "well": nothing can give this story a happy ending. Human life, for Freud, is thus fundamentally tragic in its most important dimension.

Freud was often critical of other psychologists such as Jung and Adler because, as he scathingly remarked, they "attempted to provide the meaning of life for their clients." What Jung and others meant by the meaning of life was in fact a positive meaning, a purpose for life that created hope in the client. Psychoanalysis has in contrast often claimed to be, in some important sense, neutral about the meaning of life: "objective." Presumably, psychoanalysts are only concerned with making buried material conscious, with an "impartial" analysis of the mind, and they abjure such biased and teleological notions as self-realization.

However, from a narrative point of view, it is clear that Freud's fundamental assumptions constitute a narrative meaning for interpreting the mind—namely, that of tragedy: of stories that end "badly," however "noble" the characters may be. Like the ancient Greeks, modern man is pursued by psychological "furies" of whose existence he is as unaware as Achilles was of his heel. In the context of Northrop Frye (1957), we can interpret Freud's pessimistic, stoical, and sometimes cynical mental outlook as making him a man of autumn and winter, for his narrative modes are essentially rooted in tragedy and irony.

Psychoanalysis and Narrative: Schafer

This "tragic" interpretation of Freud is fully supported by the prominent psychoanalyst Roy Schafer (1976) who explicitly uses the literary typology of Frye and others—comedy, romance, tragedy, and irony—in an extensive interpretation of psychoanalysis. His focus is on the process of psychoanalysis and its underlying assumptions and attitudes, not explicitly on Freudian theory itself. Schafer's analysis so illuminates the basic narrative character of psychoanalysis that it is well worth summarizing and discussing here.

To begin, Schafer notes that his purpose is to investigate "the guiding vision of psychoanalysis" (25) and that in doing this through literary categories he is drawing attention to the "roots of psychoanalysis in the humanities" (25). Schafer is very much an advocate of psychoanalysis as a hermeneutic investigation of the personal history of the analysand. And he is quite disillusioned with the previously noted scientific language drawn from biology, chemistry, and physics as applied to psychoanalysis.

Schafer, working from Frye, notes that the comic vision

> seeks evidence to support unqualified hopefulness regarding personal situations.
> . . . It serves to affirm that no dilemma is too great to be resolved . . . no evil so unmitigated and entrenched that it is irremediable . . . and no loss so final that it cannot be undone or made up for. The program is reform, progress, and tidings of joy. (26)

For Schafer, the protagonist's confidence in worldly success, sexual gratification, and selfhood without guilt or pain is utopian. All this optimism is simplistic and illusory. Such successes and happy endings are what "[a]nalysts might call . . . manic defense, hypomanic denial, or quasi-hallucinatory fulfillment of infantile, libidinal, and aggressive wishes" (27). Nevertheless, psychoanalysis itself is not without its modest optimism. After all, the fact that analysis itself "is offered and accepted as a treatment for a troubled life implies a shared melioristic orientation" (28). Schafer rejects calling psychoanalysis a cure, but it certainly does promise at least some relief and other positive benefits.

Furthermore, implicit in the beginning of psychoanalytic treatment is that it represents "another chance, another time around, an end to the winter of discontent, and a fresh blossoming" (29). All this implies that psychoanalysis can, to some extent, redo the past and thus deny the passage of time. From Schafer's perspective, however, even the modest optimism or early "comic" mentality is quickly transformed (one might say "corroded") by the process of analysis itself. The analysand soon recognizes that all the obstacles to his happiness that he had thought were external were in fact internal: part of himself. As Pogo put it some years ago: "We have met the enemy—and he is us." In this inexorable movement, "the analysand moves beyond the comic vision of self . . . into the tragic and ironic world of inescapable conflict and costly and uncertain reconciliations" (31).

Likewise, Schafer identifies modest romantic elements to psychoanalysis. Like Frye and others, Schafer conceptualizes the romantic vision as a quest or a journey, often perilous and heroic, with a goal that combines the "qualities of mystery, grandeur, sacredness, love, and possession by or fusion with some higher power or principle (Nature, Virtue, Honor, Beauty, etc.). . . . The seeker is an innocent, adventurous hero, and the quest ends, after crucial struggles with exaltation" (31). But again, the classic romantic quest is undermined in psychoanalysis since it is seen as an expression of an underlying wish-fulfilling daydream or, as Schafer remarks, "a masturbatory fantasy" (32). That is, psychoanalysis interprets the romantic ideal as "regressive and childlike." It represents a nostalgia for a past golden age. The romantic vision, according to Schafer, idealizes individuality and self-expression. This uncritical emphasis on autonomy and triumph is understood as fundamentally narcissistic. Like the comic elements, the romantic—or quest—aspects of psychoanalysis also erode as the analysis proceeds. But modest romantic components do persist: Schafer notes that "the analysand's quest for purification, absolution, and redemption through analysis can hardly be overemphasized" (33). (In view of Schafer's emphasis on tragedy, one wonders how psychoanalysis in any way satisfies these quests.)

The problem with the romantic vision, for Schafer, is that it too dissolves as the dragons are discovered to be part of oneself, at war with another part. It is no longer an external enemy or challenge that we face; instead, the struggle is internal and deals with repressed fantasies, infantile defenses, and other unconscious motivations. This disturbing inner world is not subject to adventurous solutions in the mode of Indiana Jones. The best one can do is a heroic working through of one's own conflicts and other things that still go bump in the night.

Schafer clearly underlines the weakness of both comic and romantic elements in psychoanalysis by writing that "insofar as the analysis has genuinely deepened, all the terms have also changed in the direction of the complex, ambiguous, paradoxical, and inexorable. Changed, that is, in the direction of the tragic and ironic visions" (34).

For Schafer, the tragic vision is the underlying narrative bedrock of psychoanalysis. He describes this as follows:

> The tragic vision is expressed in a keen responsiveness to the great dilemmas, paradoxes, ambiguities, and uncertainties pervading human action and subjective experience. It manifests itself in alertness to the inescapable dangers, terrors, mysteries, and absurdities of existence. (35)

It is also the tragic vision that, as Schafer claims, is the most "remorselessly searching, deeply involved, and, along with the ironic, impartial" (35). Schafer emphasizes very heavily the tragic character of analysis. For example, " . . . the person comes to analysis caught in a tragic situation. This tragic situation exists with greatest force in his or her inner world, although the external world may have its own share of partly independent tragic elements. . . . One may say, therefore, that the analysand is a tragic hero" (39). All this is summed up by Schafer's statement that "it is the work of the analysis . . . to bring out into the open the analysand as tragic hero" (40).

Schafer understands irony as closely related to tragedy, and he sees much of the ironic character of psychoanalysis as being supported by the same arguments that he used with tragedy. Schafer, like Frye and others, understands the ironic vision as

> a readiness to seek out internal contradictions, ambiguities, and paradoxes. In this respect it overlaps the tragic vision. . . . The ironic vision considers the same subject matter as the tragic but aims at detachment, keeping things in perspective, taking nothing for granted, and readily spotting the antithesis to any thesis so as to reduce the claim of that thesis upon us. In this respect the ironic vision tends to limit (not minimize) the scale of involvement in human difficulty while continuing to insist on the inherent difficulties of human experience. (50–1)

Schafer sees tragedy and irony as similar in the emphasis that they put on reflective thought and inner articulation of feeling. He acknowledges the much greater propensity of romantic and comic visions to action in the world, to "people making their places or losing themselves in something outside themselves—in society, nature, a cause, or a conquest" (52). Finally, Schafer notes the tragic and ironic visions that so deeply imbue psychoanalytic thought that a characteristic of health is the "capacity to suffer and to be depressed" (54).

An additional and obvious narrative aspect of the psychoanalytic story is that it is always a story of the patient's past. The Oedipus complex and early object-relations have been lived out in the patient's childhood and earlier years, however much it still manifests itself. In short, Freudian narratives are biographies of the patient up until the moment of therapeutic interpretation. And because of Freud's emphasis on childhood, with its different stages of development—stages that are essentially completed in adolescence—Freud's narratives are always retrospectives.

Narrative Critique of Psychoanalysis

An obvious major narrative weakness of psychoanalysis is its overemphasis on tragedy and irony at the expense of comedy and romance. For all practical purposes, it ignores or excludes comedy and romance, and in so doing it seriously truncates human psychology. A psychology primarily devoted to fall and winter is half a psychology, at best.

Even more disturbing is the clear implication within psychoanalysis that the tragic and ironic modes represent superior forms of truth; that somehow being impartial and realistic is intrinsically grounded in tragic and ironic attitudes. Certainly, such large claims should be explicitly defended or at least their problematic character acknowledged. This view of Schafer, and of psychoanalysis, is a kind of stoicism—and however venerable a tradition this is, it is far from being the only respectable philosophic or metaphysical position.

Let's focus on some of the obvious weaknesses of psychoanalysis when tragic and ironic mentalities are used to conceptualize its fundamental vision. The most deeply disturbing characteristic of the tragic and ironic psychoanalytic vision is its fundamental passivity, and associated with this, its equally fundamental pessimism. The psychoanalytic perspective interprets all longing, all striving, all love, all hope as expressions of wish-fulfillment, as naive variations of a masturbatory fantasy. This attitude easily lends itself to a reductionistic cynicism, as represented by the familiar psychoanalytic joke: Patient: John and Mary are so much in love! Psychoanalyst: Yes, John with himself and Mary with herself. To reduce all ideas to their origins is like reducing flowers to the dirt from which they emerge. It is a reductionist illusion—and it is largely untrue.

In addition, the passivity found in so much of psychoanalysis excludes from life the great truths of hope, of purpose, of reform. In many respects, this depressed mentality undermines most action of any kind. To act is to have a purpose; and to act greatly is to have a great purpose. From a psychoanalytic perspective, all purpose, all telos is derived from our earliest years and must involve illusions; therefore, it must be infantile. No doubt, most purposes that initiate action are somewhat simplistic. After all, we know in advance only a small fraction of what may actually happen.

When, as is often true, the profound suspicion that pervades psychoanalysis seeps out of the analytic session into the life of the analysand, the result can be a life of paralysis—a paralysis that is supported by the common rule that during analysis the analysand is to refrain from any major decisions or life changes.

In any case, without action, there is little or nothing to life since knowledge itself is a response to action; even psychoanalysis is a reflection on the past actions of the self and others. Much of what we mean by truth is gained only through action. This form of truth is unavailable to those who only sit and watch and analyze. Thus, the overly developed tragic and ironic mentalities within the constraints of psychoanalysis constitute the triumph of impotence over power, of castration over fecundity, of despair over hope.

Carl Jung and Narrative

We begin with some general comments on Jung and his psychology. As a rule, Jung's psychology has not been found especially useful with seriously disturbed patients. The only real psychology that has been developed to address the clinical problems found in people categorized as borderline personality disorder, as seriously neurotic, or even those suffering from significant physical and sexual abuse have been psychoanalytic. That is, it has been Freud and especially later students in his tradition such as ego and object-relations theorists who have developed the only existing psychologies for describing and interpreting the effects of childhood psychological trauma. One reason for Jung's lack of utility here is that he has no developmental psychology. Neither Jung nor Jungians have presented a model of the psychological stages of childhood and how these stages are affected by early traumas and express themselves in particular psychological pathologies and suffering.

Jung's influential psychology has appealed largely to relatively well-functioning adults, commonly well-educated, who have been seeking meaning in their lives. These are people over thirty or forty who usually already have some psychological "savvy": thus, they know about and are interested in dreams, they are students of mythology and of the symbolic meanings of rituals, and so on. One important difference between Freud and Jung was in their relationship to religion. All his life Freud saw religion in a reductionistic framework as a kind of infantile gratification. Jung's understanding of religion evolved throughout his life. In his early years, somewhat like Freud, he dismissed religion with psychological interpretations, but by the end of his life, Jung was almost certainly a believer in God's existence. In the intervening years he had a complex relationship to religion and spirituality, but in general was positively disposed toward it. Jung was a friend of religion—through often an ambiguous and unreliable one. Jung's psychology is in basic respects the narrative opposite of Freud's: where Freud is a well-known pessimist, Jung is an optimist. Where Freud spoke of the past as controlling our lives—and our stories as controlled by that past—Jung emphasized teleology: the goal or future toward which we strove as the central psychological motive. For Jung provided a clear purpose to life, namely, the process of individuation, often described as "self-realization." The process of individuation, however, is not just a general one, but takes on implicit narrative aspects in the case of individuals in Jungian psychotherapy. Jung's most famous contributions are known as "archetypes," which are assumed to be unconscious structures having their origin in the collective experience of all humanity and modified to some extent by each person's individual experience. As an example, take the archetype of the "feminine." In Jung's view, the most ancient and (presumably) prehuman mental representation of the feminine is that which is receptive, symbolized in a very primitive way by "night." At a somewhat more "advanced" stage, the feminine might be experienced as sea, water, earth, or mountains—these are all classic feminine symbols. Yet other such representations of the feminine are caves, depths; at a somewhat higher level, dragon or spider. Still higher, fairy princess, witch, divine maiden. At a higher level still, the ancestral mother, then grandmother, and finally one's own mother. In moving from the lowest level, we are moving from a deep inherited concept of the feminine, linked with our prehuman ancestry—according to Jung. By the time we come to cave or underworld, divine maiden, fairy princess, or witch, we are into the realm of the collective unconscious. These figures, assumed to be inherited, are part of the divine feminine archetype for all humanity, with somewhat specific versions becoming modified by culture, as in the goddess Aphrodite, or at a slightly higher (or more psychologically specific) level, Marilyn Monroe. Finally, we move from the collective unconscious to the personal unconscious when we reach the archetype of grandmother and the particular image of one's own mother.

These mental structures, or archetypes, are experienced in dreams, fantasies, and symbolic understandings of the world. It is important to note that by the time you get to the level of the personal unconscious, and even in much of the collective unconscious, archetypes of the feminine—and of the masculine, and other archetypes—are typically personified. That is, they become "types" or characters, such as the earth mother, the wise old man, the fairy godmother, the trickster, that operate in an equally "symbolic" setting of mountains and trees and oceans and rivers and so on. Take also a person's "shadow" that symbolizes part of the personality which has been repressed or denied or unfulfilled in some way. For example, a shy, mousy woman might dream of being a flamenco dancer or a quiet professor might be fascinated with old Errol Flynn movies. Like archetypes, the shadow is typically experienced in dreams and other symbolic events as a character or a personification.

The process of individuation which is the goal of Jungian therapy requires that the person become familiar with his unconscious archetypes, both personal and collective. After familiarization, the person individuates by learning how to express the previously denied, repressed, ignored aspects of their unconscious. Typically, unconscious archetypes are defined by Jung and experienced by the client as characters operating in a symbolic environment. The client's ego must learn to liberate and to allow expression to these various archetypal characters. As a result, Jungian therapy can be thought of as a group of characters in search of an author—the author, of course, is the patient in a successful Jungian analysis. The particular narrative structure of this process is unique to each individual, but it can be assumed that the process is narratively a comedy or a romantic adventure, in the sense that Jung's theory is devoted to fulfillment of the self. The only tragedy Jungians allow is to fail to fulfill oneself; to fail at the process of expressing one's archetypes; to fail to individuate. Within the Jungian framework, the narrative structure is clearly that of what Northrop Frye would call spring and summer.

There is, however, no end point to Jung's process of individuation: no goal that must be reached. Instead, it is the harmonious process of expressing these characters that constitutes individuation—and a successful individuation is a lifelong process. Success is defined as the maintaining of an integrated self, as an expression of all the person's major archetypes in an integrated and developing fashion.

Narrative Critique of Jung

As far as I can discover, no one has identified the narrative aspects of Jungian analysis as thoroughly as Roy Schafer has for psychoanalysis. Nevertheless, certain basic narrative characteristics of Jung are obvious enough for comment and critique. The basic weakness of Jung is almost the opposite of that which we found for Freud and psychoanalysis. Jung provides a psychology for spring and summer, for comedy and romance. In contrast to Freud, he downplays tragedy and irony by focusing on quests, journeys, self-transformations: in short, on self-realization. Although self-realization is difficult, painful, and involves struggle, these are ultimately the struggles of romantic adventure and the conflicts of comedy. Jung's psychology is basically a description of the psychological road to success. Its relative neglect of tragedy and irony therefore represent its major weakness. One important example of this limitation is that Jung does not seriously treat death which brings all individuation to an end. Large sections of human psychology associated with unredeemed suffering are omitted. In short, Jung's comic and romantic emphases remain relatively untainted by serious tragic experiences. And, obviously, a psychology of spring and summer is just as truncated as one of fall and winter.

This very fundamental narrative difference between Freud and Jung makes it no surprise that these two psychologists were so opposed to each other. Their conflict was more than just personal: it was a conflict between two worldviews: the difference between tragedy and comedy. One of the peculiar features of the Jungian understanding of the purpose of life is its view of narrative as primarily internal: that is, most of what matters is taking place inside your head, not in your relationship with external reality. In this sense, Jung is similar to Freud. For example, narratives make sense to most of us because the hero crosses real rivers, kills real monsters, climbs real mountains, and wins a real princess. The Jungian internal landscape of one's dreams and other archetypal experiences is an example of modern subjectivity replacing traditional objectivity. You become a "saved self" within your own self; your own psyche saves itself within an arena of the self.

Jung, as I said, gives us narrative theories that are comic or romantic, but, unlike Freud, he does not give us one specific plot—thus my remark that Jung's is a psychology of characters in search of an author. His plot outlines are forward-looking, but he never provides a particular model-story, such as the Oedipus story. Nor does Jung propose how the hero actually reaches his goal in some identifiable sense. Jung's motivations and characters contain, however, implicit plots or stories for the *future*, in marked contrast to Freud's stories of the patient's *past*.

There is another narrative critique to be made of Jung, and, again, it is the opposite of the weakness found in Freudian psychoanalysis. Jung's psychology of purpose and transformation is optimistic — to the point that at times it can be rightly criticized as naively narcissistic. The Jungian self in the process of its realization is often in danger of being nothing more than disguised selfishness. Jung, as noted, has no developmental psychology, and therefore, to whatever degree childish and infantile motivations are operating, the Jungian framework is unable to recognize them.

This danger is even more prevalent in more recent humanistic psychologies, such as those of Rogers and Maslow, where there is almost no recognition, as there is with Jung, of the person's unconscious. In summary, then, if Freud's thought often gives rise to a hermeneutic of pessimistic suspicion, Jung's thought seems to give rise to a hermeneutic of optimistic credulity. Nevertheless, there is no doubt that Jung presents probably the only psychology appropriate for the major themes of human comedy and quest: in short, he is a psychologist of hope.

Christian Narrative Reflections on Freud and Jung

An important thing to note in the preceding analyses is that narrative concepts are being used to describe and analyze psychological concepts. By looking at Freud and Jung through the lens of narrative theory, for instance, Frye, we have moved from psychology as the subject to psychology as the object. We have shifted from psychological interpretations of literature to literary interpretations of psychology. Implicit in such a shift is the notion that literary and narrative concepts are more fundamental and of a higher explanatory order than psychological concepts. As long as Freudian and Jungian theories were thought of as "science," they were largely immune to direct critique of a literary kind. But today it is clear that, in most respects, such psychology is anything but scientific. It is increasingly seen as part of the humanities, as an intrinsically literary or hermeneutical phenomenon. Psychotherapy can be viewed as a lengthy oral biography or autobiography in which we describe, confess, and interpret our past life in hermeneutic terms (e.g., see Schafer, 1980, and Spence, 1982, 1987).

It is also clear, from a narrative point of view, that however useful Freud's and Jung's psychological perspectives might be, they are both severely limited. One does not have to accept Northrop Frye's model as universal to readily see this. Both these theorists claim to be presenting a universally descriptive and appropriate psychology. The failure of Jung to incorporate tragedy as an important part of human psychology, and conversely, the failure of Freud to conceptualize anything other than sorrow and irony severely limit the approach of each.

Another way to think of this is to understand that in accepting a particular plot or narrative structure as characteristic of one's psychology one makes philosophical assumptions of a fundamental kind about human nature. These assumptions are certainly not part of any kind of science nor are they part of "clinical observation" in any plausible sense of the term. Such basic differences are probably best accounted for by temperament and personal experience.

We now turn to our final purpose, which is to develop a brief critique from the perspective of narrative models embodied in Christianity. The general relevance of a narrative framework to Christianity is, I assume, obvious, since Christianity is based on a historical narrative. First, I propose that Christianity has a broader and richer narrative matrix than either Freud or Jung, for it combines, in a great synthesis, all the "seasons." Let's look at the four categories of comic, romantic, tragic, and ironic, as found in the Christian worldview.

We will begin with the seasons that Schafer and Freud have suggested are absent from the Christian worldview: tragedy and irony. Christianity and tragedy are in fact deeply linked. Tragedy in this world is a central part of the Christian message. Not only is the Old Testament filled with tragic themes, of which the fall is the first, but also the very life of Christ is understood as a tragedy in this world. It is the story of betrayal, abandonment by friends, a sentence of death, humiliation, a *via dolorosa*, the painful and bloody crucifixion, "My God, My God why have you abandoned me," death, the pietà with the sorrowing mother, and finally entombment. And this is a narrative framework that all Christians are called to imitate: all are to take up their cross and follow Christ. The themes of comedy and romance that we will come to shortly do not deny the reality of this tragic dimension. So much for the psychoanalytic claim that Christianity is naively optimistic.

As to irony, which emphasizes ambiguity, the complex mixture of good and evil, the ultimate sense of our unimportance, and the great tendency to human self-delusion with respect to our motives, here again Christianity is filled with deep ironic understandings about human nature. Many a great saint—many a great reformer—has recognized his own sinful motivations and actions. Depravity—whether total or not—is understood as a major part of human nature. One of the curious aspects in the spiritual development of many great Christians is that with their increased self-knowledge came an increased recognition of their own odiousness. The struggle with pride—which psychoanalysts would call narcissism—is at the very center of the Christian life. Doubt is another central feature of the ironic mode and of the Christian life, for no Christian escapes from doubt. As an early follower of Jesus said (and many have repeated his words), "I believe, help thou my unbelief!" The very meaning of faith is belief in the face of uncertainty, belief in the face of doubt.

What of Christian romance? Here, there is no problem, even in the eyes of its cultured despisers. The quest provides the classic Christian stories. From St. Paul's "race" to heaven, to the Grail legends, to the spiritual journeys of the Mystics, to the great religious "romances" such as that of St. Francis with his love of "Lady Poverty," *The Way of a Pilgrim*, to the countless, nameless Christians who still today seek Christ, there is no shortage of romance in the Christian tradition.

Finally, comedy—and we must end with comedy because although Christianity contains and exemplifies all the seasons and the narrative modes, ultimately, comedy is the dominant narrative principle. But Christian comedy promises a happy ending only in the next world—and not for all! Tragedy is permanent for those who end in hell—and hell, for the Christian, is not empty. Those who enter hell must abandon hope (even more fully apparently than those who enter psychoanalysis). The great Christian comedy is one that ends with a new society in heaven, with a marriage feast, with unending fellowship and eternal joy. Dante's great work, *The Divine Comedy*, perhaps exemplifies all the narrative aspects of Christian faith better than any other single literary work. *Inferno* is Dante's story of tragedy and irony; *Purgatory* is the story of pain relieved by hope; and his *Paradise*, reached at the end of the romantic quest, provides the happy ending: the story of fulfillment and joy. Truly, a divine comedy.

Again, briefly let us look at the Freudian and Jungian mentalities through a different narrative and a more theological lens.

First, the psychoanalytic tragic and pessimistic stories of oedipal conflict, the triumph of the death instinct, of primary narcissism, of primal rage and envy can all be seen as much needed explications of the fall—of the truly ugly and depressing nature of our basic psychology. In short, psychoanalysis gives us a realistic set of stories for understanding the doctrine of original sin—for understanding the size of the tragic problem we all face. (A number of psychologists have already begun discussing this issue, e.g., Vitz and Gartner, 1984; Bridgeman and Carter, 1989.) It is relevant to note that Freud accurately used the term "original sin" in reference to oedipal motivation (Freud, 1913/1950, p. 154).

Jung, on the other hand, gives us a psychologically sophisticated narrative structure for a positive response to our problem—namely, the comedy or quest with its ultimately happy ending. Of course, from a Christian perspective, it is not a story of the self seeking its own actualization, it is the story of the self seeking its rest in God. Still, Jung, understood in this way, does have narrative theological utility.

In conclusion, what I have been trying to show is the usefulness—indeed, the necessity—of narrative concepts in understanding Freudian and Jungian psychology. These great psychologies are, I believe, more strongly rooted in narrative "visions" than in (what would be called today) psychological observation and theory. Finally, Christianity's own great narrative framework certainly has nothing to fear from either the Freudian or Jungian stories. Indeed, Christianity's synthetic narrative vision may eventually enable it to absorb—enfold—these two modern psychologies as narrative contributions to the Greatest Story Ever Told.[1]

Notes

1. See L. P. Bridgeman and J. D. Carter, "Christianity and Psychoanalysis: Original Sin—Oedipal or Preoedipal?" *Journal of Psychology and Theology*, 17 (1989), 3–8; S. Freud, *Totem and Taboo*, trans. J. Strachey (New York: Norton, 1913; reprint, 1950); N. Frye, *Anatomy of Criticism* (Princeton, N.J.: Princeton University Press, 1957); P. Ricoeur, *Freud and Philosophy* (New Haven, Conn.: Yale University Press, 1976); R. Schafer, *A New Language for Psychoanalysis* (New Haven, Conn.: Yale University Press, 1976); R. Schafer, "Narration in the Psychoanalytic Dialogue," *Critical Inquiry* 1 (1980), 29–53; D. Spence, *Narrative Truth and Historical Truth: Meaning and Interpretation in Psychoanalysis* (New York: Norton, (1982); D. Spence, *The Freudian Myth: Toward Paradigm Change in Psychoanalysis* (New York: Norton, 1987); R. S. Steele, *Freud and Jung: Conflicts of Interpretation* (London: Routledge & Kegan Paul, 1982), Paul C. Vitz and J. Gartner, "Christianity and Psychoanalysis, Part 1: Jesus as the Anti-Oedipus," *Journal of Psychology and Theology* 12 (1984), 4-14; Vitz and Gartner, "Christianity and Psychoanalysis, Part 2: Jesus as Transformer of the Superego," *Journal of Psychology and Theology* 12 (1984), 82–90; Paul C. Vitz, *Psychology as Religion: The Cult of Self-worship* (Grand Rapids: Wm. B. Eerdmans, 1988).

9

JON N. MOLINE

Words, Deeds, and Words about Deeds

As I was quietly thinking about this paper one evening, my wife, as she often does, read aloud a sentence from the book she was reading. It was attributed to George Eliot: "Blessed is the man who, having nothing to say, abstains from giving in words evidence of the fact." Fortunately, she did not know that I was thinking about this paper and did not sense the momentary alarm I felt. The Eliot quotation expresses the writer's beatitude that each of us naturally fears substantiating. The alarm was only momentary, however, because it quickly occurred to me that in moral philosophy Eliot's saying is no beatitude. If it is possible to violate it, I hope to do so most egregiously in this paper.

The reason is that in moral philosophy anything one has to say in the sense that it is merely one's own and totally original will be at best misleading and probably false. There is nevertheless much to be said, and, while slightly elusive, it is in a sense common property. Nine-tenths of it is the accumulated common-sense wisdom—perhaps a tragic, this-worldly wisdom—wisdom the love of which gave philosophy its name.[1] But like all common property, it is easily neglected and therefore in a messy state when found. There is now some uncertainty even about where to find this common property or who, if anyone, cares for it. My approach to the search for it is Aristotelian and Christian in orientation, and it comes from one deeply concerned with the education of undergraduates. That the elements in this approach are complementary will, I hope, be illustrated in what follows, although it is no part of my purpose to argue this here.

Wisdom is always related to questions. The most profound question of moral philosophy is still the one posed by Socrates in the *Gorgias*: How ought one to live?[2] It was and is a commonplace that one ought to live a good life, as a good person would live it. But there is perennial uncertainty about how to interpret such commonplaces.

This uncertainty is heightened by Alasdair MacIntyre's argument that since the Renaissance there has been serious disarray in our moral language.[3] In effect, he suggests that without common terminology there cannot be commonplaces or common opinions. Iris Murdoch also has observed what she regards as a loss of moral concepts.[4] Such disarray or loss might appear to pose severe problems for Aristotle's method and for the method of anyone who, like John Rawls, relies upon considered convictions.[5] Aristotle's work in ethics and in other areas of philosophy as well is rooted in what he terms, variously, *ta legomena* ("the things we say"), *ta phainomena* ("the things that appear to be so"), and *ta endoxa* ("the opinions found among us"). But if there is no serious agreement on what to say, no common opinions on issues of importance, and no common language in which to express common opinions if they existed, then this method would be most unpromising.[6]

Various jeremiads against our age, and especially against undergraduates, reinforce the suggestion that there are no *endoxa* or *phainomena* worth considering today.[7] To the degree that young people have become moral relativists, they may share only the opinion that their differences of opinion—marked, perhaps, by differences in vocabulary—are in principle irreconcilable. The writers of these jeremiads have called attention to issues needing discussion and have made many penetrating observations about what undergraduates today do not know. Nevertheless, the best-known were written by academics under the conditions of university life, and this feature is not reassuring as a basis for constructive work in moral philosophy.

Perhaps many of us who are academics should remind ourselves in all humility that we are not ideally placed to consider the *phainomena*, the things that appear to be so to undergraduates. Most of us encounter these students chiefly in the artificial environment of the university classroom, where structural obstacles such as anonymity and enormous classes may make it difficult or at least unnecessary for them to say what they seriously think.[8] Even where these structural obstacles do not exist, years of secondary school experience have convinced many undergraduates that articulating silly theories offering little guidance on any serious decisions they may face is often expected in the classroom and perhaps even rewarded. They may also have become convinced that saying what they really think may bring harassment from immature classmates and may occasionally even endanger their grades. What they seriously think, when they do, will emerge elsewhere, in the way they seek to live, and in what they say about this in nonclassroom settings.

The audience for the sort of moral philosophy that interests me probably will not be found—or found in an appropriate frame of mind—in the university classroom. It will be found in residence halls, dining halls, offices, stores, homes, workplaces, and churches. This audience is also a source of anecdotes, narratives, and insights. It transcends sex, race, nationality, ethnicity, and socioeconomic status. However, it does not include everyone, or everyone in every frame of mind, at least. This audience consists of those who are grappling personally with the question, "How should one live?" and are serious enough to relate this personal quest to the general question, if asked, rather than treat the general question as a strange, isolated classroom exercise. This is an audience far more confident of what a good roommate is than of what a good theory is, but one capable of bringing its enacted, applied, and hence serious views about roommates to bear on general questions about the way one ought to live. As a consequence, this audience does not include hardened moral skeptics, those who lack experience of life, those who are so impulsive that what they know does not connect with what they do, sociopaths, or those who see a quandary in every situation.[9] It does not consist of people who lack a sense that some things are absolutely wrong, and that avoiding these is a given for serious discussion of the problematic things that aren't.[10] It does not consist simply of moral critics—the Monday-morning quarterbacks of life. It consists of agents who must decide what to do and *be* or refrain from doing and being under conditions of great variability and uncertainty.[11]

What appears to be so to those who are left when the above people are omitted is not easy to discern unless, like a biblical translator scanning another language for promising expressions, one is attentive to the uses to which their own expressions are being put.[12] If one listens for the standard vocabulary of this or that ethical theory or tradition, one will probably be disappointed. Either one won't hear it at all, or, as MacIntyre points out, one will hear a potentially confusing mixture of terms drawn from allegedly incompatible theories.[13]

Nevertheless, serious people of all ages and places sense a need for guidance on the major questions of life, and they do still come equipped with eyes, ears, and brains. If they do not inherit terminology that helps them in responding to these questions, they will struggle to develop their own. They will reinvent the wheel. Perhaps its style won't exactly complement your conceptual vehicle or mine, and it may be out-of-round, but it will be recognizably a wheel in the way it functions. Let's listen for some wheels that are still turning, some convictions that are *phainomena* suitable for grounding moral philosophy today. A few of the difficulties these raise will be reviewed along the way. These *phainomena* will perhaps sound banal, but so does most of life, by definition. As my wife's sagacious undergraduate roommate, Jane Boyle, once remarked, "Life is so daily!"

To introduce our first *phainomenon*, consider the responses that a group of undergraduates gave to the following story I told them recently one evening over dinner. To the best of my recollection, all but the first sentence is true. One of my friends from undergraduate days appeared to me to be a good human being. He was, however, engaged to three women at once, unbeknownst to them or to his friends. In addition, he was arrested for corrupting the morals of a minor, theft, and several other offenses. Friends found that his promises were almost worthless. Money left lying around in dormitory rooms occasionally disappeared if he was around. I personally saw him commit one senseless theft of a small item. Although he was fun to be around at first—disarmingly pleasant and charming without seeming slick or manipulative—those who trusted him in any capacity stood a significant risk of betrayal. When found out, as he was more and more often, he never showed remorse or shame—just perplexity at what he would characterize as a small misunderstanding. After graduation, the grapevine had him guilty of transcript forgery and a series of small thefts collectively serious enough to get him expelled from graduate school.

Having related this tale to the group of young people over dinner, I asked them if I had said anything strange. The first said, "Yes. Why did you think he was a good human being?" Another said, "Right. What was good about him?" A third said, "Good for what?" They went on to reflect that they certainly would not wish a roommate or friend like that on anyone, still less a fiancé, and they wondered how anyone could put up with him for long. They wondered how I could describe him as a friend. He appeared to them a person they would choose to avoid if given the chance—one who was perhaps good for nothing.

In a more positive vein, these young people would find it equally strange to characterize someone as a bad human being while conceding that this person was a gentle, faithful, and loving mate and parent, a dependable and constructive employee, scrupulous about paying debts, a thoughtful neighbor, a responsible citizen, and a cheerful, loyal, and helpful friend. They would ask, "What is bad about him?" or "Bad for what? One might express the general import of these undergraduates' responses in the following way:

> *Phainomenon* 1: A good friend, roommate, spouse, counselor, club-member, office-holder, neighbor, etc. is a person who is worth choosing as a friend, roommate, counselor, club-member, office-holder, etc. A bad—— is a person who is worth avoiding as a——.

It may be tempting to raise a difficulty about good hit-men, but recall the Aristotelian exclusionary clause introduced earlier: absolute wrongs are not covered by these remarks, nor are roles that consist in undertaking to commit them. In such roles, "good" means merely "efficient," not "worthy of choice," since nobody is worth choosing for a role that is absolutely unworthy.

> *Phainomenon* 2: We aren't hermits. What humans do is done in relationships.[14] How one ought to live is surely conditioned by how one will in any case *have* to live. Human life is lived in, through, and sometimes for relationships. They require our choosing or avoiding people (and our being chosen or avoided) for such relationships.

The young people who heard the story of my undergraduate friend plainly knew that life inescapably involves choices relating to persons—to room with them, get engaged to them, marry them, live in their neighborhoods, be friends, colleagues, or coworkers. If what I said about my friend after the first sentence was true, it appeared to them that the first sentence itself could not be. All important human relationships demand some measure of trust, and these students saw reason to deny that my friend was worth choosing for roles or positions of trust. They concluded that unless I had left out a lot of the story, he must have been worth avoiding. They would also ask how one can be a good human being if one is worth avoiding in every important human relationship. It appears to them that human life is largely a tissue of such relationships among mutually interdependent people.

If we substitute *haireton* for "worth choosing" and *pheukton* for "worth avoiding," I have described to you a group of fairly ordinary young twentieth-century Americans who not only understand important parts of Aristotle's language but also speak a roughly functional counterpart to it and guide their lives in large part by its use. I submit that most of the rest of us do the same in our serious, practical moments. I do not wish to deny that students might sound like sophomoric relativists if asked the wrong questions or prompted for canned classroom responses. Nor would I wish to claim that among themselves they would always express their decidedly Aristotelian convictions in the standard English I have used in giving voice to their *phainomena*. In the variable language they employ, we might not recognize these views for what they are at first, but we might not recognize them if they were translated into Arabic, either.[15]

It is important to consider what these young people are *doing* with their language. They use it—especially in response to anecdotes—to express *phainomena* and guide their choices. In this respect that language is functioning much as Aristotle's did, and functional equivalence is the most plausible construal of sameness of meaning.[16] It may be objected that emotivists do as much with their language, and that this is scarcely a cause for cheer. But the function being performed here turns on implicit notions lacking in emotivist discourse. It turns on a wonderfully durable implicit notion of character, and therefore of virtue.[17]

That these undergraduates use no single word corresponding to "character" or to "virtue" is not decisive. As Bernard Knox recently pointed out in his Jefferson lecture, the English language itself has no word for *Schadenfreude*, either, but who would wish to claim that speakers of English who do not know the German word therefore do not feel, notice, or understand the phenomenon? Function, not gnostic pedigree or ecclesiastic authority, determines meaning, and the same function can be performed in ways that sound vastly different.

These young people choose roommates, friends, mates, club-members, mentors, teachers, employers, etc., and they badly want people whom they can trust. If accused of breaching trust themselves they would be upset, and if guilty, they would feel remorse. Such people quietly contribute and attend to the local grapevine on who can and cannot be trusted and in what spheres: "Don't date Robert; you may get raped." "Watch out for Professor Offenreden; if you confide in him, the whole campus will know your secrets within a week." "If you are looking for a serious relationship, stay away from Alison; there is no give and take with her when it comes to her future career; it's all take." "Don't go to work for the Whiztech Corporation; they rip off their customers and their employees."

The popularity of gossip is often thought to be a discreditable thing, but the telling of illustrative and cautionary anecdotes has always been one of the chief tools of moral education.[18] Aristotle remarked that moral judgment lies with perception, and so it does, but perception is made more accurate by prior reflection on such anecdotes.[19] Trading such stories has by no means disappeared among undergraduates. These are stories—micronarratives, if you will—of *choices*. In their serious moments, when they are grappling with real problems in their own lives or reflecting on how their friends grapple with them, they speak quite a bit of good and bad relationships. They share stories of people who are worth choosing or worth avoiding in key roles such as friend, teacher, advisor, fiancée, roommate, mate, or even parent. With Aristotle they are aware that being worth avoiding in one or two roles probably does not make one an evil person.[20] But how wide a variety of botched relationships and instances of broken trust can one enumerate for a given person without concluding that this person is simply worth avoiding as a human being?[21]

Like Edmund Pincoffs, these young people may not move from Aristotle's remarks about good flute players and good harpists to a teleological view of human nature, or at least to the same teleological view that Aristotle appears to embrace. But they certainly hold that one cannot avoid expecting people to function in certain ways—to produce certain kinds of works or fruits, if you will—in key human relationships and praising them if they do, blaming them if they don't.

The language of relationships should not conceal the Aristotelian substance of what these young people were saying. Aristotle insisted in both the *Nicomachean Ethics* and *Politics* that humans are social animals—that is, that we are born into, sustained by, and incapable of existing without human relationships.[22] Not all of the people in these relationships can be chosen, but even for those that cannot be chosen, we employ the notion of the sort of person we *would* choose if we could. We do this by way of making clear who we think worth choosing and therefore good. This reflects Aristotle's notion of who or what is *haireton*, worthy of choice. If we could, we would not choose to have alcoholic parents or dangerous neighbors, although we may be born with both. What makes a person worth choosing? To some extent, this must depend upon the particular type of relationship for which the person is being chosen, hence, despite a congenital mistrust of the sophists, I find congenial Pincoffs's quip, "Two Cheers for Meno."[23] Good teachers, good neighbors, and good parents need not have precisely the same traits, however much they may have in common, and despite whatever generic term one might find to cover all of these. But, as Pincoffs noted, Socrates gets two and one-half cheers, for the common ground is striking. Where do we look for this common ground?

> *Phainomenon* 3: People are worth choosing or avoiding on the basis of their dispositions, or, as undergraduates today might put it, a little elliptically, on the basis of "what they are like as persons."

Iris Murdoch once referred to what she termed "the opacity of persons."[24] This is what worries any prudent person in choosing another—or in being chosen—for a relationship. We know from experience that "what you see is not necessarily what you will get." A virtue is simply a praiseworthy disposition, a disposition worth choosing, but just as all children appear to be angels when asleep, so, no doubt, do all devils; their dispositions are not being manifested. Not every disposition one has *can* be manifested at the same time even in waking life, since some have physically incompatible manifestations. One can't laugh in amusement and cry in grief or rage at the same time. Perhaps not every disposition one has can be displayed even in the same year, since circumstances inviting the manifestation may not occur in that time period. In choosing people for relationships we are taking chances on tendencies and propensities we may not yet understand and may not yet have seen evinced. Wise choices tend to be founded on long acquaintance under a wide array of circumstances.[25]

In choosing people for relationships we are also projecting that the tendencies we *have* seen called forth in the limited circumstances in which we have encountered the person we are considering are good indications of what we can expect from this person in other circumstances. We could be wrong, and if we have lived long enough, we have been wrong embarrassingly often and with painful consequences. Recall various job interviews you may have conducted. Those of the young who are serious—and they do exist—know that it is well worth their while to sharpen their sense of "what people are like." They want to enhance their ability to diagnose trustworthy and untrustworthy dispositions on limited and potentially misleading evidence.

> *Phainomenon* 4: It is important to distinguish between what a person seems to be like here and now, and what that person will be like in other circumstances, or is really like deep down.[26]

As a basis for trust, dispositions must be stable, deeply engrained, and difficult to change.[27] Stability in dispositions is one necessary condition for trustworthiness or dependability in any important relationship. This ranks high among the desiderata for important associates of the young people I know today, as it did among Aristotle's criteria for what makes someone *haireton*. This stability is not stasis, as Aristotle's treatment of changes in friends suggests. One relevant form of stability is continuous growth in experience, insight, understanding, and maturity. Friendships can end, as Aristotle points out, for no deeper reason than that one party fails to mature and the other continues to mature[28]. Young people today are acutely aware of acquaintances who are not ready to grow up, and serious young people try not to trust such people in important relationships that demand maturity. They have quite an array of slang terms for such people, as well as the most elegant form of nonverbal communication—avoidance itself.[29] While the terms used change, a felt need for their function evidently remains, since the behaviors they guide—avoidance of relationships of trust with certain people—are almost inevitable.[30]

> *Phainomenon* 5: Self-knowledge is, in large part, knowledge of one's own dispositions, and this knowledge is a prerequisite for wise choices in relationships of trust.

Consider a relationship of trust with another person, for instance, a close friendship. One cannot enter into such a relationship with much confidence unless one knows that one can probably fulfill the trust one is undertaking. If a friend trusts me with a personal secret, I will need to be disposed not to tell it for personal advantage or for the amusement of others and the humiliation of my friend. If I am not so disposed, I cannot responsibly listen to secrets. If I cannot responsibly listen to secrets, I cannot be—or remain—a close friend.

Not having reflected on one's own dispositions precludes clear awareness of one's own identity and character. This in turn precludes one's being able to enter responsibly into a relationship of trust requiring that one have a certain disposition or character. Today the words, "She doesn't know who she is" can be a damaging claim, even if tempered by a sympathetic concession that "she is trying to find out." Responsible people who are trying to find out who they are, not wishing to hurt others, may be understandably wary of commitments, and others who are perceptive may be understandably wary of them. Much of the admittedly fatuous-sounding talk one hears these days about "finding out who one is," or "getting in touch with one's feelings" would not get the hearing it does were it not for the need young people have to grope for the self-knowledge required for entering responsibly into important relationships. That there is fortunately almost as much to *choose* as there is to *find out* about one's identity is perhaps an insight that comes later than one would wish, but it often does come.[31] There is an element of decision—of self-formation—here as well as self-knowledge. How does this self-formation—this formation of the sorts of dispositions that facilitate or preclude trust—take place?

Phainomenon 6: Dispositions grow out of like activities.[32]

Like Aristotle, serious young people are curious about the sources of stability in dispositions, especially so since they are typically surrounded by others whose character is not as yet fully formed or deeply rooted and is therefore at least a bit unstable. Many do learn that dispositions and the identity they help comprise are built out of like activities—out of countless small choices that eventually have a big effect. And they do know at least dimly that they should watch the trends shown by those choices, comparing these with expressed wishes. People become alcoholics by drinking a great deal of alcohol, regularly. People become great pianists by practicing the piano a great deal, self-critically and regularly. People become kindly by acting in kindly ways, regularly. We become reflections of what we practice daily. Students' participation in athletic training, their study of musical instruments or voice, and their everyday study itself also reinforce their awareness of the effects of practice. In my experience, serious young people have been less willing to excuse a student's having overlooked this obvious fact than faculty and staff are.

Phainomenon 7: We are not always ourselves.

A disposition is not a guarantee of the relevant like activity, nor is an instance of the relevant like activity a guarantee of the disposition. Anomalies must be expected and interpreted carefully in the broadest possible context. One of the most difficult sorts of judgment one has to make about another person or about oneself is the true significance of an anomalous piece of behavior—an act or omission that, if generalized, would falsely suggest a disposition worthy of avoidance or, in the case of a charlatan or fake, a disposition worthy of trust. Such anomalies can make us wonder what the agent really wishes for. It is natural to ask, "What kind of person would do that?" and to try out various answers, flattering and unflattering.[33] One asks this knowing that there are actions that are out of character, actions that should be discounted as indications of the agent's dispositions.[34]

We are especially attuned to this difficulty in an election year, when what is now called "the character issue" figures prominently in voters' assessments of candidates, more prominently perhaps than what, if anything, they say about their proposed policies and their preferred diagnoses of the world's problems. We all suspect that instability in wishes can be masked and bad character more or less successfully concealed only to emerge later in disastrous ways.[35] The opacity of human beings remarked on by Murdoch is especially unsettling when we are choosing leaders who will be entrusted with enormous power.

We know that since the days of Gorgias, if not before, political candidates have managed their images. They have put the most favorable "spin" they could devise on stories about their past, sometimes deceiving others about their character. We disregard such stories at our peril and seek out the as-yet-unedited ones. In the *Rhetoric*, Aristotle describes a charge brought by one Callistratus against Melanopus. Melanopus is said to have kept back three consecrated half-obols—a very small sum—from the temple-builders, the point evidently being that one who would give in to temptation by stealing so small an amount dedicated to a sacred purpose surely could not resist larger temptations.[36] We, too, look for signs and portents of untrustworthy dispositions, preferably far in the past, where the person who may be contriving to deceive us perhaps has less chance of editing the story.

We may also ponder the possibility that a trait can appear stable without being deeply rooted in the way required.[37] Recently a friend who knows one of the presidential candidates told me that he admires this person very much. He regards the candidate as a person of integrity, but believes he would make a terrible president because he is impatient. That is, he concludes that the candidate's desire to work with fallible human beings to achieve a hard-won solution to a problem does not run deep enough, although at the level of consciousness it is quite sincere. His concern is that what this candidate thinks or wishes in sober conversation and even on the campaign trail may be irrelevant to what he would actually do when confronted with the necessity of working with flawed people for whom he has inconcealable contempt.[38] If asked hypothetical questions about this future relationship, the person questioned may answer consistently and sincerely, but may simply be unable to live by those answers under circumstances he has reportedly neither faced successfully nor cultivated the dispositions to face.[39] Perhaps we shall see.

Good intentions or noble wishes alone do not constitute a disposition, although they help one distinguish dispositions that might temporarily yield similar behavior. Talk of intentions or wishes should not suggest that conscious deliberation is necessary for a disposition worthy of choice—kindness, for example—to be manifested.[40] There are habits of attentiveness, thought and thoughtfulness.[41] Yet even these have their limits, and it is crucial to recognize the importance of manifesting trust-related dispositions both *within* and *beyond* these limits. Suppose we are considering a candidate for a relationship or position that demands courage. Even the most frank armchair answers about hypothetical situations posed in an interview at best demonstrate good intentions, not courage. Aristotle shrewdly observed that there is a difference between frightening situations for which we can make specific preparations, psyching ourselves up in advance, and those for which we cannot prepare. Sudden frights test courage better than situations one anticipates, Aristotle argues, for one's response in sudden frights springs more from one's disposition and less from calculation.[42] One might decide to face a danger for the good repute it might bring. One might decide to face it out of a misconception of one's own strength or of the enemy's weakness. Such decisions are no indication of what one might do without time to think. Even question and answer will not disclose *how* one will react in an emergency or under stress of the sort that can impede or even preclude careful analysis.[43] Such emergencies provide the most compelling signs of what I will now term *dispositions of manner*.

> *Phainomenon* 8: Dispositions of manner provide the most suggestive and wide-ranging indications of a person worth choosing for a relationship of trust.

In describing the various ways in which we can go wrong with regard to fear, Aristotle noted that we may do so because we fear things we ought not, or fear things we ought to fear but at the wrong time, or in the wrong manner.[44] He gave great prominence to *how* one does things, to one's *manner* of behavior, and the importance of this needs greater stress than it has received from moral philosophers. I submit that serious young people today—like many of their elders—are aware of the importance of manner, and that *phainomenon* 8 is central in their thinking even if not well articulated.

When we consider what we know of others—or even of ourselves—and attempt to project this into the future, specific actions may be less revealing than the manner in which they are undertaken. Even the phrase "doing what one ought" proves to be ambiguous. It could cover simply the overt actions one is morally obligated to perform, even if they are performed grudgingly, reluctantly, churlishly, and under moral duress. Or it could cover doing what one ought in the way one ought to do it—cheerfully, willingly, generously, clearly wishing to be of help, giving observers reason to believe that this sort of behavior is not precarious in one's moral economy even though it is not automatic.

It is a sign of being more admirable to do what one ought in the second way—cheerfully, willingly, and the like—and, unwelcome as this may have been to Kant, it marks a character more worthy of trust and of choice.[45] It is wholly implausible to think that moral *worth* is not dependent on one's being *worth choosing* for relationships of trust, and therefore unrelated to the complex dispositions that make one reliable in such a relationship. Kant patronized acts that are both dutiful and amiable as backed by inclination, saying they deserved "praise and encouragement but not esteem."[46] But his doing so is based on an indefensible distinction. What we esteem or treasure most highly *for important moral relationships* will not be a grudging demonstration that some Scrooge-counterpart can, out of a belated sense of duty, bring a turkey to the Cratchetts' at Christmas, but rather a demonstration of an easy, unforced, authentic love that has proven itself reliable.

A better distinction could be made between what is morally *welcome* (our Scrooge counterpart's behavior, however belated) and what is morally *treasured* most highly. We can surely welcome—and even throw a party over—the return of a prodigal, but this does not necessarily imply that of all human behaviors, the return of the prodigal is to be treasured most highly. It elicits rejoicing at a moral windfall, but not the quiet satisfaction of what we treasure most. The word "treasure" suggests an attempt to keep, to make secure, reliable, and thus available to answer routine expectations. It excludes windfalls.

We treasure integrity—the diversity in unity in the image of which we are made, according to Trinitarians. On this view, lack of pleasure in or inclination toward doing the right thing is a sign of a deficiency in personal integrity, a further distortion of the image of God in us.[47] Not all the parts of such an agent are singing in harmony, as Plato would have said.[48] Aristotle remarked, in the same vein, the good person *feels and acts* as the circumstances merit.[49] Unless a person displays the relevant "feeling," we will find trust more difficult. We know very well that emergencies precluding principled calculations will reveal a disposition that is more than a matter of Kantian will or utilitarian calculation. Virtue need not be precarious to be virtue.[50] The disposition must, however, be the product of choice.[51] Cheerfulness in doing the right thing is reassuring about the reliability of the agent because it is reassuring about the motives and the personal integrity involved in the agent's doing it. It is not only the Lord that loves a cheerful giver.

"Manner" is an elusive and little-examined notion, yet morally central in the *phainomena* of the moral life in this age as it was in the age of Aristotle and the age of Jesus. The term's etymology suggests a relationship to the hand—specifically, a mode of *handling* situations, issues, or tasks. Manner in the relevant sense is dispositional, and akin to style in the sense of fashion only as blushes are akin to ruddy complexions or mere conditions (Aristotle's *diatheseis*) to dispositions (*hexeis*). An artist may have a style that endures for her entire career. So, too, an admirable person may have a characteristically graceful manner of handling difficult situations, a way of responding even to unanticipated problems or challenges. This manner of response can convince us that he or she is worth choosing for an enduring relationship of trust. Often manner is called *attitude*.[52]

The display of a manner or attitude can be characterized adverbially, but the manner itself is so subtle and so versatile that it may take a series of stories or parables to illustrate the difference between the manner worth choosing and a more typical manner. Looked at in this way, the parables of Jesus are often parables of manner, contrasting one way of responding to an issue with another, more conventional way.

The parable of the prodigal son can be viewed as contrasting the father's manner of greeting the return of the prodigal with the quite understandable manner of the older brother.[53] The parable of the good Samaritan can be viewed as contrasting the manner of the Samaritan with that of the other travelers who ignored the robbery victim and passed by on the other side.[54] The parable of the laborers in the vineyard can be viewed as contrasting the manner of legalistic employees whose view of justice appears to leave no room for generosity or grace with that of a generous but unpredictable employer who sometimes pays more but never less than contracted for.[55] The parable of the king and his debtor can be viewed as contrasting the manner of a compassionate creditor with that of a harsh and inflexible one.[56] Even Jesus' saying that he was leaving peace with his disciples, but that he did not give as the world gives, points up not just the difference between ordinary peace and Jesus' peace, but the difference in the manner of giving: as a pure gift, with nothing expected—indeed, nothing possible—as a quid pro quo.[57]

Such parables and stories are not allegories to be read as offering detailed guidance on all points of what to do in a given sort of situation—for example, on killing a fatted calf, not ordering pizza to be delivered; offering a ring, not a watch, and a robe, not a shirt and trousers; or pouring wine and oil but not hydrogen peroxide over wounds; or listening to pleas not to be sold into slavery but not pleas to be spared bankruptcy. They make a far more elusive point about a preferred but attentive and flexible *way* of responding to unpredictable challenges. They speak about joyous virtuousity, not grudging minimalism, about grace, not law, about a disposition or attitude that marks off one entire way of life from another, an attitude common to all of these parables.

As dispositional, a given manner can connect in a single pattern events that, considered simply on the basis of overt action, have little in common. Treating the wounds and paying the expenses of a stranger who is a crime victim may seem not very like forgiving a wastrel of a son and welcoming him home with clothing, food, jewelry, and a celebration. A king's giving a debtor a second chance to pay off his enormous debt, apart from manner, seems to have nothing in common with throwing a party for a son or with treating a crime victim. Yet viewed through the lens of manner, these three stories illustrate the same manner, putting it in sharp contrast with a more conventional manner. Plainly this manner inspires trust.

> *Phainomenon* 9: If a disposition of manner inspires trust, it does so in part owing to the steadfast wish of the person possessing it. This is the dual wish to (A) promote actively and intelligently the good of the other party, and (B) promote actively and intelligently a relationship of trust with the other party.[58]

Aristotle made a useful distinction between what he called *eunoia* or "good will" and what he usually, if awkwardly, termed *philia*, "affection." He devoted two entire books of the *Nicomachean Ethics* to various types of *philia*, types so disparate that it is worse than misleading to translate the term *philia* in the usual way as "friendship."[59] A person who feels good will for another wishes that person well but is unlikely to go to any trouble or expense on behalf of the other person.[60] Good will may make one safe from being robbed and is thus preferable to ill will, but it will not impel a stranger to help if one is robbed or welcome one back if one is the prodigal. A person of good will may wish one well, but this is not a wish to *do* good things for one personally; it amounts to a wish that *someone else* help one out in need. It does not involve a wish to be helpful personally and actively. This latter wish is characteristic of quite a different disposition of manner.

> *Phainomenon* 10: The manner central to the life of trust is characterized by agape, unconditional love, love given for the sake of the recipient and without thought of return.

It has been objected that it is implausible to make love into an adverb, since it requires not just a "how" of action but a "what."[61] Put in this way, the construal of agape as a virtue or disposition of manner is perhaps grammatically shocking, but surface grammar is often misleading. Consider how misleading it is to construe "love" as a verb. What action or actions does it name? There is no finite list, and any reasonably inclusive list will be incoherent. It will include both giving money and declining to give, telling the truth and keeping quiet, feeling and showing righteous indignation and also responding mildly, with great forbearance. The behaviors that could be listed as signs of love could equally well be listed as signs of some disreputable disposition such as contempt, manipulation, or even hatred, depending on the manner or attitude displayed in them.

One might object to an adverbial construal of love if one forgets either that adverbs modify and thus require verbs (works are essential signs of love), or that not all adverbs can be linked with all verbs. One cannot sleep slowly or bludgeon gently and lovingly. Hence, some content—the content that involves absolute wrongs—is ruled out. Love requires action, but it is at bottom a *way* of acting that avoids absolute wrongs, even as it brings to realization the two wishes mentioned in *phainomenon* 9. Only in this way can one explain the extraordinarily broad range of things that love can have us do or avoid doing when we are attentive to the circumstances in which we are placed. A verbal interpretation fails. Interpreting love as a noun is simply interpreting it as a name for the actions denoted by the verb, hence, this interpretation fails with the verbal one. We are left with the adverbial one. Love, then, is not another distinct thing to do, like carrying out the garbage, or to have, like pizza in the freezer, although, for the sake of grammatical convenience, we sometimes talk as if it were. It is rather the *way* in which we must do or have everything else if the doing or having is to be of any value. That way an adverbial filter or membrane is ruling out many acts (sexual assault, e.g.) and ruling in others (first-aid for crime victims, e.g.). Even apparently heroic acts of self-sacrifice are worthless unless done in this way.[62]

Perhaps it might be argued that *phainomenon* 10 is uniquely Christian and confined therefore to precisely the sorts of young people I am likely to run into at St. Olaf. This would, I fear, be a slight exaggeration both about the uniqueness of the point and the range of young people I encounter. Interpreted in one way, *phainomenon* 10, while characteristic of Christian thought, is not quite uniquely Christian.[63]

In his characterization of friendship, in his characterization of maternal love, and in a few other places, Aristotle plainly had glimpses of the importance of unconditional love. He remarked that *philia* seems to consist more in giving than in receiving affection and advanced as a striking example of this the pleasure that mothers take in loving (*philein*) their children. He noted that some mothers will put their children up for adoption, loving them, but not asking or expecting it to be possible to be loved in return.[64]

One may wonder, however, whether love ought to be called unconditional simply because it is not expected to be reciprocated. Not expecting the love to be reciprocated is still consistent with an important unstated condition, namely, that one expects it not to be repaid by its opposite. If so, the phrase "given without thought of return" in the expression of *phainomenon* 10 is ambiguous.

Suppose one is prepared to receive in return the very opposite of one's loving treatment. Here we encounter something that goes well beyond any affection discussed in Aristotle's works or indeed in common sense, something that may be uniquely Christian: a love that not only expects no like return, but also continues indefinitely in the face of an unlike return.

How is such a love connected with relationships of trust? It amounts to being trustworthy to the untrustworthy and treating them *as if* they were already trustworthy themselves. It amounts to acting *as if* a relationship existed that has not as yet come into existence with the recipient of the love, and perhaps will not immediately, or ever, come into existence. Does this make any sense? I shall argue that it does as a natural extension of *phainomenon* 9.

Phainomenon 9, you will recall, involves a dual wish, the second part of which is promoting actively and intelligently a relationship of trust with the other party. Recognizing human fallibility, one cannot wish this without wishing to promote the trustworthiness of the other party. Promoting this trustworthiness may require giving the other party an opportunity to change. But how is this possible? What, if anything, changes the relative trustworthiness of a person? Suppose one senses that the love of another is conditional upon one's own actions and hence upon one's being judged worth choosing in virtue of the dispositions one's acts evince. One who knows his or her own fallibility cannot entirely trust the person who bestows this love not to change his or her mind about one's fitness for it. One is loved on probation, so to speak, under an implicit contract requiring reciprocity as a condition of its continuation. One is loved for better, but not for worse, with many grounds for parting other than death. Agape is unique in that it does not put anyone on probation. It is a sheer gift, not a trade. It does not love in recognition of worthiness for any recognized Aristotelian or common-sense relationship.

There is immense room for misunderstanding at this point. It is crucial to the understanding of *love without conditions* that it not be confused with *indulgence without limits*. Love without conditions is not only consistent with but *requires* limits to the indulgence of others' preferences. The wish to promote the good—and also the trustworthiness—of the other party can be a very *tough* love, a love that can say "No." It is not the mushy sentimentality of enablers and codependents. Even in Psalm 23, I see no reason to think that the comfort provided by the Shepherd's rod and staff derive from thinking they will be used only on wolves. Part of the comfort comes of knowing that they may be used to give us unpleasant warnings when we have strayed from the fold. From a Christian perspective not every personal relationship is simply a relationship with other humans. Christians believe that one can enter a new type of relationship with a divine Shepherd, not with an indulgent fairy godmother, a sucker for all our tricks. In interpreting this belief we must resist naive urban interpretations of the bucolic sheepherding imagery here, with its suggestion of wimpy shepherds and warm, fuzzy, little lambs. I was fortunately disabused of any romanticism about sheep or shepherds at the age of eight, when, having just fed a large and ostensibly amiable sheep, I turned my back on it, only to find myself face down in a pile of manure. I had been butted hard in the back by the ungrateful beast. This particular sheep proved representative of the others I met. Sheep are not only ungrateful, but they are also smelly, stubborn, loud, sneaky, complaining, moblike, quick to panic, and not very bright. For their own good they sometimes need a little firmness, just as we do, and the good shepherd provides this.

Like any free gift, unconditional love, however tough it may be, can, I think, be refused.[65] But if the gift is received, the recipient may well be changed. If this happens, a new relationship ensues with the giver—a nonprobationary one. Such a relationship of absolute trust and absolute willingness to forgive one's lapses of trustworthiness can be enormously moving. Many will not have experienced this since they were small infants in the arms of their parents, if then. But something of the relative serenity of children who are loved in this way and sense it is restored in adults. This relationship amounts to a deep trust in the giver, a certain faith in the giver as true and constant. While this lamentably does not transform the loved one instantly into a person worthy of trust, it commonly does get across—perhaps for the first time—what it is to *be* worthy of trust. It can start a process of fundamental change that can in the end engender greater trustworthiness. The key point here is that a *model* of trust has been provided where there may have been none. Much as mistrust inspires mistrust, so trust inspires trust, and trustworthiness can inspire trustworthiness.

The world is appallingly well stocked with people who are worth avoiding, many of whom seem altogether worth avoiding. There are so many, in fact, and the rest of us are so like them, that despite emigration, massive flight to the suburbs, and other such contrivances, such people are virtually unavoidable, and many appear not to learn anything constructive from the experience of being avoided. What recourse do we then have? The first nine *phainomena* do not suffice to extricate us from unavoidable associations with the altogether avoidable, nor do they suffice to keep us from becoming altogether avoidable ourselves by combatting such people in the hateful ways that make us like them. Common sense is not enough.

Only the command to love others in an unconditional way, as we have been loved, has the slightest promise of ending the series of reprisals that mark relationships founded on doing good only for one's friends and harm to one's enemies. Trading atrocities in a series stereotypes enemies, attributing to all of them a certain hated identity regardless of any of their personal acts or characteristics. Each additional atrocity traded feeds a sense of outrage at the suffering of the subset of innocents with which one identifies and increases determination to victimize any available member of the stereotyped enemy—witness any number of struggles in the Middle East, the Balkans, or Northern Ireland. The futility of such relationships might have been the subject of a bumper sticker I saw once; it said, "There is no they; only us." The task of *making* enemies as well as ourselves worthy of choice for positions of trust is not addressed effectively by any non-Christian moral philosophy that I know of.

I do not say that there are no hints or intimations elsewhere of the ideas or even the models in this moral philosophy. See, for example, Socrates' extraordinary remarks on not repaying evil with evil at *Crito* 49 A–E, or Pliny the Younger's thoughtful comment:

> My own idea of the truly good and faultless man is one who forgives the faults of others as if he were daily committing them himself, and who keeps himself free of faults as if he could never forgive them. This, then, should be our rule at home and abroad, in every walk of life: to show no mercy to ourselves and be ready with it for others, even for those who excuse no failings but their own. Let us always remember what was so often said by Thrasea, whose gift of sympathy made him the great man he was: "Anyone who hates faults hates mankind."[66]

Nevertheless, no non-Christian moral philosophy known to me provides not only a good idea but also a model who *both* shows how to live consistently in this manner *and* promises to those who have faith the power of the Spirit to sustain emulation. Socrates, by contrast, could only tell poor Cebes and Simmias that when he died they would be on their own. Far from being promised the Paraclete or comforter, the sustaining power of the Holy Spirit, each was told, poignantly, I think, to "sing charms to himself" (*epadein*).[67]

In the end, the Christian answer to the question, "How should I live?" is, "In the manner of Jesus *and* by the Spirit Jesus promised—that is, cultivating and being sustained in the disposition of *agape* for all human beings." Christ-likeness is Christ-manneredness in action sustained by a unique power. It is the attitude of Christ reflected in the exigencies of daily life, an attitude best known through the New Testament narratives. That we should live in this way is itself a *phainomenon* to Christians, something that appears to be so, that appears to offer the only promise we have of a peace worth the name, of a life worth living, of a way to break a cycle of vengeance. It is not the *unexamined* life that is not worth living, as Socrates mistakenly claimed.[68] It is the unloving life, the life bereft of agape. It is nevertheless good to examine one's life precisely because doing so can reveal our own lapses in—or even our lack of—agape, break our hearts, and lead to repentance.[69] The narratives of the life of Jesus, sketchy as they may seem, provide a good picture of this manner of dealing with others in action. This, I submit, is an important role for narrative in moral philosophy and in moral education: elucidating and bringing to life virtues of manner, showing what it would be like to embody them in an array of challenging situations. Narrative, in the end, must have something worth narrating, and is wholly dependent on this for its value.

In conclusion, I can well imagine some hearers or readers responding to these ten *phainomena* about as enthusiastically as Abraham Lincoln did to the book he reviewed. He said, simply, "People who like this sort of thing will find this the sort of thing they like." I have employed Aristotelian methodology to sketch a route from the sorts of stories or narratives that I hear young people sharing in an attempt to pick their way through the moral minefields of human relationships to *the* Christian story that changed the world for all time by adding to it a new type of relationship, one transcending both the admirable powers and the fatal limits of common sense. That route, as I see it, is still open to anyone prepared to learn not simply *about* the Christian narratives but *from* them.

Notes

1. Such common-sense wisdom is perhaps one of the most important forms of common grace.

2. Plato, *Gorgias* 500C.

3. Alasdair MacIntyre, *After Virtue* (Notre Dame, Ind.: Notre Dame University Press, 1981), 2, 66.

4. Iris Murdoch, "Against Dryness: A Polemical Sketch," in *Revisions: Changing Perspectives in Moral Philosophy*, ed. Stanley Hauerwas and Alasdair MacIntyre (Notre Dame: Notre Dame University Press, 1983), 46.

5. John Rawls, *A Theory of Justice* (Cambridge: Harvard University Press, 1972), 47–51.

6. In describing his method, Aristotle at *Nichomachean Ethics* (hereafter NE) 1145b 1ff. remarked, "Here, as in all other cases, we must set down the appearances (*phainomena*) and, first working through the puzzles (*diaporesantes*), in this way go on to show, if possible, the truth of all the beliefs we hold (*ta endoxa*) about these experiences and, if this is not possible, the truth of the greatest number and the most authoritative. For if the difficulties are resolved and the beliefs (*endoxa*) are left in place, we will have done enough showing." The translation is that of Martha Craven Nussbaum, in *Language and Logos*, ed. Malcolm Schofield and Martha Craven Nussbaum (Cambridge: Cambridge University Press, 1982), 267.

7. The best-known of these works is Allan Bloom, *The Closing of the American Mind* (New York: Simon and Schuster, 1987). See especially pp. 25–43.

8. One of the chief advantages of the liberal arts college is the rarity of such structural obstacles.

9. Edmund Pincoffs's seminal article, "Quandary Ethics," *Mind* 80 (1971), 552–71 was an especially revealing diagnosis of the tendency in ethical theory that encourages dilemma-mongering, the failure to recognize that moral perplexity must be exceptional in the living of an everyday moral life, and therefore inattention to what makes such perplexity exceptional.

10. People who deny that there is anything that is absolutely wrong are almost never serious. That is, they are not prepared to live by this view as judged by what they say and do when confronted, e.g., with stories of people feeding broken glass to babies for amusement, or gunning down people at random on the street because they like the sight of blood. If one meets a person who is serious about this, one is in peril. Aristotle compared the task of a moral agent to that of archers who have a sizable target to hit in shifting winds and are praised for hitting it anywhere, since this is difficult, and hitting outside it is both wrong and easy (*NE* 1109a 32–b1). He listed murder, theft, and adultery as outside the moral target entirely, and therefore not covered by every feature of what one might say to help guide shots toward the bullseye (*NE* 1107a 8–26). No doubt we could expand his list.

11 Stuart Hampshire, "Fallacies in Moral Philosophy," in Hauerwas and MacIntyre, 52, notes one of the most refreshing and striking features of Aristotle's moral philosophy, one that leads people to consult it again and again: "Aristotle is almost entirely concerned to analyse the problems of the moral *agent*, while most contemporary moral philosophers seem to be primarily concerned to analyze the problems of the moral *judge* or critic."

12. Hampshire (ibid., 65) remarked, rightly, in my opinion, "If we wish to clarify our own or someone else's use of moral terms, the discovery of verbal equivalences or paraphrases among these terms is not an answer, but, at the most, a preliminary step towards an answer. I can be clear about what somebody means by saying 'this is the right action in these circumstances' only by finding out under what conditions he makes this judgment, and what reasons (and there may be many) he regards as sufficient to justify it."

13. MacIntyre, *After Virtue*, 8–10.

14. Aristotelian as this is, it also calls to mind Paul's saying, "Individually we are members of one another" (Romans 12:5b, NRSV).

15. The slang that undergraduates use varies too much from place to place and year to year to make any review of it here useful. My point is that one and the same function can be performed by widely varying, nonstandard terminology. I do not wish to deny that this variability can impede the making of subtle but important distinctions or that it can lead to considerable unnecessary confusion. As verbivores, to use Robert Roberts's apt term, we will, of necessity, cultivate our own words if not provided serviceable ones. My point is not that standardization of vocabulary is a bad thing, but rather that lack of it does not completely frustrate the communication of morally important points.

16. Ernest A. Nida, "Science of Translation," *Language* 45 (1969), 483–98, esp. 494; also E. A. Nida and C. Taber, *The Theory and Practice of Translation* (Leiden: E. J. Brill, 1969), 14.

17. It was tempting to entitle this chapter, "After Virtue? Not yet."

18. Indeed, as Hampshire remarked, "An informative treatise on ethics—or on the ethics of a particular society or person—would contain an accumulation of examples which are said to be right in various circumstances, and the reasons given and the arguments used in concluding that they are right" (Hampshire, "Fallacies in Moral Philosophy," 65–66).

19. Aristotle, *NE* 1109b 23.

20. Aristotle remarked that we do not regard bad doctors or bad carpenters as bad people simply for that reason. *NE* 1148b 7–9.

21. The question is not rhetorical. I shall return to it at the end of the chapter in considering one final kind of relationship for which people who are otherwise entirely worth avoiding can be chosen.

22. Aristotle, *NE* 1097b 11, 1169b 18.

23. Edmund Pincoffs, *Quandaries and Virtues* (Lawrence: The University of Kansas Press, 1986), 73–74.

24. Murdoch, "Against Dryness," 49.

25. This is perhaps why we treasure old friends so highly. I am particularly indebted to three such friends for comments on earlier drafts of this essay: Steven Tigner, Keith Yandell, and Ed Langerak, who will not agree with what they will view as the errors I have stubbornly retained despite their best efforts.

26. The distinction is familiar from Plato's story of the Ring of Gyges (*Republic* 359D–360D) and from the tests of Job's integrity in Job 2:3–10.

27. In *Categories* VIII, Aristotle set out a useful distinction between a disposition or "habit" (*hexis*) and what he called a *diathesis* or "condition." An example of a *diathesis* might be a blush; the corresponding ruddy complexion would be a *hexis*. A *hexis* is difficult to displace, lasting, and stable.

28. *NE* 1165b 23–30.

29. Here I am indebted to Dan Cybyske.

30. The reason for the "almost" will emerge at the end of the chapter.

31. For Christians, the decision to accept or not to accept God's grace is a fundamental life-shaping one.

32. *NE* 1114a 6–10.

33. Here see "Aristotle on Praise and Blame," *Archiv für Geschichte der Philosophie* 71 (1989), 1–2.

34. Aristotle, in discussing this issue, goes so far as to ask whether the act itself makes any difference at all (*NE* 1134a 19). Apparently it does, but only because deeds done are (fallible) signs of dispositions (*Rhetoric* 1357b1–3, 12–17, 20–24). Where deeds are misleading as signs of character, Aristotle expects to find pain and remorse in the agent (*NE* 1110b 17–1111a 20). Absence of pain and remorse are signs of viciousness, showing the act was not a misleading sign.

35. We also know that political rivals seek to find acts of their opponents that are out of character and misrepresent them as in character and representative of the opponent's true disposition. Deciding where the truth lies often turns on deciding the sincerity of expressed remorse.

36. Aristotle, *Rhetoric* 1374b 26–1375a 3.

37. Stability is always demonstrated under certain conditions, and thus within certain implicit thresholds, which later observation sometimes demonstrates to have been situated just beyond the values of critical variables of temptation previously experienced to date in a given person's life. Cynicism consists in the view that there is always a threshold or breakdown point for every virtue for every person. Master Rich gave voice to such cynicism in Robert Bolt's *A Man for All Seasons*, saying "there's always something . . ."—houses, fortunes, honors, sexual encounters, etc.—for each person. That this is a question-begging assumption and not anything one could establish by actual observation is clear. Cynics meet putative counterexamples with a priori certainty that if only the temptation index had been turned up a bit, the person in question would have given in.

38. Not concealing such feelings is vastly overrated by partisans of spontaneity and openness. As Leon Botstein has noted, civilization itself consists in part in a certain reluctance to say exactly what one thinks, since this may be inflammatory.

39. The disposition to deal respectfully with deeply flawed but well-entrenched human beings for whom contempt comes all-too-easily is one of the virtues required of politicians under a working system of separation of powers. Unfortunately, the campaign trail is the last place to look for evidence that a candidate has this disposition. The ability to appeal quietly and effectively to the best even in the worst is a prerequisite for getting constructive things done when the worst have a great deal of influence. This disposition may be almost incompatible with dispositions corresponding to the crusading zeal suggested—perhaps

falsely—by the polarizing campaign behavior most likely to be rewarded with media and voter attention.

40. If this suggestion were sufficiently difficult to resist, it would almost be preferable to translate Aristotle's term *hexis* as "habit" rather than "disposition," since "habit" suggests the greater likelihood of manifestation, even if the term "habit" wrongly suggests that the manifestation is a thoughtless response.

41. As W. F. R. Hardie observed,

> We tend to label as habitual, or as merely habitual, activities which are performed without effort and also without attention or care. Actions which proceed from a *hexis* are effortless but careful and attentive. As in the case of an accomplished tennis player, the things that are done automatically are the basis of heedful performances at a higher level. Here virtue, as conceived by Aristotle, resembles the virtuosity of the accomplished games player or craftsman. Mere drill teaches a man to do the same thing in the same circumstances without attending to what he is doing, but virtuosity, like virtue, involves doing the appropriately different thing in varying circumstances. The virtuous action is second nature and not against the grain; but it is not mechanical. (W. F. R. Hardie, *Aristotle's Ethical Theory* [Oxford: Clarendon, 1968], 104)

42. Aristotle, *NE* 1117a 15–17. See also 1111b 9.

43. Aristotle remarks (*NE* 1117a 19–20) of courageous behavior in such circumstances, *apo hexeos gar mallon*, i.e., it proceeds more from the disposition, because there is less time for preparation.

44. Aristotle, *NE* 1115b 11ff.

45. The Kant text in question here is the well-known passage in the *Grundlegung zur Metaphysik der Sitten* (Akademie Textausgabe, b. IV, s. 398): "Wohlthaetig sein, wo man kann, ist Pflicht, und ueberdem giebt es manche so theilnehmend gestimmte Seelen, dass sie auch ohne einen andern Bewegungsgrund der Eitelkeit oder des Eigennutzes ein inneres Vergnuegen daran finden, Freude um sich zu verbreiten, und die sich an der Zufriedenheit anderer, so fern sie ihr Werk ist, ergoetzen koennen. Aber ich behaupte, dass in solchem Falle vergleichen Handlung, so pflichtsmaessig, so liebenswuerdig sie auch ist, dennoch keinen wahren sittlichen Werth habe . . ." James W. Wellington (Immanuel Kant, *Grounding for the Metaphysics of Morals* [Indianapolis: Hackett, 1981], 10) translates: "To be beneficent where one can is a duty; and besides this, there are many persons who are so sympathetically constituted that, without any further motive of vanity or self-interest, they find an inner pleasure in spreading joy around them and can rejoice in the satisfaction of others as their own work. But I maintain that in such a case an action of this kind, however dutiful and amiable it may be, has nevertheless no true moral worth."

46. Kant's phrase was "*Lob und Aufmunterung, aber nicht Hochschaetzung*," 398.

47. Epistemologically, Kant's case of the joyless but dutiful person is no more interesting or revealing than that of a person who knows what duty requires but, by the smallest of margins, fails to do it owing to an inclination toward some pleasure that precludes doing it. Kant's epistemologically clear case also marks a failure, in Judeo-Christian terms, to love with one's entire personality (Deuteronomy 6:5, 30:6; Luke 10:27). One would say of such a person, "His heart wasn't in it" even if he did the "right" thing. He did not love others *as* (in the manner that) he had been loved.

48. Plato, *Republic* 443D–E. For an interpretation of the psychological theory at work here and in other middle dialogues, see *Plato's Theory of Understanding* (Madison: University of Wisconsin Press, 1981), chapter 3.

49. Aristotle, *NE* 1115b 19.

50. Aristotle would apparently praise a person of bestial disposition who refrained from giving in to bestial inclinations (*NE* 1149a 12—5), but there is no indication that he regards such a person as worthy of choice for relationships of trust.

51. Aristotle is both a libertarian and an incompatibilist. See *NE* III, Chapter 5, 1113b 3–1115a 2. His view is not incompatible with candor about what it is now fashionable to call "moral luck." At bottom, "moral luck" is no more than a special case of the problem of evil. His stated goal for a *polis* that incorporated the best of his ethical views is a society in which each person present could live the best life that it was possible for him or her to live, recognizing that this will vary with circumstance.

52. Charles Swindoll remarked,

> The longer I live, the more I realize the impact of attitude on life. Attitude, to me, is more important than facts. It is more important than the past, than education, than money, than circumstances, than failures, than successes, than what other people say and do. It is more important than appearance, giftedness, or skill. It will make or break a company . . . a church . . . a home. The remarkable thing is we have a choice every day regarding the attitude we will embrace for that day. We cannot change our past . . . we cannot change the fact that people will act in a certain way. We cannot change the inevitable. The only thing we can do is play on the one string we have, and that is our attitude. . . . I am convinced that life is 10% what happens to me and 90% how I react to it. And so it is with you . . . we are in charge of our attitudes. (Charles Swindoll, taped sermon on Phil. 2)

53. Luke 15:11–34.

54. Luke 10:29–38.

55. Matthew 20:1–16.

56. Matthew 18:23–36.

57. John 14:27–28: "Eirenen aphiemi hymin, eirenen ten emen didomi hymin; ou kathos ho kosmos didosin ego didomi hymin." The RSV translation reads: "Peace I leave with you; my peace I give to you; not as the world gives do I give to you."

58. I am conscious of a debt to feminist philosophers at this point, most especially to my former Ph.D. student at the University of Wisconsin-Madison, Markate Daly.

59. *Philia* as Aristotle employs the term in the *Nicomachean Ethics* VIII and IX includes such disparate phenomena as a mother's love for her child, a father's love for his child (not the same as the mother's, he suggests), a host's kindly treatment of a guest, the affection siblings feel for one another, the esprit de corps of members of the same ship's crew, club, or association, the affection that a student has for a teacher, the affection that the teacher has for the student (not the same as the former), and a wide range of types of affection that friends have for one another. *Philia* and its verb-cognates were Aristotle's most generic expressions for affection, but where necessary, he could be more precise, as when he used *erao*, *stergo*, or *agapao*.

60. Aristotle, *NE* 1166b 30–1167a 21.

61. I am indebted to Steven Tigner for this objection.

62. 1 Corinthians 13 strongly points to love as showing itself in a manner that can pervade or be wanting in a wide variety of acts. It describes this manner as patient, kind, not jealous or boastful, not arrogant or rude, not insistent on its own way, not irritable or resentful, not malicious, etc.

63. Unfortunately, this *phainomenon* appears to be neither unique to nor universal among those who call themselves Christians, if one is to judge by reports of the behavior of Phalangist forces in Lebanon. One winces when reading of "Christian atrocities," a phrase

that ought to be an oxymoron if agape is universal among Christians. It is best, perhaps, to use the term "Christian" normatively, not sociologically. Using it normatively puts one in a position to see that no system of beliefs is refuted by the hypocrisy or weakness of some of its alleged adherents. Otherwise, the claims that Socrates and Plato make on behalf of dialectic would have to be considered refuted by the appalling use made of dialectic by Athenian negotiators with the Melians just before committing genocide against them in the name of a "necessity of nature," a "law" (*nomos*) that, in Thucydides' chilling report, they said they were bequeathing to all humankind (*History of the Peloponnesian War*, vol. V, 85–116, esp. 89 and 105). Similar consequences would follow for Judaism, Islam, and probably for any major system of thought. But these consequences involve the same fallacious pattern of reasoning Socrates identified in his diagnosis of *misologia*, misology, hatred of discussion, hatred of reason, in Plato's *Phaedo* 89D.

64. Aristotle, *NE* 1159a 26–35.

65. Universalism requires, I think, the belief that this gift cannot be refused, and may imply either that God has not created us sufficiently in the image of his omnipotence to have the power to choose to reject the gift, or that God lacks the power to create beings who can reject divine grace. The latter would suggest that God is not omnipotent. Such a view is untenable both on the evidence of human choices and on doctrinal grounds.

66. "Atque ego optimum et emendatissimum existimo, qui ceteris ita ignoscit, tanquam ipse cotidie peccet, ita peccatis abstinet tamquam nemini ignoscat. Proinde hoc domi hoc foris hoc in omni uitae genere teneamus, ut nobis implacabiles simus, exorabiles istis etiam qui dare ueniam nisi sibi nesciunt, mandemusque memoriae quod uir mitissimus et ob hoc quoque maximus Thrasea crebro dicere solebat: 'Qui uitia odit, homines odit'" (C. Pliny Caecili Secundi, *Epistulae* VIII.22).

67. Plato, *Phaedo* 77D–78A. For additional aspects of the psychology that is beginning to emerge here in the *Phaedo*, see "Plato on Persuasion and Credibility," *Philosophy and Rhetoric* 21, no. 4 (1988), 260–278.

68. Plato, *Apology* 38A.

69. I found David Jeffrey's distinction between a hard-hearted reader and a broken-hearted reader precisely the one needed to distinguish between the frame of mind in which reading can be a liberating experience and other frames of mind. The redemptive power of suffering consists partly in its power to put one in this frame of mind.

10

GABRIEL FACKRE

Narrative Theology from an Evangelical Perspective

Observation on the many meanings of "narrative" are a commonplace of narratology. And with reason. The variety of disciplines and fields of interest from which commentary on it now rises is striking, as is the diversity of points of view within each discipline and field. The extent to which the various perspectives have or have not taken one another into account makes a good story in itself. "Narrative theology," a subset of the larger narrative discussion, has the same variety and diversity. With it has come a predictable interest in sorting out its types and models. A current typology is the division of narrative theology into the views of Hans Frei and Paul Ricoeur, "biblical narrative" and "story theology," "pure narrative" and "impure narrative," or against the background of larger questions of theological method, the cultural-linguistic versus the experiential-expressivist approaches (also identified as the "post-liberal" and "revisionist" options).[1] One of the characteristics of current typology-making—including this one—is the absence of a tradition that has been the mother of narrative sensibility for large sections of the nineteenth- and twentieth-century church. I am referring to what I shall call "evangelical narrative." One of the ironies of this absence, incidentally, is the prominent role C. S. Lewis, a mentor to many evangelicals, plays in the larger literary discussion of narrative.

The missing evangelical voice impoverishes the current theological conversation about narrative. This circumstance may soon be altered as evangelical throats are being cleared and hands raised.[2] Their number includes the essentially critical interventions of Carl Henry on current forms of narrative theology, the Yes and No reactions of Millard Erickson to the same,[3] the "perhaps, with alterations" assessments of Alister McGrath and I. M. Wallace,[4] and the approving responses of Mark Ellingsen and Clark Pinnock to one or another type.[5] Current evangelical commentary, along with the historic presence and practice of evangelical narrative, has gone largely unnoticed in the academic discussion of the subject.[6] One aim of this paper is to raise the evangelical decibel count so its voice will be heard. Another purpose is to examine specific features of evangelical narrative that can serve as a corrective to present views. And yet another is to investigate places where evangelical narrative can learn from its conversation partners. First, we must be clear about the words, "evangelical" and "narrative theology." In an entry on "Evangelical, Evangelicalism" in the *Westminster Dictionary of Christian Theology*,[7] I attempt a definition by first tracing the terms to their sixteenth-century Protestant habitat. Evangelical meant then (and still does in some denominations that derive from the Reformation) the espousal of the authority of Scripture and justification by grace through faith—the so-called formal and material principles of Protestantism. "Evangelicalism," as the word functions widely today, however, refers to a varied movement characterized by the *intensification* and *interiorization* of these two Reformation commitments. Scripture is Scripture interpreted with a rigorist hermeneutic—"inerrancy" or "infallibility"[8]—and read with an accent on personal disciplines and applications. Justification becomes a datable conversion experience decisive for life and thought—a "born-again" Christianity. Accompanying marks of an evangelical are a sense of urgency about sharing the message of Scripture and the experience of justification (thus the inextricability of evangelism and evangelicalism), an intense piety, and adherence to strict codes of personal morality. While evangelicals share these characteristics, they do so in a variety of subcommunities that include *fundamentalists*, for whom hyperinerrancy becomes the test of faithfulness to Christ in a world of Manichaean "us and them" divisions; *old evangelicals*, for whom the born-again experience and its replication through evangelism are focal; *new evangelicals*, for whom apologetics and social concern are features added to the former's commitments; *justice and peace evangelicals*, for whom social action directed toward systemic change of established structures is a crucial mark of piety; *charismatic evangelicals*, for whom a "second blessing" of exuberant worship, healing, and glossolalia are the stigmata of a full faith; *ecumenical evangelicals*, who are hospitable to kindred souls and minds beyond the self-defined evangelical circle, and thus often in coalition with evangelical *ecumenicals*.

Each of these subcommunities is identifiable by its network of churches and parachurches, journals, publishing houses, educational institutions, advocacy movements, mailing lists, etc. Of course, there is fluidity, a mobility within and among the evangelical camps. And there are subsets of the subsets, as for example, the divisions within fundamentalism between the political fundamentalism of the Christian Right and the apolitical posture of more traditional fundamentalists, or the difference between apocalyptic fundamentalism (especially, premillennialist, and within this "pretrib," "midtrib," and "posttrib") and nonapocalyptic fundamentalism (viz., postmillennial Reconstructionists). For all this diversity (regularly lost on outside commentary, both secular and religious), the commonalities noted do give evangelicalism its identity and constitute the perspective in which narrative theology shall be viewed. Building toward our definition requires an initial distinction between a broader and narrower understanding of "narrative." In the most general sense, literary narrative is "an account of events and participants moving over time and space, a recital with beginning and ending patterned by the narrator's principle of selection. . . . Narrative in the narrow sense (is) an account of characters and events in a plot moving over time and space through conflict toward resolution. While narrative broadly conceived includes history, as action patterned according to some interpretive horizon, the narrator in a *story*—the term to be used here for narrative in this narrow sense—plays a plotting role; the narrative defers to the intention of the author rather than the purposes of 'ostensive reference'" (Hans Frei). This does not mean that historical referents are excluded from the story, even crucial ones on which the tale turns, but rather that the coherence, meaning, and the direction of the events are acknowledged to be the expression of the narrator's vision. Pattern becomes plot, participants become characters, and movement has directionality through conflict toward resolution. Furthermore, the elements of tension and surprise in the unfolding drama and the free play of the imagination in the recital have an evocative power unattainable by either bare chronicle or abstract analysis.

Narrative *theology*, as the concept is used here, is the discernment of a plot in the ways of God and the deployment of story as a means of describing it. To be noted is the variety encompassed in this idea and its current practice, ranging from narrative theologies that focus on our personal or social stories, to those whose subject matter is the study of Scripture's manifold tales, to those who are concerned about the overarching "cult epic" that gives the church its identity.[9] How "evangelical narrative" does and does not fit into this wide-ranging conversation is our subject of inquiry.

Perceptions of Evangelical Narrative

While references to the evangelical perspective on narrative are rare in the current discussion of narrative theology, two of the formative figures in its development have commented passingly on it. Their perceptions provide our entry point. Karl Barth speaks appreciatively of the lasting influence upon him of an evangelical narrativity:

> "I must interpose at this point a small but sincerely grateful tribute. It is to a theologian, who cannot be called great, but to whom I am greatly indebted. I refer to Abel Burckhardt, who a hundred years ago—a contemporary of the more famous Jacob Burkhardt—was the second pastor at the minster here in Basel. He composed and edited a collection of songs for children in the local district. This was the textbook in which, at the beginning of the last decade of the last century, I received my first theological instruction in a form appropriate to my then immaturity. And what made an indelible impression on me was the homely naturalness with which these very modest compositions spoke of the events of Christmas, Palm Sunday, Good Friday, Easter, the Ascension, Pentecost, as things which might take place any day in Basel or its environs like any other important happenings. We took our mother's hand, as it were, and went to the stall at Bethlehem, and to the streets of Jerusalem where, greeted by children of a similar age, the Saviour made his entry, and to the dark hill of Golgotha, and as the sun rose to the garden of Joseph."[10]

Here a European pietism is remembered for its stewardship of biblical stories, especially of those that compose the New Testament portrait of Jesus. Barth rightly identifies the first characteristic of evangelical narrative to be discussed: the immersion in *biblical stories*. In passing, we note also his appreciation for the musical form in which evangelical narrative is often carried forward, a clue that we shall follow up.

Hans Frei, like Barth, alludes to an evangelical presence, though less charitably, in his account of the decline of biblical hermeneutics in eighteenth-century hermeneutics:

> Such sense of a narrative framework as continued to exist among religious . . . readers was now no longer chiefly that of providentially governed biblical history. In that scheme . . . every present moral and historical experience had been fitted into it by bestowing on the present experience a figural interpretation that adapted it into the governing biblical narrative. All this had now changed. Such narrative sense as remained in the reading of the Bible found the connective tissue which served simultaneously as its own effective thread to the present experience in the "present history" of the soul's conversion and perfection. . . . In evangelical piety [the] relation is reversed; the atoning death of Jesus is indeed real in its own right and both necessary and efficacious for the redemption of the sinner. Nonetheless, though real in his own right, the atoning Redeemer is at the same time a figure or type of the Christian's journey; for this is the narrative framework, the meaningful pattern within which alone the occurrence of the cross finds its applicative sense. What is real, and what therefore the Christian really lives, is his own pilgrimage; and to its pattern he looks for the assurance that he is really living it.[11]

Frei finds narrative still at work, but it has been relocated from the Scripture to the believer's spiritual journey. Bracketing an evaluation of Frei's judgment that personal appropriation constitutes relocation, it is surely right that evangelicalism brings to the fore subjective soteriology, the personal "application of the benefits" of the Work of Christ. Here then is a second aspect of the evangelical story tradition, its *pro me* accent, the emphasis on "my story." Its background is the conversion experience and/or the continuing companionship of the believer with Christ. A third feature of evangelical narrative is missing in both these characterizations: "the God Story," the encompassing biblical narrative.

Evangelical theology and piety never lost this story and expressed it in its hymnody.[12] Let us take a closer look at some of these songs, and those that may not use the story terms but actually tell a tale. The most prominent feature of Gospel song narratology is the note of *personal* story. Thus, the practice of evangelical "testimony" happens in singing as well as saying. In its songs, the language of the soul's salvation story is everywhere: C. H. Morris's "Calvary" — "I love the story sweet and old, of Christ who died for me; the sweetest story ever told, of pardon bought on Calvary"; F. H Rowley's "I will sing the wondrous story of the Christ who died for me. How he left his home in glory for the cross of Calvary"; Fanny Crosby's "Blessed Assurance" with its chorus line, "This is my story, this is my song, praising my saviour all the day long"; James Rowe's "His Grace is Satisfying Me" — "The story telling, His praises swelling, for grace is satisfying me." and his "Everywhere I Go" — "The lost shall hear the story of my Saviour's love for me"; and more and more, without the language of story as well as with it: "Wounded for Me," "He Lifted Me," "Jesus Loves Even Me."

Along with the subjectivity of evangelical piety is its commitment to Scripture, a second feature of evangelical narrative. Thus, the entreaty to 'tell me the stories of

Jesus'. And the telling of them, and other stories as well in the songs themselves: Catherine Hankey's "I love to tell the story of unseen things above, of Jesus and his glory of Jesus and his love"; Jemima Luke's "I think when I read that story of old when Jesus was here among men, how he called little children as lambs to his fold. I should like to have been with them then"; Fanny Crosby's "Tell me the story of Jesus, write on my heart every word. Tell me the story most precious, sweetest that ever was heard"; Charlotte Homer's "Awakening Chorus," "Awake and sing the blessed story . . . the Lord Jesus reigns and sin is backward hurled." (Notice the prominence of women storytellers throughout the Gospel song tradition.) A. H. Ackley's "Let God use you to tell the old, old story . . . some heart needs a friend like Jesus, some sin-sick soul that stumbles alone"; A. P. Cobb's "Do you know the story that the wise men heard as they journeyed afar?" And stories that range throughout the Bible as in Carl Boberg's "How Great Thou Art—My God when I in awesome wonder consider all the worlds thy hands have made . . . And when I think that God his Son not sparing sent him to die, I scarce can take it in." Black Gospel songs—"slave songs," "spirituals"—are especially focused on biblical stories, with all their powerful implications for present circumstances: "Go down, Moses," "Joshua Fit the Battle of Jericho," "Go Tell it on the Mountain," "My Lord delivered poor Daniel," "Mary don't you weep," "Jesus walked the water and so raised the dead," "Were you there when they crucified my Lord?"

Latent in the individual stories told is a larger plot. The tale of creation, the fall, the covenant with Noah, God's election of Israel, the coming and redemptive deed of Jesus Christ, the birth of the church, the salvation of souls and sometimes society, the hope for the final resolution in the End—all this is the Big Story.[13] The overarching tale makes its presence felt from time to time in the Gospel song: Arthur Spooner's eschatological "Sometime, somewhere, over the hill-tops of glory, shine the fair streets of gold; wonderful, wonderful story, never has half been told." The full sweep of the Big Story is found in the title, verses, and refrain of the well-known hymn, "We've a Story to Tell to the Nations." At its center is the chapter on which tales turn, "The Lord who . . . hath sent us His Son to save us . . . who the path of sorrow has trod. . . ." God's saving deed in Christ is set within a history of alienation that moves toward final reconciliation, as in the summary themes of the refrain: "For the darkness shall turn to dawning, and the dawning to noon-day bright. And Christ's great kingdom shall come on earth, the Kingdom of love and light." I must admit that it is much harder to find the overarching biblical narrative in the Gospel song, as the mood of testifying puts the personal and the specific tales of Scripture to the fore. Hence, the themes picked up by Barth and Frei. Nevertheless, the Big Story is integral to evangelical faith and is presupposed in its piety. For rendering explicit what is implicit in the Gospel song, the systematic tradition of evangelical theology is revealing. A review of standard textbooks will show that evangelical theologians follow the familiar loci: after prolegomena, God/Trinity, creation, fall, Christology, soteriology, ecclesiology, eschatology. These are, of course, expositions of the doctrines that rise from the narrative sequence in both Scripture and the ancient creeds. In the former case, the Story runs from Genesis to Revelation (as in the 1909 multivolumed evangelical work, *The Bible and its Story: Taught by One Thousand Picture Lessons*). In the latter—the Apostles' and Nicene

Creeds—the drama moves from the mission of the Father in creation (paragraph one, Act I), to the mission of the Son (paragraph two, Act II), to the mission of the Spirit (paragraph three, Act III). Scottish divine James Orr (1844–1913) went a step further in discerning the overall narrative pattern in evangelical faith, as pointed out by Peter Toon. He observed:

> What a singular parallel there is between the historical course of dogma, on the one hand, and the scientific order of the text-books on systematic theology on the other . . . (after prolegomena) follow the great divisions of the theological system—Theology proper, or the doctrine of God; Anthropology, or the doctrine of man, including sin (sometimes a separate division); Christology, or the doctrine of the Person of Christ; Soteriology (Objective) or the doctrine of the Work of Christ, especially the Atonement; Subjective Soteriology, or the doctrine of the application of redemption (justification, Regeneration, etc.); finally Eschatology, or the doctrine of last things.[14]

As Toon points out, the analogy is somewhat forced (it leaves out the doctrine of the church and the place of Israel and is only one possible reading of the history of doctrinal distillation). However, it exemplifies the working assumption of evangelical theology regarding the sequence of the loci and an imaginative proposal that the narrative of divine deeds is repeated in the history of doctrine. Carl Henry, today's best-known evangelical theologian, has written a six-volume work on "religious epistemology," *God, Revelation and Authority*. In fact, it is a systematics that covers the loci, albeit with the problematic of revelation/authority as the organizing principle. At a crucial juncture in the argument, Henry reflects on the skeletal structure of Scripture. It turns out to be the Story—albeit with Henry-like accents:

> The unity of the Bible is not to be found in its literary genres nor in its human writers. It is found in the message and meaning of the book, namely, that the living sovereign God stands at the beginning of the universe—man and the worlds—as Creator and Governor, and at the end of history as final Judge; that he made mankind in his likeness for moral rectitude and spiritual fellowship and service; that human revolt precipitated disastrous consequences for humanity and the cosmos; that the manifested mercy of God, extended first to the Hebrews, proffers the only prospect of salvation; that the divine promise of deliverance, disclosed in the course of Hebrew redemptive history to the prophets, finds its fulfillment in Jesus of Nazareth; that the incarnation, crucifixion and resurrection of the Logos of God marks the beginnings of the new and final age; that the church is a new society of regenerate persons of all races and nations over whom Christ presently rules; that the history of mankind has a dual track, issuing in final and irreversible doom for the impenitent and in eternal blessing for the righteous; that Christ will return in awesome vindication of the holy will of God, to judge men and nations, and will in the resurrection of the dead conform the people of God to his moral image; that the benefits of redemption will embrace all creation both in a final subordination of evil and of the wicked, and in the eternal vindication of righteousness.[15]

So we have turned up the third feature of evangelical narrative, latent in its hymnody and patent in its systematic theology. Together these themes provide us with a working definition. Evangelical narrative is the linkage of the Christian Story to the believer's story through biblical stories. It is the Christian faith lived at the juncture of personal, ecclesial, and biblical narrative.

How then does this definition and how do these refrains relate to the current discussion of narrative theology?

Evangelical Story and Narrative Theology

First to be noted, my story, biblical stories, the Great Story—the three dimensions of evangelical narrative—bear a marked resemblance to three types of current narrative theology. I would identify the latter as *life story, canonical stories,* and *community story.* The life story model is a response to what William Doty describes as "the cloture of science, the emptiness of massspeak . . . the tyranny of definitions and dogma."[16] Theologies of this stripe challenge modern captivity to the cerebral, rationalistic, and technocratic, call upon both individuals and victim communities to resist oppressive structures and authoritarian systems by honoring and telling their own stories, personal or collective, and reread or redo Christian faith in the context of experiential narrative.[17] For some, retrieval of narrative identity means recovery of the very narrative shape of human existence.[18] Narrative theology so conceived not only urges the telling of personal and social tales, but also probes autobiography and biography for their revelatory significance. A second constellation of narrative theologies is found in the field of biblical studies. Here the special dynamisms of scriptural story are explored: the creation of an alternative world into which the reader is drawn; the honoring of ambiguity, complexity, indeterminacy; the construction of imaginative cumulative narratives, the expressive and transformative power of story, especially parable. Features of the life story model reappear in the last version, as the biblical stories are held to be polyvalent in meaning with a richness commensurate with myriad life situations. Thus, the Bible comes alive as I let it "look me in the eye."

Community story is a third type distinguished by its view of narrative as the tale that gives unity to Scripture and shapes, as well, ecclesial identity. It is accessed, or speaks its own Word, only within its rightful hermeneutical community, the church. This biblical-cum-community narrative may be the overarching Story that runs from Genesis to Revelation, or the "central story" within in it—the life, death, and resurrection of Jesus Christ. To tell this Story is to assure its faithful proclamation in the teaching and preaching of the church, to embody it in its worship, prayer, and praise, and to conform the behavior of the community to it, resisting all efforts to displace it by the culture's agendas. We shall give attention to one version of community story that developed in the Frei-Lindbeck tradition. Evangelical narrative can enter into fruitful encounter with each of these constituencies. As the conversation develops, it has a word to speak and also one to hear. Let us eavesdrop on the exchange.

The *pro me* character of evangelical narrative suggests its readiness to affirm and appropriate aspects of personal life story narrative theology. Giving one's personal testimony is in the family of storytelling that includes such diverse progeny as therapy that requires the sharing of one's journey in addiction and feminism that asserts the dignity of women by refusal to allow the oppressors' agendas to define reality. In principle, evangelicals should be ready to acknowledge these siblings, although the therapeutics of the former may be given a more ready welcome than the politics of the latter, to judge by the fare on the shelves of the Christian bookstore. Indeed, a case might be made that the twelve-step version of storytelling is traceable to evangelical roots by way of the pietism of the former's Oxford group lineage. Ownership of origins apart, a doctrine of general revelation, usually associated with evangelicalism, can provide a warrant for acknowledging these secular graces.

Evangelical narrative will be critical, however, of any point of view that rests its narrative case with celebrations of affect, autobiography or biography, or reads the Christian story as a species of the genus, universal experiential story. Biblical narrative has an integrity of its own and cannot be absorbed into human experience as such. While Christian faith and personal journey are inseparable, they are also distinguishable. One is "redemption accomplished" and the other is "redemption applied." Behind this fundamental distinction lies the evangelical assessment of the human condition, fallen and therefore both soteriologically and epistemologically wanting. Only the Person and Work of Christ can make possible the soul's saving story. An evangelical No must be spoken to construals that reduce narrative theology to life stories of one kind or another.

The strengths of evangelical narrative carry with them related weaknesses. The tradition of personal testimony does not easily lend itself to social, indeed, sociological, awarenesses and actions. Personal piety can fall prey to a pietism innocent of corporate and systemic realities. Evangelicalism, with significant exceptions, past and present, has too often left it to others to call to account tyrannical social systems and do the difficult long-term work of organizing power to contest privilege. Its individualistic tendencies need to be challenged by the advocates of "social life story." ("Justice and peace" evangelicals who carry forward a long minority tradition of social witness are proof that this kind of expanded vision is possible.)

Evangelicalism's sometime absorption in personal story also needs to be regularly reminded that Christian narrative has to do first and foremost with the God Story—indeed, its own working assumption. Hence, the custodians of the community story, with their emphasis on the defining deeds of God, have a word to speak here, as well. The "I, me, and mines" so prominent in Gospel songs in general, and story hymnody in particular, can be the sign of a narcissistic piety if not held firmly in relationship to what—God did, is doing, and will do. Canonical Stories and Evangelical Narrative Evangelicalism challenges reductionist tendencies in literary-critical, critical consciousness, and historical-critical readings of the canonical stories. Evangelicals contend that scriptural stories mean just what they say. Hence, "plain meaning" becomes a working principle of interpretation in association with "the analogy of faith," clearer texts in canonical context clarifying murkier ones. Evangelical hermeneutical commitments here can be identified as the "common sense" and the "canonical sense" of a biblical story. The former means reading Scripture as one would a news report—or an essay arguing the literary-critical, historical-critical, or critical consciousness points of view: word in sentence, sentence in paragraph, paragraph in the next defining literary unit, and so on. The latter means that what is discerned as plainly the case coheres with, and is illumined by, comparable Scripture and by the overall pattern of canonical teaching. Narrative theologies that look to Scripture essentially for reinforcement of political, social, or economic agendas—usually on the grounds of a hermeneutics of suspicion that holds texts are always read and, indeed, written, perspectively by the wielders of power—eliminate the authorial intention of the story proper (the common sense) and the authorial intention of the story discernible within the overall biblical pattern of teaching (the canonical sense).

In the same way, narrative theologies that fix on the evocative and expressive functions of biblical stories, with their ethical and aesthetic fertility—often on the grounds of the inherent inaccessibility of textual intentions—regularly turn exegesis into eisegesis. Evangelicals bring to this encounter a doctrine of the inspiration of Scripture which compels respect for the authority of the intended meaning and resists captivity of the Bible to any extraneous program.

In both cases, ironies abound. Forms of narrative theology that reject evangelical allegiance to textual intentions as a dehistoricized, illusory objectivism insist on equivalents to common and canonical senses in the act of publically presenting their own hermeneutical theories. A serious textual argument for a historicist or a subjectivist perspective assumes the public discussability of the intended meaning of the words and sentences employed. What's sauce for the goose is sauce for the gander. Evangelical narrative also collides with a reduction of biblical stories to "the world in back of the text." The hermeneutic that delimits the meaning of Scripture to "the assured results of historical criticism" turns the Bible over to a new magisterium. The universality of access presupposed by the evangelical belief in perspicuity must challenge elitist exegesis. Furthermore, the character of biblical literature is self-involving and as such requires the *pro me* encounter to which an evangelical hermeneutic is also committed and for which no historical critical approach, standing alone, is adequate.

While evangelical narrative has its just complaints against reductionist readings of biblical stories, it also has things to hear from these sources. An application of evangelicalism's own acknowledgment of human finitude and sin, on the one hand, and the majesty and mystery of God, on the other, should make for more restraint in claims about the ease with which the plain meaning of biblical stories is accessed. Thus, critical scholarship rightly makes a contribution when it seeks to discover the literary or historical context, while being self-critical about its own ideological possibilities. It can so enrich (*bene esse*, not *esse*) our grasp of a text's meaning. Also, a critical consciousness can alert us to the social location and vested interests that skew readings of what biblical stories appear to say or have been said to mean in evangelical exegesis. A corrective to this is a *community* reading of bibilical texts, an ecumenical conversation among the many parts/perspectives in the Body of Christ. The unearthing of "hidden histories" and the finding of untold stories in Scripture by oppressed peoples are genuine gifts to be received. So too, personal significances can be richer and more unpredictable than the standard framework of evangelical interiority allows. Thus, in the canonical stories type of narrative theology, there is a take as well as a give.

Community Story and Evangelical Narrative

In this category the Big Story comes center stage. We have given attention to the ways in which evangelical narrative is focused on both the comprehensive Story and its central chapter. In recent years, the "Yale theology" has been a prominent exponent of the community model of narrative theology. Hans Frei's comparison of Scripture to a nineteenth-century realistic novel and George Lindbeck's argument for a cultural-linguistic understanding of Christian doctrine are standard features of its exposition. In both cases, "narrative" functions as a way of faithfulness to the Word and a key to preserving the integrity of the Christian community. The biblical narrative creates a world of its own, one not knowable by, or translatable into, the culture's regnant assumptions, with the identity of its chief Character, God incarnate in Jesus Christ, rendered only as the story unfolds. Its lineaments are discernible in the lore and life together of the Christian community and through the agency of its interpretive skills. Faithfulness entails loyalty to its language world and the behavior commensurate with it. Peril to the community, its charter, grammar, and conduct comes from proposals to substitute experiences, concepts, methodologies, and moral norms alien to the tale and its telling. On the face of it, there are marked similarities between evangelical narrative and this kind of community narratology: the concern for the integrity of the comprehensive Christian story and its christological center; the wariness about external categories taking the Gospel hostage; the retrieval of a common sense reading of Scripture; the assertion of the unity of Scripture; and the acknowledgment of the role of classical tradition in the formulation of faith. However, the cultural resources on which both Frei and Lindbeck draw to state the case for narrative—the nineteenth-century novel genre, cultural anthropology, and language theory—can play such a decisive role in the interpretation of Christian faith, and do so among some of its advocates, that fundamental assumptions of historic Christian belief can be either obfuscated or eliminated. We confront here another irony: a point of view wary of standard apologetics because of its tendency to accommodate to its culture itself flirts with this same possibility. How is this so?

Does the espousal of the Gospel as a narrative along the lines of a realistic novel require, as such, a reality that corresponds to it? Mark Ellingsen, an interpreter of this version of narrative theology says: "As preachers and teachers, when reading and telling biblical stories, our first responsibility is to expound them with the same literary style and imagination with which they were written. . . . there is no insistence as an article of faith or presupposition that the biblical accounts must have happened."[19] Ellingsen's judgment reflects Hans Frei's insistence on the distinction between the "history-like" accounts of the realistic novel and historical writing accountable to "ostensive" referents. If this principle is pressed to its limit, it would mean that key events in the history of Israel, Jesus Christ, and the church would not be empirically necessary for the overall narrative to serve its function of assuring the integrity of the message and defining the boundaries of Christian community. In principle, the nonnecessity of ontological correspondence would include metaphysical as well as physical referents. Does a narrative theology so conceived require that the chief character in the story correspond to the one who is and does? Parallel to the logical nonnecessity of physical-metaphysical referents in the Frei tradition of narrative theology is the implication in Lindbeck's version of the Yale theology that "propositions" with their entailment of objective truth claims represent an alternative view of doctrine to the proffered cultural-linguistic framework.

As Roman Catholic theologian Avery Dulles, with similar interests on this point as evangelical theology, observes: "For me, the church's claim to impose a doctrine in the name of revelation implies a claim of conformity to the real order, rather than a mere claim of power to regulate language."[20] Evangelical theology sharply opposes any understanding of narrative theology that does not require the correspondence of the chapters in the Christian story to "the real order." The story is "true to life," as well as "true for us." As I. M. Wallace states it: "Clearly, the Yale theologians . . . are not threatened by the 'scandal of particularity' characteristic of the biblical texts and Christian doctrines (e.g., the belief that Jesus Christ is the Son of God)."[21] But what truth claims, if any, do such faith-specific statements make? Can we ever say that such claims are statements about the world "out there" beyond the church's "in here" appropriation of its founding persons and events? Is theological discourse something more than a witness that instantiates certain grammatical rules (Lindbeck, Holmer), something more than a literary interpretation of biblical stories (Frei)? Does not theology also make assertions that refer extra nos to realities that exist independently of this grammar and these stories? An important distinction must be made here between both Lindbeck's and Frei's own use of the cultural-linguistic model of doctrine and the requirements of the model as such. Bruce Marshall has shown that Lindbeck's "postliberal" understanding of doctrine does not exclude propositional truth claims. That is, the way correspondence truth claims for doctrine/story are warranted is coherence with the "web of Christian belief and behavior." Lindbeck agrees with Marshall's interpretation, commending him for saying it better than he succeeded in doing in *The Nature of Doctrine*. In his exchange with Carl Henry about the ontological touchstones of Scripture, Frei questions Henry's "clear and distinct ideas" about both physical and metaphysical truth but does affirm key christological referents:

> "Reference" is a difficult thing to get hold of even though one wants to refer. . . . I did not mean to deny reference at all, as Henry worries I do. . . . I don't think any of us want to. . . . Of course, I believe in the "historical reality" of Christ's death and resurrection, if those are the categories we employ. . . . If I am asked to speak in the language of factuality, then I would say, yes, in those terms, I have to speak of an empty tomb. In those terms I have to speak of a literal resurrection. But [with this qualification] I think those terms are not privileged theory neutral, trans-cultural, an ingredient in the structure of the human mind and of reality always and everywhere for me, as I think they are for Dr. Henry.[22]

Usage made of the interpretive categories aside, even by their initiators, an evangelical critique of this type of narrative theology questions the logic of a perspective that does not require ontological truth claims for the decisive historical and transcendent referents in its story.

Evangelicalism has its own limitations in its deployment of features of community narrative. The often-hidden character of the overarching biblical narrative invites misunderstanding. Its lower profile may have to do with these factors:

1. The entry point to faith for evangelicals is Christian experience, a "heart strangely warmed." So the personal appropriation of the Gospel becomes paramount. It is a short step from this to the anthropomorphism about which Frei complains.

2. Suspicions about the role of tradition in evangelicalism mean that the resource role of the church in identifying the essentials of evangelical faith can become neglected. In the community model of narrative theology, the church plays an active part in discerning and carrying forward the centralities through its confessions of faith and liturgical traditions. Thus, the Big Story is embedded in the classical creeds, the lectionary readings of the church year, and the sacramental life (e.g., the eucharistic prayer in ecumenical liturgies, an act of thanksgiving that takes the worshipper from creation to Christ to consummation).

3. When evangelical theologians speak about "the basics," they often do so in strict propositional form. Thus, what is historically "an unfolding drama" (Bernhard Anderson) is discursively organized and methodically classified. Evangelical insistence that revelation is what God says as well as what God does is a crucial point being made here. But propositions, while necessary, are not sufficient. When the Epic of God is "pinned and classified like a butterfly in a collector's case" (J. B. Metz), the narrative quality of faith is dissolved into propositionalism.

In each of these respects, evangelicalism's case for narrative would be strengthened by insights garnered from advocates of community narrative.

Conclusion

For all its limitations, evangelical narrative has a corrective word to speak to the narrative theologies on the present scene. More than that, its attempt to hold together the three features of personal story, biblical stories, and the Great Story contrasts with the reductionist tendencies found in each of these types. A Christian story worth telling is an encompassing one that rises out of Scripture's intentions as interpreted and lived out by a faithful church and personally appropriated by the believer. May the evangelical voice be heard and its presence welcomed at the table of today's raconteurs.

Notes

1. On these kinds of distinctions see Gary Comstock, "Two Types of Narrative Theology," *Journal of the American Academy of Religion* 55, no. 4 (Winter 1987), 687–717, and Mark Ellingsen, *The Integrity of Biblical Narrative* (Minneapolis: Fortress Press, 1990), 53–61. On the distinction as it relates to larger questions of theological method, see William Placher.

2. Carl F. H. Henry, "Narrative Theology: An Evangelical Appraisal," *Trinity Journal* 8 NS (1987), 3–19.

3. Millard Erickson, "Narrative Theology: Translation or Transformation?" in *Festschrift: A Tribute to Dr. William Hordern*, ed. Walter Freitag (Saskatoon: University of Saskatchewan Press, 1985), 30–34 and *The Word Became Flesh* (Grand Rapids: Baker Book House, 1991), 359–379.

4. Alister McGrath, "The Biography of God," *Christianity Today* 35, no. 8 (July 22, 1991), 22–24 and *The Genesis of Doctrine* (Oxford: Basil Blackwell, 1990), 14–34, 52–65, I. M. Wallace, "The New Yale Theology," *Christian Scholars Review* 17, no. 2 (Dec. 1987) 154–170.

5. Mark Ellingsen, *Integrity of Biblical Narrative*, and *The Evangelical Movement* (Minneapolis: Augsburg Press, 1988), 364, 388, and Clark Pinnock, *Tracking the Maze* (San Francisco: Harper & Row, 1990), passim.

6. Hans Frei did respond to Carl Henry's views when the latter presented them to an evangelical gathering at Yale: "Response to 'Narrative Theology: An Evangelical Appraisal'," *Trinity Journal* 8 NS (1987), 21–24.

7. "Evangelical, Evangelicalism," *The Westminster Dictionary of Christian Theology*, ed. Alan Richardson and John Bowden (Philadelphia: Westminster Press, 1983), 191–192.

8. For an exploration of these categories see Gabriel Fackre, *Authority: Scripture in the Church for the World* vol. 2 of *The Christian Story* (Grand Rapids, Mich.: Eerdmans, 1987), 61–73.

9. Excerpted from Gabriel Fackre, "Narrative Theology: An Overview," *Interpretation* 37, no. 4 (Oct. 1983), 341.

10. Karl Barth, *Church Dogmatics*, vol. 4, pt. 2, ed. G. W. Bromiley and T. F. Torrance (Edinburgh: T & T Clark, 1958), 112–113. David Ford calls attention to this tribute in *Barth and God's Story* (Frankfurt am Main: Verlag Peter Lang, 1981), 16.

11. Hans Frei, *The Eclipse of Biblical Narrative* (New Haven: Yale University Press, 1974), 141–142.

12. So in an early Christian hymn, *Phos hilaron*, the church's teaching about the unity of first and second Persons of the Trinity is preserved: Serene Light of the Holy Glory of the Father Everlasting Jesus Christ. On this and the use of light imagery in doctrine, see Jaroslav Pelikan, *The Light of the World* (New York: Harper & Brothers, 1962), 31 and passim.

13. As in the older systematics works of Charles Hodge, *Systematic Theology*, Augustus Strong, *Systematic Theology*, Edgar Young Mullins, *The Christian Religion in its Doctrinal Expression*, and the current ones of Millard Erickson, *Christian Theology*, James Leo Garrett, *Systematic Theology*, and Gordon Lewis and Bruce Demarest, *Integrative Theology*.

14. Peter Toon, *The Development of Doctrine* (Grand Rapids, Mich.: Eerdmans, 1979), 62–70.

15. Carl F. H. Henry, *God, Revelation and Authority* (Waco: Word Books, 1979), 468.

16. William G. Doty, "The Stories of Our Times," in *Religion as Story*, ed. James B. Wiggins (New York: Harper & Row, 1975), 94.

17. See Wiggins, *Religion as Story*; Lonnis Kliever, *The Sheltered Spectrum* (Atlanta: John Knox, 1981); John Navone and Thomas Cooper, *Tellers of the Word* (New York: LeJacq, 1981); Johan Baptist Metz, *Faith in History*, trans. David Smith (New York: Seabury Press, 1980); and Robert McAgee Brown, "My Story and 'The Story,'" *Theology Today* 22 (July 1975), 166–173.

18. Stephen Crites, "The Narrative Quality of Experience," *Journal of the American Academy of Religion* 39, no. 3 (Sept. 1971), 291–311. Also, John S. Dunne, *A Search for God in*

Time and Memory (Notre Dame: University of Notre Dame Press, 1977), and Robert Roth, *The Theater of God* (Philadelphia: Fortress Press 1984).

19. This is a major emphasis of Ellingsen's *Integrity of Biblical Narrative*.

20. Avery Dulles, "Observations on George Lindbeck's *The Nature of Doctrine*" (paper presented at Yale Divinity School, New Haven, Conn., Sept. 1984), 10.

21. Wallace, "The New Yale Theology," 124–170.

22. Frei, "Response to Narrative Theology," 22.

11

NICHOLAS WOLTERSTORFF

Living within a Text

In a well-known passage from his book, *Mimesis,* Erich Auerbach, speaking of "the Biblical narrative," says that

> far from seeking, like Homer, merely to make us forget our own reality for a few hours, it seeks to over-come our reality: we are to fit our own life into its world, feel ourselves to be elements in its structure of universal history. . . . The Homeric poems present a definite complex of events whose boundaries in space and time are clearly delimited; . . . The Old Testament, on the other hand, presents universal history: it begins with the beginning of time, with the creation of the world, and will end with the Last Days, the fulfilling of the Covenant, with which the world will come to an end. Everything else that happens in the world can only be conceived as an element in this sequence; into it everything that is known about the world, or at least everything that touches upon the history of the Jews, must be fitted as an ingredient of the divine plan.[1]

This passage, though it occurs in a "secular" study of the origins of realism in Western literature, has had a deep impact on the reflections and recommendations by Christian theologians in recent years concerning the role of the Bible in the Christian community. The theologians I have in mind include, but are not limited to, those who belong to the so-called Yale school of theology.

At the beginning of his book, *The Eclipse of Biblical Narrative,*[2] Hans Frei offers a characterization of a "Western Christian reading of the Bible in the days before the rise of historical criticism." It was, he says, strongly realistic, at once literal and historical, making prominent use of figural, or typological, interpretation. Then, just before he himself cites the Auerbach passage I have just cited, Frei says that

> . . . since the world truly rendered by combining biblical narratives into one was indeed the one and only real world, it must in principle embrace the experience of any present age and reader. Not only was it possible for him, it was also his duty to fit himself into that world in which he was in any case a member, and he too did so

in part by figural interpretation and in part of course by his mode of life. He was to see his disposition, his actions and passions, the shape of his own life as well as that of his era's events as figures of that storied world. A story such as that of man's creation and "fall" (Genesis 1–3) made sense in its own right and as part of the larger story into which it was incorporated by Christian interpreters, beginning with St. Paul. But in addition, figuration made sense of the general extrabiblical structure of human experience, and of one's own experience, as well as of general concepts of good and evil drawn from experience. The point is that such experiences, events, concepts were all ranged figurally into the smaller as well as the overarching story. Biblical interpretation became an imperative need, but its direction was that of incorporating extrabiblical thought, experience, and reality into the one real world detailed and made accessible by the biblical story—not the reverse.

Frei goes on to argue that one of the effects of historical criticism was that "the direction of interpretation now became the reverse of earlier days. Do the stories and whatever concepts may be drawn from them describe what we apprehend as the real world? . . . even [for those] who had no doubt of the historicity of the narrated events: their meaning is nonetheless referable to an external more general context, and the story now has to be interpreted into it, rather than that external pattern of meaning being incorporated—figurally or in some other way—into the story" *(Eclipse,* 5–6). A corollary of this reversal of direction was the demise of typological interpretation. "Typology or figuration simply could not cope with this reversal," says Frei *(Eclipse,* 6).[3] This reversal of direction was inherently a diminution of the authority of the Bible. But Frei sees it as having harbored the potential for a further diminution of that authority. Before the days of biblical criticism, most members of the church regarded the Bible as offering an *infallible* narration of ancient events; biblical evidence for ancient events was totally reliable evidence. But once scepticism on that score settled in, the Bible lost even what authority it still had for those infallibilists who had already reversed the direction of interpretation. Yet those who were members of the church still wanted from the Bible a message that was true and edifying; accordingly, a whirling search was set going for alternative interpretations. Frei argues in detail that these proved usually to be interpretations in which the realistic character of the narrative that constitutes the literal sense of so much of the Bible, the gospels in particular, was 'eclipsed.'

The recovery of biblical authority requires undoing the eclipse of biblical narrative; and that can only be achieved, Frei thought, by interpreting the narrative with techniques characteristic of literary scholars, resolutely postponing questions of truth and reference until one has finished interpreting. "When I wrote *The Eclipse of Biblical Narrative*," he says,

I had liberals much more than conservatives in mind. And what I had in mind was the fact that if something didn't seem to suit the world view of the day, then liberals quickly reinterpreted it, or as we say today, "revised" it. And my sense of the matter, though I'm not antiliberal, was that you can revise the text to suit yourself only just so far. There really is an analogy between the Bible and a novel writer who says something like this: I mean what I say whether or not anything took place. I mean what I say. It's as simple as that: the text means what it says.[4]

But undoing the eclipse of the narrative, though necessary for recovering the authority of the Bible in the Christian community, is not by itself sufficient. There must also be a reversal in the direction of appropriation characteristic of us in the modern world—a rereversal, if you will—so that once again "extrabiblical thought, experiences and reality [are incorporated] into the one real world detailed and made accessible by the biblical story. . . ." Or as George Lindbeck, one of Frei's colleagues, puts it in one of his essays: ". . . the issue which concerns us is the extent to which the Bible can be profitably read in our day as a canonically and narrationally unified and internally glossed (that is, self-referential and self-interpreting) whole centered on Jesus Christ, and telling the story of the dealings of the Triune God with his people and his world in ways which are typologically (though not, so at least the Reformers would say, allegorically) applicable to the present."[5] (It is no surprise that this metaphor of *reversing the direction* is used by the Yale theologians not only to characterize the relation of the modern way of using the Bible to its predecessor and their own response to the modern way, but also to characterize the relation of 'liberal' theology to its antecedents and their own response to that, in turn.) "In the Middle Ages," says Lindbeck, "Platonism and Aristotelianism . . . were assimilated into the scriptural framework and thus Christianized. . . . Now, however, the interpretive direction is reversed: the biblical message is translated into contemporary conceptualities. This always happens unconsciously in varying degrees . . . but from Schleiermacher through Karl Rahner and to liberation theologies, translation into nonbiblical idioms has been done deliberately and systematically."[6]

In this chapter I wish to set off to the side analysis and assessment of the proposals concerning interpretation of the biblical texts that are contained in the above remarks and reflect instead on the recommendation to the Christian community that it reverse the direction of its appropriation, and once again practice inhabiting the world of the biblical text. Of course it's true, as Lindbeck remarks, that "a habitable text need not have a primarily narrative structure."[7] Though human beings, in his opinion, do need "texts projecting imaginatively and practically habitable worlds," he thinks that it's not required in general that the text be narrative in structure but only that it "in some fashion be construable as a guide to thought and action in the encounter with changing circumstances. It must supply followable directions for coherent patterns of life in new situations. Obviously, this comment is relevant to our appropriation of the Bible; for, even if we grant that the Bible as a whole presents a narrative, there are large parts which are clearly not narrative in structure; and those parts—for example, the prophetic literature of the Old Testament and the epistolary literature of the New Testament—have traditionally been used by the church as guidance for its life. Likewise, the Psalms have been, and still are, used by the church to express its praise, its lament, its thanksgiving. In using them thus, we inhabit these texts. But without denying any of that, the Yale theologians are calling our attention to the narrative components of Scripture; it is the world of these parts of the total text that they are urging us who are Christians to inhabit. With the narrativity of those components clearly in view, we are to inhabit, "imaginatively and practically," the worlds projected. Before we set out on our journey, let me express my conviction that the Yale theologians are pointing to something true and important for the Christian community with their metaphor of *inhabiting* the world of the biblical narrative. I shall be critical of certain details of their proposal, especially of what they say concerning the use of figural interpretation. But mine are the comments of a friendly critic.

Historically, the identity of the church has been constituted in good part by its being that community which takes the Scriptures of the Old and New Testaments as canonical under interpretation. To use the words of Lindbeck already quoted, as a "narrationally unified and internally glossed . . . whole centered on Jesus Christ, and telling the story of the dealings of the Triune God with his people and his world. . . ." What goes into taking as canonical is rich and complex; but a rather good metaphor for expressing that complexity is that one inhabits the biblical text and its world. The signal contribution of the Yale theologians is their insistence that this holds not only for the doctrinal and ethical passages of the Bible but also for the narrative passages. If the church no longer inhabits the biblical story, or inhabits it only so far as such habitation is compatible with inhabiting some other more fundamental story, then its identity, at least as traditionally secured, is threatened. The church's identity has been a *story-constituted identity*. I shall not here ask whether its identity could be reconstituted, nor why it is important that its identity be preserved. I shall limit myself to reflecting on those provocative comments about inhabiting the world of the biblical narrative—paying particular attention, as I mentioned, to the claims made for figural interpretation.

To make the points I wish to make, I must draw a distinction between three different modes of habitation. There is a tendency in Frei and Lindbeck to use "typological interpretation," along with its synonym, "figural interpretation," as catchall phrases for that activity whereby we discern or achieve habitation. That will not do. But before I can make the necessary distinctions among modes of habitation, I must briefly explain what I take the *world* of the biblical narrative to be, saying something both about the concept of the sense of a text, and something about the concept of the world of a text. This part of my discussion will be mostly ontological, and accordingly, rather abstract; worse yet, it will be somewhat dogmatic in character, since I lack the time here to display its motivations.

We speak of sentences and sequences of sentences as having senses. What, ontologically, is a *sense*? For anyone acquainted with Frege's famous essay, "*Sinn und Bedeutung*," the thought comes immediately to mind that a sense is a proposition—or as Frege called it, a Gedanke. However, in speaking, we not only express propositions but also take up various stances toward the propositions expressed—the assertive, the interrogative, the optative, the imperative, the fictive; and I think it best to regard these as also belonging to the sense. So I propose that we take senses to be *speech actions*; more specifically, speech actions which are what J. L. Austin called *illocutionary actions*. "Expressing the wish that the weather were warm" is an entity of the right sort to be a sense, as is "asserting that this has been a cold spring." That gives us the categorial status of senses. But we want also to know which, of all the speech actions, is that action which is the sense of some specific sentence—for example, of the sentence, "This has been a cold spring." A crucial thing to note here is that senses do not just come associated with sentences relative to uses of sentences in such a way that the speech action is a *sense* of that sentence relative to that use.

Frei is very much aware of the fact that a given text can have a number of different kinds of senses—literal, metaphorical, allegorical. And he observes that in a given community at a given time, a rule may be in force to the effect that for certain texts, the community is to attend to just one kind of sense; those texts in that community then have an established kind of sense. What Frei does not note—it would in fact cause some havoc in his theory if he did—is that there are not only different kinds of senses but that the literal sense of a sentence relative to one use thereof may differ from the literal sense of that same sentence relative to another use thereof and so also for metaphorical sense, allegorical sense, and whatever other kinds there are. Frei regularly speaks of the literal sense of the text of the gospels; in doing so, he remained imprisoned within the New Critical way of thinking.

Let us move on now from senses to *worlds*. Clearly, the illocutionary actions performed by some linguistic utterances do not have propositional content; cries and greetings are examples: "Whew," Howdy," "Ugh," "Whoa." But let us set such actions off to the side; henceforth, when I speak of senses, let us confine our attention to those senses that do have propositional content. And let us also confine our attention to those senses in which the stance taken up toward the propositional content is either assertive or fictive or a sequence thereof. With these restrictions in mind, consider then the propositional content of a sense of some text. The *world projected* by that text for that sense can then be thought of as that propositional content, plus whatever else is appropriately extrapolated therefrom. We all, when dealing with texts, extrapolate beyond the propositional content of the sense; we 'flesh it out.' If we read in a contemporary realistic novel that someone traveled from New York to Chicago in two hours, we extrapolate to his having taken a plane between these two cities, even though there are no *words* in the text that even so much as carry the suggestion that he took a plane. It will help our discussion to regiment the terminology here a bit and speak henceforth of *elucidation* as the activity of figuring out what belongs to some sense of a text, and *extrapolation* as the activity of figuring out what, in addition to the propositional content of that sense, belongs to the world projected by that text for that sense. Observation of the practice of extrapolation makes clear that different practitioners operate with different principles; and obviously, different principles of extrapolation will normally yield different worlds. Thus, when I speak of the world projected by a text for a sense, this must be understood as relative to some practice of extrapolation and the rules embedded in that practice. As to choosing among practices of extrapolation and the principles embedded therein, let me here say no more than that the choice cannot be made in terms of truth and falsehood of such principles; it can only be made in terms of how well the practice embodying some principle serves one and another value. Of course, practitioners will often not really choose among such practices and their principles; they will simply engage in some practice as they were taught.

With this theoretical equipment in hand, let me now distinguish between three broadly different ways of inhabiting the world projected by a text, calling them the *component mode*, the *narrative-continuation mode*, and the *conformation mode*. One way of inhabiting the world projected by a text (relative to a sense) consists of oneself being a component of that world; and more generally, one way in which contemporary reality 'fits into' some projected world consists of that reality being a component of that world. By something being a *component* of a world, I mean that that world could not occur without that item of reality existing. This form of habitation, if and when it occurs, will be an objective fact; interpretation will bring it to light, not bring it about. Clearly, Frei and Lindbeck think that a great deal of contemporary reality inhabits the biblical world in the component mode; that is one of the most interesting and provocative suggestions contained in their writings. I think close scrutiny will reveal, however, that there is less here than meets the eye.

You and I are, of course, never referred to in the biblical narrative. If we are nonetheless components of its projected world (relative to some sense), that will come about by virtue of what is extrapolated from the sense, rather than by virtue of the sense itself. Extrapolation, not elucidation, will be the relevant mode of interpretation uncovering our 'componenthood'. The mode of extrapolation to which Frei and Lindbeck most frequently appeal, when discussing our inhabiting the world of the biblical text, is *figural* or typological extrapolation. So let us begin there — asking first what figuration, or typology, is, and then, what constitutes figural or typological *interpretation*.

Frei repeatedly insists that typological interpretation is not a species of allegorical interpretation. "Far from being in conflict with the literal sense of biblical stories, figuration or typology was a natural extension of literal interpretation" (*Eclipse*, 2), he says. I think he is right about that. An allegorical text is a text for which there are two senses and two worlds, a literal sense and a literal world, and an allegorical sense and an allegorical world, with the latter projected by way of the former's projection. Allegorical interpretation then consists of elucidating the allegorical sense and appropriately extrapolating thereon, so as to arrive at a knowledge of the allegorical world. By contrast, figural interpretation normally focuses on the literal sense and its associated world; and what defines it as a distinct mode of interpretation is that it is the attempt to puzzle out, by elucidation and extrapolation, the *relations of signification* that hold among the (nonlinguistic) entities in the projected world.

The principles that we in the modern world make use of for extrapolation are almost exclusively principles of logic and principles of causality. If the twenty-first birthday of some character is described for us, we extrapolate to his having had a twentieth birthday, even if it is neither said nor verbally suggested that he did. And, to repeat the example offered earlier, if we are told in a contemporary realistic novel that someone traveled from New York to Chicago in two hours, we extrapolate to his having done so by plane. In the former case, we tacitly appeal to a principle of logic; in the latter case, to a principle of causality.

But suppose one's vision of historical reality is such that one not only regards entities as standing in causal relations to each other but also as standing in relations of *signification*: this historical thing, person, or event signifies that one. Then, in all likelihood, if one is concentrating on the literal sense of some text and that text is 'historylike', one will conduct one's extrapolation not only by appealing to logical and causal principles, but also by appealing to one's convictions as to the signification relations which hold among entities. Such extrapolation is figural, or typological, extrapolation. Of course, if this vision of reality as charged with signification was shared by the writer of the text before one, then in all likelihood he himself will have pointed to some of the signification-relations among the entities in his projected world. Discerning those demands no more than elucidating the sense; it requires no extrapolation. That is why I said that figural interpretation is a mode of interpretation that comprises both elucidation and extrapolation; it consists, to say it once again, in trying to discern the signification-relations among the entities in some projected world. Auerbach, in two passages cited by Frei, offers a lucid and compact description of figural interpretation. Figural interpretation

> establishes a connection between two events or persons in such a way that the first signifies not only itself but also the second, while the second involves or fulfills the first. The two poles of a figure are separated in time, but both, being real events or persons, are within temporality. They are both contained in the flowing stream which is historical life, and only the comprehension, the *intellectus spiritualis*, of their interdependence is a spiritual act. (*Mimesis*, 73)
>
> In this conception, an occurrence on earth signifies not only itself but at the same time another, which it predicts or confirms, without prejudice to the power of its concrete reality here and now. The connection between occurrences is not regarded as primarily a chronological or causal development but as a oneness within the divine plan, of which all occurrences are parts and reflections (*Mimesis*, 555).

The word "predicts" introduces a false note here; I shall return to the matter shortly. Suppose, now, that the urgings of theologians like Frei and Lindbeck have been successful, and that, like our forebears, we in the Christian community regard reality as laced through with figural meaning; we think of reality as a book to be read. More specifically, we think of reality as laced through with figures of persons, things, and events in the *biblical narrative*. I, and my various doings and undergoings, are seen as figuring persons, doings, and undergoings contained in the literal sense of the biblical narrative; and the same for you. Your suffering, for example, may be seen as a figure of Christ's suffering. If such a renewal of vision did occur among us, one would expect that we, when dealing with narrative texts, would make use of our figural convictions in our practice of extrapolation. Whether it is at all likely that such a renewal of vision can occur is a matter I shall consider shortly. For now, suppose it happened.

The question I wish to pose is whether it would be at all plausible to suppose that the revised practice of extrapolation which accompanied this recovery would be such that I and you, along with our doings and undergoings, would prove to be components of the world of the biblical text? I think not. To extrapolate, one starts with the propositional content of a sense and then asks what else would be the case if that were the case, or what else the *author thought* would be the case if that were the case, or what else the *original audience thought* would be the case if that were the case, or what else a present audience thinks would be the case if that were the case, or what else *contemporary science and logic tell* us would be the case if that were the case—or some such principle. Now if one believed that reality was laced through with figural meaning, then asking what else would be the case if the (propositional content of the) text's sense were the case would quite naturally lead one to extrapolate from mentioned signifiers to unmentioned signifieds. If Charlemagne were a component of the (propositional content of the) sense, and one brought to the text the conviction that Charlemagne was a figure of King David, then one would naturally extrapolate to the existence of King David. If the story was about you, and I brought to the text the conviction that your suffering is a figure of Christ's suffering, then I would naturally extrapolate to the existence of Christ. But it seems to me most implausible to suppose that the practice would license extrapolation in the reverse direction, from signified to signifier—from a story about King David to Charlemagne and all the other figures of David, from a story about Christ's suffering to your suffering and all the other figures of Christ's suffering. Accordingly, I don't think that recovering the figural vision of reality will do anything at all to bring it about that I and my contemporaries are revealed to be components of the biblical world.

But might it be that you and I, and contemporary realities in general, are components of the biblical narrative world by virtue of biblical prophecy—in particular, by virtue of the foretelling component of biblical prophecy? I have mentioned that Frei and Lindbeck regularly treat prophecy as a species of typology, following Auerbach in this regard; prophecy is treated as forward-directed figuration. This seems to me a mistake. Typology, as we have seen, consists of figural relations among persons, things, and events, whereas prophecy consists of speech. To use our theoretical terminology, strange though it sounds in this context: prophecy consists of the performance of illocutionary actions.

Now suppose that in a novel someone foretells something—using "foretell" as a catchall word to cover predicting, promising, threatening, assuring, and so forth. Then that person's (or character's) foretelling that particular thing is a component in a sense of that novel and in its corresponding world. But is *the thing foretold*, as well as the *foretelling*, a component? That depends on the principle of extrapolation used and on whether the foretelling is accurate or thought by the relevant persons to be accurate. Suppose that the principle which guides extrapolation is that we are to extrapolate to whatever else would occur if the sense in question occurred; then if the foretelling is accurate or trustworthy, it does follow that the thing foretold is a component of the novel world, for that sense.

Frei comments on a passage from Calvin in which the distinction between prophecy and figuration is clearly assumed, though he does so without, so it seems to me, himself fully seeing the significance of the distinction. Frei has just cited Calvin's interpretation of Genesis 3:15: "I will put enmity between you and the woman, and between your seed and her seed; he shall bruise your head, and you shall bruise his heel." Calvin denies that this is a prophetic reference to Christ; "Gladly would I give my suffrage in support of [this] opinion," he says, "but that I regard the word 'seed' as too violently distorted by [it]; for who will concede that a collective noun is to be understood of one man only?" Frei then says the following: "If a literal reading leads [Calvin] to a general rather than specific prophecy of the course of events as the meaning of this verse, the same kind of reading of Isaiah 7:14 brings him to the opposite conclusion. 'Therefore the Lord himself will give you a sign, Behold, a virgin [Calvin opts for this disputed interpretation] shall conceive and bear a son, and shall call his name Immanuel.' Calvin rejects, among other referential interpretations of this prophecy, its merely figural application to Christ, as if 'the Prophet spoke of some child who was born at that time, by whom, as by an obscure picture, Christ was foreshadowed.' His interpretative claim once again is literal, though this time to the opposite effect: 'This name Immanuel could not be literally applied to a mere man; and, therefore, there can be no doubt that the Prophet referred to Christ'" (*Eclipse*, 26).

It is clearly the case that not all foretelling reported or expressed in the biblical writings is accurate; there were, after all, false prophets. The Bible itself, however, by and large sorts things out for us. So suppose that as one facet of taking the Bible as authoritative, the Christian community trusts the Bible's sorting out of true from false prophecies; we believe that those foretellings to which the Bible gives its stamp of approval are accurate or trustworthy. Then, if the principle of extrapolation to which we adhere is the one cited above, it follows that not just the foretellings but whatever is foretold by an approved foretelling is a component of the world of the biblical text (for the sense in question). If the existence of the same reality contemporary with you and me was foretold, those contemporary realities are to be regarded as belonging to the world of the biblical text. They inhabit that world, in the component mode. It appears to me, however, that there isn't very much contemporary reality that fits into the biblical world by virtue of biblical prophecy. My existence was not foretold, neither was yours. It's true that the existence of sinners was foretold, or at least it was assumed that there would be sinners in the future; and I am one of those. But it's not the case that it was foretold, *of me*, that I would be a sinner, since nowhere am I referred to.

Let me move on now to the second mode of habitation which I call the *narrative-continuation* mode. The mode I have in mind is suggested by these words of Auerbach, already quoted: "The Old Testament . . . presents universal history: it begins with the beginning of time, with the creation of the world, and will end with the Last Days, the fulfilling of the Covenant, with which the world will come to an end. Everything else that happens in the world can only be conceived as an element in this sequence; . . ." To understand the thought here we have to change our focus. Instead of focusing on the narrative world of the biblical text and the realities which are components of that world, we have to turn our attention to the whole sweep of human history. All of history, so the Bible suggests, is the story of the dealings of God with humanity. To this great sweeping story, the Bible bears a variety of distinct relationships. For one thing, its composition is itself part of the story. But also, the Bible is about that story in various ways. It details for us certain parts of the story, especially those parts that are redemptively decisive; it tells in sketchy fashion what we can expect for the future. And one way of inhabiting the biblical narrative is telling the story of our contemporary reality in accord with the lines of interpretation exhibited and suggested by the biblical narrative—and more generally, telling the story of those parts of history of which the Bible does not directly speak in accord with the lines of interpretation there laid down.

Consider an analogue: Suppose one comes across a century-old history of America whose line of interpretation one finds illuminating and insightful. One might then consider bringing its history of America up to date, following the line of interpretation there exhibited and suggested—not updating that history, which is quite a different enterprise, but bringing it up to the present time. That is the sort of thing I have in mind by the *narrative-continuation* mode of inhabiting: Telling the story of one's own life and time—in accord with the lines of interpretation exhibited and suggested in the Bible's narration—in that way, bringing the biblical story up to date. Here again Frei's emphasis on the importance of typology enters the picture; for, of course, typology is one of the lines of interpretation exhibited in the biblical narrative. And lest there be confusion on the point, let me emphasize that my earlier argument, that the recovery of figural interpretation will not have the consequence that you and I are revealed to be components of the world of the biblical narrative, implies nothing at all against either the possibility or desirability of using typological interpretation in bringing the biblical narrative up to the present.

Nonetheless, I have my doubts. For one thing, I myself, so far as I can tell, simply lack any concept of *signification* according to which it is plausible to hold that Charlemagne signifies King David, that Mother Theresa signifies Christ, that Billy Graham signifies St. Paul, and so on. I know indeed what it is for the thought of Charlemagne to *suggest* the thought of King David to me, what it is for the thought of Mother Theresa to *suggest* the thought of Christ to me, what it is for the thought of Billy Graham to *suggest* the thought of St. Paul to me. It may be important to allow such suggestions to do their work; it may even be important to cultivate such suggestions. But suggestion is not signification.

Perhaps, though, there is a concept of *signification* according to which these things are true; if so, perhaps it is possible to recover it. But why would it be important to do so? Why does Frei think it important to recover this way of thinking? He doesn't say. Presumably, he thinks it's a true way of thinking; there are all those significations in reality. But even if he were right about that, lots of true things aren't worth spending much time on. The heyday of typological interpretation was probably the fifteenth and sixteenth centuries; hundreds of thousands of books of so-called emblems were published in Europe, offering readings of the "book of nature." Why is it important to recover those habits? Is it important to recover them? What would have to happen to enable us to recover them? It appears to me that figural interpretation when genuinely embedded in one's life-practice—so that for example as one walks through the woods on a spring day one takes note of what the Dutchman's-breeches mean, of what the bloodroots mean, of what the trillions mean, of what the hepaticas mean, of what the marsh marigolds mean—requires or strongly encourages an Augustinian type of spirituality. For presumably, the point of God's filling the world with signifiers of biblical reality would be that God wants our attention directed to the things signified. And that fits the spirituality which comes to expression so vividly in Book Ten of the *Confessions*, where Augustine imagines the things of the world all saying to him, "Go away from us, to our Creator." Frei often stresses that figural interpretation leaves the 'reality' of both poles of the figure 'intact'. That's true, of course; Charlemagne and King David are equally real. Nonetheless, the intended function of figural signification is to direct us away from the hepaticas and bloodroots to what the hepaticas and bloodroots signify. It's my guess that among the causes of the decay of figural interpretation was the decay of Augustinian spirituality. Though the theology of the Reformers was deeply Augustinian, their spirituality was significantly different.

All of us, when children, inhabited the worlds of stories we read or were told in such a way that our perceptions, our imaginations, our emotions, our actions, our descriptions, were shaped thereby: a story about wolves at the bottom of the stairs led us to 'hear wolves' at the bottom of the stairs in the night, stories about Superman led us to run about wearing a cape over our shoulders. The same is true, though perhaps less obviously so, for us as adults: we all live story-shaped lives. The issue is not *whether* we will do so; the issue is rather, which are the stories that will shape our lives? Frei's point is that recovering the authority of Scripture in the life of the Christian community must include recovering the practice of inhabiting the world of the biblical narrative in the *conformation* mode. More than that: the story that *most decisively shapes* our lives must be the biblical story.

My own conviction is that Frei's contention here is both important and correct. Naturally, there will be some, even in the Christian community, who have their doubts; it would be eminently appropriate to address those doubts: What is it about the biblical story that makes it important to conform our lives to that story? But rather than using this occasion to address that fundamental question and also without using it to explore the fascinating topic of how stories in general work on us so as to shape our lives—both these topics are too large for engaging here—I wish to raise a question about the proposal itself, a question which obtains, actually, to both the narrative-continuation mode and the conformation mode.

The 'I' and the 'YOU' who seek to conform our lives to, and guide our interpretations by, the biblical story are twentieth-century members of the modern West, shaped by our society and culture; as such, we experience a great many points of collision when we come up against the biblical narrative. At many of these, our modern Western mentality ought to bend and give; otherwise, they are a harbinger. In fact, they are ancient. The early Fathers, confronted with biblical sentences ascribing change and emotions to God, said that these must be interpreted metaphorically, since we know that God does not change and that God is apathetic. How did they know that? And in the face of such a move as this, wherein lies the authority of the Bible? If the church no longer feels obligated to conform its life to, and guide its narrative interpretations by, the biblical story, the authority of the Bible in the life of the church is seriously impaired; and when the authority of the Bible in the life of the church is seriously impaired, the church's identity is endangered. These claims seem to me important and correct. Yet allowing oneself to be shaped by the biblical narrative is only one facet of a complex picture. For the shaping has to be a *discriminate* shaping. But how does one justify one's discriminations? And what marks the difference between discriminating conformation and guidance, on the one hand, and going one's own way, on the other? Those are the big questions on the agenda.

Notes

1. Erich Auerbach, *Mimesis* (Princeton: Princeton University Press, 1968), 15–16.

2. Hans Frei, *The Eclipse of Biblical Narrative* (New Haven: Yale University Press, 1974), 3.

3. Cf. the following passage from George Lindbeck, "Scripture, Consensus, and Community," in *Biblical Interpretation in Crisis*, ed. R. J. Neuhaus (Grand Rapids, Mich.: Eerd-

mans, 1989): "The laity learned the fundamental outline and episodes of the scriptural drama through liturgy, catechesis, and occasional preaching. That drama defined for them the truly real world, and within it they inscribed their own reality (as the products of the popular imagination from paintings, sculpture, and Mystery plays to oaths and proverbs make evident). Nor was this absorption of ordinary life by the Bible simply an imaginative matter. Charlemagne's typological identification of himself as a Christian King David set over God's people, for example, was not an empty metaphor but a history-transforming trope" (79).

4. "Response to 'Narrative Theology: an Evangelical Appraisal'," *Trinity Journal* 8 NS (1987), 21–24.

5. Lindbeck, "Scripture, Consensus, and Community," 75.

6. Ibid., 86–87.

7. Ibid., 97.

PART IV

THE PROBLEMS OF NARRATIVE

12

PAUL GRIFFITHS

The Limits of Narrative Theology

Prolegomena

I assume in this essay the truth of the following claims. First, that religious communities typically either explicitly claim or implicitly assume the truth of some descriptive statements about the nature of the world and of human persons. Second, similarly, that such communities typically do the same in regard to the truth of some broadly axiological statements, statements as to what is of value. And third, that such communities typically regard doing these things as both proper and essential to their function as religious communities. I shall call a community's descriptive and axiological claims its *doctrines*.[1] These are often, though not always and not necessarily, preserved and displayed in authoritatively binding collections of natural language sentences that I shall call creeds. Though both *doctrine* and *creed* are terms used by Christians for their artifacts, and therefore have a specific cultural and conceptual history, they can usefully be used to pick out artifacts used by non-Christian religious communities; in fact, I would argue that religious communities necessarily have doctrines (though the degree and manner of their articulation varies), and that many of them have creeds. I shall not argue these claims; instead, they will inform and be ingredient to the argument I do make.

Each of these assumptions is a broadly descriptive claim about what religious communities typically do. Stated in a more general way, I am assuming that religious communities cannot perform their typical functions without making some set of descriptive claims about how the world is, and about how human persons ought to behave in it. While I am aware that these claims, innocuous though they might seem, can be and have been challenged on a wide variety of grounds, I shall not here attempt to meet any of these challenges (which does not mean that I think them without merit or significance). I shall simply treat these three claims and their corollaries as axiomatic for a discussion of the questions that concern me here.

Let me unpack these axioms a little more. Some of the claims made by religious communities about the nature of human persons and of the world they inhabit are typically—and, in the end, necessarily—claims not indexed to a time. That is, they are true (if they are) always and everywhere. So, for example, when an intellectual representative of some Buddhist community claims that "all existents are impermanent" or that "everything has a cause," and moreover represents such claims as possessing religious significance for the community, it is clear that these are universal claims: their subject is all things at all times, and so their truth, if they have any, is not indexed to a time or to a place. (It might also be argued, as it has been by some Buddhists, that if these claims are true they are so necessarily, and that they are therefore properly metaphysical claims. But I shall not argue this here, though I do think it true that no religious community can in the end avoid making properly metaphysical claims.)

Of course, religious communities also typically make many descriptive claims with doctrinal force that are indexed to a time. Christians, for instance, make such claims about a historical individual, Jesus of Nazareth, as well as about various other paradigmatic figures and events in their tradition. Since the object of such claims is a (theoretically) datable event or set of events, they are necessarily indexed to a time; and so sentences representing such temporally indexed states of affairs may often have doctrinal force for religious communities.

A community's axiological doctrines, those by means of which it attributes value to something or to some course of action, will also often be of a universal kind, a kind that recommends some course or courses of action as desirable for all human persons at all times, or that predicates what William Christian would call an "unrestricted primacy-ranking predicate" of something.[2] Of this kind is the Buddhist claim that Nirvana is the proper end of all human persons or the Christian claim that "the service of God is the proper end of all human persons." Ethical principles, of which religious communities typically have many among their doctrines, are also of this broadly universalistic kind: "love your neighbor as yourself" is an example. These broadly universalistic axiological claims are true, if they are, atemporally: this is so because they are not indexed to a time. Finally, I understand theology to be the tradition- and community-specific enterprise of exhibiting, elucidating, systematizing, and (where necessary) defending or justifying the descriptive and axiological claims ingredient to and presupposed by some community's religious practice.[3] This definition is meant to include theological practice as part of a community's religious practice; which entails the conclusion that theological practice, unlike most other kinds of religious practice, is interestingly recursive: part of its subject-matter is itself, and it therefore includes, necessarily, those procedural claims that the community takes to govern its own proper performance.

Given these preliminary ground-clearing definitions—and I am profoundly aware of how controverted and controversial they are—my central concern in this essay will be with the question of what the deployment of narrative discourse by religious communities can contribute to the furtherance of the theological enterprise, bearing in mind that prosecuting this enterprise is an unavoidable and proper part of the function of such communities. Treating this question will involve asking whether the use of narrative discourse by religious communities can give their members knowledge whose kind or content is available in no other way. That is, does narrative discourse have epistemic or cognitive significance not possessed by other kinds of discourse, and, if it does, how might this significance best be stated? To put this in yet another way: Are there conceptual contents, axiological or de-scriptive, presentable only through the medium of narrative, and if so what are they? I take this to be the same as asking whether it is true that translations or para-phrases of narrative discourse into other kinds of discourse may or must lose some of the narrative's conceptual contents. It is obvious (though far from uninteresting) that such translations or paraphrases inevitably lose much in the way of affective and aesthetic effect; and I also take it to be self-evident that there will often be a de facto loss of conceptual contents; but it is not self-evident (though it may nonethe-less turn out to be true) that there is necessarily a loss of this latter kind.

These are issues of considerable theoretical interest in their own right. Answer-ing them fully would require an attempt at resolution of numerous controverted questions, including: how to define narrative discourse, and whether it is possible to offer a characterization of it with sufficient specificity to make it useful (or: is there such a thing as narrativity?); what other kinds of discourse there are to which the label "narrative discourse" might serve as a contrastive term; and various difficult topics in the epistemology and hermeneutics of narrative. I shall say or imply some-thing about all these questions, but my main interest here is not in any of them but rather in the much more specific issue of what contribution narrative discourse can make to the theological enterprise.

Narrative: A Definition

I understand a narrative to be a diachronically ordered representation of a series of events or states of affairs, a representation that makes it possible for an appropriately skilled consumer to perceive the series (and its representation) as meaningful.[4] There are many kinds of diachronic ordering; a minimal one is the simple chrono-logical list, represented best in what historians call annals.[5] Annals list events and give them temporal location, either relatively, so that we know how the events are temporally related to one another in the series, or absolutely, according to when they occurred in some calendrical system (or, more often, both). Examples of an-nals understood in this sense are a schoolchild's diary ("had breakfast, went to school, came home, had tea, did homework, went to bed"); a chart of a hospital pa-tient's body temperature with hourly entries represented in graphic form; and, using Hayden White's example, the *Annals of St. Gall*, in which the entry for the year 709 CE reads "Hard winter. Duke Gottfried died," and for 710 reads "Hard year and deficient in crops."[6] More complex diachronic orderings include not just chronological sequence, but also teleological orderings, flashbacks, and flashfor-wards, temporal nesting or embedding of various kinds, and the like. Examples of these more complex orderings are found, obviously, in novels—consider, for exam-ple, the bildungsroman in its various incarnations from Goethe to Henry James— and in various kinds of historical writing, perhaps most especially in those works of history like Spengler's *Decline of the West* or Gibbon's *Decline and Fall* whose overt goal is precisely to present a series of historical events in such a way that, to the ap-propriately skilled consumer, order, purpose, or telos are evident in them.

It will be necessary, in order for some work to be considered a narrative that, as a whole, it represents a series of events indexed to a time, and that, for each of its component parts (down to the level of sentences), those parts are either implicitly or explicitly also so indexed. In the case of sentences, this means that each sentence in a narrative must either be an explicit and direct representation of a temporally indexed state of affairs in a sentence whose ideal type is: *At time t* . . . ; or it must be a direct representation of a state of affairs without a temporal index, but one that is given such an index by courtesy, as it were, in virtue of its relations to the temporal structure of the narrative as a whole. (Of course, the temporal indexing may be possible only relative to the chronological schema of the narrative as a whole, and not to any broader chronological scheme.) This requirement will usually be met by the use of tense; but it need not be. It seems reasonable to suggest that any series of events or states of affairs can be represented narratively in an infinitely large number of ways. The act of producing a narrative is precisely the act of selecting and describing events in accord with some criterion or criteria of significance; the significance thus represented is not an essential property of the events. This means that narratives, fictional, fabulist, or historical, neither theoretically can nor actually do show us *wie es eigentlich gewesen ist*. Rather, they show us one way among infinitely many of attributing significance to how it really was (or is).[7] Fictional and nonfictional narratives do not differ from one another in this regard. That is, the principle that events are ordered according to criteria of significance and not according to their intrinsic properties is operative equally in both kinds of narrative.[8] This is true even if, as Paul Ricoeur would probably want to argue, all events involving human persons necessarily have (what he calls) the attributes of temporality and historicality, and that these attributes can only be represented narratively. For then, although there will be some properties intrinsic to all states of affairs out of which a narrative can be made, these properties will act only as necessary conditions for the possibility of the narrativization of the states of affairs to which they belong; it will not be in virtue of them that some particular narrative will be constructed.[9]

Of course, to say that any sequence of events or states of affairs can be narrativized in an infinite number of ways is not to say that it can be narrativized in just any way. Constraints are placed by the nature of the events or states of affairs: a sequence of events that can be narrativized both as a subtle and challenging presentation of ideas and as an arrogant and puerile act of self-aggrandizement is unlikely also to be capable of narrativization as an especially thrilling final over in a test-match, or as a dramatic forest fire.

There are many kinds of discourse whose content is not diachronically ordered, and which are therefore formally distinct from narrative discourse. Some of these kinds of discourse have a logical rather than a temporal structure: that is, they are ordered to represent to their consumers the logical relations among states of affairs or claims about states of affairs, and so are ordered according to these logical relations. Aside from narrative discourse, it is these kinds of discourse that have the greatest significance for theology as understood in this chapter. Such relations include (at least) causality, entailment, consonance, abstraction, generalization, and the like. I take it that many philosophical works are of this kind—Locke's *Essay*

Concerning Human Understanding, Kant's *Critiques*, and Vasubandhu's *Abhidhar-makosabhasya* are good examples.[10] I shall call this kind of discourse 'systematic' and shall take its objects to be those states of affairs, together with the relations among them, that are not described in sentences indexed to a time.

An example of a state of affairs in principle not statable in a sentence indexed to a time (*At time t . . .*) is the principle of material implication (though, of course, instantiations and examples of it are so statable). Similarly, if God is strictly atemporal, then both this fact and everything there is to know about God's properties can be stated only in sentences not indexed to a time. (This might be taken as a strategic disadvantage inherent in the view that God is atemporal.) I take it, also, that many, perhaps most, of the sentences comprising this essay are of this kind. For example, if it is true that Locke's *Essay Concerning Human Understanding* is an artifact best characterized by the property "consisting of systematic discourse," then this fact cannot be directly stated in a sentence indexed to a time (though, again, instantiations of it can), and so the sentence used in this essay to express this fact is, correspondingly, not indexed to a time, either relatively or absolutely.

All states of affairs describable in temporally indexed sentences can be embedded in sentences with no such index, and so deployed systematically; and all states of affairs describable in sentences not indexed to a time can be embedded in sentences so indexed, and so deployed narratively. So, for example, the temporally indexed claim "Jesus Christ was crucified and resurrected under Pontius Pilate" (taking the reference to Pilate as our temporal index) may be of use and interest for narrative purposes (as it arguably is for the Gospels). But it may also be of use for purely systematic purposes, where, appropriately embedded in a discourse that removes its temporal index or makes such indexing of secondary interest, it may be used, as it arguably was by Anselm in *Cur Deus Homo*, either as an axiom in or as the conclusion of an argument whose interests are exclusively systematic. A possible embedding of this statement that would, as it were, prepare it for systematic use, is "the fact that Jesus Christ was crucified and resurrected under Pontius Pilate." In the first, temporally indexed, sentence the state of affairs (of Jesus Christ having been crucified and so forth) is represented directly; this is possible because the state of affairs obtained (if it did) at a time. In the second sentence, it is represented indirectly, by being mentioned or embedded in the context of a different state of affairs, one that neither requires nor can have temporal indexing.

Similar moves can be made with nontemporally indexed sentences deployed for systematic purposes. Consider the sentence "'snow is white' is true if and only if snow is white." This is a paradigmatic example of such a sentence. The state of affairs—or, better, the set of semantic facts—to which it refers can easily be prepared for narrative use by embedding similar to that used to prepare narrative sentences for systematic use. Consider the (implausible) sentence "Anna contemplated '"snow is white" is true if and only if snow is white' as she threw herself under the train." Here, as with "the fact that Jesus Christ was crucified and resurrected under Pontius Pilate," a direct representation of one state of affairs has been transformed into an indirect representation by embedding it in the context of another, though in the case of Anna's contemplation of the 'snow is white' sentence, the transformation is from a lack of temporal indexing to the possession of such, rather than the other way around. In these ways all narrative sentences may be systematized and all systematic sentences may be narrativized.

In addition to narrative and systematic discourse there is also, for example, discourse structured neither by temporal nor logical relations, but rather by atemporal relations among states of affairs or existents. Such discourse is typically descriptive of the spatial relations, physical properties, and aesthetic attributes of physical objects—Thomas Hardy's description of the Wessex moors at the beginning of *The Return of the Native* is a good example; or it is descriptive of the states of mind of narrative actors—Charlotte Bronte's description of Jane Eyre's emotional response when her schoolfriend Helen Burns dies of consumption is a good example.[11] Such discourse is typically employed for narrative purposes when found in the context of a narrative. That is, it is given an implicit temporal index by its location in a broader context, and it is usual to find occasional explicit traces of emplotment within even the most narrowly descriptive passages. Whether exclusively descriptive prose is possible is a nice question, but I shall not be able to pursue it here.[12]

Works that are, as a whole, properly considered narratives will typically contain nonnarrative passages. This is obvious in the case of the kinds of descriptive passage just mentioned, but it is also the case that narratives may contain lengthy passages structured according to logical relations. There may, therefore, be cases in which it is difficult to decide whether a particular work should, as a whole, be classified as a narrative. We might, for instance, wonder this about some of the Platonic dialogues, or about some Buddhist Sutras, since these often have a narrative frame and occasional narrative interjections, but are nonetheless largely nonnarrative in form. It should also be clear that narratives, if taken as defined here, need not use words. They may use three-dimensional images, as in the case of the carved stone panels at Borobudur in Central Java: these panels represent scenes from Buddha's lives arranged chronologically; or they may use two-dimensional images, as in the case of wordless visual sequences in cinema (think of Chaplin's or Laurel and Hardy's sight gags); or they may use sound, as in the case of program music (I think of Tchaikovsky's *Romeo and Juliet*). I suppose they might also use smells or tactile stimuli, though I find it difficult to see how these sensory stimuli alone could be used to represent a complex narrative.[13]

But I shall be concerned in what follows only with narratives whose instruments are words, whether written or spoken. The characterization of narrative given here is minimalist. I have said nothing as to whether and to what extent narratives need to be marked by closure in order to achieve their goal, as Hayden White puts it, of presenting "the moral under the aspect of the aesthetic." Nor have I said anything about how we should understand such complex ideas as plot, the presence in a narrative of a narrator, the distinctions made by narratologists among such categories as theme *(fabula)*, discourse *(sluzet)*, and genre *(forma)*, or the interesting question of whether a formalist/structuralist approach to narrative is more or less productive than, say, a Foucauldian analysis, according to which narratives should be understood primarily as acts of power in a particular cultural context. But I think, in spite of these large lacunae and the many cases in which it will be difficult to decide whether a particular work should as a whole be thought of as a narrative, that the rough formal characterization of narrative given here will suffice to demarcate narrative discourse from other kinds. It now needs to be asked explicitly what kind of properly cognitive significance such discourse has, and also what significance it has for the theological enterprise.

The Cognitive Significance of Narrative

Let me begin by affirming, as both obvious and important, that narratives are capable of representing things that can be effectively represented in no other way. The formal properties that characterize complex and subtle narratives—the devices of plot, the complex interactions between story time and discourse time, the dramatic and aesthetically pleasing depiction of a series of events as bearing meaning—all these (and more) make possible the representation of states of affairs otherwise effectively not capable of representation. I shall, for the sake of convenience, mention three kinds of phenomena that narratives are able to represent better than any other kind of discourse. This list may not be exhaustive, but it appears to cover most of the relevant ground.

First, narratives are especially good at representing the flavor of what Jerome Bruner calls "lived time"[14] and what Paul Ricoeur calls "temporality" or "historicality."[15] More abstractly, it seems proper to say that narratives are especially good at—because precisely developed and deployed for—the detailed representation of specific instances of the phenomenal properties of many kinds of human experience, including affect, conation, and the like. [16]

All this begins to make narrative sound like phenomenological analysis, and while it is true that good phenomenology edges toward narrative,[17] it is better to preserve the distinction by saying that narrative tends to be more concerned with specific cases of the phenomenal properties of such experience than does even the richest phenomenology. (But it is no accident that phenomenologists often draw so heavily on fictive narratives for their work.) It seems likely, then, that the best way to understand what it is like to be a deceitful and disturbed female adulterer is to read *Madame Bovary* and *Anna Karenina*, just as the best way to understand what it is like to be a weak and destructive man with too many daughters is to read *Pride and Prejudice*. Phenomenological studies of lust, depression, and the abdication of responsibility can tell us a good deal about these phenomena, but not, with enough rich and specific detail, what it is like to be a particular lustful, depressed, or weak individual; such studies move, quite properly, at a higher level of abstraction and generality. Second, narratives, whether fictive, historiographic, or ethnographic, are also especially good at, again because designed for, communicating a detailed sense of the fabric of physical and social life in particular places and times. In the realm of ethnography, consider Clifford Geertz's description of the Balinese cockfight (in large part a narrative description);[18] in that of historiography, consider Peter Gay's history of sex and love in the Victorian period;[19] and among fictive narratives, consider the description of the financial, practical, and emotional details of the life of a hack writer who has ambitions to transcend his condition in George Gissing's *New Grub Street* (1891). There is clearly significant overlap between this first and second function of narrative. Ethnography, historiography, and fiction that narratively represent the fabric of physical and social life will almost always do so in part by representing the phenomenal properties of human experience.

Third, narratives are especially effective at getting their consumers to perceive meaning in historical events. The selection of certain key events and their presentation under certain descriptions is capable of convincing consumers, for example, that the English-speaking peoples have had and will continue to have a role to play in world history whose significance is of a different order than that open to any other ethnic or linguistic group;[20] that Sri Lanka is a country the meaning of whose history is indissolubly linked with Buddhism; or that the whole of human history is given meaning by and finds its proper culmination in the establishment of democratic societies.[21] This third function of narrative is best understood, I think, as the production in its consumers of a certain kind of seeing-as rather than a systematically statable knowing-that (although, of course, all seeing-as implies some systematically statable knowing-that). So, for instance, appropriately skilled consumption of the narratives of the Bible will produce in the consumer the skill of seeing history as the arena of God's action to a degree and in a way that no other kind of discourse (and perhaps no other instance of narrative discourse) is capable of doing. I shall return to this. If these examples of the three kinds of things narratives can represent better than any other kind of discourse are supportable, we already have a partial answer to our question as to the cognitive significance of narrative. Narratives, it appears, can give us detailed acquaintance with the phenomenal properties of lived human experience; with the fabric of human social life in particular settings; and with history as possessing meaning. And no other kind of discourse can do this to the same degree and in the same way.

Can stronger claims than this be made for the cognitive significance of narrative? Some philosophers and literary theorists appear to want to claim more than I have claimed in the immediately preceding paragraphs. They want to claim not only that narrative discourse is a splendidly effective instrument for representing certain kinds of conceptual contents (including the kinds mentioned) and for bringing about certain kinds of cognitive transformation in its consumers, but also (perhaps) that the narrative form in itself has special additional cognitive significance that cannot be stated systematically. Louis Mink, for example, says that "the complex form of the narrative itself" makes a claim to truth that cannot be stated nonnarratively, but must instead be shown by displaying or retelling a narrative.[22] This is, at least in part, a claim as to the limits of translatability, a claim that no attempt at a nonnarrative paraphrase of a narrative can communicate all the claims to truth made by that narrative. Martha Nussbaum has made similar claims, sometimes quite lyrically. For example, she says:

> A paraphrase . . . even when reasonably accurate, does not ever succeed in displacing the original prose; for it is, not being a high work of literary art, devoid of a richness of feeling and a rightness of tone and rhythm that characterize the original, whose cadences shape themselves inexorably on the heart . . . the only way to paraphrase this passage [Nussbaum refers to a passage from Henry James's The Golden Bowl] without loss of value would be to write another work of art. [23]

In order to assess these and similar claims some distinctions may be useful. First, there is the distinction between efficacy and possibility; and second, there is the distinction between effect and content. Suppose we take the efficacy of a particular kind of discourse to be what it is particularly good at doing, what its peculiar genius is. And suppose we take the possibilities of a particular discourse to denote those things that can be done with it. It will surely always be true that the possibilities of a discourse-type are more extensive than its efficacy: what can be done with it is more than what should be done with it. This is especially obvious in the case of discourse that doesn't use words. Suppose, for example, one wants to assemble a child's toy that comes in many pieces. Consider what diagrams can do in the way of explaining how to assemble the toy. Typically, discursive prose, narrative or otherwise, will be able to achieve the same ends only with great clumsiness and great difficulty. The genius of visual representations is useful in such contexts; that of discursive prose is not. If the goal is to produce in the consumer a certain kind of behaviorally evidenced knowing-how—that is, the consumer is able to put the toy together successfully—then visual aids are good for achieving this aim and discursive prose is not. But discursive prose has possibilities in this area also: it can do something, even if its efficacy doesn't lie here. Analogously and presumably Mink and Nussbaum mean at least this much: that the genius of narrative discourse lies precisely in its ability to give its consumers detailed acquaintance with the phenomenal properties of lived human experience and so forth. But it is not clear that this is something in principle beyond the capacity of nonnarrative discourse. I have already suggested that the kind of rich systematic discourse we call phenomenological analysis may go a good way toward producing such acquaintance. It may be natural and proper to become impatient at certain points with the limitations of systematic or descriptive discourse, and as a result to turn to narrative. But this is a practical rather than a theoretical necessity, just as when giving directions to someone it may be practically necessary to draw a map rather than to write a letter. This is very different from claiming that it is in principle impossible to give spatial directions in discursive prose. In just the same way, the claim that no paraphrase of a richly textured narrative artifact into systematic prose can replace the narrative is, by itself, no argument that the undoubted efficacy of narrative discourse for certain things requires one to conclude that narrative discourse necessarily has cognitive significance that systematic discourse does not.

Suppose we look, then, at the second distinction, between effect and content. This is a distinction between what a particular discourse does to its consumers (what it evokes in them, how it transforms them ethically, cognitively, behaviorally, and the like) on the one hand, and what it claims, the conceptual contents it represents, on the other. It is abundantly clear that narrative discourse, both fictive and historiographic, can produce effects that are, both theoretically and practically, beyond the reach of systematic discourse. This capacity on the part of narrative discourse is partly caused by its efficacy at representing the kinds of conceptual contents discussed above, but is, I think, theoretically separable from it. The point here is that what narrative discourse calls to the attention of its consumers is, strictly, without limit.[24] This is in part because of the literary devices that are its stock-

in-trade, devices such as metaphor, metonymy, synecdoche, and the like are consti-
tutively suggestive and evocative and open-endedly so. But it is also because the
kind of effect produced by the appropriately skilled consumption of narrative is a
cognitive transformation that consists in a kind of seeing-as. The consumer of the
Bible's narratives learns to see history as the arena of God's action; the consumer of
the narratives that constitute Balzac's *Comedie Humaine* learns to see human action as determined largely by greed, lust, and ambition; and the consumer of Anita
Brookner's careful narrative representations of despair begins to see human action
as, in large part, determined by fear, lassitude, and lack of vision. Seeing things in
terms such as these is a skill that can, as Nussbaum and others claim, only be fully
learned narratively, as well as being a skill whose exercise and application itself has
narrative form.

   Donald Davidson, in the course of an analysis of what metaphors mean, says
this:

> It's not only that we can't provide an exhaustive catalogue of what has been at-
> tended to when we are led to see something in a new light; the difficulty is more
> fundamental. What we notice or see is not, in general, propositional in character.
> . . . Seeing as is not seeing that . . . [and] since in most cases what . . .
> metaphor prompts or inspires is not entirely, or even at all, recognition of some
> truth or fact, the attempt to give literal expression to the content of the metaphor is
> simply misguided.[25]

Substituting 'narrative' for 'metaphor' here, I would wish to say the same. If,
through properly skilled consumption of the biblical narrative, I come to see history
as the arena of God's action, this is certainly not the same as my coming to know
that history is the arena of God's action—though it may entail and require that I
have such knowledge. Instead, it is the open-ended transformation of my capacity to
see historical events as a certain kind of thing, to experience them under the rubric
of a certain narrative description. This transformation can be labeled proposition-
ally, and its conceptual contents can be elucidated systematically; but what I experience in virtue of it is not accessible in detail to systematic discourse. This is because
such experience has an infinitely large set of phenomenal properties whose flavor is
both produced by consumption of narratives and capable of further display and development only narratively. With these distinctions and conclusions in mind, I return to Mink's and Nussbaum's suggestions that narrative form itself makes a claim
to truth that cannot be stated or represented nonnarratively. I would restate this to
say that the unique effect of narrative discourse is to produce cognitive transformations in its consumers whose content is neither exhaustively statable in systematic
discourse, nor effectively capable of display in any discourse other than narrative.
But I would deny that any claim about the nature of things is made by narratives,
considered either as wholes or in their parts, whose content cannot also be represented in systematic discourse. If this is right then it is indeed true that no nonnarrative paraphrase of a narrative can replace it. But this is true not because narratives
make claims to truth of a special kind, but because their peculiar genius is to produce transformative effects of a properly cognitive and affective kind: consumed
skillfully, narratives shape the phenomenal properties of lived experience; they cre-

ate and foster perceptions of value in the temporal succession of events; they provide, at the most general level, a set of perceptual and cognitive skills, the exercise and application of which in a specific life itself has narrative structure.

Similar claims should be made—and, increasingly, are being made—by philosophers concerned with the analysis of moral knowledge and moral action.[26] Moral knowledge—that is, knowledge both of what right action is and of how to perform such action—is, it may be said, available principally through detailed acquaintance with specific instances of morally significant decision-making; and such detailed acquaintance is, in turn, possible only through the skilled consumption or construction of narrative. Put in terms of virtue theory, such claims will be interpreted to mean that the development of virtue is either contingent upon or symbiotically linked with the use of narrative discourse. But one need not be a virtue theorist in order to hold strong views about the importance of narrative in the development of a moral life.[27] If it is right that there is an irreducible particularity about what makes a morally right action right,[28] a particularity to which the general moral principles stable in systematic discourse are not only an insufficient guide, but also a guide that may be actively misleading, then it is easy to see how narrative can be taken to be indispensable to the development of moral perceptions that are adequately precise and responsive to the demands of specific situations. For it is precisely and only narratives that are capable of providing "an account of the careful, detailed fashioning of a moral action,"[29] and therefore precisely and only narratives that can develop the moral imagination in such a way as to produce appropriately specific moral skills.

It is important to distinguish this view of the cognitive importance of narrative discourse from one implicit in another common way in which philosophers (including ethicists) use narrative: as illustrative example. In this use, since the point is to depict a situation in such a way as to "elicit shared beliefs about *particular* situations so as to resolve *disputed* beliefs about *general* claims,"[30] ambiguity is not a virtue. The point is heuristic power, effectiveness in posing or solving some set of problems; and for this goal to be realized, ambiguity must be reduced as much as possible (though complexity may be extended as much as seems beneficial). When narratives are used illustratively or heuristically in such ways, they tend not to be works of literary art; this is just because such works of art value and represent the potent and irreducible ambiguity of lived experience in a manner that is itself ambiguous. The reverse is true, for instance, of Hilary Putnam's stories about brains-in-a-vat[31] and of Derek Parfit's imaginative use of stories about matter transmitters and brain transplants.[32] This use of narrative as a device to disambiguate rather than to explore the cognitive implications of ambiguity is paralleled by the cavalier way in which many anglophone philosophers treat the history of philosophy. Very often such philosophers have no interest in giving a nuanced and historically informed reading of texts in the history of philosophy. For them, the names 'Aristotle' or 'Aquinas' designate only particular positions, the less ambiguous and the more precisely stated the better, and so the adjectives 'Aristotelean' or 'Thomistic' become not markers for serious historiographic (and so more-or-less narrativized) reconstructions and restatements, but rather calques for positions capable of exhaustive statement in systematic discourse. But even in the sphere of ethics, where perhaps the most attention has been paid to the philosophical significance of narrative and the strongest claims made for it, it does not seem that narrative discourse can do everything the moral philosopher might want it to do. Certainly, it can, as Nussbaum claims, give access to the processes through which moral imagination is developed and moral decisions made; it can also act, as Daniel Brudney (following Stanley Cavell) suggests, as a means for projecting some of the concepts of moral philosophy, a means for showing "a new context for applying a concept, one that reveals new dimensions and resonances."[33] But suppose the moral philosopher wants to state principles, to elucidate a metaethic, or to give an argument to show that a particular action in a particular context is right or wrong? Since the objects of such claims and such arguments are nontemporally indexed states of affairs, making them is among the paradigmatic functions of systematic discourse; the deployment of narrative discourse to perform them is likely to be about as successful as the use of discursive prose in place of musical scores to get an orchestra to play the slow movement of Beethoven's seventh symphony. The efficacy of discursive prose for such a purpose is just about zero; and so also, I suggest, is the efficacy of narrative discourse for the elucidation of some specific metaethic or the construction and contestation of arguments whose conclusion is that some ethical principle has universal validity. And it appears that those who extol the virtues of narrative for engaging in moral philosophy recognize nonetheless that systematic discourse has its proper functions in this sphere also, even if there is considerable disagreement as to the nature and scope of those proper functions. I shall return to this last question in a moment, when I come to discuss what it is that narrative discourse can and cannot do for theology.

Narrative discourse, then, to summarize my conclusions to this point, can represent things that systematic discourse can represent only with great difficulty (if at all). And some of these representative capacities may have considerable cognitive import for properly skilled consumers of narrative. Furthermore, narrative discourse is capable of producing effects upon its consumers analogous to the effects produced by metaphorical discourse, effects that are altogether beyond the scope of complete restatement in systematic discourse. But the peculiar efficacy of narrative discourse in these spheres does not suggest that it is capable of simply replacing systematic discourse. What, then, of the significance of narrative discourse for theology?

Narrative Discourse and Theology

That the deployment of narrative discourse is indispensable to at least Christian theology (and possibly, though I shall not argue this here, to all forms of theology) should be clear from all that has been said so far about narrative. If one of theology's functions is to exhibit the community's descriptive and axiological claims, and by so doing to transform the perceptual, affective, and cognitive habits of its members, it is clear that the genius of narrative discourse makes it indispensable: How else could the appropriate kinds of skill be fostered and developed? The indispensability of narrative here is of the same logical kind as the indispensability of narrative for the formation of moral knowledge and moral action, discussed above. And exponents of narrative theology have emphasized this kind of indispensability almost ad nauseam.[34]

But to claim that the deployment of narrative discourse will suffice for the prosecution of the theological enterprise is a much stronger and very different claim. It is not clear that anyone makes it. Even the most vociferous advocates of narrative discourse as an instrument for carrying out the tasks of Christian theology acknowledge that other kinds of discourse have their place and purpose in performing those tasks. The real question, then, is how to understand the nature of the relations between narrative discourse and systematic discourse within the theological enterprise. If each is necessary, which is basic or foundational and how does the one relate to the other? And on this question narrative theologians speak with a much more unified voice: so far as theology is concerned, they say, narrative discourse is prior to and independent of systematic discourse; and that the functions of systematic discourse within theology are thus based upon and an epiphenomenon of the functions of narrative discourse. Here is a programmatic and abstract example of such a claim, taken from Michael Goldberg's exegetical essay on two verses from the first chapter of Exodus.

"The central claim of 'narrative theology' is the contention that virtually all our basic convictions about the nature and meaning of our lives find their ground and intelligibility in some sort of overarching, paradigmatic story."[35] The claim here seems to be that properly skilled consumption of certain narratives is a necessary condition both for having certain kinds of axiological beliefs and for being able to specify what they are.

Stanley Hauerwas says exactly this in his defense of casuistry as a narrative art: narratives, he says, give the meanings of terms in moral discourse and so also the possibility of their use; the appropriately skilled consumption of narratives is therefore among the conditions for the possibility of engagement in systematic moral discourse. And narrative discourse therefore has both practical and logical priority over any attempt to "justify the rightness or wrongness of certain actions abstracted from their narrative context" and, by extension, priority also over all attempts at systematic justification of properly metaphysical claims independently of the narrative context in which they are represented to and consumed by the community of the faithful.[36]

Some version of these claims to priority may well be defensible. I have already suggested that properly skilled consumption of narrative discourse has cognitive effects attainable in no other way; and I also think it true that exposure to narratives, and the gradual process of learning to use them skillfully, has, in almost everyone's life, temporal priority over learning to manipulate systematic discourse. All religious persons, or almost all, know the stories before they learn the theology (if they ever do the latter). But it also seems clear that theology has certain needs—most especially those for systematization, precision, universalization, and justification—that cannot easily be met, if they can be met at all, by the deployment of narrative discourse. Let's try and see why.

First, and most generally, the fact that religious communities typically—and Christians most certainly—have found it necessary to develop and deploy doctrines and creeds expressed in systematic discourse and not in narrative discourse strongly suggests that such communities have felt called to engage in intellectual activities whose ends cannot be realized solely by the use of narratives. Most basically, such communities have felt they could not avoid making nontemporally indexed claims of universal axiological and descriptive import.[37] It is the making of just such claims that constitutes doctrinal practice. Consider the claims "God is three persons in one substance; all human persons are made in the image of God; the literal sense of Scripture must always have priority for the believing community over the allegorical sense." These are, in my sense, claims made in systematic discourse. They are claims made and argued for by Christian theologians, who have frequently seen them as theological claims. And they are claims to the statement and elucidation of which narrative discourse is paradigmatically unsuited—though they can, of course, be instantiated and deployed narratively.

But religious communities have not felt called upon only to make such abstract, generalized, nontemporally indexed claims. They have also attempted to justify them in the face of opposition, to argue for them against competitors, and to do so by deploying the abstract and denaturalized schemata of systematic discourse[38] rather than the unsubstitutable specificities of narrative discourse. The name for this activity has traditionally been "apologetics," and it is an activity that those narrative theologians, who deny either the need for or the possibility of justification in any terms other than those given by the community's narratives, must eschew. Apologetics, for a "pure narrative theologian like Hauerwas or (perhaps) Hans Frei,"[39] is a mere act of recital meant for the sustenance, means, and benefit of the believing community;[40] it cannot mean an intellectual engagement with persons for whom the narratives of the Christian community are both unknown and insignificant. Furthermore, it seems that narrative discourse is unsuited not only to the systematic and apologetical needs of religious communities, but also to many of their catechetical needs. While insufficient work has yet been done on the genres or kinds of discourse in and through which catechesis is done—I suspect that there is rich material here for cross-cultural comparative work—it is clear that catechesis is done only partly through the medium of narrative. At least as often, and for very good reasons, it is done through the medium of systematic discourse, for only such discourse can provide the requisite level of precision and systematization. A good catechism does both more and less than retell the sacred narratives, just as a creed does: insofar as it uses what is made available by skilled consumption of narrative, it does so under a redescription that makes it available for systematic use. In general, the characteristics of narrative as defined in this chapter make it an instrument for the presentation to its consumers of a unique singularity—that of this unsubstitutable person, or this unsubstitutable set of ambiguous moral decisions, or this unsubstitutable catena of events. It is precisely not designed to answer questions at the level of generality and abstraction applicable to properly anthropological or metaphysical questions. And, I would argue, treatment of such questions is unavoidable because in part it is constitutive of theology. The argument to this point has been simple: narrativists typically either deny that the needs of religious communities traditionally met by their deployment of systematic discourse are actually needs at all; or they reconstrue those needs, and so also the meaning of the use of systematic discourse in meeting them, in such a way that such discourse is seen as epiphenomenal to narrative discourse. This latter move is most easily made when considering the abstraction, generalization, and systematization of scholastic theological system-building, or when considering the use of such abstractions in catechesis. Here, without denying that religious communities typically do feel the need to use such discourse to engage in such enterprises, the claim can still be made that such discourse issues only in rules for the governance of the inner life of the community, and not in any properly metaphysical claims as to the nature of reality or of human persons. This, I take it, is the point of George Lindbeck's attempt to state a theory of doctrine, in which all systematic doctrinal discourse has an exclusively regulative function for the community that produces it and is thus incapable of making claims to truth that extend beyond the boundaries of the community.[41] The merits of such theories have been extensively discussed during the past decade, and I have no space here to engage this discussion fully; all I can do is to point out that even if such a theory turns out to be defensible as a theory about the systematic and catechetical practices of Christian communities, it cannot do justice to their apologetical practices since these require the possibility that systematic discourse might engage and make claims upon those who do not share the narratively constituted practices that gave rise to it in the first place. So, even if the regulative theories of doctrine, which are the necessary resort of the narrativist who does not want simply to reject the whole enterprise of systematic theology as a mistake, turn out to be defensible (though I do not think they are), their use must entail the conclusion that the entire apologetical enterprise rests upon a mistake.

The inability of narrativists to provide an account of the significance of systematic discourse that will do justice to the ways in which religious communities have understood—and still largely continue to understand—their use of it is by itself a powerful reason to reject their view of systematic discourse as epiphenomenal to narrative discourse. But there is another, and I think decisive, argument that can be brought to bear. This is an argument to the conclusion that a pure narrativist program is self-referentially incoherent. To see how this argument goes it is important to understand one of the basic motivations of the narrativist program. Narrativists tend to think, on the basis of a relatively uncritical appropriation of the Kantian critique of metaphysics and of the postmodernist rejection of foundationalism in all its forms (metaphysical and epistemological), that what religious communities have typically wanted to do with systematic discourse cannot be done, and that it ought therefore either to be jettisoned or radically reconstrued.[42] What religious communities should want to do instead, they think, is to retell their stories with ever more passion and seriousness and recapitulate the narrative structure of those stories in their own lives as witnesses to it; and to do these things without using categories extraneous to the narrative to frame, explain, or justify them. The self-referential incoherence in this kind of antifoundationalist narrativism is surely, given this explanation, easy to see. If the narrativist claim is that narrative discourse is all the theologian needs to do theology, or that everything important to theology must be done without introducing categories extraneous to a master narrative, and that procedural claims governing the practice of theology are themselves part of theology (recall my claim that the theological enterprise is recursive in this way), then it is hard to see how the claims being made by narrativists either are or could be stated (much less argued for) solely in narrative discourse. These claims are true (if they are) atemporally: they provide a theory of value and a set of procedural claims intended to govern the community's theological practice (which is part of its religious practice) always and everywhere; or they make claims as to the capacities of narrative discourse which are true (if they are) for all narratives everywhere. And yet, in tension with their own agenda they do not make their claims narratively: they make them systematically. And when challenged they produce not narratives but arguments, arguments stated in systematic discourse. And they do this for the very good reason that narrative presentation of such claims could only instantiate them, not argue for them. If, then, apologetical needs must be met even for pure narrativists, how much more is this the case for religious communities? The arguments I've offered are suggestive rather than demonstrative. They do indicate, I think, some strategic disadvantages inherent in some versions of the strong narrativist program, most striking among which are the inability to account for what religious communities actually do with the discourse they employ, and the inability to state and argue for the program itself without producing a damaging variety of self-referential incoherence.

My own view is that narrative discourse is extremely important for theology: it has cognitive powers and transformative capacities not available to religious communities in any other way. But it cannot be the case that narrative discourse can fulfill all theological needs. This could only happen if theologians made the procedural decision to dispense with their goal of making nontemporally indexed universalizable descriptive, and axiological claims and to engage instead solely in the production and manipulation of narrative discourse. And, as I have suggested, this procedural decision cannot be argued or even presented without incoherence. So the conclusion is that theology done by deploying narrative discourse narratively has both strengths and limits, just as moral philosophy done in the same way has both strengths and limits. A properly developed and flexible theology will recognize and use both narrative and systematic discourse, according to the particular needs of the community engaging in it; and such a community's use of systematic discourse need not be limited to, nor even strongly constrained by, the stories it tells itself. Only then can the truly universal and properly metaphysical ambitions of Christian (and every other variety of) theology be served and realized.

Notes

1. In putting matters in this way I am indebted to William A. Christian, Sr.'s works, especially *Oppositions of Religious Doctrines* (London: Macmillan, 1972), and *Doctrines of Religious Communities* (New Haven & London: Yale University Press, 1987).

2. See Christian, *Oppositions of Religious Doctrines*, 60–86.

3. Compare the definition given by Kathryn Tanner in "Theology and the Plain Sense," in *Scriptural Authority and Narrative Interpretation*, ed. Garrett Green (Philadelphia: Fortress Press, 1987), 59–78, at 60–61. In spite of the distinctive differences in focus of interest between Tanner's definition and mine, I take them to be congruent.

4. I draw here upon the definitions and descriptive analyses of narrative found in Tzvetan Todorov, *The Poetics of Prose* (Oxford: Blackwell, 1977), 233; Oswald Ducrot and Tzvetan Todorov, *Encyclopedic Dictionary of the Sciences of Language*, trans. Catherine Porter (Baltimore: Johns Hopkins University Press, 1979), 297; W. T. J. Mitchell, ed., *On Narrative* (Chicago & London: University of Chicago Press, 1981), 80, 11, 205; Hayden White, *The Content of the Form: Narrative Discourse and Historical Representation* (Baltimore: Johns Hopkins University Press, 1987), x–xi; Jerome Bruner, *Actual Minds, Possible Worlds* (Cambridge: Harvard University Press, 1986), 3–43; Gabriel Fackre, "Narrative Theology: An Overview," *Interpretation* 37 (1983), 340–352, at 341–343.

5. White, *Content of the Form*, 5.

6. White, *Content of the Form*, 6.

7. See Louis O. Mink, "Narrative Form as Cognitive Instrument," in *The Writing of History*, ed. R. Canary and H. Kozicki (Madison: University of Wisconsin Press, 1978), 129–149, at 143.

8. In "The Narrative Function," *Semeia* 12 (1978), 177–202, at 186, 195. Ricoeur argues that historical and fictional narratives are similar in terms of both sense and reference. The similarity in sense is given by the "structural factor" of the fact of emplotment; the similarity in reference is given by the fact that both are ineluctably fictive and mimetic (i.e., narrativized), and that both therefore have historicality-temporality as their ultimate referent. Compare Ricoeur, *Time and Narrative*, 3 vols., trans. Kathleen McLaughlin and David Pellauer (Chicago: University of Chicago Press, 1984–88), vol 2, 156. See also Edward T. Oakes, S.J., "Apologetics and the Pathos of Narrative Theology," *Journal of Religion* 72 (1992), 37–58, at 44–45.

9. "I take temporality to be that structure of existence that reaches language in narrativity, and narrativity to be the language structure that has temporality as its ultimate referent. Their relationship is therefore reciprocal." Ricoeur, "Narrative Time," in Mitchell, ed., *On Narrative*, 165–186, at 165.

10. See Mitchell, ed., *On Narrative*, 118, and Bruner, *Actual Minds, Possible Worlds*, 12–14. Bruner calls this kind of discourse "paradigmatic." Mink, "Narrative Form," calls it "theory." There are important differences between their ways of distinguishing narrative discourse from other kinds and that stated here, but the purpose of making the distinction is the same.

11. See the analysis of Maupassant's "Une Partie de campagne" in terms of these distinctions in Mitchell, ed., *On Narrative*, 119–120.

12. It should be obvious that the categorization of kinds of discourse given here is not meant to be exhaustive. It is intended to suffice only for the task of exploring what significance narrative has for theology.

13. For some interesting thoughts on the cognitive significance of olfactory stimuli, see Dan Sperber, *Rethinking Symbolism*, trans. Alice Morton, *Studies in Social Anthropology* 11 (Cambridge: Cambridge University Press, 1975), 115–123.

14. On which see Jerome Bruner, "Life as Narrative," *Social Research* 54 (1987), 11–32, at 17–18, drawing from Roman Jakobsen and Vladimir Propp.

15. Ricoeur, "Narrative Time," 165. White, *Content of the Form*, 170–181, provides a useful discussion of Ricoeur's work on narrative.

16. For some specifically theological applications of this in terms of the "tensed modalities" of human experience, see Stephen Crites, "The Narrative Quality of Experience," *Journal of the American Academy of Religion* 39 (1971), 291–311.

17. One might make that case, for instance, about the best of Merleau-Ponty's or some of Edward Casey's work, especially *Remembering: A Phenomenological Study* (Bloomington: Indiana University Press, 1987).

18. Clifford Geertz, "Deep Play: Notes on the Balinese Cockfight," in *The Interpretation of Cultures*, ed. Clifford Geertz (New York: Basic Books, 1973), 412–453.

19. Peter Gay, *The Education of the Senses* (New York: Oxford University Press, 1984); idem, *The Tender Passion* (New York: Oxford University Press, 1986).

20. I think here of Winston Churchill's *History of the English-Speaking Peoples*, first published 1956–58.

21. I have in mind here the uses made of the *Mahavamsa* and the *Dipavamsa* by contemporary Sinhalese Buddhist intellectuals.

22. Mink, "Narrative Form," 144–145.

23. Martha Nussbaum, "'Finely Aware and Richly Responsible': Literature and the Moral Imagination," in *Literature and the Question of Philosophy* ed. Anthony J. Cascardi, (Baltimore: Johns Hopkins University Press, 1987), 167–191, at 177. Nussbaum has made similar claims in her "Flawed Crystals: James's *The Golden Bowl* and Literature as Moral Philosophy," *New Literary History* 15 (1983), 25–50; idem, "Perceptive Equilibrium: Literary Theory and Ethical Theory," *Logos* 8 (1987), 55–83; idem, "Narrative Emotions: Beckett's Genealogy of Love," *Ethics* 98 (1988), 225–254. See also Daniel Brudney, "Knowledge and Silence: *The Golden Bowl* and Moral Philosophy," *Critical Inquiry* 16 (1990), 397–437, at 424–425. See also Philip Quinn's claim: "A life is a process with a narrative structure. The extent to which an ethical theory made in the image of the theories of science can generate a blueprint or model of a life is problematic. Theoretical descriptions of a life plan are usually very schematic and lacking in concrete detail; they seldom cast much light on what it would be like to lead a life as planned." ("Tragic Dilemmas, Suffering Love, and Christian Life," *Journal of Religious Ethics* 17 [1989], 151–183, at 151.) Compare Arthur Danto's discussion in "Philosophy As/And/Of Literature," in Cascardi, ed., *Literature and the Question of Philosophy*, 3–23. Hans Frei makes a very similar point when he refers, glancingly, to the "heresy of paraphrase": see "'Narrative' in Christian and Modern Reading," in *Theology and Dialogue: Essays in Conversation with George Lindbeck*, ed. Bruce D. Marshall (Notre Dame: University of Notre Dame Press, 1990), 149–163, at 155.

24. In this I take narrative discourse to be, semantically, just like metaphor. I draw here upon Donald Davidson's work on metaphor, especially "What Metaphors Mean," in *Inquiries Into Truth and Interpretation*, ed. Donald Davidson (Oxford: Clarendon Press, 1984), 245–264. Ricoeur also emphasizes the strong connection between what one can say theoretically about narrative discourse and what one can say about metaphor. See *Time and Narrative*, vol. 1, preface. See also George Steiner, *Real Presences* (Chicago: University of Chicago Press, 1989), 83, who says that literary objects demand and produce infinite response, even though the description of their formal components may be finite.

25. Davidson, "What Metaphors Mean," 263.

26. Alasdair MacIntyre, *After Virtue*, 2d ed. (Notre Dame: University of Notre Dame Press, 1981); idem, *Whose Justice? Which Rationality?* (Notre Dame: University of Notre Dame Press, 1988); Brudney, "Knowledge and Silence"; Quinn, "Tragic Dilemmas," 151, 152.

27. Nussbaum, for instance, is not such a theorist, and yet she wants to claim that the use of the moral imagination, requisite for moral action, depends upon the development of "moral attention and insight," and that this is available only by looking closely at "the specificity and . . . the emotional and imaginative richness of . . . [the] individual moral effort" ("Finely Aware," 170).

28. This claim was made by Aristotle, who says that to respond "at the right times, with reference to the right objects, towards the right people, with the right motive, and in the right way, is what is appropriate and best, and this characterizes virtue" (*Nichomachean Ethics*, 1106b 21–23).

29. Brudney, "Knowledge and Silence," 425.

30. Brudney, "Knowledge and Silence," 417.

31. Hilary Putnam, *Reason, Truth and History* (Cambridge: Cambridge University Press, 1981), 1–21.

32. Examples of such stories are scattered throughout Parfit's *Reasons and Persons* (Oxford: Clarendon Press, 1984).

33. Brudney, "Knowledge and Silence," 429, drawing on Stanley Cavell's work in the philosophy of language, especially as represented in *The Claim of Reason: Wittgenstein, Skepticism, Morality, and Tragedy* (New York: Oxford University Press, 1979).

34. Useful surveys of work in narrative theology and collections of representative essays include Fackre, "Narrative Theology"; Garrett Green, ed., *Scriptural Authority and Narrative Interpretation*; Gary L. Comstock, "Two Types of Narrative Theology," *Journal of the American Academy of Religion* 55 (1987), 687–717; Stanley Hauerwas and L. Gregory Jones, ed., *Why Narrative? Readings in Narrative Theology* (Grand Rapids, Mich.: Eerdmans, 1989).

35. Michael Goldberg, "Exodus 1:13–14,11" *Interpretation* 37 (1983), 389–391, at 389.

36. Stanley Hauerwas, "Casuistry as a Narrative Art," *Interpretation* 37 (1983), 377-388, at 378-379.

37. David Kelsey puts this clearly when he says that "theological anthropology is a set of questions about human personhood that are fully as general as the questions about human being addressed by the human and physical sciences." ("Biblical Narrative and Theological Anthropology," in Green, ed., *Scriptural Authority and Narrative Interpretation*, 121–143, at 134.) He goes on to argue (implausibly in my view) that theological anthropology in this general sense is "materially derivative from almost all other theological topics" (139), that it is secondary to and derivative from theological elucidation of what narrative tells us (140–141), and that it is "rooted in and ordered to practical theology" (136). Though none of these positions is at all likely to be correct (and this can be shown historically not to be how the general run of Christian theologians have conceived the enterprise of theological anthropology), Kelsey does at least clearly recognize and acknowledge that theological anthropology—and by extension other dimensions of the theological enterprise—requires generalized abstractions in order to do its work.

38. See my "Denaturalizing Discourse: Abhidharmikas, Propositionalists, and the Comparative Philosophy of Religion," in *Myth and Philosophy*, ed. Frank E. Reynolds and David Tracy (Albany, N.Y.: State University of New York Press, 1990), 57–91.

39. I rely here on Comstock, "Two Types of Narrative Theology." See also idem, "Truth or Meaning: Ricoeur versus Frei on Biblical Narrative," *Journal of Religion* 66 (1986), 117–140, where it is argued that Ricoeur preserves the possibility of allowing the biblical narratives to make claims to truth of universal import, while Frei denies this. It is not quite so clear to me that Frei does deny this. His comments in "'Narrative' in Christian and Modern Reading" seem to leave it open. But I am in basic sympathy with Comstock's rejection of what he calls "pure narrativism," at least when questions of justification arise.

40. Oakes, "Apologetics and the Pathos of Narrative Theology," 58. See also William Werpehowski, "Ad Hoc Apologetics," *Journal of Religion* 66 (1986), 282–301; William C. Placher, *Unapologetic Theology: A Christian Voice in a Pluralistic Conversation* (Louisville, Ky.: Westminster/John Knox Press, 1989); and my own *An Apology for Apologetics: A Study in the Logic of Interreligious Dialogue* (Maryknoll, N.Y.: Orbis, 1991). Much of this discussion has been sparked by George Lindbeck's attempts to provide a place for ad hoc apologetics within the framework of a cultural-linguistic theology that is broadly sympathetic to some version of narrative theology. See Lindbeck, *The Nature of Doctrine: Religion and Theology in a Postliberal Age* (Philadelphia: Westminster Press, 1984), 128–134.

41. See the discussions of Lindbeck's work in *The Thomist* 49 (1985), and in *Modern Theology* 4/1 (1988).

42. Comstock, "Two Types of Narrative Theology," and Oakes, "Apologetics and the Pathos of Narrative Theology," outline the historical story behind these assumptions on the part of (at least) "pure narrativists." Joseph A. DiNoia, O.P., "Philosophical Theology in the Perspective of Religious Diversity," *Theological Studies* 49 (1988), 401–416, makes a powerful argument that the rejection of foundationalism need not issue in a retreat from the deployment of systematic discourse, nor from the universalistic aspirations inherent in such deployment.

13

KEITH E. YANDELL

Narrative Ethics and Normative Objectivity

Introduction

Professor Stanley Hauerwas begins the first chapter of *The Peaceable Kingdom* (Notre Dame: University of Notre Dame Press, 1983) by claiming that

> all ethical reflection occurs relative to a particular time and place. Not only do ethical problems change from one time to the other, but the very nature and structure of ethics is determined by the particularities of a community's history and convictions. From this perspective the notion of "ethics" is misleading, since it seems to suggest that "ethics" is a definable discipline that is constant across history; in fact, much of the burden of this book will be to suggest that ethics always requires an adjective or qualifier—such as, Jewish, Christian, Hindu, existentialist, pragmatic, utilitarian, humanist, medieval, modern—in order to denote the social and historical character of ethics as a discipline. (1)

It is not lucid what this claim amounts to. The principle of noncontradiction tells us that for any property, thing, and time, that thing cannot both have and lack that property at that time, and that anything timeless or eternal cannot both eternally have and eternally lack any property. This expression of the principle occurs in English, in Washington, in the twentieth century, but none of those facts about its expression entails that the truth of the principle of noncontradiction is relative to when or where some expression of it occurs, and plainly it does not so depend. As Mircea Eliade is reputed to have said, "Nonsense is nonsense, even in Sanskrit." Nor is its truth discernible only if one knows who said it, where, and when.

I take it that Professor Hauerwas denies that the analogous things are true for any ethical principle or rule or theory or claim. It is not obvious why anyone should deny this. It is banally true that every assertion of, say, a moral principle by a human being occurs in some language at some time in some cultural context. Nothing whatever follows from that about how, if at all, ethical principles can be assessed, or whether if an ethical principle is true, it is true exceptionlessly over time and space and societies. The view expressed in the quotation wavers between that banal truth and the nonbanal (and, I shall argue, false) thesis that in order to understand and assess any ethical principle (rule, theory, claim) one must appeal only to some set of facts about the particularities and peculiarities of some specific historical individual or community. Indeed, it seems to me perfectly plain that one could not possibly *confirm* or *disconfirm* any moral claim by any such appeal. Such appeal is relevant if we want to know what the *mores* of some community amount to, including what their beliefs are about matters ethical. Without making any suggestion about intentions, it is highly convenient that a view be stated so as to be ambiguous between the banal truth and nonbanal thesis, and even so put as to make it seem that the thesis follows from the truth, as of course it does not. For then one can appeal to the banal truth when one is defending one's view, and to the thesis when one wants substantial conclusions. I shall not inquire into whether Professor Hauerwas, intentionally or not, is involved in such a dubious enterprise. My interests are broader than that.

Enthusiastic Narrativism

Enthusiasts for narrative ethics contend that we receive our identity as persons and derive the content of our obligations, rights, and responsibilities from the narratives embraced by our communities. They contend that the notion of an ethic based on consideration of rational agents as ends in themselves or of duties derived from the nonnarratively defined nature of such agents is fiction in the pejorative sense. Kant, whom narrative ethicists do not much love, says that concepts without experiences are empty and experiences without concepts are blind. The narrativist position is that ethics without narrative is empty though presumably narrative without ethics is possible since it is actual. The view just sketched is popular these days, and it serves to underline the oft-ignored ethical relevance of religious traditions. Nonetheless, it is fundamentally flawed, trying (among other things) to have second mile ethics without first mile. It is one among many views held by scholars so impressed by the importance of concrete historical and cultural details that they ignore, or do not even see, that these details gain significance only from structures that (in contrast to their concrete expressions) are cross-cultural and ahistorical. They even are capable of ignoring that were their own position true, it could be so only due to precisely such structures.

   In discussing enthusiastic narrativism, one faces a dilemma of sorts. One can discuss particular versions of it and run the risk of being judged unfair in one's account of someone's views, and no doubt I have already risked one professional colleague's ire. Or one can discuss the view in the abstract and run the risk of apparent irrelevance to actual dispute. For reasons that I hope will become obvious, I choose to run the latter risk. The sort of discussion that I take to be required if we are to assess enthusiastic narrativism is unrepentantly abstract, for we must ask whether in fact the notion of an ethic more basic and general than the opening quotation sanctions is a genuine possibility. But I take its application to actually held views to be accessible to those who know the literature.

   Since the argument to be offered here is necessarily abstract in content, we may as well make a virtue of necessity. My hope is that by the time we have made the distinctions necessary for a responsible direct assault on our topic, enough tolerance to abstract reasoning will have built up so that the limits as well as the contributions of narrative to ethics can be seen. While I grant the importance of narrative for ethics, I deny the derivability of all of ethics from narrative. I will argue that enthusiastic narrativism is an incoherent narrativist imperialism.

Morality and Ethics

By "ethics" I shall mean the philosophical discipline whose purpose is to answer at least three questions:

1. *the watershed question*: When is ethical reflection appropriate?
2. *the action question*: What makes an action right and what makes an action wrong?
3. *the person question*: What makes a person good and what makes a person evil?

Of course, one must answer other questions in order to answer those questions. What makes something a person is not irrelevant to the person question; what makes something an action is not irrelevant to the action question. Different accounts of right and wrong, and of good and evil, will have different entailments regarding an answer to the watershed question. Furthermore, ethics endeavors to answer another question:

4. *the bottom line question*: What has ultimate value (God, God and created persons, actions, etc.)?

Answers to those fundamental questions do not typically take, and never require, a narrative format. Ethics, so construed, is to be distinguished from what I shall mean by morality and from mores. By "morality" I will mean the ontological conditions of ethics—what there is, if anything, about our world that gives an ethic purchase on it. By "mores" I shall mean ethics as embedded in institutions, practices, and whatever is character-and-conduct-and-lifestyle-evaluating-and-guiding in a culture. Since there are nonethical factors also embedded in cultures that guide and assess character and conduct and lifestyle, what I mean here by "mores" probably is narrower than what is usually intended. I confess to thinking of the discipline of ethics as largely and properly populated by competing ethical theories, and the theoretical task of the ethicist as largely a matter of articulating and assessing these theories. As casuist, the ethicist applies theories to particular actions, policies, persons, ends, and lifestyles. I see no reason why casuistry should be a dishonorable enterprise for an ethicist; why should the practical consequences of ethical theories be drawn only by those who are not expert concerning them? But ethics is not inherently utilitarian or consequentialist or concerned only with quandaries. Particular ethical traditions endeavor to answer some or all of the indicated questions.

If there is no way to rationally assess competing answers to the four indicated questions, then there is no such thing as ethics. This inelegant situation might obtain for either of two reasons. It might be that there was no such thing as morality—

that the conditions which must obtain for ethics to apply to our world simply do not obtain. (It is an interesting question that I will not pursue here whether in a world in which it seemed to its inhabitants that ethics did apply, it is possible that it really did not.) It might also be that while there was such a thing as morality, we had no way whatever to discover what it was—that when we came to trying to understand what the conditions were that made ethics in principle applicable to our world, we simply could not come to tell what those conditions were. (It is an interesting question that I will not pursue here, whether in a world in which its inhabitants understood enough to wonder whether ethics had purchase on it, it could be the case that they could not tell.) Ethics might be precluded, then, by either metaphysical or epistemological factors. Narrative discourse in the sense of stories can illustrate answers to our four questions. Insofar as it is particularistic and story-specific it cannot give general answers to, let alone provide rational assessment of, those answers. But such generality and assessment are essential to ethics.

If there is no logical possibility of ethical disagreement and no logical possibility of making a mistake in ethics, then there is no such thing as ethics. It cannot be the case that a sentence of the form "Ethical claim C is true" is replaceable (translatable without remainder) by a claim of the form "Someone believes that C," for to believe something is to believe that it is true; if truth is a casualty, so are knowledge and belief. It is important to distinguish between ethical principles and ethical rules. An ethical rule specifies something as right or wrong, good or bad, without telling one why it is so, and either prescribes or proscribes what it specifies. Thus, "Truthtelling is obligatory" tells us that saying what is true with intent to inform is a duty without saying why it is, and "Stealing is wrong" tells us that not surreptitiously appropriating for our use that to which another has prior proper claim is a duty without saying why it is. (If some other account of truthtelling or stealing is correct, let it replace the ones just offered.) Ethical rules are produced by applying ethical principles to concrete circumstances, and their ethical rationale is exposed by appealing to an ethical principle. An ethical principle tells us what makes something right or wrong, good or bad, without telling us what specific sorts of things are right or wrong or good or bad. "One ought always to treat others as ends, and never as a means only" and "One ought to love the Lord God with all of one's heart, mind, and strength, and to love other created persons as one loves oneself" do not tell us what ways of acting show respect or manifest love. Rules that fall under the principles provide at least part of that content. Nothing in ethical theory is more ultimate than an ethical principle, and unless such a principle can be derived from other basic claims, its defense must come in terms of intrinsic plausibility, absence of counterexample, and explanatory power relative to cases. The epistemology of ethics is not our focus here, so I will not defend the claim that one can rationally assess ethical principles, though I believe that claim to be true. Ultimate disagreements in ethics concern principles, not rules, and the question as to what there is by way of deep ethical diversity either cross-culturally or intraculturally has essentially to do with principles. Acceptance of an ethical principle by two parties who diverge as to the nonethical facts may yield different ethical rules where the difference is essentially about nonethical matters. Since there is genuine disagreement only if there is something to disagree about, cross-cultural disagreement regarding ethical principles presupposes that there is some true ethical principle. So does the telling of moral narratives.

Finally, ethical deliberations are inherently trivalent. An action, for example, is right, wrong, or neutral. It is ethically neutral not only if ethical considerations are not relevant to it but also if the relevant ethical considerations in its favor are balanced by those against it. If there is such a balance, so far as one can tell after careful reflection, then the judgment "It does not ethically matter what you do" or "Doing is no more justified than refraining" is a legitimate result of ethical deliberation. This is different from a case in which one cannot tell what is the right thing to do. Failure to recognize the full range of possibilities can lead one to mistake a justified verdict of neutrality for a case of failure to obtain a justified result. Ethics, as just characterized, is a human artifact. If no humans (at least, no rational agents of any sort), then no ethics. Analogous things could be said regarding physics and theology. It does not follow that ethics, any more than physics or theology, creates what it is about. Indeed, if it does so, it is not ethics—not a truth-seeking discipline, in which people make claims that are either true or false and in which there are ways of rationally assessing competing claims.

In looking through the sale books in our local university bookstore recently, I discovered a book entitled *Greek Insects*. For better or worse, I have the kind of mind that responds to a title like *Cooking Chinese* by thinking "Isn't that immoral?" I find it puzzling that a book entitled *Before and After Socrates* be about Socrates. So I found *Greek Insects* an interesting title, and my response was "There aren't any." Anything bright enough to speak Greek and be a citizen in a polis would not be an insect. But, of course, the author disappointingly meant "insects the Greeks wrote about." *Greek Ethics* is like *Greek Insects*. It means "what the Greeks wrote about ethics." What gives entomology purchase on our world, of course, is different from what gives ethics purchase on it, but that is irrelevant to the argument. If there were nothing inherently non-Greek and indeed ahistorical that the Greeks wrote about when they wrote about ethics, then a book entitled *Greek Ethics* would be like a book entitled *Greek Insects*, in a world in which there was a Greece but it lacked all insectile inhabitants. It would be a fraud. The same thing holds, of course, if one uses some other qualifier than "Greek." The rest of this essay argues for what I have just asserted.

Metaphysics and Ethics

Metaphysics is not a narrative discipline. It does not consist of stories. It contains non-narrative claims—for example, that there are abstract objects, determinism is true, there are both minds and bodies that belong to distinct ontological kinds, or God exists, and of course the denials of these claims. It contains nonnarrative arguments—for example, (i) if it is logically possible that there exist necessarily existing things, then there are necessarily existing things; (ii) it is logically possible that there are necessarily existing things; so (iii) there are necessarily existing things. This argument is obviously valid. Premise (i) is true. Modal propositions—propositions that ascribe logical necessity, possibility, or contingency—to other propositions are, if true, then necessarily true. To say that there are necessarily existing things is to say that there is something X about which it is true that "Necessarily, X exists" is true. Consider the claim that "Necessarily, God or abstract objects exist" is possibly true. If (iv) is true, it is necessarily true; if (iv) is false, it is necessarily false. Now (iv) does not appear to be a necessary falsehood. If it isn't, then (iv) is possibly true. Any proposition of the form "Necessarily, P" is either necessary true or necessarily false, and if it is possibly true then it is not necessarily false and hence is necessarily true. To the degree that one is rightly confident that (i) is possibly true—i.e. that (ii) is true—one can properly infer from (i) to (iii). Such abstract arguments, and counters to them, obviously are not narratives—not stories.

Ethics and metaphysics are indissolubly linked. Ethics applies only to worlds of which certain things are true. There is, of course, disagreement about which things these are. In what follows, I will consider what some of these things may be.

The overall strategy of my argument is simple. The fact is that, whether or not they include the ones I suggest in what follows, ethics has purchase on a world only if certain nonnarrative things are true of it. (For ethics to have purchase on a world is a mattrer of its principles being applicable to it.) These things being true of a world are both necessary and sufficient for ethics having purchase on that world. While if these things are true of a world, moral narratives will also be true of it, these things are true of it whether or not the narratives are ever told. The conditions that a world must meet in order for ethics to have purchase on it hold constant across worlds. They do not vary.

There is an analogous argument to be made regarding ethics itself—an argument within ethics, not one that deals with the relations between metaphysics and ethics. If it is a true moral principle that a person ought to be treated with respect (or, perhaps, ought to be so treated in any case in which he or she has not so acted as to temporarily have forfeited that right, or the like), then this is universally true—true under all possible conditions, under all circumstances. If it is instead true that what ought to be aimed at is the greatest degree possible of preference satisfaction, then that is always true. Ethical principles are precisely the sort of things whose scope of truth cannot be limited in the way favored by enthusiastic narrativists. Further, much of the dispute in ethics concerns, directly or indirectly, which moral principle is, or which moral principles are, true. These disputes themselves are not narrativist or particularist nor are the arguments for and against the contenders narrativist or particularist. True, stories are often told as ways of expressing counterexamples, but any story that makes the counterexample clear will do and there are always a plethora of stories (from different particular traditions) that might be used. The point is the counterexample, not the story that expresses it, and of course the defect an apt counterexample exposes can be stated, and seen to be a defect, without the accompanying story.

What follows, then, is an account of at least some of the nonnarrative things that must be true if ethics is to have purchase on a world, and whose truth is sufficient as well as necessary for ethics having purchase on a world.

Worlds and Necessity

I want to talk about *narrative worlds*. A narrative world is a world of which some narrative is true. The notion of a narrative is not lucid, nor is the notion of a world. Perhaps we can gain some lucidity regarding the latter notion by borrowing from talk of possible worlds. A proposition is anything either true or false; typically, declarative sentences (or uses of same) express propositions. The same proposition can be expressed by more than one sentence in the same language or by sentences in different languages. A proposition A entails a proposition B if it is logically impossible or self-contradictory that A be true and B be false. Consider, then, the notion of a "maximal proposition," namely, a proposition that has this feature: for any proposition you like, a maximal proposition entails either it or its contradictory.

Thus, a maximal proposition either entails "Al Gore is elected in 2000" or entails "Al Gore is not elected in 2000," and the same holds for any other pair of propositions. A maximal proposition describes a possible world. The actual world is what corresponds to whatever maximal proposition is true, and, of course, not more than one such proposition can be true. So by "world" I will mean "possible world." One might think that for every possible world, there was a corresponding narrative. One would be wrong in so thinking.

In a way, necessity and narrative are enemies. Narrative requires contingencies. If not every narrative, at least more than minimal narrative requires, not only contingencies but also certain sorts of contingencies. Necessity is notoriously treacherous terrain, and I will only skirt its borders in an attempt to forage sufficiently for our needs. Some philosophers think of necessity as an artifact of our language or our conceptual systems; they talk about conceptual truths and mean truths that arise simply from the ways in which we use words or perhaps from the ways we think about things. It seems typical for these philosophers to use "All bachelors are unmarried" and "If something is a unicorn then it has one horn" as examples of conceptual truths; the idea is to emphasize that conceptual truths are not informationally significant. This is hardly a fair sampling, since (say) Gödel's Theorem, and the thesis that every modality (necessity, possibility, contingency) that a proposition possesses, it possesses necessarily, are necessarily true but informationally nontrivial propositions. On the "necessity is an artifact" line of reasoning, necessary truths are simply conceptual truths, and if languages and conceptual systems were to vanish from our world, necessity would vanish with it, just as necessity entered the world only as it was carried in along with our linguistic devices or arose from our conceptual capacities. While not everyone who speaks of conceptual truths means what has been suggested here, those who do embrace *logical conventionalism*. It is easy to reason that if one can produce necessity by fiat, then necessity lies "in us" and not "out there." If I define a "wable" as "anything that is a washcloth or a table," then it is conceptually necessary that "All wables are washcloths or tables" and the necessity that results must be invented, not discovered.

Even this defense of conventionalism is misguided. Of course, what "wable" means is decided by my fiat, and what terms of natural language mean, if not typically fiated, does arise from our cultural activities; any mark or sound might have had no meaning (been no word) at all or had some meaning other than the one it has (been some other word). All that is conventional. But what "All bachelors are unmarried" says is that "Anything that has the property of being unmarried and the property of being adult and the property of being male (three properties that we designate by the one word "bachelorhood") has the property of being unmarried" and of course any proposition of the from "If X has A,B, and C, then X has C" is true whether we like it or not. It is true "out there" and all that is "in here" is how we say it.

The opposing view to conventionalism is *logical realism*. If conventionalists locate the grounds or conditions of necessity in human language or concepts, realists locate it outside of human commerce or contrivance. The English sentence "If Sandra draws a pentagon then Sandra draws a figure," used to make an assertion, expresses a necessary truth. Typically, realists argue as follows: a truth has truth conditions—something makes it true. A necessary truth has necessary truth conditions—something that cannot fail to obtain that makes it true. If what makes it true could fail to obtain, it could fail to be true. Hence, the grounds or conditions of necessity lie in something that exists with complete security—abstract objects, ideas in the mind of God, or the like.

Without entering into the metaphysics of necessity, one can recognize that the principle of noncontradiction, in contrast to some particular way of expressing it, is a discovery and not an invention, something true long before human language and concepts graced the creation. If this is so, then presumably some form of realism rather than conventionalism is true. It is plainly true that necessity is expressed or reflected in language; "Nothing can have but also lack the same property at a given time, or timelessly both have and not have a property" expresses what is necessarily so regarding properties and things, and no decisions or inventions of ours can change that. But "A is reflected in B" does not entail "A is dependent on B." Nor does "We can learn that A only because A is reflected in B" entail that "A is true only because of B." The importance of the "reflected in" versus "dependent on" distinction is relevant to the relations between morality and narrative, as well as the relations between necessity and language.

Philosophers also speak of metaphysical necessity and (if they speak kindly of it) mean to say that not all necessity concerns concepts or propositions. "Socrates is necessarily self-conscious" ascribes to Socrates "being self-conscious" as an essential property, as "Being two atoms of hydrogen to one atom of oxygen is water's essence" ascribes an essential property to water. Such propositions assert that certain things necessarily have certain properties. Philosophers refer to this as *de re* necessity— necessity concerning properties and things—rather than *de dicto* necessity concerning propositions. There are metaphysically necessary categorical or nonhypothetical *de re* propositions only if there are existing things that have essential properties; there are metaphysically necessary hypothetical *de re* propositions only if there might be things that have essential properties, and of course, if there are metaphysically necessary categoricals, then there are metaphysically necessary hypotheticals. Some ethical theories have application to our world only if there are things that have essential properties—only if there are true metaphysically necessary categorical propositions. Aristotle's virtue ethics, and Kant's ethic of respect for persons, are examples. In what follows, I shall assume logical realism and use the term "logically necessary proposition" to cover both *de re* and *de dicto* necessary truths. I will suppose that while every proposition whose denial, once properly symbolized in some standard and unobjectionable system of formal logic, is reducible to something of the form "P and not-P" is necessarily true, the converse is false.

Finally, some philosophers speak of causal necessity. One way of approaching this notion involves noting that there are true propositions (e.g., "Acid dissolves zinc"), knowledge of which justifies one in accepting some true counterfactuals into one's theories and leaving other true counterfactuals out. Conditional statements, on the canonical analysis, are true if their antecedents are false. A counterfactual is a conditional and it has a false antecedent, so all counterfactuals are true. But not all are useful in our theories, and the problem often expressed as telling which ones are true in fact is the problem of telling which true ones we can nonmisleadingly embed in our theories. The useful ones—the ones that together with accurate reports of what has happened entail true accounts of what will happen—express laws. For example, the known truth of "Acid dissolves zinc" justifies us in using "If this bit of zinc were to be placed in that beaker of acid, it would dissolve" rather than "If this bit of zinc were to be put into that beaker of acid, it would not dissolve," since it is that conditional which, when conjoined with "This bit of zinc is placed in that beaker of acid" will yield the proper prediction. There is a problem with this way of putting things. Consider our two alleged truths: (Z_1) "If this bit of zinc were to be placed in that beaker of acid, it would dissolve," and (Z_2) "If this bit of zinc were to be put into that beaker of acid, it would not dissolve." Then add a true report: (A) "This bit of zinc was put into the beaker of acid." Plainly, (A) and (Z_1) entail (B) "This bit of zinc dissolves," whereas (A) and (Z_2) entail (not-B) "This bit of zinc does not dissolve." Since (not-B) is false, at least one of (A) and (Z_2) is false; but ex hypothesi (A) is true; so (Z_2) is false. Hence, either the canonical account of conditionals is mistaken or it does not apply to counterfactuals.

One way of dealing with this problem is to think of laws as grounded in the essences of the things the laws range over. Consider the *de re* statement "Dissolving zinc is a power that is essential to acidity" or the *de re* statement "It is the nature of acid to dissolve zinc." The nature of a thing is in part defined by its causal powers, and laws, on this account, define the causal powers essential to things of a kind, perhaps a very broad kind like "being material" or perhaps a much smaller kind like "being mammalian." Laws will be true in virtue of the essential causal powers of the kinds of physical things that the world contains. "If zinc is placed in acid, it dissolves" is true because of the natures of zinc and acid. Newton's laws of motion abstractly express consequences that follow from true descriptions of the causal powers of material objects. Alternatively, some philosophers take laws to express necessary connections among properties, construed as abstract objects, that thus also hold among their instances. In any case, the core idea of causal necessity is that if for every change C_2 in the world at any time T_2, there is a condition C_1 and a law L such that "C_1 obtains at T_1" is true, and "C_1 obtains at T_1" plus L entail "C_2 obtains at T_2," then the past determines a unique future. This will be so, even if the law is contingently true—if the lawlike proposition has neither a contradictory denial nor a single exception. Among possible worlds, some exhibit causal necessity.

Stories and the Epistemology of Ethics

Counterexamples are common and crucial in philosophy, including ethics. Furthermore, examples of what seem plainly justified moral judgments play an important role in ethics—an ethical theory worth its salt must either explain why moral judgments that seem plainly correct are so, or else explain why in this case the judgment that seems correct only seems so. There are moral appearances to be saved, and others to be jettisoned for principled reasons, and part of the rational assessment of an ethical theory deals with its handling of the ethical phenomena. The counterexamples and phenomena can be described in brief and crisp ways perhaps too short to count as stories. Typically, however, they are expressed in terms of stories (fictional stories are often better than biographically true stories here, though there is considerable prejudice to the contrary). As conveyors of counterexamples and phenomena, stories (or something like them, only briefer) are exceedingly useful in the epistemology of ethics.

Some Possible Worlds

Consider a possible world in which there exist only eternal abstract objects all of whose nonrelational properties are essential. Something is eternal only if it has no temporal properties at all. For example, "X is eternal" entails "It is false that X exists now" and "For any temporal item Y, X bears no temporal relation to Y." Every true proposition that ascribes existence or some nonrelational property to any of these abstract objects is necessarily true. Assuming that the relational properties of these objects are entailed by their nonrelational properties, every true proposition that ascribes a relational property to any of these objects is also necessarily true. In this sort of world, change is impossible and nothing happens. I assume that narrative is true of a world only if something happens in that world. In our first sort of world, nothing can (and so nothing does) happen. Hence, no narrative is true of that world. While this sort of world is describable, there can be no narration concerning it. A world composed of abstract objects that are whole numbers can be described in great detail in ways that we are aware of; it is not paucity of information but lack of happenings that renders such a world immune to narrative treatment. If there are abstract objects of the sort described, their description is contained in every maximal proposition. They exist in every possible world.

I am assuming that there is a maximal proposition that entails that all and only abstract objects exist, and it is perfectly compatible with this that the description of these objects—though not of course the claim that they are all there is—be contained in every maximal proposition. It is not an argument against this assumption that some contingent proposition must be true. Indeed, presumably there are an infinite or indefinite number of contingent propositions, exactly half of which are true; if the world of abstract objects were the actual world, all positive contingent existential statements would be false and their negations true.

Suppose instead that our abstract objects are everlasting rather than eternal. An everlasting X has lots of temporal properties; it exists now and at every other time, and for any other temporal item Y there are temporal relations between X and Y. Of course, the *same* set of abstract objects could not be eternal and possibly everlasting or everlasting and possibly eternal, since presumably whatever is eternal (or everlasting) is necessarily eternal (or everlasting); but perhaps abstract objects come in two brands, one eternal and one everlasting, or perhaps the truth about abstract objects is that they are everlasting rather than eternal. Then perhaps, in a certain minimal sense, there can be change, even if every property of these objects is essential. Suppose that one of these objects is the number two. Perhaps we can distinguish between the property "being everlastingly even" and the properties "being even at time T_1" and "being even at time T_2." The number two has the property "being everlastingly even" only by virtue of its having such properties as "being even at time T_1" and "being even at time T_2" and ever so many more such properties. Then the number two can change from "being even at T_1" to "being even at T_2" but not with respect to "being everlastingly even." If so, in this world things happen.

It does not follow that this is a narrative world. For one thing, the subjective conditions of narrative are lacking; there are no narrators. Furthermore, while something happens, its description hardly makes a story, and, according to narrative enthusiasts, it is stories that are crucial to ethics. In our world of everlasting abstract objects, there is no natural science. There exist neither the subjective conditions of natural science (there are no scientists) nor its objective conditions (there are, for example, no physical events, and hence, no physical events did occur but might not have occurred, generalizations over which can be discovered only through experiments). However exactly scientific method should be described, there is nothing in this world for it to operate on.

Consider instead a Lucretian world in which physical atoms fall endlessly through infinite space in paths described by exceptionless lawlike statements and causal necessity reigns. Here the objective conditions of natural science exist. Narrative, even broadly construed, has little scope in this world and story none whatever. This is so, even though logically contingent happenings abound.

Lucretian Idealism

Suppose Lucretius is converted to metaphysical idealism, holding that all that exists is minds, mental states, properties of minds, and relations among minds. Each pellet in his old world is traded for a mind in his new. Minds being unlocated, space disappears unless one counts spaces private to an individual's mental images. But time remains, as does causal necessity, though it reigns over the relations between mental states at one time and those at the next, for each sequential temporal pairing. (Whether these minds interact so that A's states can affect and be affected by B's, or have no causal concourse, does not matter here.) We now have a world in which there are thoughts. Each thought in each mind is the product of a previous thought (or of some other) in a beginningless progression. If an account of a sequence of mental events, each caused by a previous mental event, in a causally necessary system, is a narrative, then there is a narrative that is true of this world. Have we now reached a world in which the conditions of morality are found? That is a contentious question.

One perspective on values thinks in terms of a metaphysical hierarchy, the great chain of being. Since the chain's members are thought of as coming in ascending ranks, it seems to me that what is conceived is not so much a chain as a ladder of being, each rung being occupied by something both metaphysically more complex and possessed of greater worth than anything on a lower rung. Some who think in these terms do not countenance a point on the ladder at which morality begins; there is just goodness and badness, not any distinctively *moral* goodness or badness. I take it that Aristotle thinks along these lines. Others, Kant perhaps preeminent among them, thinks in terms ironically much more like those who, whether exactly narrative imperialists or not, find narrative in some manner central to ethics. The Judeo-Christian tradition, I take it, finds value in all that God has created (agreeing with that feature, at least, of ladder of being thought) but also finds a particular sort of value in those it conceives as particularly created in the divine image, associating that value with responsibility (there agreeing with Kant). If the prehuman creation is properly pronounced good, the creation with human occupants is very good. What makes the difference?

Stories and Agency

Professor Alasdair MacIntyre, in *After Virtue*, contends that

> the narratives which we live out have both an unpredictable and a partially teleological character. If the narrative of our individual and social lives is to continue intelligibly—and either type of narrative may lapse into unintelligibility—it is always both the case that there are constraints on how the story can continue and that within those constraints there are indefinitely many ways that it can continue. (216)

On MacIntyre's account, the particular sort of contingence that narratives with ethical relevance—namely, stories—require is (partly) absence of causal necessity. A world in which causal necessity reigns is one in which the past, physical or mental, determines a unique future. There are not indefinitely many ways in which a biographically true story can go. There are not even two ways.

The importance, in turn, of the presence of this sort of contingency has to do with agency. Typically, at least, the relevant stories will have to do with agents. Thus, a light touch on agency is required if we are to be specific about the conditions that must obtain in a world if ethics is to have a place in it. On one account, agents are self-conscious beings possessed of libertarian freedom regarding morally significant actions. (Those convinced of other notions of agency are free to see if their notion of agency can fit into my overall argument.) Moral universes are those that contain agents.

Determinism, Compatibilism, and Incompatibilism

Determinism can be stated along these lines. Let a "tensed universal description" be a statement that expresses every nonlawlike proposition that is true of the universe at a specific time. Let "the perfect science" be a statement that expresses all lawlike truths. Then determinism claims that any universal description tensed to a time T, plus the perfect science, logically entails the universal description tensed to time T+1 (and a fortiori any later time, since whatever may be the case about causality, entailment is transitive). In slogan form, every past determines a unique future.

A compatibilist holds that even if determinism is true, we can be responsible for our morally significant actions and hence be free in any sense required by responsibility. This seems to me demonstrably false. Peter Van Inwagen's *An Essay on Free Will* offers perhaps the best recent critique of compatibilism, which essentially is this. Suppose that determinism is true. Then the universal description of the world at a time, say, when the first dinosaur appeared entails the universal description of the universe that is true at any moment during my lifetime. I have no control over what universal description is true thousands upon thousands of years before my birth. I have no control over the content of the perfect science. I have no control over the laws of logic or over what logically entails what. And I have no control over what is determined by what I have no control over. So I have no control over what universal descriptions are true during my lifetime. But whatever is true regarding what I think, choose, or do is part of some universal description that is true of some moment during my lifetime. So I have no control over anything that I think, choose, or do. If I have no control over what I think, choose, or do, then I am not free regarding what I think, choose, or do — not unless one joins Spinoza in saying that the freedom of the will is merely ignorance of the causes of the will, which of course is a determinist position. Compatibilism, then, is false.

Compatibilism is the sort of position that no one seems to rush to embrace for its own sake. It is like an unpleasant person whom you want with you when you visit tough neighborhoods; the value of association lies in what is prevented, not what is accomplished. If compatibilism is true, ethicists can work in their discipline without worrying about the metaphysics of freedom. Furthermore, of course, many take determinism to be either a deliverance or else a presupposition of science.

In a certain sense, ethics does not depend on metaphysics. One can develop one's work in ethics in terms of adopting (say) a particular account of what a person is and then ask: Supposing persons are of this sort, what is it right or wrong to do regarding them, and what is it right or wrong for them to do? What will count as flourishing for a being of this sort? If one construes persons as economic agents, whose only basis for choice is preference satisfaction, one set of answers will arise — one that Professor John Elster's *Sour Grapes* subjects to scathing critique. If you think of persons as created in the *imago Dei* to live lives that progressively approximate tough unconditional love of others as oneself, one's ethic will be different. The same will hold for other alternatives. Then one's work in ethics is entirely hypothetical — here is what is good for X's, should there be any X's, a matter into which we ethicists don't inquire. So construed, ethics, it seems to me, is restrictedly though not fully autonomous. Once one shifts from the hypothetical to the categorical, then even this restricted autonomy vanishes, and since part at least of a dispute over what there is, and particularly over the nature of persons, will involve metaphysical claims, ethics will not be separable from, or autonomous in regard to, metaphysics. Nonetheless, strictly speaking, one of the things that attracts ethicists to compatibilism is available even if compatibilism is false, namely (in the restricted sense just explained) the autonomy of ethics. Of course, the fuller autonomy available to ethics if compatibilism is true will continue to lead some ethicists to hope that it is.

Unfree, Nonfree, and Free Stories

In some worlds—not, for example, those of which Berkeleyan idealism is true— there are physical states that are causally necessitated by other physical states and serve as physical conditions for embodied agency. There will be physical descriptions of such states and the laws relevant to them; let such descriptions, by an extension of the term "story," be physical stories. As descriptions of causally necessitated states, these accounts will concern states that lack freedom; I will call these stories "unfree" stories because they are about unfree things.

If a world contains moral conditions, it contains self-conscious creatures. If unfree stories are true in a world in which the conditions for morality obtain, it will contain beings that have such properties as "having memories," "being capable of sensory perception," "being able to identify other persons," and the like. There will be cognitive psychological descriptions of such varieties of sentience, and there being sentience allows for there to be subjects and objects of stories in something closer to the proper sense of the term. Let us call these "nonfree" stories because it is at least arguable whether "being self-conscious" or "being sentient" entails "being free." A nonfree story is a story concerning self-conscious beings that does not, unless supplemented by an argument to the effect that "being self-conscious" entails "being free," entail that the story's characters are free.

Free stories, then, are stories that are true because of the choices and actions of libertarianly free agents, either described explicitly as free or recounted in a context that assumes such freedom so that it need not be explicitly mentioned. I suspect that most stories occur in exactly this sort of context.

Biographical Stories and Fictional Stories

Biographical (including autobiographical) free stories are stories that are true of actual free agents; they recount the free and morally significant choices and actions of libertarian agents. But it is helpful that there also be fictional accounts of free choices, for one can consider the consequences of proposed courses of conduct without actually carrying them out, warn of the inelegance of vice without exhibiting it, and show the praiseworthiness of virtues that one has not achieved.

Relevant concern with science is not limited to worries about determinism. Consider the perspective offered by a formal argument that expresses the views of a distinguished biologist with whom I recently teamtaught a course. His views are not idiosyncratic, and it perplexed him how to fit them together consistently with his concerns about the environment. Explanations have two parts. One part is an explicandum or to-be-explained—an explainee, if you like—that tells you what the explanation is an explanation of. This must be described in terms that are accessible to the other part of the explanation. The other part is an explicans or explainer that tells you what is the reason for the explainee; this by itself is often called "the explanation." A genuine explainee is one that can be related to a genuine explainer. If all explanations are explanations in physics, then all explainers can be described in all ways relevant to explanation only by the concepts of physics. Then all explainees must be related by the laws of physics to the explainers. For all purposes relevant to explanation, the explainees must be described only by the concepts of physics. Here, then, is the argument.

1. All explanation is scientific explanation.
2. All scientific explanation is explanation in physics.
3. Explanations in physics use no concepts and no laws save those of physics. [true by definition]
4. All explanation is explanation in physics. [from 1 and 2]
5. All explanations use no concepts and no laws save those of physics. [from 3 and 4]
6. For all purposes relevant to explanation, one needs nothing other than physical concepts and laws to explain or describe anything. [from 5]
7. Any property that a thing has is a property for which there is an explanation.
8. One needs nothing to describe or explain any property that anything has except the laws and concepts of physics. [from 6 and 7]
9. If one needs nothing other than physical concepts and laws to explain or describe any property of anything, then questions (should any still arise) about what is right or wrong can be answered by reference only to physical descriptions and explanations of things. [necessary truth]
10. Questions (should any still arise) about what is right or wrong can be answered by reference only to physical descriptions and explanations of things. [from 8 and 9]
11. "Right" and "wrong" do not refer to any physical properties of anything, and so reference to them appears in no physical descriptions of anything.
12. If 11 is true, then questions about what is right or wrong cannot be answered by reference only to physical descriptions and explanations of things.
13. Questions (should any still arise) about what is right or wrong cannot be answered by thinking that there is anything that is right or wrong. [from 10, 11, and 12]
14. If 13 is true, anything is permissible.
15. Anything is permissible. [from 13 and 14]

No one who thought that there was anything to ethics could consistently accept the perspective that this argument defines. The argument has its defects. Note that the first claim that "all explanation" is scientific explanation is not itself justifiable by appeal to science alone; it is a view in theory of knowledge or epistemology—a piece of philosophy, not a piece of science, as it were. If the claim were true, one could not know that it was true.[1] While this does not entail that the claim is false, it does entail that even if it were true no one could know this, nor (if reasonable belief must rest on knowledge) could anyone reasonably believe it. Try replacing "right" and "wrong" in the argument with "true" and "false" or by "believed on the basis of evidence" and "believed without evidence" or any similar pairing. *These* terms no more refer to physical properties than do religious or moral terms.

Some Metaphysical Alternatives

Of course, one need not be a materialist in order to insist on this. One might be a dualist and yet maintain that mental states have a basically physicalistic sufficient explanation. Consider, for example, a *state dualism*, which holds that mental states and physical states are of irreducibly different kinds, or a *substance dualism*, which holds that mental substances and physical substances are of irreducibly distinct kinds, where in both cases it is added that for every mental state M of any kind K that S is in at t, S's being in M is causally determined by, or is otherwise entirely a function of, the physical state S is in at t. Then it will be held that (iii) "Every mental state is correlated to some physical state on which it, in some fashion, completely depends," and (iv) "If S is in mental state M of kind K at t, S's being in M is entirely due to S's being in some physical state N of kind K_1 at t." Given a purely physicalistic explanation E of S's being in physical state N of kind K_1 at t, plus (iii), plus (iv), one will have a nonepistemic explanation of S's being in M at t. For such varieties of dualism as these, there will also be overdetermination or overexplicability of beliefs if any beliefs are rationally or reasonably held. The general sorts of dualism briefly described above, given their views concerning the tight dependence of mental states on physical states, might be called *physicalistic dualism*. If materialism, or physicalistic dualism, is true, and if any beliefs are rationally or reasonably held, then some mental states (beliefs) are overdetermined or overexplicable. I do not offer this as a criticism, much less a refutation, of materialism or physicalistic dualism, though it does seem to me that materialism is—at least in the respect specified—less parsimonious than might have been thought, and some of its proponents have leaned heavily on its alleged allegiance to explanatory simplicity as one of its particular virtues.

In any case, one alternative to holding that beliefs (at least, reasonably held beliefs) are overdetermined or overexplicable is to hold that every explanation of a belief—even if it has a physicalistic component—must also have an epistemic component of a sort not countenanced by physicalism or physicalistic dualism. If S is in mental state M, and M is a belief that S is reasonable in having, then while S's being in some physical state N may be a necessary condition of S's being in M, S's having some ground or reason (and so S's being, or at least having been, in some mental state M_1) is also a necessary condition of S's being in M. One might allow that references to both N and M_1 appear in the same seamless explanation. Or one might require that reference to N occur in one explanation and reference to M_1 in another, and view these explanations as belonging to different kinds such that no single explanation could participate in both kinds, but hold that a *full* explanation of M will conjoin both explanations into an account of S's being in M whose component parts cannot commingle. Whichever alternative is chosen, on this view a physicalistic explanation of a mental state of S at t is not a sufficient explanation of that state in the sense that crucial features of the state— features that render the state *mental* rather than physical, and/or features that render it the *sort* of mental state it is—are not determined by the physical states S is in at t (and/or *was* in before t). Such a view seems properly referred to as *idealistic*, or at least nonphysicalistic, dualism.

The other alternative would be to hold that all explanation is epistemic and none physicalistic—that apparently physicalistic explanations are all translatable into, or that all physicalistic explanations are replaceable by, epistemic explanations, and that there is good enough reason in each case to make the translation or replacement.[2] Presumably, this view is most at home in, and perhaps it is required by (and requires), mind-body idealism (the view that all there is are minds, mental states, and properties, i.e., qualities and relations of minds and mental states). Idealism and idealistic or nonphysicalistic dualism relevantly share the view that the mental states of S at t are not completely causally determined by, or otherwise purely functions of, the physical states of S at, and/or before, t so that a mental state can be epistemically explicable without its being overdetermined.

Reductive and Nonreductive Perspectives

It is widely assumed that physical states stand in relations of causal necessity to prior physical states. The most important scientific exception to this, of course, is the demise of classical determinism in favor of indeterminacy at the subatomic level and the resulting probabilistic conception of physical laws. In the face of more than enough complexity already, I will leave this aside save for two comments. One is that randomness is no more a friend of freedom than is necessity. The other is that probabilistic laws no more relate an agent to his actions in a libertarianly free manner than do deterministic laws. If there is a defense of metaphysical libertarianism, it does not lie in filling in the cracks in an otherwise merely probabilistic account. For simplicity, I shall assume a causal necessity unconstrained by indeterminacy considerations, granting that a final account must be expanded to deal with them.

While it is false in some possible worlds, it seems plainly true in the actual world that ordinary human cognitive activities as manifested in choice and action have physically necessary conditions and are inhibited or prevented by physical malfunction. One vexing metaphysical question is how to conceive the relationship between physical descriptions of human behavior and descriptions of actions by human beings—of how to relate "Jim's arm rose" (which can be dealt with in purely physical terms) and "Jim raised his arm" (which cannot). Suppose each physical state is related by causal necessity to prior physical states, and the physical past determines a unique physical future. How, then, can there be freedom of choice? It was this problem that led Kant to take the transcendental turn, perhaps the classic example in philosophy of a solution vastly worse than the problem it was intended to solve.

Replacing causal necessity by some weaker notion of connection will be of no help as long as the conditionals expressing causal laws are assumed to be unexceptionably true. The conjunction "A occurred" and "If A then B" entails "B occurs" even if the conditional is nonnecessary in every possible sense. One possibility is to claim that laws of science are true only on the whole—they are statements of how things generally go, analogous to "Your average senior fears exams less than your average sophomore" rather than to "Every circle has a circumference" or "Ninety-nine and forty-four-hundredths percent of your Ivory soap bar is pure." Another is to hold that physical states and mental states typically are in one-many relationships. Still another is to hold that physical descriptions are necessitarian regarding items all of whose properties are physical (regarding the items that they describe fully) but nonnecessitarian regarding beings not all of whose properties are physical (regarding the items that they only partially describe). None of these proposals is worth much until laid out in a carefully developed manner. The libertarian, I take it, holds that some such alternative is the truth of the matter, even if she currently is unprepared to say which of these is correct or to add some more promising further account of the matter.

Professor Nancy Cartwright, in *How the Laws of Physics Lie* (Oxford: Clarendon Press, 1983), writes:

> The metaphysical picture that underlies these essays is the Aristotelian belief in the richness and variety of the concrete and particular. Things are made to look the same only when we fail to examine them too closely. Pierre Duhem distinguished two kinds of thinkers: the deep but narrow minds of the French, and the broad but shallow minds of the English. The French mind sees things in an elegant, unified way. It takes Newton's three laws of motion and turns them into the beautiful, abstract mathematics of Lagrangian mechanics. The English mind, says Duhem, is an exact contrast. It engineers bits of gears, and pulleys, and keeps the strings from tangling up. It holds a thousand different details all at once, without imposing much abstract order or organization. The difference between the [scientific] realist and me is almost theological. The realist thinks that the creator of the universe worked like a French mathematician. But Duhem thinks that God has the untidy mind of the English. (19)

Libertarianism

It, of course, is controversial that libertarian freedom is required for moral responsibility. The standard definition of free agency runs:

> (F1) Person S is free with respect to action A at time T if and only if, at T, it is actually within S's power to do A and actually within S's power not to do A, though of course it is not actually within S's power both to do A and not.

A standard qualification to (F1) is "unless S has done something earlier than T that results in S's doing A or not doing A at T, and in S's lacking the power to act other than S does act at T."

A famous sort of objection to (F1), qualified or not, supposes that Jim is seated in a room that is locked. Jim has promised his mother to stay in his room until it is clean, which will not be for some time even if Jim works long and hard. Not knowing the room is locked, he considers sneaking out to the movies, thinks better of it, and works away until his job is finished. By then, the room has been unlocked, and Jim leaves with a clean room and conscience. Jim is praiseworthy for not having left the room, even though he could not have left it. So he is praiseworthy for acting as he did in a case in which he could not have done otherwise.[3]

Another famous sort of objection supposes that Kim, furious at her older sister, is contemplating breaking her sister's favorite vase. She is unaware that her sister, advanced in science if not in ethics, has implanted in Kim's brain an electrode that allows her to tell what Kim is thinking and has intentionally both angered Kim and left the vase within Kim's reach. If Kim's deliberations go against vase-breaking, her sister will not activate the reverse function of the electrode. If Kim's deliberations are about to end in a decision to break the vase, however, her sister will activate that function and Kim will "decide"—that is, Kim's sister will cause her to decide—not to break the vase. So Kim has but one choice. Yet if she makes up her mind on her own and decides to leave the vase alone, she has made the praiseworthy decision. Hence, choices not made under the conditions that (F1) specifies can be praiseworthy and so choices that one is responsible for having made.

It is worth considering these objections carefully. In the first objection, Jim considers leaving the room and does not know that he cannot leave it. The most that Jim can do is try to leave; then what (F1) entails is that what Jim is responsible for is merely not trying to leave, and he is praiseworthy for that, and he would be blameworthy for trying to leave if he had tried. He can be praised for refraining from leaving, for he did not and chose not to. But he could not be blamed for leaving, for he could not do so, though he could try and be blamed for trying. Here what Jim can be praised and blamed for seem exactly to correspond to what he can do and can try to do.

Turning this material into an objection against (F1) seems to require some such principle as this:

> (F*) If S can be morally praised for doing A, then it was within S's power not to do A.

In Jim's case, it is in his power not to try to leave the room, and a consequence of his not trying is that he will not leave it, whether the room is locked or not. There is a relevant disparity between what he could be praised for (for not trying to leave the room, and hence for not doing so) and what he could be blamed for (for trying, though not for leaving). There is also a relevant parity (between trying to leave and not trying to leave). The only reason that Jim is praiseworthy for staying is that there is something that Jim can do that does satisfy (F1) and that, in the circumstances, is sufficient for staying. The relevant principle, then, is not (F*) but

> (F2) If S can be morally praised for doing A, then either it was within S's power not to do A, or there was something B that it was within S's power to do, and within S's power not to do, such that S's doing B is, in the circumstances, sufficient for doing A.

So long as (F2) is satisfied, it does not matter whether it is also in S's power to do something that is sufficient for not doing A. But S is responsible for doing A only through being responsible for doing B under conditions that satisfy (F1).

Consider now the second objection. Here, one will make the right choice—at least, the sister's favored choice—no matter how one's deliberations go. But Kim is not praiseworthy for choosing to leave the vase in one piece if her sister causes that choice, while she is if she causes it. But now Kim is able to deliberate—to freely undergo a process of thought that will result in a choice if it is allowed (as it may, or may not, be) to mature and flower. Strictly, what she is responsible for is how her deliberation goes. Her deliberation occurs under considerations that satisfy (F1). She is praiseworthy for leaving the vase alone precisely and only because she is responsible for the deliberation that results in that choice. She cannot, under the circumstances, be responsible for choosing to break the vase, though she can be responsible for deliberations that would have ended up in that choice had they then not been quenched or reversed. Once we conjoin (F1) and (F2), rejecting (F*), there is nothing in these objections that endangers libertarianism.

It is worth noting that while the discussion has been cast in terms of praise-worthiness and blameworthiness, it is the agent's ability to participate in the forming of his or her own character that is of central moral significance.

In Plato's *Phaedo*, Socrates is reported as saying:

> It seemed to me . . . very much as if one should say that Socrates does with intelligence whatever he does, and then, in trying to give the causes (*aitias*) of the particular thing I do should say first that I am now sitting here because my body is composed of bones and sinews . . . and so, as the bones are hung loose in their ligaments, the sinews, by relaxing and contracting, make me able to bend my limbs now, and that is the cause of my sitting here with my legs bent. Or as if in the same way he should give voice and air and breathing and countless other things as the causes for one talking with each other, and should fail to mention the real causes, which are that the Athenians decided it was best to condemn me, and therefore I have decided it was best for me to sit here, and that it is right for me to stay and undergo whatever penalty they order. For, by the dog, I fancy that these bones and sinews of mine would have been in Megara or Boeotia long ago, carried hither by an opinion (*doxes*) of what is best, if I did not think it was better and nobler to endure any penalty the city may inflict rather than to escape and run away. But it is most absurd to call things of that sort causes. If anyone were to say that I could not have done what I thought proper, if I had not bones and sinews and other things, he would be right. But to say that those things are the cause of my doing what I do, and that I act with intelligence but not from the choice of what is best would be an extremely careless way of talking. (98c–99b)

The Minimum Conditions of Morality

What must exist in a world if there is to be any morality there? As we have noted, it seems plain that there are possible worlds on which ethics has no purchase. If all there is is empty space, or if every space is occupied by inert sand and nothing else exists, there is nothing that will give ethics a foothold; no moral conditions will obtain. But suppose there exist two self-conscious, unembodied beings, Alpha and Beta. Each enjoys logically necessary existence and is everlasting rather than eternal. An eternal being cannot change, and so one eternal being cannot effect change in another eternal being. But let us suppose Alpha and Beta can change. They have essential properties, but not all of their properties are essential. They are essentially self-conscious, but they are not essentially happy or essentially sad, essentially kind or essentially unkind, or the like.

Value and Morality

It is admittedly contentious where along the continuum of Worlds of greater and greater contingency morality first dawns. Worlds characterized by *no happenings* and *unrelieved randomness* presumably are failed candidates. I have suggested that moral conditions obtain, and so ethics has purchase, only in worlds graced by libertarianly free agents who are capable of morally significant activity. This seems to accord with narrativist proclivities and to be a narrative-friendly suggestion in that stories, whose relevance to ethics narrative enthusiasts exaggerate, concern just such creatures. Other suggestions could be made that, while less in accord with a view I actually hold, would do as well or better by my current overall argument.

What gives ethics purchase on a world is that moral conditions hold in it. Whatever is the case about the possibility of telling stories, stories actually told or even thought are not among those conditions. Let us supose that Alpha and Beta can so act as to affect their own flourishing as self-conscious creatures. They can knowingly affect each other's well-being. They can affect for weal or woe the conditions of their sentient but nonself-conscious colleagues. Given any of these capacities, and given all of them, Alpha and Beta are moral agents. That they share stories, enjoy a common culture, or embrace the narratives of a community, is not required. They need not even share a physical environment. If it is false that they are mutually obligated by virtue of standing in these relationships, it is hard to see what further, story-dependent relations they might stand in that would create a moral environment.

It is logically possible that there be such an Alpha and Beta. I suspect that it is also causally possible even in our world; what law of natural science would God contravene or qualify by creating an Alpha and Beta pair in our world? (There are of course pictures of our world into which Alpha and Beta would not fit, but that is different from any laws being challenged. Perhaps those pictures should be challenged.) Furthermore, *we* are related to one another in the morally relevant ways in which Alpha and Beta are related, and it is that fact that gives ethics purchase on our world. Were we not so related, we would not be joint members of a moral community defined in terms of our sheer abilities to affect our own flourishing and the well-being of others. Such relations do not require, but are presupposed by, any further and narrative-elicited obligations there may be.

It can be argued that we cannot have obligations to one another if we do not have the notion of an obligation and such notions as flourishing, harming, well-being, and the like. If we lack such concepts, at most it is true that we would be obligated if we had them. This seems correct so far as it goes, but while telling stories is *a* way of communicating such concepts, and typically is a congenial and effective way, it is not the only way, logically or causally, of teaching them. It is not beyond the human capacity to master codes of ethics neither laced with narrative nor proffered in a narrative context; they need not even have pictures.

I am not insensitive to the utility, and more significantly the humanity, of the telling and hearing of ethically relevant stories, of the value of traditions, or of the importance of placing oneself in relation to and inside of a community. My concern here is not at all to deny the value of narrative but to gauge its value realistically. It is proper to note that my argument has proceeded in part by telling rather abstract stories and asking what is true concerning them. Thought experiment is standard philosophical fare and has its proper uses in both metaphysics and ethics. Nothing that I claim here is incompatible with thought experiment being a philosophically legitimate enterprise and stories a tool of thought experiment. Further-more, both the ethical appearances there are to save and the counterexamples that often are so effective in revealing defects in ethical theories play important roles in the epistemology of ethics and can be exhibited in story form. Nothing that I argue is incompatible with any of this.

It is a sufficient condition of ethics having purchase on a world that free bio-graphically true stories can be told in it. It is not required that the free stories that are true actually be told or have some sort of specific content other than that which makes them biographically true free stories in the first place. It follows that the vari-eties of ethical theory that derive ethical content that applies to all rational agents from conditions of free agency are entirely justified.

It does not follow that it makes no ethical difference which particular free or nonfree stories are true. This is so in a variety of ways that I will illustrate without trying to be exhaustive. Suppose that "One ought always to treat rational agents with respect" is a moral principle. What counts as "treating with respect" will some-what depend on what particular stories are held true. It will depend *only* somewhat on that—killing them for pleasure and torturing them for fun cannot be modalities of respect for rational agents. But whether, even if my right hand is injured, I may offer you my left hand in greeting will depend on how the left hand (and, for that matter, handshaking) fares in your culture. What will and will not cause pain, give offense, provide reassurance, express concern, be perceived as a threat, and the like depend on which particular unfree, nonfree, and free stories are true. I cannot op-erate responsibly in your environment without knowing something considerable about which physical stories are true and what anthropological, sociological, and psychological stories are true or held true.

It is time to draw some consequences. Narrative, as story, presupposes agents. A narrative world in which free stories are true concerning morally significant actions is a moral world. Also, a moral world is a narrative world. Ethics has purchase in a world only if it is a moral world. While it follows that ethics has purchase in a nar-rative or story world of the sort characterized, this is so only because such a narra-tive or story world is a moral world. Ethics can have purchase on a world, even if no narratives are ever offered in that world, for morality (the ontological conditions of ethics) can obtain in a world in which no story is ever told. It is the occurrence of morally significant free choices in a world that give ethics application in it, not sto-ries about choices or about anything else. The choice to tell a story may itself be raw material for ethical reflection, which may occur without telling a story about a story being told. Any moral world provides the conditions for ethics, no matter what stories are true in it and whether or not stories occur within its culture.

One can object that a person gets her identity from the stories with which she identifies. This claim combines an important point with overblown rhetoric. Only something that is already a person can get a *sense* of identity by identifying with a story. What identifying with the story typically does is to further define a sense of identity already possessed, but a sense of identity is one thing and identity as a per-son is another, and however intimately they may be related, they are not identical. Again, anything lacking an identity cannot so much as hear a story, let alone get an identity from hearing it.

The last paragraph, of course, cries out for someone to say what is *meant* by identity. On one account—one I think correct, but defending that claim is not my task here—a person is a self-conscious mental substance possessing libertarian freedom of action on morally significant occasions. Anything with those properties has an identity as a person—that is, he *is* a person—whether he ever hears any stories or not. The existence of such persons in a world makes that world a moral world (and arguably nothing else does). The existence of such persons in a world also makes that world a narrative world—a world in which actual biographically true free stories can be told. But such a world is a moral world, and so one in which ethics has purchase, whether or not stories are told in it. Persons, already possessed of the properties that make them persons and so already proper subjects of ethical discourse, may take as their own (identify with) various things talked about in a story—they may come to participate in institutions, practices, liturgies, rituals, and lifestyles recounted in a story, or come to act for ends, goals, reasons, and purposes commended by a story. But they do not literally become persons by so doing, and could not, since they would already have to be persons in order to do any of these things. These banal truths would not need utterance were there not narrative imperialists whose enthusiastic support of narrative ethics ignores them. All of this is true, even if a person flourishes best, or only, if she does identify with certain stories—only if her sense of identity, her robust self-image, includes her embracing certain sorts of stories, or certain particular stories of some sort—as her own. Narrative ethics is plausible, even possible, only as second-mile ethics, requiring as its context and basis the very sort of ethics whose possibility its imperialistic proponent denies.

Conclusion

It is plain that narrative has its use in ethics. A story can present an ideal in the concrete form of a saint or a hero. It can paint vice in its ugliness and virtue in its beauty. Actual biography can show that what is right or good is also accessible. As one identifies oneself with a tradition, interpreting (and thereby making) one's autobiography part of its biography, one affects who one is and how one may behave. Seeing one's life as part of a larger whole that is partially defined by stories, mythical or historical, can answer a longing for meaning and make it possible for one to interact suitably with one's peers. Narrative is not irrelevant to ethics. Chief Justice Warren once aptly remarked that law floats on a sea of ethics. Enthusiastic narrativists claim that ethics floats on a sea of narrative. It does not. The telling of stories—free and nonfree—assumes that narrative conditions are met. One could argue that any world in which free stories can be told is one in which those conditions are met, but it seems noncontradictory that there be storytellers who thought that they (or the subjects of their stories) were free when this was not so. If this is impossible, an argument is needed to show that. It is harder to see how nonfree narrative conditions could appear to obtain when they actually did not. But some philosophers have thought otherwise, and if they are mistaken it is argument, not narrative, that shows this. Some philosophers have contended that what I (perhaps misleadingly) have called the nonfree conditions of narrative cannot obtain unless what I have called the free conditions of narrative also obtain; again, this is a matter decidable only by argument. If one likes buoyancy metaphors, then narrative floats on a sea of metaphysics. Both the nature of the sea, and of the floating, prevent ethics from being as the enthusiastic narrativist conceives it.

Notes

1. For an elegant, thorough argument for this, see Paul K. Moser and David Yandell, "Farewell to Philosophical Naturalism," in *Naturalism: A Critical Analysis*, ed.William Lane Craig and J. P. Moreland (London: Routledge, 2000).

2. I here use "epistemic" in the nonstandard sense: x is epistemic only if x is mental and x has propositional content.

3. These sorts of alleged counter-examples receive detailed discussion in Chap. 14 in my *Philosophy of Religion* (London: Routledge, 1999).

Index